THE HIDDEN PLACES OF

EAST ANGLIA

Including Norfolk, Suffolk, Essex and Cambridgeshire

By Peter Long

Regional Hidden Places

Cornwall
Devon
Dorset, Hants & Isle of Wight
East Anglia
Lake District & Cumbria
Northumberland & Durham
Peak District and Derbyshire
Sussex
Yorkshire

National Hidden Places

England
Ireland
Scotland
Wales

Hidden Inns

East Anglia
Heart of England
North of England
South
South East
Wales
West Country
Yorkshire

Country Pubs and Inns

Cornwall
Devon
Sussex
Wales

Country Living Rural Guides

East Anglia
Heart of England
Ireland
North East of England
North West of England
Scotland
South
South East
Wales
West Country

Other Guides

Off the Motorway

Published by: Travel Publishing Ltd, 7a Apollo House,
Calleva Park, Aldermaston, Berks, RG7 8TN

ISBN 1-904-434-31-2

© Travel Publishing Ltd

First published 1989, second edition 1993,
third edition 1994, fourth edition 1996,
fifth edition 1999, sixth edition 2001, seventh edition 2003,
eighth edition 2005

Printing by: Scotprint, Haddington

Maps by: © Maps in Minutes ™ (2005)
© Crown Copyright, Ordnance Survey 2005

Editor: Peter Long

Cover Design: jpbstudio, Whitchurch, Hampshire

Cover Photograph: Denver Windmill near Downham
Market, Norfolk Fens © www.britainonview.com

Text Photographs: © www.britainonview.com

Foreword

This is the 8th edition of the **Hidden Places of East Anglia** which has been fully updated. In this respect we would like to thank the many Tourist Information Centres in East Anglia for helping us update the editorial content. Regular readers will note that the pages of the guide have been extensively redesigned to allow more information to be presented on the many places to visit in Norfolk, Suffolk, Essex and Cambridgeshire. In addition, although you will still find details of places of interest and advertisers of places to stay, eat and drink included under each village, town or city, these are now cross referenced to more detailed information contained in a separate, easy-to-use section of the book. This section is also available as a free supplement from the local Tourist Information Offices.

East Anglia offers plenty for the visitor to explore in real *Hidden Places* country. **Norfolk** is rightly famous for the Norfolk Broads, but also possesses gentle rolling hills, delightful pastoral scenes and a beautiful coastline rich in wildlife. **Suffolk** is blessed with incomparable rural beauty. Meandering tidal rivers and numerous streams, brooks and gullies intersect a land blended with low hills and vast open spaces. Suffolk was made famous by the brush of John Constable and his paintings reflect the sheer beauty and tranquility of this attractive county. **Essex** with its large estuaries and fishing communities, has a rich maritime tradition going back as far as Roman times. The county is equally well endowed with pretty stone-built villlages and contains the oldest recorded town in England, namely Colchester. **Cambridgeshire** is most famous for its ancient university as well as being the birthplace of Oliver Cromwell and Samuel Pepys. The county offers a wealth of peaceful and attractive countryside with many towns and villages steeped in history and tradition.

Our books contain a wealth of interesting information on the history, the countryside, the towns and villages and the more established places of interest. But they also promote the more secluded and little known visitor attractions and places to stay, eat and drink many of which are easy to miss unless you know exactly where you are going.

We include hotels, inns, restaurants, public houses, teashops, various types of accommodation, historic houses, museums, gardens, and many other attractions throughout the area, all of which are comprehensively indexed. Most places are accompanied by an attractive photograph and are easily located by using the map at the beginning of each chapter. We do not award merit marks or rankings but concentrate on describing the more interesting, unusual or unique features of each place with the aim of making the reader's stay in the local area an enjoyable and stimulating experience.

Whether you are visiting the area for business or pleasure or in fact are living in the counties we do hope that you enjoy reading and using this book. We are always interested in what readers think of places covered (or not covered) in our guides so please do not hesitate to use the reader reaction forms provided to give us your considered comments. We also welcome any general comments which will help us improve the guides themselves. Finally if you are planning to visit any other corner of the British Isles we would like to refer you to the ordr form for other **Hidden Places** titles to be found at the rear of the book and to the Travel Publishing website at **www.travelpublishing.co.uk**.

Travel Publishing

Contents

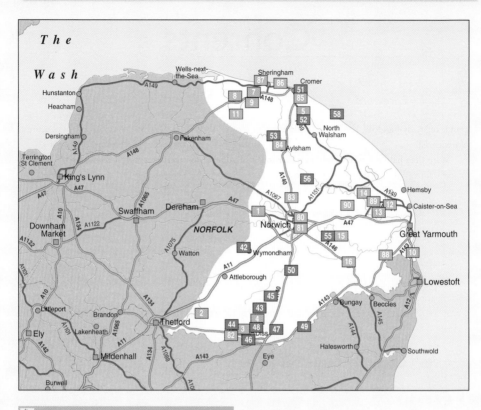

Norwich and East Norfolk

Norwich has the most Dickensian atmosphere of any city I know' declared J B Priestley in his *English Journey of 1933*. 'What a grand, higgledy-piggledy, sensible old place Norwich is!'

More than half a century later, in a European Commission study of 'most habitable' cities, Norwich topped the list of British contenders, well ahead of more favoured candidates such as Bath and York. The political, social and cultural capital of Norfolk, Norwich has an individual charm that is difficult to define, a beguiling atmosphere created in part by its prodigal wealth of sublime buildings, and partly by its intriguing dual personality as both an old-fashioned Cathedral town and a vibrant, modern metropolis.

The central part of East Norfolk that surrounds Norwich is effectively a plateau, where the gentle contours never rise or fall more than a few metres. The valleys of the Rivers Nar and Wensum display some of the most enchanting scenery in the county, and the area boasts two of the finest Gothic parish churches in England, at Cawston and Salle (Norfolk is blessed with more than 600 medieval churches – perhaps as many as any county). In prehistoric times, this was the most wooded part of Norfolk, and a good number of medieval natural woods still remain, a feature which adds another visual attraction to this pastoral area of the country. Dotted throughout these rural pleasures is a wealth of quiet, unspoilt villages hidden away on minor roads.

The northeast coast makes up the Highlands of Norfolk - the Cromer Ridge, which attains a modest height of 330 feet above sea level and does little to gainsay Noel Coward's observation in *Private lives*. Substantial stretches of the coast are, happily, in the care of the National Trust, but anyone in search of a beach holiday will probably want to focus attention on the coastline east of Sheringham. From this decorous resort, a broad strip of excellent sands runs almost uninterrupted past Cromer and southwards to Great Yarmouth.

Visitors who want to experience a bird's-eye view that encompasses the essence of the Norfolk Broads should climb the tower of the 'Cathedral of the Broads', the Church of St Helen's at Ranworth. Spread out beneath lies a vast panorama of glittering waterways, acres of marshland dotted with windmills, reed beds which are still harvested for thatch, grand churches and farmhouses of warm, red brick.

This is Britain's finest wetland area, a National Park in all but name. Broadland covers some 220 square miles, in a rough oval to the northwest of Great Yarmouth. Three main rivers, the Ant, the Thurne and the Bure, thread their way through the marshes, providing some 120 miles of navigable waterways. The Broads remain a refuge for many species of endangered birds and plants, and during the spring and autumn they are a favourite stopping-off place for migrating birds.

Boats on the Norfolk Broads

3

NORWICH

Back in prehistoric times, there were several settlements around the confluence of the Rivers Wensum and Yare. By the late fourth century, one of them was important enough to have its own mint. This was *Northwic*. By the time of the *Domesday Book* 700 years later, Northwic/Norwich, had become the third-most populous city in England, only outnumbered by London and York. To the Norman conquerors, such a major centre of population (about 5,500 residents) needed a **Castle** to ensure that its Saxon inhabitants could be kept in order.

The first castle structure, in wood, was replaced in the late 1100s by a mighty fortress in stone which, unlike most blank-walled castles of the period, is decorated with a rich façade of blind arcades and ornamental pilasters. This great fort never saw any military action, and as early as the 13th century was being used as the county gaol, a role it continued to fill until 1889. From its walls, in December 1549, the leader of the rebellion against land enclosures, Robert Kett, was hung in chains and left to starve to death.

The Castle is now home to the **Norwich Castle Museum and Art Gallery**, which contains some of the most outstanding regional collections of fine art, archaeological exhibits and natural history displays. The former dungeons contain a forbidding display of instruments of torture, along with the death masks of some of the prisoners who were executed here. Among the countless other fascinating exhibits are those devoted to Queen Boudica (Boadicea), which features the life of the Iceni tribe with an interactive chariot ride, the Egyptian gallery with its mummy Ankh Hor, and new and interactive displays in the Castle keep and keep basement, recently made accessible to the public.

The Art Gallery's incomparable collection of paintings by the celebrated Norwich artist, John Sell

Elm Hill, Norwich

Cotman (1782-1842), and others in the group known as the Norwich School. Their subjects were mostly landscape scenes, such as John Crome's *The Poringland Oak*. Quite apart from the artistic quality of their works, they have left a fascinating pictorial record of early 19th century Norfolk.

The **Bulwer and Miller** collection of more than 2,600 English china teapots makes its home in a brand new gallery called the Twinings Gallery, while the museum's Langton collection of around 100 cats fashioned in porcelain, ivory, bronze, glass and wood, originating from anywhere between Derbyshire and China, and Margaret Elizabeth Fountaine's mind-boggling accumulation of 22,000 butterflies which she had personally netted during her travels around the world, are available to view by appointment at the Shirehall Study Centre, next door to the Royal Norfolk Regimental Museum on Market Avenue.

The great open space of the Market Square, where every weekday a colourful jumble of traders' stalls can be found, offers just about every conceivable item for sale. Dominating the western side of the Market Square is **City Hall**, modelled on Stockholm City Hall and opened by King George VI in 1938. Opinions differ about its architectural merits, but there are no such doubts about the nearby **Guildhall**, a fine example of 15th century flintwork that now houses a tea room.

Around the corner from London Street, in Bridewell Alley, is the **Bridewell Museum**, a late 14th century merchant's house now dedicated to Norfolk's crafts and industries.

Millennium Plain just off Theatre Street is where visitors will find **The Forum**, an architecturally stunning modern building designed by Sir Michael Hopkins. Combining a unique horseshoe shape with an all-glass façade, this spectacular

●

An interesting museum/ shop, located in the Royal Arcade, a tiled riot of Art Nouveau fantasy, celebrates the county's great contribution to world cuisine: mustard. Back in the early 1800s, Jeremiah Colman perfected his blend of mustard flours and spice to produce a condiment that was smooth in texture and tart in flavour. Together with his nephew James he founded J & J Colman in 1823; 150 years later The Mustard Shop was established to commemorate the company's history. The shop has an appropriately late-Victorian atmosphere and a fascinating display of vintage containers and advertisements, some of them from 'Mustard Club' featuring such characters as Lord Bacon of Cookham and Miss Di Gester, created by no less distinguished a writer than Dorothy L Sayers. All in all, a most appetising exhibition.

●

Market Square, Norwich

The Assembly House in Theatre Street is one of the city's finest historical houses and also a leading venue for the arts. With two concert halls, three galleries featuring changing exhibitions and a restaurant and tea rooms, this magnificent Georgian home must be included in any visit to the city.

structure has, at its heart, the **Atrium** and **Bridge**, meeting places where you can enjoy a meal or drink anytime through to midnight, seven days a week. At the **Origins Visitor Centre**, an attractive multimedia display on three floors affords the opportunity to experience the life and times of Norwich and the wider Norfolk region. Here can also be found the Tourist Information Centre. The new **Norfolk & Norwich Millennium Library** houses 120,000 books and offers the best in information and communication technology.

While the Castle has been used for many purposes over the years,

the **Cathedral** remains what it has always been: the focus of ecclesiastical life in the county. It's even older than the castle, its service of consecration taking place over 900 years ago, in 1101. This peerless building, its flint walls clad in creamy-white stone from Caen is, after Durham, the most completely Norman cathedral in England, its appeal enhanced by later Gothic features such as the flying buttresses. The Norman cloisters are the largest in the country and notable for the 400 coloured and gilded bosses depicting scenes from medieval life. Another 1,200 of these wondrous carvings decorate the glorious vaulted roof of the nave.

It's impossible to list all the Cathedral's treasures here, but do seek out the **Saxon Bishop's Throne** in the Presbytery, the lovely 14th century altar painting in St Luke's Chapel, and the richly carved canopies in the Choir.

Outside, beneath the slender 315-feet spire soaring heavenwards, the **Cathedral Close** is timeless in its sense of peace. There are some 80 houses inside the Close, some medieval, many Georgian, their residents enjoying an idyllic refuge free from cars. At peace here lie the remains of Nurse Edith Cavell. A daughter of the rector of Swardeston, a few miles south of Norwich, Nurse

Norwich Cathedral

Cavell worked at a Red Cross hospital in occupied Brussels during the First World War. She helped some 200 Allied soldiers to escape to neutral Holland before being detected and court-martialled by the Germans. As she faced execution by firing squad on 12 October 1915, she spoke her own resonant epitaph: 'Standing as I do, in the view of God and eternity, I realise that patriotism is not enough. I must have no hatred or bitterness towards anyone.'

A stroll around the Close will take you to **Pull's Ferry** with its picturesque flint gateway fronting the River Wensum. In medieval times a canal ran inland from here so that provisions, goods and, in the earliest days, building materials, could be moved direct to the Cathedral. Along the riverside walk is **Cow Tower**, built around 1378 and the most massive of the old city towers.

At the western end of the Cathedral Close is the magnificent **Erpingham Gate**, presented to the city in 1420 by a hero of the Battle of Agincourt, Sir Thomas Erpingham.

Beyond this gate, in Tombland (originally Toom or wasteland), is **Samson and Hercules House**, its entrance flanked by two 1674 carvings of these giants. Diagonally opposite stands the 15th century Maid's Head Hotel.

Norwich is home to some 32 medieval churches in all, every one of them worth attention, although many are now used for purposes other than worship. Outstanding

among them are **St Peter Mancroft**, a masterpiece of Gothic architecture built between 1430-55 (and the largest church in Norwich), and **St Peter Hungate**, a handsome 15th century church standing at the top of **Elm Hill**, a narrow, unbelievably picturesque lane where in medieval times the city's wool merchants built their homes, close to their warehouses beside the River Wensum.

St Gregory's Church in Pottergate is another Norwich church to have been deconsecrated, and its fate might well have been a sad one. Happily, it is now the home to an arts centre where local artists, actors, musicians, dancers and other arts groups stage a variety of performances and exhibitions throughout the year.

When the basic structure of the present St Gregory's was built in the late 14th century, the general rule seems to have been that any parish of around 1,000 people would have its own place of worship. St Gregory's was founded on the site of a Saxon church in 1210 and rebuilt in its present form in 1394. The church takes it name from Gregory the Great, the 6th century Pope best known for his campaign to convert the heathen Anglo-Saxons of 'Angle-land' to Christianity, despatching a party of 40 monks to Angle-land in AD 596, led by Augustine, whom the Pope consecrated as the first Archbishop of Canterbury.

The Inspire Discovery Centre, housed in the medieval church of St Michael in Coslany Street, just across

There are a large number of beautiful and well-maintained parks in the city, some of which offer chess, lawn tennis and hard tennis courts, bowls, pitch and putt, rowing and more, together with a programme of entertainments ranging from theatre to concerts. One worth particular mention is The Plantation Garden in Earlham Road, three acres of Victorian plantings restored after having fallen into disrepair, and thought to be the only one in the nation with a Grade II listing.

80 DRAGON HALL

King Street, Norwich

A magnificent medieval timber framed merchant's house. The crown post roof features an intricately carved and painted dragon.

🏛 see page 266

81 THE PLANTATION GARDEN

Earlham Road, Norwich

A green oasis in the centre of Norwich, this three-acre site was restored in the 1980s to its former 19th century glory.

 see page 267

1 THE REMBRANDT

Easton, west of Norwich

Fish & chips and home-made pizzas head the menu at **The Rembrandt**, a short drive outside Norwich on the Dereham Road.

 see page 239

83 CITY OF NORWICH AVIATION MUSEUM

Horsham St Faiths, Norwich

A museum dedicated to keeping Norfolk's aviation history alive with displays on its development and a collection of aircraft.

 see page 267

the Wensum northeast of the city centre, is full of exciting hands-on displays and activities that make scientific enquiry come to life.

On the western edge of the city stands the **University of East Anglia**. It's well worth making your way here to visit the **Sainsbury Centre for Visual Arts**. Housed in a huge hall of aluminium and glass designed by Norman Foster, the Centre contains the eclectic collection of a 'passionate acquirer' of art, Sir Robert Sainsbury. For more than 50 years, Sir Robert purchased whatever works of art took his fancy, ignoring fashionable trends. Thus the visitor finds sculptures and pictures by Henry Moore, Bacon and Giacometti, along with African and pre-Columbian artefacts, Egyptian, Etruscan and Roman bronzes, works by Native Americans and Inuit Eskimos, and sculptures from the Cyclades, the South Seas, the Orient and medieval Europe. This extraordinary collection was donated to the University by Sir Robert and Lady Lisa Sainsbury in 1973; their son David complemented his parents' generosity by paying for the building in which it is housed.

To the south of Norwich in the village of Caistor St Edmund are the remains of **Venta Icenorum**, the Roman town established here after Boudica's rebellion in AD 61. Unusually, this extensive site has not been disturbed by later developments, so archaeologists have been able to identify the full scale of the original settlement.

Most of the finds discovered during excavations in the 1920s and 1930s are now in Norwich Castle Museum, but the riverside site still merits a visit.

AROUND NORWICH

HORSHAM ST FAITHS

1 mile N of Norwich on the A140

Brown tourist signs from the A140 lead to the **City of Norwich Aviation Museum**, dedicated to keeping Norfolk's aviation heritage alive. The most impressive craft on display is a massive Avro Vulcan bomber that saw service in the 1982 Falklands conflict, but there are several other aircraft as well as displays showing the development of flying in Norfolk. The major roles played by Norfolk-based aircraft during the Second World War are remembered by exhibitions on the RAF and USAAF.

WYMONDHAM

9 miles SW of Norwich off the A11

The exterior of **Wymondham Abbey** presents one of the oddest ecclesiastical buildings in the county; the interior reveals one of the most glorious. The Abbey was founded in 1107 by the Benedictines - or Black Monks, as they were known because of the colour of their habits. The richest and most aristocratic of the monastic orders, the Black Monks apparently experienced some difficulty in respecting their solemn vows of poverty and humility. Especially the latter. Constantly in dispute with the people of

Wymondham, the dissension between them grew so bitter that in 1249 Pope Innocent IV himself attempted to reconcile their differences. When his efforts failed, a wall was built across the interior of the Abbey, dividing it into an area for the monks and another for the parishioners. Even this drastic measure failed to bring peace, however. Both parties wanted to ring their own bells, so each built a tower. The villagers erected a stately rectangular tower at the west end; the monks an octagonal one over the crossing, thus creating the Abbey's curious exterior appearance.

Step inside and you find a magnificent Norman nave, 112 feet long. (It was originally twice as long, but the eastern end, along with most of the Abbey buildings, was demolished after the Dissolution of the Monasteries.) The superb hammerbeam roof is supported by 76 beautifully carved angels. There's also an interesting 16th century tomb, of the last Abbot, in delicate terracotta work, and a striking modern memorial: a gilded and coloured reredos and tester commemorating the local men who lost their lives in the First World War.

The rectangular western tower of the Abbey was the setting for one of the last acts in the ill-fated Kett's Rebellion of 1549. From its walls,

William Kett was hung in chains and left to die: his brother Robert, the leading figure in the uprising, suffered the same fate at Norwich Castle.

Although many of Wymondham's oldest houses were lost in the fire of 1615, when some 300 dwellings were destroyed, there are still some attractive Elizabethan buildings in the heart of the town. The **Market Place** (Friday is market day, and on the first Friday of every month there's an antiques and collectors' fair held in Central Hall) is given dignity by the picturesque octagonal Market Cross, rebuilt two years after the fire. Crowned by a pyramid roof, this appealing timber-framed building is open on all sides on the ground floor, and its upper floor is reached by an outside stairway. Also of interest is **Becket's Chapel**, founded in 1174 and restored in 1559. In its long

42 KIMBERLEY HOME FARM

Wymondham

Three spacious rooms provide quiet, secluded B&B accommodation at **Kimberley Home Farm**.

see page 254

Wymondham Abbey

45 OAKBROOK

Great Moulton, nr Long Stratton

Oakbrook is a fine redbrick house with 9 bright, spacious rooms for B&B.

 see *page 254*

2 THE SWAN

East Harling, nr Norwich

The Swan is a convivial village inn catering well for both thirsts and appetites.

see *page 239*

•

Railway buffs will want to visit the historic Railway Station at Wymondham, built in 1845 on the Great Eastern's Norwich-Ely line. At its peak, the station and its section employed over 100 people. Still providing a rail link to Norwich, London and the Midlands, the station has been restored, and its buildings house a railway museum, restaurant and tearoom, and a piano showroom.

•

history it has served as a pilgrim's chapel, grammar school, and coal store. Currently, it houses the town library. **The Bridewell**, or House of Correction, in Bridewell Street was built as a model prison in 1785 along lines recommended by the prison reformer, John Howard, who had condemned the earlier gaol on the site as 'one of the vilest in the country'. Wymondham's Bridewell is said to have served as a model for the penitentiaries established in the United States. Now owned by the town's Heritage Society, Bridewell is home to several community projects, including the **Wymondham Heritage Museum**.

ATTLEBOROUGH

14 miles SW of Norwich off the A11

The greatest glory of this pleasant market town is to be found in its church of **St Mary**. Here, a remarkable 15th century chancel screen stretches the width of the church and is beautifully embellished with the arms of the 24 bishoprics into which England was divided at that time. The screen is generally reckoned to be one of the most outstanding in the country, a remarkable survivor of the Reformation purging of such beautiful creations from churches across the land.

Collectors of curiosities will be interested in a strange memorial in the churchyard. It takes the form of a pyramid, about 6 feet high, and was erected in 1929 to mark the grave of a local solicitor with

the rather splendid name of Melancthon William Henry Brooke, or 'Lawyer' Brooke as he was more familiarly known. Melancthon was an amateur Egyptologist who became convinced by his studies of the Pharaohs' tombs that the only way to ensure an agreeable after-life was to be buried beneath a pyramid, precisely placed and of the correct physical dimensions. Several years before his death, he gave the most punctilious instructions as to how this assurance of his immortal existence should be constructed and located.

BANHAM

18 miles SW of Norwich on the B1114

Banham Zoo provides the opportunity to come face to face with some of the world's rarest wildlife - many of the animals who find a home here otherwise face extinction. The Zoo is particularly concerned with monkeys and apes, but in the 25 acres of landscaped gardens you'll also come across tigers, cheetahs, lemurs, penguins and many other species. There are educational talks and displays, a children's play area, Shire Horse dray rides, and a restaurant.

BRESSINGHAM

22 miles SW of Norwich off the A1066

Bressingham Gardens and Steam Museum boasts one of the world's finest collections of British and Continental locomotives, some of them on loan from the National Railway Museum at York. All are housed under cover in the museum's extensive locomotive sheds, which also contain many steam-driven industrial engines, traction engines, and **The Fire Museum**, whose collection of fire engines and fire-fighting equipment could form a complete museum in its own right. Visitors can view the interior of the Royal Coach and ride along five miles of track through the woods and gardens. Bressingham is renowned for its special 'Steam Days' when the engines can be seen in full steam on the three narrow-gauge lines, and talks and footplate rides are given on the standard-gauge locomotives. It is also home to the National Dads Army Collection.

DISS

20 miles S of Norwich on the A1066/A140

The late Poet Laureate, John Betjeman, voted Diss his favourite Norfolk town, and it's easy to understand his enthusiasm. The River Waveney running alongside forms the boundary between Norfolk and Suffolk, but this attractive old market town – winner of Best Kept Market Town in Norfolk, whose town centre is now a designated conservation area - keeps itself firmly on the northern bank of the river. The town is a pleasing mixture of Tudor, Georgian and Victorian houses grouped around **The Mere**, which gives the town its name, derived from the Anglo-Saxon word for 'standing water'.

The old town grew up on the hill above The Mere, perhaps because, as an 18th century resident observed, 'all the filth of the town

centring in the Mere, beside the many conveniences that are placed over it, make the water very bad and altogether useless ... it stinks exceedingly, and sometimes the fish rise in great numbers, so thick that they are easily taken; they are chiefly roach and eels.' A proper sewerage system was finally installed in 1851.

There's a public park beside the six-acre Mere, and from it a narrow street leads to the small **Market Place**. This former poultry market is dominated by **St Mary's** church. The oldest parts date back some 700 years, and the St Nicholas Chapel is particularly enjoyable with its wonderful corbels, angels in the roof, and gargoyles. In the early 1500s, the Rector here was John Skelton, Court poet and tutor to Prince Henry, later Henry VIII. A bitter, quarrelsome man, Skelton was appointed Poet Laureate through the patronage of Cardinal Wolsey, despite the fact that most of Skelton's output has been described as 'breathless doggerel'. Appointed Rector of Diss in 1502, he appears to have been suspended nine years later for having a concubine. Not far from his church is the delightful Victorian **Shambles** with a cast-iron veranda and a small museum inside.

SCOLE

2 miles E of Diss on the A140

Scole's history goes back to Roman times, since it grew up alongside the Imperial highway from Ipswich to Norwich at the point where it bridged the River Waveney. Traffic

82 BRESSINGHAM GARDENS

Bressingham

World renowned garden, famous for its collection of nearly 5,000 species of hardy perennials.

 see page 267

44 HAZEL BARN

Bressingham, nr Diss

Hazel Barn has three beautifully appointed ground-floor bedrooms in a quiet country setting.

see page 254

3/46 FAYRE VIEW RESTAURANT & ROOMS

Lower Denmark Street, Diss

Fayre View Restaurant & Rooms is a stunning setting for enjoying superb food and wine and an overnight stay.

see pages 239 and 255

48 WALCOT GREEN FARM

Walcot Green, nr Diss

Walcot Green Farm Cottage is a three-bedroom self-catering base on a working farm.

see page 255

4 THE BURSTON CROWN

Burston, north of Diss

Home cooking and real ales are both very special at the 16th century **Burston Crown**.

 see page 239

43 GROVE FARM

Gissing, nr Diss

The luxurious modern bungalow at **Grove Farm** provides very comfortable self-catering accommodation for up to 5 guests.

 see page 254

47 MOOR VIEW

Semere Green Lane, Dickleburgh

Moor View is a quiet, civilised base for a B&B or self catering break in lovely countryside.

 see page 255

49 TOM, DICK & HARRY

Withersdale, nr Harleston

Tom, Dick & Harry are comfortable self-catering cottages for two in a scenic country setting.

see page 256

on this road (the A140) became unbearable in the 1980s, but a bypass has now mercifully restored some peace to the village. There are two hostelries of note: a coaching inn of 1655, built in an extravagant style of Dutch gables, giant pilasters and towering chimney stacks, and the Crossways Inn, which must have a good claim to being the prettiest pub in the county.

LANGMERE

6 miles NE of Diss on minor road off the A140 (through Dickleburgh)

Veterans of the Second World War and their families and friends will be interested in the **100th Bomb Group Memorial Museum**, a small museum on the edge of Dickleburgh Airfield (now disused). The Museum is the 'Bloody Hundredths' tribute to the US 8th Air Force, which was stationed here during the war, and includes displays of USAAF decorations and uniforms, equipment, combat records and other memorabilia and photographs. Facilities include refreshments, a museum shop, visitor centre and a picnic area. The Museum is open Saturdays, Sundays and Bank Holidays, also on Wednesdays between May and September. Closed November, January and February. Tel: 01379 740708

HARLESTON

7 miles NE of Diss off the A143

This pretty market town with some notable half-timbered and Georgian houses, and a splendid 12th century

coaching inn, was a favourite of the renowned architectural authority, Nikolaus Pevsner, who particularly admired the early Georgian Candlers House at the northern end of the town. Another writer has described the area around the marketplace as 'the finest street scene in East Anglia'. The town of Harleston lies in the heart of the Waveney Valley, a lovely area which inspired many paintings by the locally-born artist, Sir Alfred Munnings.

PORINGLAND

6 miles S of Norwich on the B1332

The name of this sizable village will be familiar to those who love the paintings of the Norwich artist John Crome (1794-1842) whose Arcadian painting of *The Poringland Oak* hangs in the Tate Gallery.

To the southwest of Poringland is **The Playbarn**, an indoor and outdoor adventure centre specially designed for the under-sevens. All the play equipment is based on a farmyard theme, with a miniature farm, bouncy tractors, soft play sheep pens, and donkey rides among the attractions. Refreshments and light lunches are available, or you can bring along your own picnic.

GREAT WITCHINGHAM

11 miles NW of Norwich off the A1067

Norfolk Wildlife Centre & Country Park is home to an interesting collection of rare, or ancient, breeds of farm livestock such as white-faced woodland and Shetland sheep, pygmy goats and

Exmoor ponies. Set in 40 acres of peaceful parkland, the Centre also has reindeer, otters and badgers, pools teeming with wildfowl and a huge colony of wild herons nesting in the trees. There are also 'Commando' and Adventure Play Areas, one of the finest collection of trees and flowering shrubs in the county, a café and gift shop. The Centre also hosts the most spectacular birds-of-prey flying display in Norfolk.

Anyone who has ever read Parson Woodforde's enchanting *Diary of a Country Parson* will want to make a short diversion to the tiny village of **Weston Longville**, a mile or so south of the Dinosaur Park. The Revd James Woodforde was vicar of this remote parish from 1774 until his death in 1803, and throughout that time he conscientiously maintained a daily diary detailing a wonderful mixture of the momentous and the trivial. 'Very great Rebellion in France' he notes when, ten days after the fall of the Bastille, the dramatic news eventually arrived at Weston Longville. More often he records his copious meals ('We had for dinner a calf's head, boiled fowl and tongue, a saddle of mutton roasted on the side table, and a fine swan roasted with currant jelly sauce for the first course. The second course a couple of wild fowl, larks, blamange, tarts etc. etc.'), the weather (during the winter of 1785, for example, the frost was so severe that it froze the chamberpots under the beds), and his frequent dealings with the smuggler Andrews, who kept the good parson well-supplied with contraband tea, gin and cognac. Inside

the simple village church there's a portrait of Parson Woodforde, painted by his nephew, and across the road the inn has been named after this beguiling character.

SWANNINGTON

11 miles NW of Norwich off the A1067/B1149

The gardens of **Swannington Manor** are famous for the 300-year-old yew and box topiary hedge. Other features of this small town are the 13th century St Margaret's church, Swannington Hall – where can be seen the remains of the former moat – and the charming thatched village water pump.

Swannington's Ketts Lane was named for Robert Kett, leader of the peasants' revolt, who reputedly was captured in a barn nearby.

REEPHAM

12 miles NW of Norwich on the B1145

Reepham is an attractive town set in the rich countryside between the Wensum and Bure Valleys. Lovely 18th century houses border the Market Place, and there is delightful walking along the Marriott's Way cycle path. Market day is Wednesday, and regular antiques fairs are held at the Old Reepham Brewery.

CAWSTON

12 miles NW of Norwich on the B1145

'Lovers of the Norfolk churches can never agree which is the best,' wrote Sir John Betjeman. 'I have heard it said that you are either a Salle man or a Cawston man.' In this county so rich in exceptionally

50 FOXHOLE FARM

Saxlingham Thorpe, nr Norwich

Two en-suite rooms provide quiet B&B accommodation at **Foxhole Farm** in a rural setting south of Norwich.

see page 256

•

Ssoutheast of Great Witchingham lies the Dinosaur Adventure Park near Lenwade. It doesn't have any living creatures, but as you wander through the woods here you will come across some startlingly convincing life-size models of dinosaurs. One of them, the 'Climb-a-Saurus', is a children's activity centre. A woodland maze, picnic area with gas-fired barbecues, a play area for toddlers, a restaurant and a 'Dinostore' offering a wide variety of dinosaur models, books and gifts are among the park's other attractions.

•

On the B1149, just before the junction with the B1145, stands a large stone on a plinth that commemorates a duel that took place in 1698 between Sir Henry Hobart and Oliver Le Neve. The former was killed in this duel, and his son John, 1st Earl of Buckinghamshire, erected the 'Duelling Stone' in his father's memory.

84 BURE VALLEY RAILWAY

Norwich Road, Aylsham

This narrow guage railway runs between Aylsham and Wroxham and operates four steam trains along the nine mile track, carrying passengers in luxurious surroundings.

 see page 268

beautiful churches, Salle and Cawston are indeed in a class of their own. **St Agnes Church** in Cawston, among many other treasures, boasts a magnificent double hammerbeam roof, where angels with protective wings 8 feet across float serenely from the roof, and a gorgeous 15th century rood screen embellished with lovely painted panels of saints and Fathers of the Church. The two churches are just a couple of miles apart, so you can easily decide for yourself whether you are 'a Salle man or a Cawston man'. Surprisingly for such a genial character, Sir John seems to have overlooked the possibility that other visitors to these two remarkable churches might define themselves as either 'a Salle woman or a Cawston woman'.

AYLSHAM

14 miles N of Norwich on the A140

The attractive little town of Aylsham is set beside the River Bure, the northern terminus of the **Bure Valley Railway**. This 15" gauge railway was built in 1990 and is operated mainly by steam locomotives. It runs for nine miles between Aylsham and Wroxham, with intermediate stations at Brampton, Buxton and Coltishall. There are several Days Out with Thomas the Tank Engine during the year, and one- and two-day steam driving courses available during off-peak periods are aimed at everyone from the absolute beginner upwards. The 15th anniversary of this charming little railway will be celebrated in grand

style on the 8th and 9th of October. Tel: 01263 733858.

Aylsham's unspoilt **Market Place** is surrounded by late 17th and early 18th century houses, reflecting the prosperity the town enjoyed in those years from the cloth trade, and a 14th/15th century church, St Michael's, said to have been built by John O'Gaunt. In the churchyard is the tomb of one of the greatest of the 18th century landscape gardeners, Humphry Repton, the creator of some 200 parks and gardens around the country.

One of Repton's many commissions was to landscape the grounds of **Blickling Hall** (National Trust), a 'dream of architectural beauty' which stands a mile or so outside Aylsham. Many visitors have marvelled at their first sight of the great Hall built for Sir Henry Hobart in the 1620s. 'No-one is prepared on coming downhill past the church into the village, to find the main front of this finest of Jacobean mansions, actually looking upon the road, unobstructed, from behind its velvet lawns' enthused Charles Harper in 1904. 'No theatrical manager cunning in all the artful accessories of the stage could devise anything more dramatic.'

From the outside, Sir Henry's house fully satisfied the contemporary architectural vogue for perfect symmetry. Four towers topped with lead-covered turret-caps rise at each corner, there are lines of matching Dutch gables and mullioned windows, and even the chimneys were placed in corresponding groups of twos, threes or fours.

Inside, the most spectacular feature is the Long Gallery, which extends for 135 feet and originally provided space for indoor exercise in bad weather. Its glory is the plaster ceiling, an intricately patterned expanse of heraldic panels bearing the Hobart arms, along with others displaying bizarre and inscrutable emblems such as a naked lady riding a two-legged dragon.

Blickling Hall

Other treasures at Blickling include a dramatic double-flight carved oak staircase, the Chinese Bedroom lined with 18th century hand-painted wallpaper, a library of over 12,000 books, an exhibition on the RAF at Blickling and the dazzling Peter the Great Room. A descendant of Sir Henry Hobart, the 2nd Earl of Buckinghamshire, was appointed Ambassador to Russia in 1746, and he returned from that posting with a magnificent tapestry, the gift of Empress Catherine the Great. This room was redesigned so as to display the Earl's sumptuous souvenir to its full effect, and portraits of himself and his Countess by Gainsborough were added later.

The Earl was a martyr to gout, and his death in 1793 at the age of 50 occurred when, finding the pain unbearable, he thrust his bloated foot into a bucket of icy water, and suffered a heart attack. He was buried beneath the idiosyncratic Egyptian Pyramid in the grounds, a 45-feet high structure designed by Ignatius Bonomi that combines Egyptian and classical elements to create a mausoleum which, if nothing else, is certainly distinctive.

Blickling also offers its visitors miles of footpaths through extensive parkland, a formal woodland wilderness garden, a Victorian parterre and a dry moat with scented plants, a plant centre, a picnic area, a superb restaurant, a shop and cycle hire.

Within a few miles of Blickling Hall are two other stately homes, both the properties of Lord and

53 ITTERINGHAM MILL

The Common, Itteringham

Itteringham Mill is a very comfortable, civilised base for touring the sights of North Norfolk.

see page 257

Mannington Hall

found walks and trails, orienteering, an adventure playground and various special events are held throughout the year. The Hall is open for tours every Friday from April.

Over 20 miles of waymarked public footpaths and permissive paths around Mannington and Wolterton link into the Weavers Way long-distance footpath and Holt circular walk.

Just north of Mannington Hall stands the village of **Little Barningham**, where St Mary's Church is a magnet for collectors of ecclesiastical curiosities. Inside, perched on the corner of an ancient box pew, stands a remarkable wood-carved skeletal figure of the Grim Reaper. Its fleshless skull stares hollow-eyed at visitors with a defiant, mirthless grin: a scythe gripped in one clutch of bones, and an hour-glass in the other, symbolise the inescapable fate that awaits us all. This gruesomely powerful *memento mori* was donated to the church in 1640 by one Stephen Crosbie who, for good measure, added the inscription: 'As you are now, even so was I, Remember death for ye must dye.' Those words were a conventional enough adjuration at that time, but what is one supposed to make of Stephen's postscript inscribed on the back of the pew: 'For couples joined in wedlock this seat I did intend'?

Lady Walpole. **Mannington Gardens and Countryside** are set around a 15th century moated manor house and feature a wide variety of plants, trees and shrubs, including thousands of roses, and particularly classic varieties. The Heritage Rose Garden and Twentieth century Rose Garden are set in small gardens reflecting their period of origin; the gardens contain more than 1,500 varieties of roses. In 2003 a sensory garden was created, with plants chosen for scent, touch, sight, taste and hearing. There are also garden shops, with plants, souvenirs and crafts, and tea rooms. The grounds are open Sundays May to September and also Wednesday to Friday June to August.

Wolterton Park, the stately 18th century Hall built for Horatio Walpole, brother of Sir Robert, England's first Prime Minister, stands in grounds landscaped by Humphry Repton. Here can be

THE NORTHEAST COAST

CROMER

As you enter a seaside town, what more reassuring sight could there be than to see the pier still standing? **Cromer Pier** is the genuine article, complete with Lifeboat Station and the Pavilion Theatre, which still stages traditional end-of-the-pier shows. The Pier's survival is all the more impressive since it was badly damaged in 1953 and 1989, and in 1993 it was sliced in two by a drilling rig which had broken adrift in a storm.

Cromer has been a significant resort since the late 1700s and in its early days even received an unsolicited testimonial from Jane Austen. In her novel *Emma* (1816), a character declares that 'Perry was a week at Cromer once, and he holds it to be the best of all the sea-bathing places.' A succession of celebrities, ranging from Lord Tennyson and Oscar Wilde to Winston Churchill and the German Kaiser, all came to see for themselves.

The inviting sandy beach remains much as they saw it (horse-drawn bathing machines aside), as does the Church of **St Peter & St Paul**, which boasts the tallest tower in

Norfolk, 160 feet high. And then as now, Cromer Crabs were reckoned to be the most succulent in England. During the season, between April and September, crab-boats are launched from the shore (there's no harbour here), sail out to the crab banks about 3 miles offshore, and there the two-man teams on each boat deal with some 200 pots.

The **Lifeboat Museum**, however, is a fairly recent addition. Housed in the former Lifeboat Station, it tells the dramatic story of the courageous men who manned the town's rescue service. Pre-eminent among them was Harry Blogg, who was coxswain of the lifeboat for 37 years, from 1910 to 1947. During those years his boat, the *H F Bailey*, was called out 128 times and saved 518 lives. In 1991, the H F Bailey was purchased by Peter Cadbury of the chocolate manufacturing family and presented

Cromer

Fishing Boats, Cromer

85 CROMER MUSEUM

Tucker Street, Cromer

A smart redbrick pub serving some of the best food in the area, with Adnams and Fullers ales to accompany.

 see page 268

to the Museum as its prime exhibit.

Cromer Museum, housed in a row of restored fishermen's cottages near the church, invites visitors to follow the story of Cromer from the days of the dinosaurs, some of whose bones were found nearby, up to the present, and access the computer for thousands of pictures and facts about this attractive town.

AROUND CROMER

AYLMERTON

3 miles W of Cromer on minor road off the A148

Aylmerton is home to one of Norfolk's grandest houses, **Felbrigg Hall** (National Trust). Thomas Windham began rebuilding the old manor house at Felbrigg in the 1620s, erecting in its place a grand Jacobean mansion with huge mullioned windows, pillared porch, and at roof-level a dedication in openwork stone: *Gloria Deo in Excelsis*, 'Glory to God in the Highest'. Later that century,

Thomas' grandson William Windham I married a wealthy heiress and added the beautifully proportioned Carolean West Wing, where visitors can see portraits of the happily married couple painted by Sir Peter Lely. Their son, William Windham II, returning from his four-year-long Grand Tour, filled the house with treasures he had collected - so many of them that he had to extend the Hall yet again. The Windham family's ownership of Felbrigg Hall came to a tragi-comic end in the 1860s when William Frederick Windham inherited the estate. William was one of the great English eccentrics. He loved uniforms. Accoutred in the Felbrigg blue and red livery, he would insist on serving at table; in guard's uniform he caused chaos on the local railway with his arbitrary whistle-blasts; dressed as a policeman, he sternly rounded up the ladies of easy virtue patrolling London's Haymarket. Inevitably, 'Mad' Windham fell prey to a pretty fortune-hunter and Felbrigg was only saved from complete bankruptcy by his death at the age of 26.

The Hall was acquired by the National Trust in 1969, complete with its 18th century furnishings, collection of paintings by artists such as Kneller and van der Velde, and a wonderful Gothic library. The 1,750-acre estate includes a traditional working walled garden containing an elegant octagonal dovecote, an orangery of 1707, a 500-acre Great Wood and a restaurant, tea room and shop.

WEST RUNTON

3 miles W of Cromer on the A149

Felbrigg Hall

The parish of West Runton can boast that within its boundaries lies the highest point in Norfolk - **Beacon Hill**. This eminence is 330 feet high, so you won't be needing any oxygen equipment to reach the summit, but there are some excellent views. Nearby is the Roman Camp (National Trust), a misleading name since there's no evidence that the Romans ever occupied this 70-acre stretch of heathland. Excavations have shown, however, that in Saxon and medieval times this was an iron-working settlement.

West Runton's major tourist attraction is undoubtedly the **Norfolk Shire Horse Centre** where twice a day, during the season, these noble beasts are harnessed up and give a half-hour demonstration of the important role they played in agricultural life right up until the 1930s. They are the largest (19 hands/6 feet 4 inches high) and heaviest horses in the world, weighing more than a ton, and for generations were highly valued both as war-horses and draught animals. Several other heavy breeds, such as the Suffolk Punch, Clydesdale and Percheron, also have their home here, along with no fewer than nine different breeds of pony. The Centre also has a video room showing a 30-minute film, a small animals' enclosure and an adventure playground for children, a café and gift shop. A horse-drawn cart will transport you around the village and at the West Runton Riding School (on site) you can hire riding horses by the hour.

SHERINGHAM

5 miles W of Cromer on the A149

Sheringham has made the transition from fishing village to popular seaside resort with grace and style. There are plenty of activities on offer, yet Sheringham has managed to avoid the brasher excesses of many English seaside towns. The beach here is among the cleanest in England, and markedly different from the shingle beaches elsewhere on this part of the coast. Consisting mainly of gently sloping sand, it is excellent for bathing and the team of lifeguards makes it ideal for families with children. Rainfall at Sheringham is one of the lowest in the county, and the bracing air has also recommended the town to sufferers from rheumatism and respiratory problems.

86 THE NORFOLK SHIRE HORSE CENTRE

West Runton, Cromer

An animal lovers paradise where the main attraction are the magnificent shire horses. A superb day out for all the family.

see page 268

Sheringham Station

SHERINGHAM
TWIXT SEA AND PINE

Station Road, Sheringham

Two of the museums three original lifeboats are on show, together with a wealth of displays on local history.

 see page 269

Bodham, nr Sheringham

The Red Hart is the popular hub of village life, with real ales, hearty home cooking and traditional pub games.

 see page 240

A small fleet of fishing boats still operates from here, mostly concentrating on crabs and lobsters, but also bringing in catches of cod, skate, plaice, mackerel and herring. Several original fishermen's cottages remain, some with lofts where the nets were mended. Sheringham has never had a harbour, so boats are launched from the shore where stacks of creels stand as they have for generations. A 'golden lobster' in the town's coat of arms celebrates this traditional industry.

Like so many other former fishing villages in England, Sheringham owes its transformation into a resort to the arrival of the railway. During the Edwardian peak years of rail travel, some 64 trains a day steamed into the station but the line became yet another victim of the Beeching closures of the 1960s. Devotees of steam trains joined together and, by dint of great effort and enthusiasm, managed to re-open the line in 1975 as the **North Norfolk Railway**, better known as The Poppy Line.

The name refers to 'Poppyland", a term given to the area by the Victorian journalist Clement Scott who visited in pre-herbicide days when the summer fields were ablaze with poppies. In 1883, Scott travelled to Cromer on the newly-opened Great Eastern Railway's extension from Norwich. Walking out of the town, he was entranced by the tranquillity of the countryside. In his dispatch to the *Daily Telegraph* he wrote: 'It is difficult to convey an idea of the silence of the fields through which I passed, or the beauty of the prospect that surrounded me - a blue sky without a cloud across it, a sea sparkling under a haze of heat, wild flowers in profusion around me, poppies predominating everywhere ...' Spurred by Scott's enthusiasm, a succession of notable Victorians made their way here - painters, writers, actors, even a youthful Winston Churchill. Later, during the Second World War, Churchill returned to the area, staying at Pear Tree Cottage in Mundesley.

Although greatly diminished in number, plenty of brilliant poppies can still be seen as you travel the scenic five-mile journey, steam or diesel operated, from Sheringham to Holt via Weybourne. Sheringham Station, just across the road from the Network Rail station on the Bittern Line, was built in 1887 and retains all the charm of steam railway days, complete with luggage piled on the platform and smartly uniformed staff. Tel: 01263 820800 for timetable details

Just to the west of the town, at Upper Sheringham, footpaths lead to the lovely grounds of **Sheringham Park** (National Trust). The Park was landscaped by Humphry Repton, who declared it to be his 'favourite and darling child in Norfolk'. There are grand views along the coast (one viewing tower is on the site of a Napoleonic lookout), many species of trees and shrubs, and banks of rhododendrons which are at their most dazzling from May to early June. New for 2005 are an exhibition barn, café-style catering and a small shop.

North Norfolk Railway

WEYBOURNE

9 miles W of Cromer on the A149

Here, the shingle beach known as **Weybourne Hope** (or Hoop) slopes so steeply that an invading fleet could bring its ships right up to the shore. Which is exactly what the Danes did many times during the 9th and 10th centuries. A local adage states that 'He who would Old England win, Must at Weybourne Hoop begin,' and over the centuries care has been taken to protect this stretch of the coast. A map dated 1st May 1588 clearly shows 'Waborne Fort', and Holt's Parish Register for that year of the Armada notes that *'in this yeare was the town of Waborne fortified with a continuall garrison of men bothe of horse and foote with sconces (earthworks) ordinaunce and all manner of appoyntment to defend the Spannyards landing theare.'*

As it turned out, the 'Spannyards' never got close, but during both World Wars the same concern was shown for defending this vulnerable beach. The garrison then became the Anti-Aircraft Permanent Range and Radar Training Wing, providing instruction for National Servicemen until the camp finally closed in 1959. It was reckoned that by then some 1,500,000 shells had been fired out to sea. The site has since been returned to agricultural use, but the original NAAFI building remains and now houses **The Muckleburgh Collection**, a fascinating museum of military vehicles, weapons and equipment, most of which have seen action in battlefields all over the world. All of the tanks, armoured cars and amphibious vehicles on display can be inspected at close quarters, and there are regular tank demonstrations. Meals and snacks

•

Pretty Corner, just to the east of the A1082 at its junction with the A148, is a particularly beautiful area of woodland and also offers superb views over the surrounding countryside.

•

8 THE RAILWAY TAVERN

Holt, North Norfolk

The Railway Tavern is a convivial pub on the main street of Holt serving lunchtime snacks and light meals.

 see page 241

•

The worst day in Holt's history was May 1st, 1708, when a raging fire consumed most of the town's ancient houses. The consequent rebuilding replaced them with some elegant Georgian houses, gracious buildings which played a large part in earning the town its designation as a Conservation Area.

•

9 THE HARE & HOUNDS

Hempstead, nr Holt

The Hare & Hounds is a 17th century pub with lots of old-world charm, a welcome for all the family and fine home cooking.

 see page 241

11 THE HUNWORTH BELL

Hunworth, nr Holt

Excellent home cooking, well-kept cask ales and a friendly, cheerful ambience keep visitors happy at the **Hunworth Bell**.

 see page 242

are available - served in a NAAFI-style canteen.

Incidentally, despite Weybourne's exposed position, it has in fact only been attacked once, by the Luftwaffe on 11th July 1940. A stick of bombs landed in the main street and badly damaged two cottages.

Weybourne is the middle station on the Poppy Line (see under Sheringham) and alongside the station are the line's locomotive and carriage & wagon workshops.

HOLT

10 miles W of Cromer on the A148

A perennial finalist in the 'Anglia in Bloom' competition, Holt's town centre always looks a picture, with hanging baskets and flowers everywhere. Back in 1892, a guide-book to the county described Holt as 'A clean and very prettily situated market town, being planted in a well undulating and very woody neighbourhood.' More than a century later, one can't quarrel with that characterisation.

The town's most famous building, **Gresham's School**, somehow escaped the disastrous conflagration of 1708. Founded in 1555 by Sir John Gresham, the school began as an altruistic educational establishment, its pupils accepted solely on the basis of their academic promise. Since then, the school has abandoned both its town centre location and its founder's commitment to educating, free, those bright children who could not otherwise afford it. Among the school's many distinguished alumni

are Lord Reith, the poets W H Auden and Stephen Spender, and the composer Benjamin Britten.

Look out for one of Holt's most unusual buildings, **Home Place**. Designed and built in 1905 by E S Prior, an architect follower of the Arts & Crafts movement, the exterior of the house is completely covered with an ingeniously contrived cladding of local pebbles. The station at Holt, on the Poppy Line, is really Stalham Station, lovingly re-erected complete with much of its original furnishings.

CLEY-NEXT-THE-SEA

12 miles W of Cromer on the A149

Cley's name is no longer appropriate. Cley-a-mile-away-from-the-Sea would be more truthful. But in early medieval times, Cley (pronounced Cly, and meaning clay) was a more important port than King's Lynn, with a busy trade exporting wool to the Netherlands. In return, Cley imported a predilection for houses with curved gables, Flemish bricks and pantiles. The windmill overlooking the harbour adds to the sense that a little piece of Holland has strayed across the North Sea. This is the famous **Cley Mill**, the subject of thousands of paintings. Built in 1713 and in use until 1921, the Mill is open to visitors during the season (afternoons only), and also offers bed and breakfast.

The village's prosperity in the past is reflected in the enormous scale of its 14th/15th century parish church, **St Mary's**, whose south porch is particularly notable for its fine stonework and 16 armorial crests. The gorgeous fan-vaulted roof is decorated with bosses carved with angels, flowers, and a lively scene of an old woman throwing her distaff at a fox running away with her chickens.

Half a mile east of Cley on the A149 coast road, the Norfolk Wildlife Trust's **Cley Marshes** has a well-earned reputation as one of the UK's premier birdwatching sites.

Cley-Next-The-Sea

GLANDFORD

12 miles W of Cromer off the B1156

Near this delightful village, the **Natural Surroundings Wild Flower Centre** is dedicated to gardening with a strong ecological emphasis. There are wild flower meadows and gardens, organic vegetable and herb gardens, nurseries, a nature trail alongside the unspoilt River Glaven, and the Centre also organises a wide range of events with a conservation theme. A short walk down the valley from the Centre is the **Glandford Shell Museum**, a

From Cley it's possible to walk westward along the shoreline to Blakeney Point, the most northerly extremity of East Anglia. This spit of land that stretches three miles out into the sea is another twitcher's paradise. Over 250 species of birds have been spotted here, and the variety of flora is scarcely less impressive.

Seals at Blakeney Point

23

lovely Dutch-style building which houses the private collection of Sir Alfred Jodrell, a unique accumulation of sea shells gathered from beaches all around the world, together with a fascinating variety of artefacts made from them.

A couple of miles south of Glandford you'll find a building of 1802 which, year after year, has been voted one of the top tourist attractions in North Norfolk. **Letheringsett Watermill** stands on the site of an earlier mill recorded in the *Domesday Book*, and was rescued from near-dereliction in the 1980s. This fully functional, water-powered mill produces 100% wholewheat flour from locally grown wheat; there are regular demonstrations of the milling process, with a running

Boating at Letheringsett Mill

commentary from the miller; and the end product can be purchased in the gift shop.

MORSTON

13 miles W of Cromer on the A149

Great stretches of salt marshes and mud flats lie between this pleasant village and the sea, which is reached by way of a tidal creek that almost disappears at low tide. Morston is a particularly pleasing village with quiet lanes and clusters of cottages built from local flint cobbles. If the church tower looks rather patched-up, that's because it was struck by lightning in 1743. It's said that local people took this as a sign that the Second Coming of Christ was imminent, and that repairing their church was therefore pointless. It was many years before restoration work was finally undertaken, by which time the fabric of the tower had deteriorated even further.

LANGHAM

14 miles W of Cromer off the A149/A148

The minor road leading south from Morston will bring visitors, after a mile or so, to **Langham Glass & Rural Crafts** where, in a wonderful collection of restored 18th century barn workshops, a variety of craftspeople can be seen practising their traditional skills. In the churchyard of St Andrew and St Mary is the grave of the novelist Captain Marryat, who wrote *Mr Midshipman Easy* and devised a signalling code for the Merchant Navy.

BLAKENEY

14 miles W of Cromer on the A149

One of the most enchanting of the North Norfolk coastal villages, Blakeney was a commercial port until the beginning of the 20th century, when silting up of the estuary prevented all but pleasure craft from gaining access. The silting has left a fascinating landscape of serpentine creeks and channels twisting their way through mud banks and sand hills. In a side street off the quay is the 14th century **Guildhall** (English Heritage), which was probably a private house and contains an interesting undercroft, or cellar, which is notable as an early example of a brick-built vaulted ceiling.

The beautifully restored Church of St Nicholas, set on a hill overlooking village and marshland, offers the visitor a lovely Early English chancel, built in 1220, and the magnificent west tower, 100 feet high, a landmark for miles around. In a small turret on the northeast corner of the chancel a light would once burn as a beacon to guide ships safely into Blakeney Harbour.

STIFFKEY

16 miles W of Cromer on the A149

Regarded as one of the prettiest villages in the county, Stiffkey lies beside the little river of the same name. Pronounced 'Stewkey', the name means 'island of tree stumps' and is most likely derived from the marshy river valley of reed beds and fallen trees, which indeed gives the village the appearance of an island. At the east end of the village is the church of St John the Baptist; from the churchyard there are fine views of the river and of Stiffkey Hall to the south. All that now remains of this once-impressive building, built by the Bacon family in 1578, are the towers, one wing of the house, and the 17th century gatehouse. The stately ruins of the great hall have been transformed into a rose terrace and sunken garden and are open to the public.

The former Rectory is a grand Georgian building, famous as the residence of the Revd Harold Davidson, Rector of Stiffkey during the 1920s and 1930s. This

A couple of miles south of Stiffkey stand the picturesque ruins of Binham Priory (English Heritage), its magnificent nave still serving as the parish church. This represents only about one-sixth of the original Priory, founded in 1091 by a nephew of William the Conqueror. The church is well worth a visit to see its unusually lofty interior with a Monk's Walk at roof level, its Seven Sacraments font, and noble west front.

Blakeney Village

25

•

At South Denes in Great Yarmouth stands the 144-feet high Nelson's Monument crowned by a statue, not of Norfolk's most famous son, but of Britannia. The fluted Doric column was based on the Monument to the Great Fire of London; its base is inscribed with the names of Nelson's great victories of Aboukir, St Vincent, Copenhagen and Trafalgar.

•

gentleman launched a personal crusade to save the fallen women of London, and caused much gossip and scandal by doing so. Despite the fact that his notoriety regularly filled the church to capacity, he constantly fell foul of the ecclesiastical authorities and eventually lost his living. There is a rather bizarre ending to his story. After handing over the keys of Stiffkey Rectory, Harold joined a travelling show and was later killed by a lion whose cage he was sharing.

To the north of the village are the **Stiffkey Salt Marshes**, a National Trust nature reserve which turns a delicate shade of purple in July when the sea lavender is in bloom. Here on the sandflats can be found the famous 'Stewkey blues' - cockles which are highly regarded as a delicacy by connoisseurs of succulent bivalve molluscs.

GREAT YARMOUTH

The topography of Great Yarmouth is rather curious. Back in Saxon times, it was actually an island, a large sandbank dotted with fishermen's cottages. Later, the narrow estuary of the River Bure at the northern end was blocked off, causing it to flow down the western side of the town. It runs parallel to the sea for two miles before joining the larger River Yare, and then their united waters curve around the southern edge of the town for

another three miles before finally entering the sea.

So Yarmouth is now a promontory, its eastern and western sides displaying markedly different characters. The seaward side is a 5-mile stretch of sandy beaches, tourist attractions and countless amusements, with a breezy promenade from which one can watch the constant traffic of ships in Yarmouth Roads. There are two fine old traditional piers, the Britannia (810 feet long) and the Wellington (600 feet long), as well as The Jetty, first built in the 16th century for landing goods and passengers. A host of activities are on offer for families: **The Sealife Centre** with many kinds of marine life including octopus and seahorses, and an underwater viewing channel passing through shark-infested 'oceans'; **Amazonia**, an indoor tropical paradise featuring the largest collection of reptiles in Britain; **Merrivale Model Village** which offers an acre of attractive landscaped gardens with over 200 realistic models of town and country in miniature, which are illuminated at dusk, and the **Pleasure Beach**, featuring over 70 rides and attractions combining all the thrills of modern high-tech amusement park rides with the fun of traditional fairground attractions.

For heritage enthusiasts, Great Yarmouth has a rich and proud maritime history. The **Norfolk Nelson Museum** on South Quay features displays, paintings and contemporary memorabilia relating to the life and times of Horatio Lord Nelson. Also on South Quay is the **Elizabethan House Museum**, built by a wealthy merchant and now a museum of domestic life, with 16th century panelled rooms and a functional Victorian kitchen. In Row 117, South Quay, the **Old Merchant's House** is an excellent example of a 17th century dwelling and a showplace for local wood and metalwork. Nearby is **The Tollhouse**, originally built in 1262 as a gaol and later used as a courthouse. It is now a museum with original dungeons. Nearby is the exciting new **Time and Tide, Museum of Great Yarmouth Life**, where visitors can find out all about the town's fishing and maritime heritage.

Most of Yarmouth's older buildings are concentrated in the western, or riverside, part of the town. Here you will find **The Quay**, which moved Daniel Defoe, in 1724, to describe it as 'the finest quay in England, if not Europe'. It is more than a mile long and in places 150 yards wide. The **Town Hall** is well known for its grand staircase, Court Room and Assembly Room; the building itself is in use by the Local Authority. **The Rows**, a medieval network of tiny courtyards and narrow alleys, are a mere 2 feet wide in places. Badly damaged during a bombing raid in 1942, enough remains to show their unique character. There were originally 145 of these rows,

The Beach, Great Yarmouth

about 7 miles in total, all of them built at right angles to the sea and therefore freely ventilated by onshore breezes which, given the urban sanitary conditions of those times, must have been extremely welcome.

The bombing raid of 1942 also completely destroyed the interior of **St Nicholas'** church, but left its walls standing. Between 1957 and 1960 this huge building - the largest parish church in England - was completely restored and furnished in traditional style largely by using pieces garnered from redundant churches and other sources. The

•

The scale of over-fishing produced the inevitable result: within the space of two decades Yarmouth's herring industry foundered, and by the late 1960s found itself dead in the water. Luckily, the end of that historic trade coincided with the beginning of North Sea oil and gas exploitation, a business which has kept the town in reasonably good economic health up to the present day.

•

27

The Pier, Great Yarmouth

10 THE WHITE HART

Hopton-on-Sea, between Lowestoft and Great Yarmouth

Traditional hospitality and fine home cooking bring visitors to **The White Hart**.

 see page 241

88 FRITTON LAKE COUNTRYWORLD

Fritton, Great Yarmouth

A superb day out in the country with outdoor activities, children's farm and local crafts.

 see page 269

28

partly Norman font, for example, came from Highway church in Wiltshire, the organ from St Mary-the-Boltons in Kensington.

Just south of the church, off the Market Place, is the half-timbered **Anna Sewell House**, built in 1641, in which the author of *Black Beauty* lived. Sewell was born in the town in 1820, but it was only when she was in her late fifties that she transmuted her concern for the more humane treatment of horses into a classic and seemingly timeless novel. Anna was paid just £20 for the rights to a book which, in the five months that elapsed between its publication and her death in 1878, had already sold an incredible 100,000 copies. (Anna Sewell, who died in 1878, is buried in the Quaker burial ground in Lamas, a village between Coltishall and Aylsham.)

Another famous author associated with the town is Charles Dickens, who stayed at the Royal Hotel on Marine Parade in 1847 and 1848 while writing *David Copperfield*. Dickens had visited the town as a child and had actually seen an upturned boat on the beach being used as a dwelling, complete with a chimney emerging from its keel. In his novel, this becomes Peggotty's house to which young Copperfield is brought following the death of his mother. 'One thing I particularly noticed in this delightful house,' he writes, 'was the smell of fish; which was so searching, that when I took out my pocket-handkerchief to wipe my nose, I found it smelt exactly as if it had wrapped up a lobster.'

In fact, the whole town at that time was pervaded with the aroma of smoked herring, the silvery fish that were the basis of Yarmouth's prosperity. Around the time of Dickens' stay here, the author of the town's directory tried to pre-empt any discouraging effect this might have on visitors by claiming that 'The wholesome exhalations arising from the fish during the operation of curing are said to have a tendency to dissipate contagious disorders, and to be generally beneficial to the human constitution which is here sometimes preserved to extreme longevity.'

Across the town, some 60 curing houses were busy gutting, salting and spicing herrings to produce Yarmouth's great contribution to the English breakfast, the kipper. The process had been invented by a Yarmouth man, John Woodger: a rival of his, a Mr Bishop, developed a different method which left the fish wonderfully moist and flavoursome, and so created the famous Yarmouth bloater.

For centuries, incredible quantities of herring were landed, nearly a billion in 1913 alone. In earlier years the trade had involved so many fishermen that there were more boats (1,123) registered at Yarmouth than at London.

AROUND GREAT YARMOUTH

FRITTON

6 miles SW of Great Yarmouth off the A143

At **Fritton Lake Countryworld**, visitors will find a large undercover falconry centre with birds-of-prey flying displays twice daily. There are also heavy horse stables and a children's farm, 9-hole golf and 18-hole putting courses, lakeside gardens, boating and a large adventure playground. Open end-March to end-September every day, and weekends and half-term in October.

BURGH CASTLE

4 miles W of Great Yarmouth off the A12 or A143

When the Romans established their fortress of *Garionnonum*, now known as Burgh Castle, the surrounding marshes were still under water. The fort then stood on one bank of a vast estuary, commanding a strategic position at the head of an important waterway running into the heart of East Anglia. The ruins are impressive, with walls of alternating flint and brick layers rising 15 feet high in places, and spreading more than 11 feet wide at their base. The Romans abandoned Garionnonum

around AD 408 and some two centuries later the Irish missionary St Fursey (or Fursa) founded a monastery within its walls. Later generations cannibalised both his building, and much of the crumbling Roman castle, as materials for their own churches and houses.

CAISTER-ON-SEA

3 miles N of Great Yarmouth off the A149

In Boudica's time, this modern holiday resort with its stretch of fine sands was an important fishing port for her people, the Iceni. After the Romans had vanquished her unruly tribe, they settled here sometime in the 2nd century and built a *castra*, or castle, or Caister, of which only a few foundations and remains have yet been found. **Caister Castle**, which stands in a picturesque setting about a mile to the west of the town, is a much later construction, built between 1432 and 1435 by Sir John Fastolf with his spoils from the French wars in which he had served, very profitably, as Governor of Normandy and also distinguished himself leading the English bowmen at the Battle of Agincourt. Academics have enjoyed themselves for centuries disputing whether this Sir John was the model for Shakespeare's immortal rogue, Falstaff. Certainly the real Sir John was a larger-than-life character, but there's no evidence that he shared Falstaff's other characteristics of cowardliness, boastfulness or general over-indulgence.

13 THE FERRY INN

Stokesby, off the A1064 west of Caister
Motorists park and boaters moor alongside to enjoy the happy, relaxed atmosphere and the fine cooking at **The Ferry Inn**.

¶ *see page 242*

12 THE KINGS HEAD

Filby, west of Caister
New tenants provide a warm welcome, a friendly ambience and good home cooking at **The Kings Head**.

¶ *see page 242*

89 THE VILLAGE EXPERIENCE

Bugh St Margaret, Fleggburgh
A huge variety of attractions, including fairground rides, junior maze and concerts make this an unmissable day out.

🏛 *see page 269*

• *About three miles west of Caister Castle, the pleasantly landscaped grounds surrounding an 1876 Victorian mansion have been transformed into the Thrigby Hall Wildlife Gardens, home for a renowned collection of Asian mammals, birds and reptiles. There are snow leopards and rare tigers; gibbons and crocodiles; deer and otters; and other attractions include a tropical house, aviaries, waterfowl lake, willow pattern garden, gift shop and café. The Gardens are open every day, all year round.* •

Thurne, 6 miles west of Caister

The pride of its family owners, **The Lion Inn** is well worth tracking down for the warmest of welcomes, real ales and super home cooking.

see page 243

Caister Castle was the first in England to be built of brick, and is in fact one of the earliest brick buildings in the county. The 90-feet tower remains, together with much of the moated wall and gatehouse, now lapped by still waters and with ivy relentlessly encroaching. The castle is open daily from May to September and, as an additional attraction, there is an impressive collection of veteran and vintage cars.

THE NORFOLK BROADS

REEDHAM
8 miles SW of Great Yarmouth off the B1140

Here in Reedham is the single remaining car and passenger ferry in the Broads. There's also an interesting craft showroom at the Old Brewery, and a great pub in The Reedham Ferry Inn.

ACLE
10 miles W of Great Yarmouth off the A47

A thousand years ago, this small market town, now 10 miles inland, was a small fishing port on the coast. Gradually, land has been reclaimed from the estuaries of the Rivers Bure, Waveney and Yare, so that today large expanses of flat land stretch away from Acle towards the sea. The town's importance as a boating centre began in the 19th century with boat-building yards springing up beside the bridge. When Acle's first Regatta was held in 1890, some 150 yachts took part. The town became known as the 'Gateway to the

Reedham

Broads' and also as the gateway to 'Windmill Land', a picturesque stretch of the River Bure dotted with windmills. The medieval bridge that formerly crossed the Bure at Acle has less agreeable associations, since it was used for numerous executions with the unfortunate victims left to dangle over the river.

Acle was granted permission for a market in 1272, and it's still held every Thursday, attracting visitors from miles around. Others come to see the unusual church of **St Edmund** with its Saxon round tower, built some time around AD 900, crowned with a 15th century belfry from which eight carved figures look down on the beautifully thatched roof of the nave. The treasures inside include a superbly carved font, 6 feet high, and inscribed with the date 1410, and a fine 15th century screen.

SOUTH WALSHAM

9 miles E of Norwich on the B1140

This small village is notable for having two parish churches built within yards of each other. Just to the north of the village is the **Fairhaven Woodland and Water Garden**, an expanse of delightful water gardens lying beside the private **South Walsham Inner Broad**. Its centrepiece is the 900-year-old King Oak, lording it over the surrounding displays of rare shrubs and plants, native wildflowers, rhododendrons and giant lilies. There are tree-lined walks, a bird sanctuary, plants for sale, and a restaurant. A vintage-style riverboat runs trips every half-hour around the Broad.

The best way to see the remains of **St Benet's Abbey** is from a boat along the River Bure (indeed, it's quite difficult to reach it any other way). Rebuilt in 1020 by King Canute, after the Vikings had destroyed an earlier Saxon building, St Benet's became one of the richest abbeys in East Anglia. When Henry VIII closed it down in 1536 he made an unusual deal with its last Abbot. In return for creating the Abbot Bishop of Norwich, the Cathedral estates were to be handed over to the King, but St Benet's properties could remain in the Abbot/Bishop's possession. Even today, the Bishop of Norwich retains the additional title of Abbot of St Benet's, and on the first Sunday in August each year travels the last part of the journey by boat to hold an open-air service near the stately ruins of the Abbey gatehouse.

RANWORTH

14 miles NW of Great Yarmouth off the B1140

This beautiful Broadland village is famous for its church and its position on Ranworth Broad. From the tower of **St Helen's** church it is possible to see five Norfolk Broads, Horsey Mill, the sea at Great Yarmouth and, on a clear day, the spire of Norwich Cathedral. Inside, the church houses one of Norfolk's greatest ecclesiastical treasures, a breathtaking early 15th century Gothic choir screen, the most beautiful and the best preserved in the county. In

16 THE KINGS HEAD

Loddon, between Beccles and Norwich

Fish and seafood specials head the varied menus at **The King's Head**, with local ales and fine wines in support.

❙❙ *see page 244*

15/55 THE NEW INN

Rockland St Mary, nr Norwich

Overnight accommodation has been added to fine dining and wining at **The New Inn**.

❙❙ ⊨ *see pages 243 and 257*

90 FAIRHAVEN WOODLAND & WATER GARDEN

South Walsham, Norwich

A wonderful natural garden with three miles of paths taking you through trees and glades, and with colourful plants and flowers to see at any time of year.

🏛 *see page 270*

Norfolk Broads

The Norfolk Wildlife Trust's Ranworth Broad is a popular family destination where interpreted boardwalks promote an understanding of Broads ecology. A thatched building with an information centre floats on pontoons on the edge of the Broad.

glowing reds, greens and golds, gifted medieval artists painted a gallery of more than 30 saints and martyrs, inserting tiny cameos of such everyday scenes as falcons seizing hares, dogs chasing ducks and, oddly for Norfolk, lions. Cromwell's men, offended by such idolatrous images, smothered them with brown paint - an ideal preservative for these wonderful paintings, as became apparent when they were once again revealed during the course of a 19th century restoration of the church.

HORNING

12 miles NW of Great Yarmouth off the A1062

The travel writer Arthur Mee described Horning as 'Venice in Broadland', where 'waterways wandering from the river into the gardens are crossed by tiny bridges.' With its pretty reed-thatched cottages lining the bank of the River Bure and its position in the heart of the Broads, there are few more attractive places from which to explore this magical area.

POTTER HEIGHAM

13 miles NW of Great Yarmouth off the A149

Modern Potter Heigham has sprung up around the medieval bridge over the River Thurne, a low-arched structure with a clearance of only 7 feet at its highest, a notorious test for novice sailors. The Thurne is a major artery through the Broads, linking them in a continuous waterway from Horsey Mere in the east to Wroxham Broad in the west. A pleasant excursion from Potter Heigham is a visit to **Horsey Mere**, about six miles to the east, and **Horsey Windpump** (both National Trust). From this early 20th century drainage mill, now restored and fully working, there are lovely views across the Mere. A circular walk follows the north side of Horsey Mere, passes another windmill, and returns through the village. There's a small shop at the Windpump, and light refreshments are available.

STALHAM

18 miles NW of Great Yarmouth on the A149 (or 13 miles NE of Norwich)

At the Staithe, Stalham, on the opposite side of the A149 from Stalham centre, lies the **Museum of the Broads**. Open from 11 to 5 Monday to Friday and also during the local school summer holidays, the Museum has boats, displays,

exhibits and videos telling the story of life in the Broads. For more details Tel: 01692 581681

WROXHAM

8 miles NE of Norwich on the A1151

This riverside village, linked to its twin, Hoveton, by a hump-backed bridge over the River Bure, is the self-styled 'capital' of the Norfolk Broads and as such gets extremely busy during the season. The banks of the river are chock-a-block with boatyards full of cruisers of all shapes and sizes; there's a constant traffic of boats making their way to the open spaces of **Wroxham Broad**, and in July the scene becomes even more hectic when the annual Regatta is under way.

Wroxham is also the southern terminus of the **Bure Valley Railway**, a nine-mile long, narrow-gauge (15-inch) steam train service that closely follows the course of the River Bure through lovely countryside to the market town of

• *Four miles southeast of Stalham, the Norfolk Wildlife Trust's Hickling Broad is the largest Norfolk Broad and is home to a spectacular variety of wildlife that includes swallowtail butterflies, bitterns, marsh harriers and other rare Broadland species.*
•

River Thurne at Bastwick, near Potter Heigham

Wroxham Broad

---

56 BRIDGE HOUSE

High Street, Coltishall

The family-run **Bridge House** is a quiet, comfortable B&B with a garden leading down to a river frontage.

 see page 258

•

A mile or so east of Wroxham Barns, Hoveton Hall Gardens offer visitors a splendid combination of plants, shrubs and trees, with rare rhododendrons, azaleas, water plants and dazzling herbaceous borders within a walled garden. There are woodland and lakeside walks, streams and bridges, plant sales, gardening books and a tea room.

•

Aylsham. A couple of miles north of Wroxham is **Wroxham Barns**, a delightful collection of beautifully restored 18th century barns set in 10 acres of countryside, and housing a community of craftspeople. There are 13 workshops, producing between them a wide range of crafts, from stained glass to woodturning, stitchcraft to handmade children's clothes, pottery to floral artistry, and much more. The complex also includes a cider-pressing centre, a junior farm with lots of hands-on activities, a traditional Family Fair (with individually priced rides), a gift and craft shop, and a tearoom.

Anyone interested in dried flower arrangements should make their way to the tiny hamlet of **Cangate**, another couple of miles to the east, where **Willow Farm Flowers** provides an opportunity

of seeing the whole process, from the flowers in the field to the final colourful displays. The farm shop has an abundance of dried, silk, parchment and wooden flowers, beautifully arranged, and more than 50 varieties of dried flowers are available in bunches or made into arrangements of all shapes and sizes, or to special order. Willow Farm also has a picnic and play area, a guided farm walk, lays on flower arranging demonstrations and also runs one-day classes.

COLTISHALL

8 miles N of Norwich on the B1150/B1354

This charming village beside the River Bure captivates visitors with its riverside setting, leafy lanes, elegant Dutch-gabled houses, village green and thatched church. Coltishall has a good claim to its title of 'Gateway to Broadland', since for most cruisers this is the beginning of the navigable portion of the Bure. Anyone interested in Norfolk's industrial heritage will want to seek out the **Ancient Lime Kiln**, next door to the Railway Tavern in Station Road. Lime, formerly an important part of Norfolk's rural economy, is obtained by heating chalk to a very high temperature in a kiln. Most of the county sits on a bed of chalk, but in the area around Coltishall and Horstead it is of a particularly high quality. The kiln at Coltishall, one of the few surviving in the country, is a listed building of finely finished brickwork, built in a style unique to Norfolk.

The top of the tapered kiln pot is level with the ground, and down below a vaulted walkway allowed access to the grills through which the lime was raked out. This was uncomfortable and even dangerous work since fresh lime, when it comes into contact with a moist surface, such as a human body, becomes burning hot. The lime had to be slaked with water before it could be used as a fertiliser, for mortar or as whitewash. Access to the kiln is by way of the Railway Tavern, but during the months from October to March you may find that the building has been taken over by a colony of hibernating bats which, by law, may not be disturbed.

WORSTEAD

12 miles NE of Norwich off the A149 or B1150

Hard to imagine now, but Worstead was a busy little industrial centre in the Middle Ages. The village lent its name to the hard-wearing cloth produced in the region, and many of the original weavers' cottages can still be seen in the narrow side-streets. Worsted cloth, woven from tightly-twisted yarn, was introduced by Flemish immigrants and became popular throughout England from the 13th century onwards. The Flemish weavers settled happily into the East Anglian way of life and seem to have influenced its architecture almost as strongly as its weaving industry.

The lovely 14th century church of **St Mary** provides ample evidence of Worstead's former prosperity. Its many treasures include a fine hammerbeam roof, a chancel screen with a remarkable painted dado, and a magnificent traceried font complete with cover.

NORTH WALSHAM

This busy country town with its attractive **Market Cross** of 1600 has some interesting historical associations. Back in 1381, despite its remoteness from London, North Walsham became the focus of an uprising in support of Wat Tyler's Peasants' Rebellion. These North Norfolk rebels were led by John Litester, a local dyer, and their object was the abolition of serfdom. Their actions were mainly symbolic: invading manor houses, monasteries and town halls and burning the documents that recorded their subservient status. In a mass demonstration they gathered on Mousehold Heath outside Norwich, presented a petition to the King, and then retreated to North Walsham to await his answer. It came in the form of the sanguinary Bishop of Norwich, Henry Despenser, who, as his

The village of Worstead stages an annual weekend of events in July to raise money for the restoration of the church. The festival started up some 35 years ago, attracting more than 35,000 visitors in 1999. The memory of Worstead's days of glory is kept alive by a still-functioning Guild of Weavers. The Guild has placed looms in the north aisle of St Mary's, and from time to time there are demonstrations of the ancient skill of weaving.

•

About four miles east of North Walsham, near the village of Erpingham on the A140, Alby Crafts & Gardens has a Crafts Gallery promoting the excellence of mainly East Anglian and British craftsmanship - lacework, woodturning, jewellery, canework and much more. The 'Plantsman's Garden' displays a fine collection of unusual shrubs, plants and bulbs in a 4-acre site; there are also workshops where you can watch craftsmen at work, a Bottle Museum (small charge for admission) and a tearoom.

•

admiring biographer recorded, led an assault on the rebels, 'grinding his teeth like a wild boar, and sparing neither himself nor his enemies ... stabbing some, unhorsing others, hacking and hewing'. John Litester was captured, summarily executed and, on the orders of the Bishop, 'divided into four parts, and sent throughout the country to Norwich, Yarmouth, Lynn and to the site of his own house.'

A more glorious fate awaited the town's most famous resident, Horatio Nelson, who came to the Paston School here in 1768 as a boy of ten. Horatio was already dreaming of a naval career and, three years later when he read in the county newspaper that his Uncle Maurice had been appointed commander of a warship, he prevailed on his father to let him join the *Raisonnable.*

The **Paston School** had been founded in 1606 by Sir William Paston. His ancestors were the writers of the extraordinary collection of more than a thousand letters, written between 1422 and 1509, which present an astonishingly vivid picture of East Anglian life at the end of the turbulent Middle Ages. Sir William himself is buried in the parish church where he personally supervised (and paid for) the construction of the impressive marble and alabaster monument he desired to be erected in his memory.

AROUND NORTH WALSHAM

MUNDESLEY

2 miles NE of North Walsham on the B1159

'The finest air in the kingdom has been wasted for centuries,' said a speaker celebrating the arrival of the railway at Mundesley in 1898, 'because nobody had the courage to bring the people to the district.' The railway has been and gone, but the fresh breezes off the North Sea remain as invigorating as ever.

After the hazards of the coastline immediately to the north where cliffs, fields and houses have all been eroded by the relentless sea, it's a pleasure to arrive at this unassuming holiday resort with its superb sandy beach, considered by

Paston School, North Walsham

many the very best in Norfolk. Mundesley village is quite small (appropriately, its Maritime Museum is believed to the smallest museum in the country), but it provides all the facilities conducive to a relaxing family holiday. Best of all, there is safe swimming in the sea, and when the tide is out children can spend many a happy hour exploring the many 'lowes', or shallow lagoons, left behind.

PASTON

2 miles NE of North Walsham on the B1159

It was in this small village that the Paston family entered historical record. The vivid collection of letters they wrote to each other during the years that England was being racked by the Wars of the Roses has already been mentioned, and the village boasts another magnificent legacy from this remarkable family. In 1581, Sir William Paston built a cavernous tithe-barn here with flint walls and a thatched roof. It still stands, its roof still thatched: 160 feet long, almost 60 feet high - the longest, most imposing barn in Norfolk. In the nearby church, the most striking of the family memorials is the one dedicated to Katherine Paston. Sculpted in alabaster by Nicholas Stone in 1628, Katherine lies dressed to kill in her Jacobean finery of starched ruff, embroidered bodice, puffed sleeves and pearl necklaces. The monument cost £340, a staggering sum of money at that time.

HAPPISBURGH

4 miles E of North Walsham on the B1159

The coastal waters off Happisburgh (or 'Hazeborough', to give the village its correct pronunciation), have seen many a shipwreck over the centuries, and the victims lie buried in the graveyard of **St Mary's** church. The large grassy mound on the north side of the church contains the bodies of the ill-fated crew of HMS *Invincible*, wrecked on the treacherous sandbanks here in 1801. The ship was on its way to join up with Nelson's fleet at Copenhagen when the tragedy occurred, resulting in the deaths of 119 sailors. Happisburgh's distinctive Lighthouse, built in 1791 and striped like a barber's pole, certainly proved ineffectual on that occasion, as did the soaring 110-feet tower of the church itself, which could normally be relied on as a 'back-up' warning to mariners.

Inside the Church is a splendid 15th century octagonal font carved with the figures of lions, satyrs and 'wild men'; embedded in the pillars along the aisle are the marks left by shrapnel from German bombs dropped on the village in 1940.

LESSINGHAM

5 miles SE of North Walsham off the B1159

From this small village a lane winds down through spectacular dunes to the sands at Eccles Beach and, a little further north, to Cart Gap with its gently sloping beach and colourful lines of beach huts.

58   THE DURDANS

Mundesley-on-Sea

The Durdans is a perfect holiday base for enjoying fine hospitality, bracing air and the many attractions along the coast and inland.

🛏 see page 258

•

About four miles south of Lessingham stands a windmill that is not just the tallest in Norfolk, but in the whole of England. Eighty feet high, Sutton Windmill was built in the year of the French Revolution, 1789, and its millstones only finally ground to a halt in 1940.

Chris Nunn bought the mill in 1976, and since then he has devoted himself to renovating this glorious nine-storey building with the ultimate aim of restoring it to working order. Chris and his family have also built up a fascinating private collection of artefacts which reflect the social history of Norfolk over the past 150 years or so. These are on display in the family's privately-owned Broadlands Museum, a magpie's nest in which you'll find anything from vintage kitchen and veterinary tools to a reconstructed Pharmacy Shop of the 1880s, complete with a fine collection of patent medicines, ointments and pills.

•

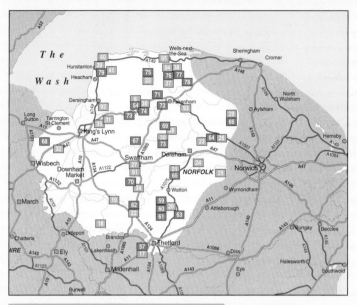

Kings Lynn & West Norfolk

Breckland, which extends for more than 360 square miles in southwest Norfolk and northwest Suffolk, is underlain by chalk with only a light covering of soil. The name 'Breckland' comes from the dialect word *breck*, meaning an area of land which has been cultivated for a while and then allowed to revert to heath after the soil has become exhausted. This quiet corner of the county is bounded by the Rivers Little Ouse and Waveney, which separate Norfolk from Suffolk.

It's surprising to find that one of England's most important ports in medieval times, King's Lynn, sat at the southern end of an underwater maze of sandbanks in The Wash. Keels were shallower then, of course, but without such modern aids as echo-sounders it must still have taken sailing skills of a high order to navigate one's way into the safety of King's Lynn harbour.

Along most of The Wash's 50-mile shoreline there is no human habitation: good news for the more than 160,000 wading birds and 51,000 wild ducks who have claimed the coast for themselves.

South of King's Lynn the countryside never quite decides whether it belongs to the Cambridgeshire fenland, with its bread-board level contours and over-arching skyscapes, or to the subtly-rounded undulations of central Norfolk where each twist of the road reveals yet another unblemished rural scene.

Within a radius of a few miles from the small town of Fakenham can be found a remarkable variety of places of interest. To the north, in the valley of the River Stiffkey, the Shrine of Our Lady of Walsingham was in medieval times second only to that of Thomas à Becket at Canterbury as a pilgrim destination. To the northeast, the Thursford Collection is home to an astonishing gathering of steam-powered engines of every description, including a monumental Wurlitzer organ. On the eastern outskirts of the town you can visit the premier collection of endangered and exotic waterbirds to be found in Europe, and over to the west stands the Marquess of Cholmondely's majestic home, Houghton Hall.

The shoreline along Norfolk's northwest coast changes from the perfect sands at Hunstanton to salt marshes threaded by winding creeks, and windswept dunes barely held in place by marram grass. It's an exhilarating coast, with huge skies, ozone-tangy breezes sweeping in from the North Sea, and an abundance of wildlife. There are three separate Nature Reserves within an eight-mile stretch, including the huge National Trust-owned bird sanctuary of Scolt Head Island. An admirable way to experience the area to the full is to walk all or part of the Coastal Footpath which begins at Holme next the Sea and follows the coastline for some 36 miles eastwards to Cromer, for most of its route well away from any roads.

Cliffs at Hunstanton

THETFORD

•

*To the west of Thetford
stretches the 90 square
miles of Thetford Forest,
the most extensive
lowland forest in Britain.
The Forestry Commission
began planting in 1922,
and although the
woodland is largely
given over to conifers,
with Scots and Corsican
Pine and Douglas Fir
predominating, oak,
sycamore and beech can
also be seen throughout.
There is a particularly
varied trail leading from
the Forestry Commission
Information Centre
which has detailed
information about this
and other walks through
the area.*

•

Some 2,000 years ago, Thetford
may well have been the site of
Boudica's Palace. In the 1980s,
excavations for building
development at Gallows Hill, north
of the town, revealed an Iron Age
enclosure. It is so extensive it may
well have been the capital of the
Iceni tribe which gave the Romans
so much trouble. Certainly, the
town's strategic location at the
meeting of the Rivers Thet and
Little Ouse made it an important
settlement for centuries. At the
time of the *Domesday Book*, 1086,
Thetford was the sixth-largest town
in the country and the seat of the
Bishop of East Anglia, with its own
castle, mint and pottery.

Of the **Castle**, only the 80-feet
motte remains, but
it's worth climbing
to the top of this
mighty mound for
the views across
the town. An early
Victorian traveller
described Thetford
as *'An ancient and
princely little town ...
one of the most
charming country
towns in England.'*
Despite major
development all
around, the heart
of the town still
fits that
description, with a
goodly number of
medieval and

Georgian houses presenting an
attractive medley of flint and half-
timbered buildings. Perhaps the most
striking is the **Ancient House**
Museum in White Hart Street, a
magnificent 15th century timber-
framed house with superb carved oak
ceilings. It houses the Tourist
Information Centre and a museum
where some of the most interesting
exhibits are replicas of the Thetford
Treasure, a 4th century hoard of gold
and silver jewellery discovered as
recently as 1979 by an amateur
archaeologist with a metal detector.
The originals of these sumptuous
artefacts are housed in the British
Museum in London.

Even older than the Ancient
House is the 12th century **Cluniac
Priory** (English Heritage), now
mostly in ruins but with an
impressive 14th century gatehouse
still standing. During the Middle
Ages, Thetford could boast 24
churches; today, only three remain.

Thetford's industrial heritage is
vividly displayed in the **Burrell Steam
Museum**, in Minstergate, which has
full-size steam engines regularly 'in
steam', re-created workshops and
many examples of vintage agricultural
machinery. The Museum tells the
story of the Burrell Steam Company,
which formed the backbone of the
town's industry from the late 18th to
the early 20th centuries, their sturdy
machines famous around the world.

In King Street, the **Thomas
Paine Statue** commemorates the
town's most famous son, born here in
1737. The revolutionary philosopher,
and author of *The Rights of Man*

St Peter's Church, Thetford

emigrated to America in 1774, where he helped formulate the American Bill of Rights. Paine's democratic views were so detested in England that even ten years after his death in New York, the authorities refused permission for his admirer, William Cobbett, to have the remains buried in his home country. And it wasn't until the 1950s that Thetford finally got around to erecting a statue in his honour. Ironically for such a robust democrat, his statue stands in King Street and opposite **The King's House**, named after James I, who was a frequent visitor here between 1608 and 1618. At the Thomas Paine Hotel in White Hart Street, the room in which it is believed that Paine was born is now the Honeymoon Suite, complete with four-poster bed.

On the edge of the forest, about two miles west of Thetford, are the ruins of **Thetford Warren Lodge**, built around 1400. At that time a huge area here was preserved for farming rabbits, a major element of the medieval diet. The vast warren was owned by the Abbot of Thetford Priory, and it was he who built the Lodge for his gamekeeper.

Still in the forest, reached by a footpath from the village of Santon Downham, are **Grimes Graves** (English Heritage), the earliest major industrial site to be discovered in Europe. At these unique Neolithic flint mines, Stone Age labourers extracted the materials for their sharp-edged axes and knives. It's a strange experience entering these 4,000 year old shafts which descend some 30 feet to an underground chamber. The experience is even better if you bring your own high-powered torch. Opening times are Thursday to Monday in March and October, daily from April to September. Tel: 01842 810656

AROUND THETFORD

MUNDFORD

8 miles NW of Thetford on the A1065/A134

Mundford is a large Breckland village of flint-built cottages, set on the northern edge of Thetford Forest and with the River Wissey running by. If you ever watch television, you've almost certainly seen Lynford Hall, a mile or so northwest of Mundford. It has provided an impressive location for scenes in *Dad's Army; Allo, Allo; You Rang My Lord?* and *Love on a Branch Line*, as well as featuring in numerous television commercials. The Hall is a superb Grade II listed mansion, built for the Lyne-Stevens family in 1885 (as a hunting-lodge, incredibly) and designed in the Jacobean Renaissance style by William Burn.

THOMPSON

10 miles NE of Thetford on minor road off the A1075

This is a quiet village with a marshy man-made lake, **Thompson Water**, and a wild common. **The Peddars Way** long-distance footpath passes about a mile to the west and, about the same distance to the northeast, the Church is a splendid early 14th century building notable for its fine carved screen and choice 17th century fittings.

17/57 THE ELVEDEN INN

Elveden, nr Thetford

The Elveden Inn is a convivial pub for food and drink and comfortable B&B rooms.

 see pages 244 and 258

18 THE LODGE

Feltwell, west of Thetford Forest

The Lodge is a friendly village pub where Mexican dishes are among the owner-chef's specialities.

 see page 244

19 THE CROWN INN

Northwold, northwest of Thetford

The owner-chef at **The Crown** is the king of Caribbean cuisine – many other dishes, too, and 4 real ales.

 see page 244

22/62 LYNFORD HALL COUNTRY HOTEL

Mundford, north of Thetford (junction of A134 and A1065)

Lynford Hall is a magnificent country mansion that combines the comfort of a top-class hotel with business, banqueting and wedding facilities.

see pages 245 and 259

59 COLLEGE FARM

Thompson, nr Thetford

College Farm provides comfort and seclusion in three very spacious bedrooms for B&B guests.

 see page 258

20/60 THE CHEQUERS INN

Thompson, nr Watton

The Chequers is a beautiful thatched village inn offering real ales, bar and restaurant menus and purpose-built guest accommodation.

 see pages 244 and 258

61 THE THATCHED HOUSE

Thompson, near Thetford

The Thatched House offers delightfully comfortable, civilised B&B accommodation in the prettiest of settings.

 see page 258

63 MANOR FARM

Great Hockham, northeast of Thetford

Outstanding breakfasts start the day at **Manor Farm**, a comfortable B&B base on a 300-acre arable farm.

 see page 260

WATTON

14 miles NE of Thetford on the A1075

Watton's striking town sign depicts the 'Babes in the Wood' of the famous nursery story. The story, which was already current hereabouts in the 1500s, relates that as Arthur Truelove lay dying he decided that the only hope for his two children was to leave them in the care of their uncle. Unfortunately, the uncle decided to help himself to their inheritance and paid two men to take the children into nearby **Wayland Wood** and kill them. In a moment of unexpected compassion, one of the men decided that he could not commit the dastardly act. He disposed of his accomplice instead, and abandoned the children in the wood to suffer whatever fate might befall them. Sadly, unlike the nursery tale in which the children find their way back home and live happily ever after, this unfortunate brother and sister perished. Their ghosts are said to wander hand in hand through the woods to this day.

Watton boasts an unusual **Clock Tower**, dated 1679, standing at the centre of its long main street.

EAST HARLING

8 miles E of Thetford on the B1111

This attractive little town boasts a beautiful 15th century church in a pastoral location beside the River Thet. Inside, a magnificent hammerbeam roof crowns the lofty nave, there's some outstanding 15th century glass and, in the Harling Chapel, the fine marble **Tomb of**

Robert Harling. Harling was one of Henry V's knights, who met his death at the siege of Paris in 1435. Since this was long before the days of refrigeration, the knight's body was instead stewed, then stuffed into a barrel and brought back to East Harling for a ceremonious burial.

Harling's church houses another equally sumptuous memorial, the **Tomb of Sir Thomas Lovell**. Sculpted in alabaster, Sir Thomas is an imposing figure, clad in armour with a long sword, his head resting on a helmet, his feet on a spray of peacock's feathers. He and his wife lie beneath a wondrously ornamented canopy, decorated with multi-coloured shields and pinnacles.

DEREHAM

One of the most ancient towns in the county, Dereham has a recorded history stretching back to AD 654 when St Withburga founded a Nunnery here. Her name lives on at St Withburga's Well, just to the west of the church. This is where she was laid to rest but, some 300 years later, the Abbot and monks of Ely robbed her grave and ensconced the precious, fundraising relic in their own Cathedral. In the saint's desecrated grave a spring suddenly bubbled forth, its waters possessed of miraculous healing properties, and St Withburga's shrine attracted even more pilgrims than before. Some still come.

In the church of St Nicholas, the second largest in Norfolk, there are features from every century from the 12th to the 16th: a magnificent lantern tower, a lofty Bell Tower, painted roofs, and a Seven Sacrament Font. This is the largest of these notable fonts, of which only 30 have survived - 28 of them in Norfolk and Suffolk.

In the northeast transept is buried a poet, some of whose lines have become embedded in the language:

"*Variety's the very spice of life, that gives it all its flavour*"
"*I am the monarch of all I survey*"
"*God made the country and man made the town*"

They all came from the pen of William Cowper who, despite being the author of such cheery poems as *John Gilpin* ("*A citizen of credit and renown*"), suffered grievously from depression, a condition not improved by his association with John Newton, a former slave-trader who had repented and become 'a man of gloomy piety'. The two men collaborated on a book of hymns that included such perennial favourites as '*Oh! for a Closer Walk with God*', '*Hark, my soul, it is the Lord*' and '*God moves in a mysterious way*'. Cowper spent the last four years of his life at Dereham, veering in and out of madness. In a late-flowering romance he had married the widow Mary Unwin, but the strain of caring for the deranged poet drove her in turn to insanity and death. She, too, is buried in the church.

William Cowper died four years

after Mary, in 1800. Three years later, another celebrated writer was born at the quaintly named hamlet of **Dumpling Green** on the edge of the town. George Borrow was to become one of the great English travel writers, producing books full of character and colour such as *Wild Wales* and *The Bible in Spain*. In his autobiographical novel *Lavengro* he begins with a warm recollection of the town where he was born: '*I love to think on thee, pretty, quiet D[ereham], thou pattern of an English market town, with thy clean but narrow streets branching out from thy modest*

23 THE ANGEL

Swanton Morley, north of Dereham

History, character and good food and drink combine at **The Angel**, where the hosts are always ready with a warm welcome.

see page 246

Dereham

43

28/69 THE MALLARD

Mileham, northwest of East Dereham

The Mallard offers the unique combination of top-quality self-catering accommodation and an exclusive wine business.

⚊ ❙❙ *see pages 247 and 261*

65 POUND GREEN HOTEL

Shipdham, between Dereham and Watton

Pound Green Hotel has 11 comfortable bedrooms, a brasserie and bar and a good-sized garden.

⚊ *see page 260*

21 THE GOLDEN DOG

Shipdham, nr Dereham

The Golden Dog is a traditional village pub with a strong local following. Home cooking, pub games, beer garden.

❙❙ *see page 244*

24 THE MUSTARD POT

Whinburgh, nr Dereham

Home cooking and traditional ales and beers bring the regulars to **The Mustard Pot**, a cosy old roadside inn.

❙❙ *see page 246*

market place, with thine old-fashioned houses, with here and there a roof of venerable thatch.' The house in which George Borrow was born, Borrow's Hall, still stands in Dumpling Green.

A much less attractive character connected with Dereham is Bishop Bonner, the enthusiastic arsonist of Protestant 'heretics' during the unhappy reign of Mary Tudor. He was rector of the town before being appointed Bishop of London, and he lived in the exquisite thatched terrace now called **Bishop Bonner's Cottages**. The exterior is ornamented with delightful pargeting, a frieze of flower and fruit designs below the eaves, a form of decoration which is very unusual in Norfolk. The cottages now house a small museum.

The **Mid-Norfolk Railway** runs through 11 miles of attractive rural Norfolk linking the ancient market towns of Dereham and Wymondham, passing through river valleys and pretty villages and hamlets. 2005 saw the first running of steam locomotives 50 years after the withdrawal of steam from passenger services. The class B12/3 61572 was operating on the line in May, on loan from the North Norfolk Railway. Tel: 01362 851723

AROUND DEREHAM

GRESSENHALL

3 miles NW of Dereham off the B1146

The **Norfolk Rural Life Museum** is housed in an impressive late 18th century former workhouse built in rose-red brick. Gressenhall Workhouse was designed to accommodate some 700 unfortunates, so it was built on a very grand scale indeed. Now one of the UK's leading rural life museums and among Norfolk's top family attractions, there's ample room for the many exhibits illuminating the working and domestic life of Norfolk people over the last 150 years. Farming the old-fashioned way is there to be discovered on Union Farm, where heavy animals still work the fields. A stroll along the 1930s village high street takes in the grocer's, post office and schoolroom. The surrounding 50 acres of unspoilt countryside are perfect for walking. The site hosts numerous special events during the season, ranging from Steam Days to an international folk dance festival with more than 200 dancers taking part.

A mile or so south of Gressenhall, the tiny community of **Dillington** is worth seeking out for **Norfolk Herbs at Blackberry Farm**, a specialist herb farm located in a beautiful wooded valley. Visitors are invited to browse through a vast collection of aromatic, culinary and medicinal herb plants, and to learn all about growing and using herbs.

NORTH ELMHAM

6 miles N of Dereham off the B1110

Near the village of North Elmham stand the sparse remains of a Saxon Cathedral. North Elmham was the seat of the Bishops of East Anglia until 1071, when they moved to Thetford (and then, 20 years later, to Norwich). Although there had been a cathedral here since the late 7th century, what has survived is mostly from the 11th century. Despite its grand title, the T-shaped ground plan reveals that the cathedral was no larger than a small parish church.

BRISLEY

7 miles N of Dereham on the B1145

Brisley village is well known to local historians and naturalists for its huge expanse of heathland, some 170 acres of it. It's reckoned to be the best example of unspoilt common in Norfolk, and at its centre are scores of pits that were dug out in medieval times to provide clay for the wattle-and-daub houses of the period. Another feature of interest in the village is Gately Manor (private), an Elizabethan manor house standing within the remains of a medieval moat, and yet another moated house at Old Hall Farm in the southwest corner of the green.

SWAFFHAM

Swaffham's one-time claim to be the 'Montpellier of England' was justified by the abundance of handsome Georgian houses that used to surround the large, wedge-shaped market place. A good number still survive, along with the **Assembly Room** of 1817 where the quality would foregather for concerts, balls and soirees. The

central focus of the market square is the elegant **Butter Cross**, presented to the town by the Earl of Orford in 1783. It's not a cross at all, but a classical lead-covered dome standing on eight columns and surmounted by a life-size statue of Ceres, the Roman goddess of agriculture - an appropriate symbol for this busy market town, from which ten roads radiate out across the county.

From the market place an avenue of limes leads to the quite outstanding Church of **St Peter & St Paul**, a 15th century masterpiece with one of the very best double hammerbeam roofs in the county, strikingly embellished with a host of angels, their wings widespread. The unknown mason who devised the church's harmonious proportions made it 51 feet wide, 51 feet high and 102 feet long. Carved on a bench-end here is a man in medieval dress accompanied by a dog on a chain. The same two figures are incorporated in the town's coat of arms, and also appear in the elegantly designed town sign just beyond the market place. The man is 'The Pedlar of Swaffham', a certain John Chapman who, according to legend, dreamed that if he made his way to London Bridge he would meet a stranger who would make him rich. The pedlar and his dog set off for London, and on the bridge he was eventually accosted by a stranger who asked him what he was doing there. John recounted his dream.

---

25 THE BELL

Barnham Broom, between Wymondhan and Dereham

The Bell is a sociable old inn with real ales, home cooking, pub games, entertainment and a warm welcome for everyone.

see *page 246*

---

26 THE FOX & HOUNDS

Lyng, northeast of Dereham

All the ingredients of a traditional country inn can be found at **The Fox & Hounds** on the main street of a charming village.

see *page 246*

---

64 COLLIN GREEN COTTAGES

Lyng, northeast of Dereham

Collin Green Cottages provide excellent self-catering accommodation in a quiet rural setting.

see *page 260*

29/66 THE BELL INN

High Street, Cawston

Good food and drink and spotless B&B rooms make **The Bell Inn** a popular choice for locals and tourists.

see *pages 248 and 260*

45

27 THE NORFOLK HERO

Station Street, Swaffham

Hearty home cooked dishes head the blackboard menu at **The Norfolk Hero**.

🍴 see page 246

34/70 THE SWAN

Hilborough, nr Swaffham

The Swan is a fine old pub of wide appeal, with good food and drink and comfortable B&B accommodation.

🍴 see page 249 and 262

91 SWAFFHAM MUSEUM

London Street, Swaffham,

The museum focuses on the history of the town with aspects of trade, industry and domestic life all represented.

🏛 see page 270

Scoffingly, the stranger said 'If I were a dreamer, I should go to Swaffham. Recently I dreamt that in Swaffham lived a man named Chapman, and in his garden, buried under a tree, lay a treasure.' John hastily returned home, uprooted the only tree in his garden, and unearthed two jugs full of gold coins.

There was indeed a John Chapman who contributed generously to the building of the parish church in the late 1400s. Cynics claim that he was a wealthy merchant, and that similar tales occur in the folklore of most European countries. Whatever the truth, there's no doubt that the people of Swaffham took the story to their hearts.

John Chapman may be Swaffham's best-known character locally, but internationally the name of Howard Carter, the discoverer of Tutankhamen's tomb, is much better known. Carter was born at Swaffham in 1874; his death in 1939 was attributed by the popular press to 'the Curse of Tutankhamen'. If so, it must have been an extremely slow-acting curse. Some 17 years had elapsed since Carter had knelt by a dark, underground opening, swivelled his torch and found himself the first human being in centuries to gaze upon the astonishing treasures buried in the tomb of the teenage Pharaoh.

Swaffham Museum in the Town Hall, recently fully refurbished, is the setting for the story of the town's past. Visitors can follow Howard Carter's road to the Valley of the Kings, see the Symonds Collection of handmade figurines, and admire the Sporle collection of locally-found artefacts.

Move on some 1,400 years from the death of Tutankhamen to Norfolk in the 1st century AD. Before a battle, members of the Iceni tribe, led by Boudica, would squeeze the blue sap of the woad plant onto their faces in the hope of frightening the Roman invaders (or any other of their many enemies). At **Cockley Cley Iceni Village and Museums**, three miles southwest of Swaffham off the A1065, archaeologists have reconstructed a village of Boudica's time, complete with wooden huts, moat, drawbridge and palisades. Reconstruction though it is, the village is remarkably effective in evoking a sense of what daily life entailed more than 1,900 years ago. The exhibits cover many centuries, up to the Second World War.

A more recent addition to Swaffham's attractions is the **EcoTech Discovery Centre**, opened in 1998. Through intriguing interactive displays and hands-on demonstrations, visitors can discover what startling innovations current, and possible, technology may have in store for us during the next millennium. Energy and a head for heights are needed to climb to the viewing platform at the top of the 220feet E66 wind turbine.

AROUND SWAFFHAM

CASTLE ACRE

4 miles N of Swaffham off the A1065

Set on a hill surrounded by water meadows, Castle Acre seems still to linger in the Middle Ages. William de Warenne, William the Conqueror's son-in-law, came here very soon after the Conquest and built a Castle that was one of the first, and largest, in the country to be built by the Normans. Of that vast fortress, little remains apart from the gargantuan earthworks and a squat 13th century gateway.

Much more has survived of **Castle Acre Priory**, founded in 1090 and set in fields beside the River Nar. Its glorious West Front gives a powerful indication of how majestic a triumph of late Norman architecture the complete Priory must have been. With five apses and twin towers, the ground plan was modelled on the Cluniac mother church in Burgundy, where William de Warenne had stayed while making a pilgrimage to Rome. Despite the Priory's great size, it appears that perhaps as few as 25 monks lived here during the

Middle Ages - and in some comfort, judging by the well-preserved Prior's House, which has its own bath and built-in wash-basin. The Priory lay on the main route to the famous Shrine at Walsingham, with which it tried to compete by offering pilgrims a rival attraction in the form of an arm of St Philip.

Today the noble ruins of the Priory are powerfully atmospheric, a brooding scene skilfully exploited by Roger Corman when he filmed here for his screen version of Edgar Allan Poe's ghostly story, *The Tomb of Ligeia*. The walled herb garden is divided into four sections containing medicinal, decorative, culinary and strewing herbs.

Castle Acre village is extremely picturesque, the first place in Norfolk to be designated a

67 LODGE FARM

Castle Acre, nr King's Lynn

Guests at **Lodge Farm** will find a warm welcome and spacious B&B accommodation in a secluded rural setting.

see page 260

Castle Acre Priory

47

30 THE BULL INN

Litcham, nr King's Lynn

Additional accommodation is coming on stream at the 17th century **Bull Inn**, a popular hostelry serving classic pub dishes.

🍴 *see page 248*

Conservation Area, in 1971. Most of the village, including the 15th century parish church, is built in traditional flint, with a few later houses of brick blending in remarkably happily.

LITCHAM

11 miles NE of Swaffham on the B1145

Small though it is, this village strung alongside the infant River Nar can boast an intriguing **Village Museum**, with displays of local artefacts from Roman times to the present, an extensive collection of photographs, some of which date back to 1865, and an underground lime kiln.

KING'S LYNN

In the opinion of James Lee-Milne, the National Trust's architectural authority, 'The finest old streets anywhere in England' are to be found at King's Lynn. Tudor, Jacobean and Flemish houses mingle harmoniously with grand medieval churches and stately civic buildings. It's not surprising that the BBC chose the town to represent early 19th century London in their production of *Martin Chuzzlewit*. It seems, though, that word of this ancient sea-port's many treasures has not yet been widely broadcast, so most visitors to the area tend to stay on the King's Lynn bypass while making their way to the better-known attractions of the north Norfolk coast. They are missing a lot.

The best place to start an exploration of the town is at the beautiful church of **St Margaret**, founded in 1101 and with a remarkable leaning arch of that original building still intact. The architecture is impressive, but the church is especially famous for its two outstanding 14th century brasses, generally reckoned to be the two largest and most monumental in the kingdom. Richly engraved, one shows workers in a vineyard, the other, commemorating Robert Braunche,

Tuesday Market, King's Lynn

represents the great feast which Robert hosted at King's Lynn for Edward III in 1364.

Marks on the tower doorway indicate the church's, and the town's, vulnerability to the waters of the Wash and the River Great Ouse. They show the high-water levels reached during the great floods of 11 March 1883 (the lowest), 31 January 1953 and 11 January, 1978.

The organist at St Margaret's in the mid 18th century was the celebrated writer on music, Dr Charles Burney, but his daughter Fanny was perhaps even more interesting. She wrote a best-selling novel, *Evelina*, at the age of 25, became a leading light of London society, a close friend of Dr Johnson and Sir Joshua Reynolds, and at the age of 59 underwent an operation for breast cancer without anaesthetic. She only fainted once during the 20-minute operation, and went on to continue her active social life until her death at the ripe old age of 87.

Alongside the north wall of St Margaret's is the **Saturday Market Place**, one of the town's two market places, where visitors can explore The Old Gaol House, an experience complete with the sights and sounds of the ancient cells. A few steps further is one of the most striking sights in the town, the **Guildhall of the Holy Trinity** with its distinctive chequerboard design of black flint and white stone. The Guildhall was built in 1421, extended in Elizabethan times, and its Great Hall is still used

today for wedding ceremonies and various civic events.

Next door to the Guildhall is the Town Hall of 1895, which in a good-neighbourly way is constructed in the same flint-and-stone pattern. The Town Hall also houses the **Museum of Lynn Life** where, along with displays telling the story of the town's 900 years, you can also admire the municipal regalia. The greatest treasure in this collection is King John's Cup, a dazzling piece of medieval workmanship with coloured enamel scenes set in gold. The Cup was supposed to be part of King John's treasure which had been lost in 1215 when his overburdened baggage train was crossing the Nene Estuary and sank into the treacherous quicksands. This venerable legend is sadly undermined by the fact that the Cup was not made until 1340, more than a century after John's death.

A short distance from the Town Hall, standing proudly by itself on the banks of the River Purfleet, is the handsome **Custom House** of 1683, designed by the celebrated local architect Henry Bell.

There's not enough space here to list all of the town's many other important buildings, but mention must be made of the **Hanseatic Warehouse** (1428), the **South Gate** (1440), the **Greenland Fishery Building** (1605), and the **Guildhall of St George**, built around 1406 and reputedly the oldest civic hall in England. The Hall was from time to time also used as a theatre; it's

The Guildhall is now home to the King's Lynn Arts Centre, active all year round with events and exhibitions and since 1951 the force behind an annual Arts Festival in July with concerts, theatre and a composer in residence. Some of the concerts are held in St Nicholas' Chapel, a medieval building whose acoustics outmatch those of many a modern concert hall.

•

At Walpole St Peter, between the A17 and A47, the church known as the 'Queen of the Marshland' is a graceful Perpendicular church with many treasures, including a font with an exotic Jacobean cover, a cobbled covered passageway and two aisle chapels in the nave; St Peter's has a rare example of a hudd, a portable cubicle to protect the priest from rain during burial.

•

known that Shakespeare's travelling company played here, and it is considered highly likely that the Bard himself trod the boards.

At **Caithness Crystal** Visitor Centre, you can watch craftsmen at close quarters as they shape and manipulate glass into beautiful objets d'art.

AROUND KING'S LYNN

TERRINGTON ST CLEMENT

5 miles W of King's Lynn off the A17

Terrington St Clement is a sizable village notable for its superb church, a 14th century Gothic masterwork more properly known as St Clement's church, and for the **African Violet and Garden Centre**, where some quarter of a million violets are grown each year, in a wide range of colour and species. This unique working nursery, an all-seasons attraction, has earned many awards since opening in 1987, including Gold Medals at the Chelsea Flower Show.

STOW BARDOLPH

8 miles S of King's Lynn off the A10

Holy Trinity church at Stow Bardolph houses one of the oddest memorials in the country. Before her death in 1744, Sarah Hare, youngest daughter of the Lord of the Manor, Sir Thomas Hare, arranged for a life-sized effigy of herself to be made in wax. It was said to be an exceptionally good likeness: if so, Sarah appears to have been a rather uncomely maiden, and afflicted with

boils to boot. Her death was attributed to blood poisoning after she had pricked her finger with a needle, an act of Divine retribution, apparently, for her sin of sewing on a Sunday. Sarah was then attired in a dress she had chosen herself, placed in a windowed mahogany cabinet, and the monument set up in the Hare family's chapel, a grandiose structure which is larger than the chancel of the church itself.

DOWNHAM MARKET

10 miles S of King's Lynn off the A10/A1122

Once the site for a major horse fair, this compact little market town stands at the very edge of the Fens, with the River Great Ouse and the New Bedford Drain running side by side at its western edge. Many of its houses are built in the distinctive brick and carrstone style of the area. One of the finest examples of this traditional use of local materials can be seen at Dial House in Railway Road, built in the late 1600s.

The parish church has managed to find a small hill on which to perch. It's an unassuming building with a rather incongruously splendid glass chandelier from the 1730s. The town square has recently been regenerated and in it stands the elegant, riotously decorated cast-iron **Clock**. This was erected in 1878 at a cost of £450 and now chimes on the hour. The tower's backdrop of attractive cottages provides a charming setting for a holiday snap.

Two great names are associated with this small town: Charles I, disguised as a clergyman, stayed at

Downham Market for a night during his flight after the Battle of Naseby, and Horatio (later Lord) Nelson, son of the parson of Burnham Thorpe, was sent to the little school here.

Near Downham Bridge on the A1122 you will find Collectors World and the Magical Dickens World. The first boasts a plethora of farming and household memorabilia, carts, carriages, radios, cameras, antique and collectible dolls, Armstrong Siddeley cars and much more, with rooms dedicated to Barbara Cartland, Horatio Nelson, the 1960s and more. Dickens World offers visitors a chance to step back in time into a maze of late 19th century streets, shops, sights and sounds.

DENVER

2 miles S of Downham Market off the A10/A1122

Denver Sluice was originally built in 1651 by the Dutch engineer, Cornelius Vermuyden, as part of a scheme to drain 20,000 acres of land owned by the Duke of Bedford. Various modifications were made to the system over the years, but the principle remains the same, and the oldest surviving sluice, built in 1834, is still in use today. Running parallel with it is the modern **Great Denver Sluice**, opened in 1964; together these two sluices control the flow of a large complex of rivers and drainage channels, and are able to divert floodwaters into the Flood Relief Channel that runs alongside the Great Ouse.

The two great drainage cuts

Downham Market

constructed by Vermuyden are known as the Old and New Bedford rivers, and the strip of land between them, never more than 1,000 yards wide, is called the Ouse Washes. This is deliberately allowed to flood during the winter months so that the fields on either side remain dry. The drains run side by side for more than 13 miles, to Earith in Cambridgeshire, and this has become a favourite route for walkers, with a rich variety of

51

Denver Windmill

•

Denver Windmill, built in 1835 but put out of commission in 1941, when the sails were struck by lightning, re-opened in 2000. This wonderful working mill set on the edge of the Fens has been carefully restored. On-site attractions include a visitor centre, craft workshops, bakery and tea shop. Holiday accommodation is also available.

•

bird, animal and insect life to be seen along the way.

HILGAY

3 miles S of Downham Market off the A10

When the *Domesday Book* was written, Hilgay was recorded as one of only two settlements in the Norfolk fens. It was then an island, its few houses planted on a low hill rising from the surrounding marshland. The village is scarcely any larger today, and collectors of unusual gravestones make their way to its churchyard seeking the last resting place of George William

Manby. During the Napoleonic wars, Manby invented a rocket-powered life-line that could be fired to ships in distress. His gravestone is carved with a ship, an anchor, a depiction of his rocket device and an inscription that ends with the reproachful words, 'The public should have paid this tribute.'

OXBOROUGH

10 miles SE of Downham Market off the A134

How many hamlets in the country, one wonders, can boast two such different buildings of note as those to be seen at Oxborough? First there's the church of **St John the Evangelist**, remarkable for its rare brass eagle lectern of 1498 and its glorious Bedingfeld Chapel of 1525, sheltering twin monuments to Sir Edmund Bedingfeld and his wife fashioned in the then newly popular material of terracotta.

It was Sir Edmund who built **Oxburgh Hall** (National Trust), a breathtakingly lovely moated house built of pale-rose brick and white stone. Sir Edmund's descendants still live in what a later architect, Pugin, described as 'one of the noblest specimens of domestic architecture of the 15th century.' Henry VII and his Queen, Elizabeth of York, visited in 1497 and lodged in the splendid State Apartments which form a bridge between the glorious gatehouse towers, and which ever since have been known as the King's Room and the Queen's Room. On display here is the original Charter of 1482, affixed with Edward IV's Great Seal of England, granting Sir

Edmund permission to build with 'stone, lime and sand', and to fortify the building with battlements. These rooms also house some magnificent period furniture, a collection of royal letters to the Bedingfelds, and the huge Sheldon Tapestry Map of 1647 showing Oxfordshire and Berkshire. Another more poignant tapestry, known as the Marian Needlework, was the joint handiwork of Elizabeth, Countess of Shrewsbury, and Mary, Queen of Scots, during the latter's captivity here in 1570. The Bedingfelds seemed always to draw the short straw when the Tudors needed someone to discharge an unpleasant or difficult task. It was an earlier Sir Edmund who was charged with the care of Henry VIII's discarded wife, Catherine of Aragon; Edmund's son, Sir Henry, was given the even more onerous task of looking after the King's official bastard, the Princess Elizabeth. After Elizabeth's accession as Queen, Sir Henry presented himself at Court, no doubt with some misgivings. Elizabeth received him civilly but, as he was leaving, tartly observed that 'if we have any prisoner whom we would have hardlie and strictly kept, we will send him to you.'

As staunch Catholics, the Bedingfelds were, for the next two and a half centuries, consigned to the margins of English political life. Their estates dwindled as portions were sold to meet the punitive taxes imposed on adherents of the Old Faith. By the middle of the 20th century, the Bedingfelds' long tenure of Oxburgh was drawing to a close. In 1951 the 9th Baronet, another Sir Edmund, sold Oxburgh to a builder, who promptly announced his intention of demolishing the house. Sir Edmund's mother, the Dowager Lady Sybil, was shocked by such vandalism and used her considerable powers of persuasion to raise sufficient funds to buy back the house. She then conveyed it into the safe keeping of the National Trust.

CASTLE RISING

5 miles NE of King's Lynn off the A148/A149

As the bells ring for Sunday morning service at Castle Rising, a group of elderly ladies leave the

The grounds at Oxburgh Hall provide the perfect foil for the mellow old building, reflected in its broad moat. There's a wonderfully formal and colourful French garden, a walled kitchen garden, and woodland walks.

Oxburgh Hall

35 THE THREE HORSESHOES

Roydon, nr King's Lynn

New hosts have raised the level of cooking to new heights at **The Three Horseshoes**, an attractive redbrick country pub.

see page 250

31 THE ANVIL

Congham, northeast of King's Lynn

Home-made pies are among the splendid dishes served at **The Anvil**.

see page 248

mellow redbrick Bede House and walk in procession to the church. They are all dressed in long scarlet cloaks, emblazoned on the left breast with a badge of the Howard family arms. Once a year, on Founder's Day, they add to their regular Sunday costume a tall-crowned hat typical of the Jacobean period, just like those worn in stereotypical pictures of broomstick-flying witches.

These ladies are the residents of the almshouses founded by Henry Howard, Earl of Northampton in 1614, and their regular Sunday attendance at church was one of the conditions he imposed on the original 11 needy spinsters who were to enjoy his beneficence. Howard also required that each inmate of his 'Hospital of the Holy and Undivided Trinity' must also 'be able to read, if such a one may be had, single, 56 at least, no common beggar, harlot, scold, drunkard, haunter of taverns, inns or alehouses'.

The weekly *tableau vivant* of this procession to the church seems completely in keeping with this picturesque village, which rates high on any 'not to be missed' list of places to visit in Norfolk. The church to which the women make their way, St Lawrence's, is an outstanding example of Norman and Early English work, even though much of it has been reconstructed. But overshadowing everything else in this pretty village is the massive **Castle Keep** (English Heritage), its well-preserved walls rising 50 feet high, and pierced by a single entrance. The Keep's towering presence is made even more formidable by the huge earthworks on which it stands. The Castle was built in 1150, guarding what was then the sea approach to the River Ouse. (The marshy shore is now some three miles distant and still retreating.)

Despite its fortress-like appearance, Castle Rising was much more of a residential building than a defensive one. In 1331, when Edward III found it necessary to banish his ferocious French-born mother, Isabella, to some reasonably comfortable place of safety, he chose this far-from-London castle. She was to spend some 27 years here before her death in 1358, never seeing her son again during that time. How could Edward treat his own mother in such a way? Her crime, in his view, was that the 'She-Wolf of France', as all her

Medieval Re-enactment, Castle Rising

enemies and many of her friends called Isabella, had joined forces with her lover Mortimer against her homosexual husband Edward II (young Edward's father) and later colluded in the king's grisly murder at Berkeley Castle. A red-hot poker, inserted anally, was the instrument of his death. For three years after that loathsome assassination, Isabella and Mortimer ruled England as Regents. The moment Edward III achieved his majority, he had Mortimer hung, drawn and quartered. His mother he despatched to a lonely retirement at Castle Rising.

The spacious grounds around the castle provide an appropriate backdrop for an annual display by members of the White Society. Caparisoned in colourful medieval garments and armed with more-or-less authentic replicas of swords and halberds, these modern White Knights stage a battle for control of the castle.

SANDRINGHAM

8 miles NE of King's Lynn
off the A149/B1140

A couple of miles north of Castle Rising is the entrance to **Sandringham Country Park** and **Sandringham House**, the Royal Family's charming country retreat. Unlike the State Rooms at Windsor Castle and Buckingham Palace, where visitors marvel at the awesome trappings of majesty, at Sandringham they can savour the atmosphere of a family home. The rooms the visitor sees at Sandringham are those used by the royal family when in residence,

complete with family portraits and photographs, and comfy armchairs. Successive royal owners have furnished the house with an intriguing medley of the grand, the domestic and the unusual. Entering the principal reception room, The Saloon, for example, you pass a weighing-machine with a leather-covered seat, apparently a common amenity in great houses of the 19th century. In the same room, with its attractively carved Minstrels' Gallery,

 92 SANDRINGHAM HOUSE

Sandringham, Norfolk
Sandringham House is the country retreat of Her Majesty The Queen and all of the ground floor rooms are open to the public, with further items to view housed in the Museum.

🏛 *see page 271*

Sandringham House

Just across from Sandringham house, the old coach-houses and stables have been converted into a fascinating museum. There are some truly splendid royal vehicles here, including the first car bought by a member of the royal family - a 1900 Daimler - and an evocative series of old photographs depicting the life of the royal family at Sandringham from 1862 until Christmas 1951. Other attractions at Sandringham include a visitors centre, adventure playground, nature walks, souvenir shop, restaurant and tearoom.

hangs a fine family portrait by one of Queen Victoria's favourite artists, Heinrich von Angeli. It shows the Prince of Wales (later Edward VII), his wife Alexandra and two of their children, with Sandringham in the background.

The Prince first saw Sandringham on 4th February 1862. At Victoria's instigation, the 20-year-old heir to the throne had been searching for some time for a country property, a refuge of the kind his parents already enjoyed at Balmoral and Osborne. A courtier accompanying the Prince reported back that although the outside of house was ugly, it was pleasant and convenient within, and set in pretty grounds. The surrounding countryside was plain, he went on, but the property was in excellent order and the opportunity of securing it should not be missed. Within days, the purchase was completed.

Most of the 'ugly' house disappeared a few years later when the Prince rebuilt the main residence; the 'pretty grounds' have matured into one of the most beautiful landscaped areas in the country. And the 'plain' countryside around - open heath and grassland overrun by rabbits - has been transformed into a wooded country park, part of the coastal Area of Outstanding Natural Beauty.

One of the additions the Prince made to the house in 1883 was a Ballroom, much to the relief of Princess Alexandra. 'It is beautiful I think & a great success.'

she wrote, '& avoids pulling the hall to pieces each time there is a ball or anything'. This attractive room is now used for cinema shows and the estate workers' Christmas party. Displayed on the walls is a remarkable collection of Indian weapons, presented to the Prince during his state visit in 1875-6; hidden away in a recess are the two flags planted at the South Pole by the Shackleton expedition.

DERSINGHAM

9 miles NE of King's Lynn off the A149

This large village just north of Sandringham was actually the source of the latter's name: in the *Domesday Book*, the manor was inscribed as 'Sant-Dersingham'. Norfolk tongues found 'Sandringham' much easier to get around. Dersingham village has expanded greatly in recent years and modern housing has claimed much of Dersingham Common, although there are still many pleasant walks here through **Dersingham Wood** and the adjoining Sandringham Country Park.

SNETTISHAM

11 miles N of King's Lynn off the A149

Snettisham is best known nowadays for its spacious, sandy beaches and the **RSPB Bird Sanctuary**, both about two miles west of the village itself. But for centuries Snettisham was much more famous as a prime quarry for carrstone, an attractive soft-red building-block that provided the 'light relief' for the walls of thousands of Georgian houses around the country, and for nearby Sandringham House. The carrstone quarry is still working, its product now destined mainly for 'goldfish ponds and the entrance-banks of the more pretentious types of bungalow'. Unfortunately, one has to go to the British Museum in London to see Snettisham's greatest gift to the national heritage: an opulent collection of gold and silver ornaments from the 1st century AD, the largest hoard of treasure trove ever found in Britain, discovered here in 1991.

HEACHAM

13 miles N of King's Lynn off the A149

Heacham Park Fishery on Pocahontas Lake is set within the original boundary of Heacham Hall. This three-and-a-half acre freshwater lake was re-established

in 1996. Spring 1997 saw the introduction to the lake of specimen carp, to be followed in 1998 by rudd, bream, perch and roach. The lake takes its name from the renowned Native American princess, who married into the Rolfe family, owners of Heacham Hall, and lived here in the 1600s.

FAKENHAM

Fakenham is a busy and prosperous-looking market town, famous for its National Hunt Racecourse, antique & bric-a-brac markets and auctions, and as a major agricultural centre for the region. Straddling the River Wensum, this attractive country town has a number of fine late-18th and early-19th century brick buildings in and around the Market Place. And it must surely be one of the few towns in England where

•

Just outside the charming village of Heacham is the famous Norfolk Lavender, the largest lavender-growing and distilling operation in the country. Established in 1932, it is also the oldest. The information point at the western entrance is sited in an attractive listed building, a Victorian watermill that has become something of a Norfolk landmark. On entering the site, visitors instinctively breathe in, savouring the unmistakable aroma that fills the air. The centre is open all year round, and guided tours of the grounds run throughout the day in the summer; and during the lavender harvest, visitors can tour the distillery and see how the wonderful fragrance is made.

As well as being a working farm, this is also the home of the National Collection of Lavenders, a living botanical dictionary which displays the many different colours, sizes and smells of this lovely plant. Among other attractions at Norfolk Lavender are a Fragrant Meadow Garden, Fragrant Plant Centre, Herb Garden, a gift shop selling a wide variety of products, and a tearoom serving cream teas and even lavender-and-lemon scones!

•

Fields of Lavender at Heacham

71 MANOR FARM

Sculthorpe, west of Fakenham

Manor Farm is a quiet, comfortable base for a B&B holiday in a handsome period house on a 500-acre farm.

see page 263

72 WENSUM HOUSE

Fakenham Hempton

Wensum House is a fine 16th century house with spacious rooms for B&B and a self-contained self-catering annexe.

see page 263

93 PENSTHORPE WATERFOWL PARK & NATURE RESERVE

Pensthorpe, Fakenham

A 200 acre site with an amazing collection of waterfowl including endangered species.

 see page 271

the former gasworks (still intact) have been turned into a **Museum of Gas & Local History**, housing an impressive historical display of domestic gas appliances of every kind. Fakenham Church also has an unusual feature, a powder room - a room over the large porch, built in 1497, used for storing gunpowder. Even older than the church is the 700-year-old hunting lodge, built for the Duchy of Lancaster, which is now part of the Crown Hotel. As an antidote to the idea that Norfolk is unremittingly flat, reinforced by Noel Coward in his *Private Lives*, take the B1105 north out of Fakenham and after about half a mile take the first minor road to the left. This quiet road loops over and around the rolling hills, a 10-mile drive of wonderfully soothing countryside that ends at Wells-next-the-Sea.

AROUND FAKENHAM

Southeast of Fakenham, off the A1067, **Pensthorpe Waterfowl Park** is home to Europe's best collection of endangered and exotic waterbirds. Over 120 species of waterfowl can be seen here in their natural surroundings, a wonderful avian refuge where you may come across anything from a scarlet ibis to the more familiar oystercatcher, along with avocets and ruff. The spacious walk-through enclosures offer close contact with shy wading birds, and in the Dulverton Aviary elegant spoonbills and bearded tits vie for your attention. There are

good facilities for children and visitors with disabilities, a Wildlife Brass Rubbing Centre, nature trails through 200 acres of the Wensum Valley countryside, a millennium garden, a restaurant and a shop.

Ten miles southeast of Fakenham, signposted from the A1067 Norwich to Fakenham road, The Norfolk Wildlife Trust's **Foxley Wood** is Norfolk's largest ancient woodland and is being restored to its former beauty.

EAST RAYNHAM

3 miles SW of Fakenham, on the A1065

Raynham Hall is another superb Palladian mansion, designed by Inigo Jones and with magnificent rooms created a century later by William Kent. The house is only open to the public by appointment since it is the private residence of the 7th Marquess of Townshend. It was his 18th century ancestor, the 2nd Viscount (better known as 'Turnip' Townshend), who revolutionised English agriculture by promoting the humble turnip as an effective means of reclaiming untended land for feeding cattle in winter, and along with wheat, barley and clover, as part of the four-year rotation of crops that provided a cycle of essential nutrients for the soil. The Townshend family have owned extensive estates in this area for centuries, and in St Mary's Church there are some fine monuments to their ancestors, the oldest and most sumptuous of which commemorates Sir Roger, who died in 1493.

TATTERFORD

*5 miles SW of Fakenham off the A148 or
A1065*
-

This tiny village is well known to
botanists for **Tatterford Common**,
an unspoilt tract of rough
heathland with tiny ponds, some
wild apple trees and the River Tat
running through it to join the River
Wensum about a mile away.

About four miles west of
Tatterford stands **Houghton Hall**,
home of the Marquess of
Cholmondely and one of the
country's most magnificent
buildings. This glorious demi-palace
was built in the Palladian style
during the 1720s by Sir Robert
Walpole, England's first Prime
Minister. The Walpoles had been
gentlemen of substance here since
the 14th century. With his family
revenues augmented by the
considerable profits Sir Robert
extracted from his political office,
he was in a position to spend
lavishly and ostentatiously on his
new house. The first step was to
destroy completely the village of
Houghton (it spoilt the view), and
re-house the villagers a mile away at
New Houghton.

Although Sir Robert
deliberately cultivated the manner
of a bluff, down-to-earth Norfolk
squire, the personal decisions he
made regarding the design and
furnishings of the house reveal a
man of deep culture and refined
tastes. It was he who insisted that
the Hall could not be built in
homely Norfolk brick, and took the
expensive decision to use the
exceptionally durable stone quarried

at Aislaby in North Yorkshire and
transport it by sea from Whitby to
King's Lynn. More than two and a
half centuries later, the Aislaby
stone is still flawless, the only sign
of its age a slight weathering that
has softened its colour to a creamy
gold.

To decorate the interior and
design the furniture, Sir Robert
commissioned the versatile William
Kent. Kent was at the peak of his
powers - just look at the decoration
in the Stone Hall, the exquisite
canopied bed in the Green Velvet
Bedchamber, and the finely-carved
woodwork throughout which made
impressive use of the newly-
discovered hardwood called
mahogany. And then there were the
paintings, an incomparable
collection of Old Masters
personally selected by Sir Robert.
Sadly, many of them are now in the
Hermitage Museum in St
Petersburg, sold by his wastrel
grandson to the Empress Catherine
of Russia.

This grandson, George, 3rd
Earl of Orford, succeeded to the
title at the age of 21 and spent the
next 40 years dissipating his
enormous inheritance. When his
uncle Horace (the 4th Earl, better
known as Horace Walpole, novelist,
MP and inveterate gossip)
succeeded to the title he found
'Houghton half a ruin ... the two
great staircases exposed to all
weathers; every room in the wings
rotting with wet; the park half-
covered with nettles and weeds;
mortgages swallowing the estate,
and a debt of above £40,000.'

73 LOWER FARM B&B

*Harpley, between King's Lynn
and Fakenham*

The bedrooms are large and
comfortable at **Lower Farm**,
a working farm in a quiet,
rural setting.

⊨ *see page 263*

36/74 THE CROWN

East Rudham, nr King's Lynn

The landlady's fine cooking
has earned a strong
following at **The Crown**,
which also offers B&B
accommodation.

⫙ ⊨ *see pages 250 and
263*

6/54 THE DUKES HEAD

West Rudham, nr King's Lynn

The Dukes Head is a classic
country pub with an exciting
menu of Cantonese dishes
with a Malaysian influence.

⫙ ⊨ *see pages 240 and
257*

59

33/75 THE OSTRICH INN

South Creake, nr Fakenham

Good food, real ales, fine wines and en suite guest bedrooms make **The Ostrich Inn** a great place for a visit.

 see pages 248 and 263

37/76 THE BLACK LION HOTEL

Little Walsingham

Visitors to Little Walsingham will find excellent home cooking and comfortable B&B rooms at **The Black Lion Hotel**.

 see pages 250 and 264

Houghton's decline was arrested when the Hall passed by marriage to the Marquess of Cholmondeley, Lord Great Chamberlain, in 1797. But it wasn't until 1913, when George, later the 5th Marquess, moved into the house with his new wife, Sybil Sassoon, that Houghton was fully restored to its former state of grace. The depleted collection of paintings was augmented with fine works by Sir Joshua Reynolds and others from Cholmondeley Castle in Cheshire, and the Marchioness introduced new collections of exquisite French furniture and porcelain.

One of the interests of the 6th Marques was military history, and in 1928 he began the astonishing Model Soldiers Collection now on display at Houghton. More than 20,000 perfectly preserved models are deployed in meticulous reconstructions of battles such as Culloden and Waterloo, and in one exhibit, re-creating the Grand Review of the British Army in 1895, no fewer than 3,000 figures are on parade.

St Martin's Church at the Hall contains the Walpole family vault, where Sir Robert and his youngest son Horace are buried.

LITTLE WALSINGHAM

5 miles N of Fakenham on the B1105

Every year, some half a million pilgrims make their way to this little village of just over 500 souls, noted for its impressive timber-framed buildings and fine Georgian façades, to worship at the **Shrine of Our Lady of Walsingham**. In 1061 the Lady of the Manor of Walsingham, Lady Richeldis de Faverches, had a vision of the Holy Virgin in which she was instructed to build a replica of the Holy House in Nazareth, the house in which the Archangel Gabriel had told Mary that she would be the mother of Christ. Archaeologists have located the original house erected by Lady Richeldis. It was just 13 feet by 23 feet and made of wood, later to be enclosed in stone.

These were the years of the Crusades, and the **Holy House** at Walsingham soon became a major centre of pilgrimage, because it was regarded by the pious as an authentic piece of the Holy Land. Around 1153,

Little Walsingham

an **Augustinian Priory** was established to protect the shrine, now encrusted with jewels, gold and silver, and to provide accommodation for the pilgrims. The Priory is in ruins now but the largest surviving part, a stately Gatehouse on the east side of the High Street, is very impressive.

For almost 500 years, Walsingham prospered. Erasmus of Rotterdam visited in 1511 and was critical of the rampant commercialisation of the Shrine with its plethora of bogus relics and religious souvenirs for sale. He was shown a gigantic bone, 'the finger-joint of St Peter' no less, and in return for a small piece of translation was presented with a highly aromatic fragment of wood - a sliver of a bench on which the Virgin had once seated herself.

In the same year that Erasmus visited, Henry VIII also made the pilgrimage that all his royal predecessors since Richard I had undertaken. He stayed overnight at the enchanting early-Tudor mansion, **East Barsham Hall**, a glorious medley of mullioned windows, towers, turrets, and a group of 10 chimneys, each one individually carved with an amazing variety of styles.

After his overnight stay at East Barsham Hall, Henry VIII, like most other pilgrims, went first to the **Slipper Chapel**, a beautiful 14th century building about a mile away in Houghton St Giles. Here he removed his shoes and completed the last stretch on foot. Despite this show of piety, some 25 years later Henry had no hesitation in closing the Priory along with all the other monastic institutions in his realm, seizing its treasures and endowments, and having its image of the Virgin publicly burnt at Chelsea.

Little Walsingham itself is an exceptionally attractive village, set in the midst of parks and woodlands, with the interesting 16th century octagonal **Clink in Common Place**, used in medieval times as a lock-up for petty offenders, the scanty ruins of Walsingham's **Franciscan Friary** of 1347, and the former **Shire Hall**, which is now a museum and tourist information centre. In the 1770s the friary was converted into the shire hall for the quarter sessions, a role it filled until 1861; the petty sessions continued until 1971.

GREAT WALSINGHAM

5 miles N of Fakenham on the B1388

English place names observe a logic of their own, so Great Walsingham is of course smaller than Little Walsingham. The two villages are very different in atmosphere and appearance, Great Walsingham displaying the typical layout of a rural Norfolk settlement, with attractive cottages set around a green watered by the River Stiffkey, and dominated by a fine 14th century church, **St Peter's**, noted for its superb window tracery, wondrously carved Norman font, and perfectly preserved 15th century carved benches.

94 WALSINGHAM SHIREHALL MUSEUM & ABBEY

Little Walsingham

The 16th century building now houses a museum which includes displays on Walsingham, as well as the entrance to the Abbey Grounds.

🏛 *see page 272*

77 BERRY HALL

Great Walsingham

Guests at **Berry Hall** have the choice of B&B in the 17th century main house and a self-catering cottage along the lane.

⊨ *see page 264*

78 FIELD HOUSE

Hindringham, nr Fakenham

Guests at **Field House** stay in top-class B&B accommodation in a charming village setting.

⊨ *see page 264*

Wighton, nr Fakenham

The Carpenters Arms is a delightful country pub with a wide and growing reputation for fine food and cask ales. Beer festival in June.

see page 251

•

A mile or so north of the Thursford museum, in the village of Hindringham, Mill Farm Rare Breeds is home to dozens of cattle, sheep, pigs, goats, ponies, poultry and waterfowl which were once commonplace but are now very rare. These intriguing creatures have some 30 acres of lovely countryside to roam around. Children are encouraged to feed the animals and there's also an adventure playground, crazy golf course, craft & gift shop, picnic area and tearoom.

•

WIGHTON
7 miles N of Fakenham, on the B1105

Just outside the village, the Wells to Walsingham Light Railway trundles its way between Little Walsingham and Wells-next-the-Sea. The longest 10¼-inch narrow-gauge steam railway in the world, it runs throughout the summer along a 20-minute scenic journey through the North Norfolk countryside.

THURSFORD GREEN
4 miles NE of Fakenham off the A148

About two minutes' walk from Thursford Green stands what is perhaps the most unusual museum in Norfolk, **The Thursford Collection Sight and Sound Spectacular**. George Cushing began this extraordinary collection of steam-powered traction engines, fairground organs and carousels back in 1946 when 'one ton of tractor cost £1'. Perhaps the most astonishing exhibit is a 1931 Wurlitzer organ whose 1,339 pipes can produce an amazing repertoire of sounds - horses' hooves, fire engine sirens, claps of thunder, waves crashing on sand, and the toot-toot of an old railway engine are just some of the Wurlitzer's marvellous effects. There are regular live music shows when the Wurlitzer displays its virtuosity. Other attractions include a steam-powered Venetian Gondola ride, shops selling a wide variety of goods, many of them locally made, and a tearoom. The Collection is open from 12 to 5 every day except Saturday. Tel: 01328 878477

GREAT SNORING
5 miles NE of Fakenham off the A148

The names of the twin villages, Great and Little Snoring, are such a perennial source of amusement to visitors it seems almost churlish to explain that they are derived from a Saxon family called Snear. At Great Snoring the main street rises from a bridge over the River Stiffkey and climbs up to St Mary's Church.

THE NORTHWEST COAST

Although the whole of Norfolk lies on a foundation of chalk, 1,000 feet deep in places, it is only in this northwest corner that it lies close enough to the surface to have been used as a building material. Once exposed to the air, the chalk, or 'clunch' as it's known, becomes a surprisingly durable material. It was widely used in medieval buildings and can still be found in many barns, farmhouses and cottages in the area. Chalk was also quarried and then burnt to produce lime, prodigious quantities of which were used in building the sublime churches of the Middle Ages.

HUNSTANTON

The busy seaside resort of Hunstanton can boast two unique features: one, it has the only cliffs in England made up of colourful levels of red, white and brown strata, and two, it is the only east

Windsurfing at Hunstanton

coast resort that faces west, looking across The Wash to the Lincolnshire coast and the unmistakeable tower of the 272-feet high Boston Stump (more properly described as the Church of St Botolph).

Hunstanton town is a comparative newcomer, developed in the 1860s by Mr Hamon L'Estrange of nearby Hunstanton Hall to take advantage of the arrival of the railway here, and to exploit the natural appeal of its broad, sandy beaches. The centre is well-planned with mock-Tudor houses grouped around a green that falls away to the shore.

Hunstanton's social standing was assured after the Prince of Wales, later Edward VII, came here to recover from typhoid fever. He stayed at the Sandringham Hotel which, sadly, has since been demolished, along with the grand Victorian pier and the railway. But Hunston, as locals call the town, still has a distinct 19th century charm about it and plenty to entertain visitors.

The huge stretches of sandy beach, framed by those multi-coloured cliffs, are just heaven for children who will also be fascinated by the **Sea Life Sanctuary**, on Southern Promenade, where an underwater glass tunnel provides a fascinating opportunity to watch the varied and often weird forms of marine life that inhabit Britain's waters. A popular excursion from Hunstanton is the boat trip to Seal Island, a sandbank in The Wash where seals can indeed often be seen sunbathing at low tide.

AROUND HUNSTANTON

HOLME NEXT THE SEA

3 miles NE of Hunstanton, off the A149

This village is at the northern end of the **Peddars Way**, the 50-mile pedestrian trail that starts at the Suffolk border near Thetford and, almost arrow-straight for much of its length, slices across northwest Norfolk to Holme, with only an occasional deviation to negotiate a necessary ford or bridge. This

---

39 GEORGIE'S RESTAURANT & CELLAR BAR

Lestrange Terrace, Hunstanton

Georgie's Restaurant & Cellar Bar offers a varied menu of snacks and meals in convivial seafront surroundings.

see page 251

---

40 NEPTUNE INN & RESTAURANT

Old Hunstanton

Superb cuisine, real ales, fine wines and stylish accommodation puts the **Neptune Inn** among the foremost in the region.

see page 251

41/79 THE GIN TRAP

Ringstead, nr Hunstanton

The Gin Trap is a fine old coaching inn with an excellent restaurant, B&B or self-catering accommodation and an art gallery.

see pages 252 and 265

Holme next the Sea is famous in part as the site of 'Sea Henge', a 4,500-year-old Bronze Age tree circle discovered on Holme Beach. This early religious monument was removed by English Heritage for study and preservation to Flag Fen, Peterborough, though after its restoration it is hoped that it will be returned to Holme.

In a region well provided with excellent nature reserves, the one on Ringstead Downs is particularly attractive, and popular with picnickers. The chalky soil of the valley provides a perfect habitat for the plants that thrive here and for the exquisitely marked butterflies they attract.

determinedly straight route was already long-trodden for centuries before the Romans arrived, but they incorporated long stretches of it into their own network of roads. It was from the Latin word *pedester* that the route takes its name. With few gradients of any consequence to negotiate, the Peddars Way is ideal for the casual walker. At Holme, the Peddars Way meets with the Norfolk Coastal Footpath, a much more recent creation. Starting at Hunstanton, it closely follows the coastline all the way to Cromer.

RINGSTEAD

3 miles E of Hunstanton off the A149

Another appealing village, with pink and whitewashed cottages built in wonderfully decorative Norfolk carrstone. A rare Norman round tower, all that survives of St Peter's church, stands in the grounds of the former Rectory and adds to the visual charm.

DOCKING

9 miles SE of Hunstanton, on the B1454 & B1153

One of the larger inland villages, Docking was at one time called Dry Docking because, perched on a hilltop 300 feet above sea level, it had no water supply of its own. The nearest permanent stream was at Fring, almost three miles away, so in 1760 the villagers began boring for

a well. They had to dig some 230 feet down before they finally struck water, which was then sold at a farthing (0.1p) per bucket. A pump was installed in 1928, but a mains supply didn't reach Docking until the 1930s.

GREAT BIRCHAM

7 miles SE of Hunstanton off the B1153

A couple of miles south of Docking stands the five-storey **Great Bircham Windmill**, one of the few in Norfolk to have found a hill to perch on, and it's still working. If you arrive on a day when there's a stiff breeze blowing, the windmill's great arms will be groaning around; on calm days, content yourself with tea and home-made cakes in the tearoom,

Great Bircham Windmill

and take home some bread baked at the Mill's own bakery.

TITCHWELL

7 miles E of Hunstanton, on the A149

Perhaps in keeping with the village's name, the church of St Mary at Titchwell is quite tiny - and very pretty indeed. Its circular, probably Norman tower is topped by a little 'whisker' of a spire, and inside is some fine late 19th century glass.

BRANCASTER STAITHE

9 miles NE of Hunstanton, on the A149

In Roman times a castle was built near Brancaster to try and control the Iceni, Boudica's turbulent tribe. Nothing of it remains, although a Romano-British cemetery was discovered nearby in 1960. In the 18th century, this delightful village was a port of some standing, hence the 'Staithe', or quay, in its name. The waterborne traffic in the harbour is now almost exclusively pleasure craft, although whelks are still dredged from the sea bed, 15 miles out, and mussels are farmed in the harbour itself.

From the harbour a short boat trip will take you to Scolt Head Island (National Trust), a three-and-a-half mile sand and shingle bar separated from the mainland by a narrow tidal creek. It was originally much smaller, but over the centuries deposits of silt and sand have steadily increased its size, and continue to do so. Scolt Head is home to England's largest colony of Sandwich terns,

which flock here to breed during May, June and July.

BURNHAM MARKET

9 miles E of Hunstanton, on the B1155

There are seven Burnhams in all, strung along the valley of the little River Burn. Burnham Market is the largest of them, its past importance reflected in the wealth of Georgian buildings surrounding the green and the two churches that lie at each end of its broad main street, just 600 yards apart. In the opinion of many, Burnham Market has the best collection of small Georgian houses in Norfolk, and it's a delight to wander through the yards and alleys that link the town's three east-west streets.

Burnham Market also boasts two excellent bookshops and probably the best hat shop in the county. Auctions are held on the village green every other Monday in summer.

•

Just to the west of Titchwell is a path leading to Titchwell Marsh, a nationally important RSPB reserve comprising some 420 acres of shingle beach, reed beds, freshwater and salt-marsh. These different habitats encourage a wide variety of birds to visit the area throughout the year, and many of them breed on or around the reserve. Brent geese, ringed plovers, marsh harriers, terns, waders and shore larks may all be seen, and two of the three hides available are accessible to wheelchairs.

•

Brancaster Staithe

A little over a mile to the south of Burnham Thorpe stand the picturesque ruins of Creake Abbey (English Heritage), an Augustinian monastery founded in 1206. The Abbey's working life came to an abrupt end in 1504 when, within a single week, every one of the monks died of the plague.

95 HOLKHAM HALL & BYGONES MUSEUM

Wells-next-the-Sea, Norfolk

A fine example of an 18th century mansion, packed with artistic and architectural treasures. Also here is the Bygones Museum with over 4,000 exhibits.

🏛 see page 272

Historically the most important room at Holkham is the Statue Gallery, which contains one of the finest collections of classical sculpture still in private ownership. In this sparsely furnished room there is nothing to distract one's attention from the sublime statuary that has survived for millennia, among it a bust of Thucydides (one of the earliest portrayals of man) and a statue of Diana, both of which have been dated to 4BC.

BURNHAM THORPE

11 miles E of Hunstanton off the B1355

From the tower of All Saints' Church, the White Ensign flaps in the breeze; the only pub in the village is the *Lord Nelson*; and the shop next door to it is called the Trafalgar Stores. No prizes for deducing that Burnham Thorpe was the birthplace of Horatio Nelson. His father, the Revd Edmund Nelson, was the Rector here for 46 years; Horatio was the sixth of his eleven children.

Parsonage House, where Horatio was born seven weeks' premature in 1758, was demolished during his lifetime, but the pub (one of more than 200 hostelries across the country bearing the hero's name) has become a kind of shrine to Nelson's memory, its walls covered with portraits, battle scenes and other marine paintings.

There's more Nelson memorabilia in the church, among it a crucifix and lectern made with wood from HMS *Victory*, a great chest from the pulpit used by the Revd Nelson, and two flags from HMS *Nelson*. Every year on Trafalgar Day, October 21st, members of the Nelson Society gather at this riverside church for a service in commemoration of the man who had specified in his will that he wanted to be buried in its country graveyard 'unless the King decrees otherwise'. George III did indeed decree otherwise, and the great hero was interred in St Paul's Cathedral.

HOLKHAM

16 miles E of Hunstanton, on the A149

If the concept of the Grand Tour ever needed any justification, **Holkham Hall**, seat of seven generations of the Earls of Leicester, amply provides it. For six years, from 1712 to 1718, young Thomas Coke (pronounced Cook) travelled extensively in Italy, France and Germany, studying and absorbing at first hand the glories of European civilisation. And, wherever possible, buying them. When he returned to England, Coke realised that his family's modest Elizabethan manor could not possibly house the collection of treasures he had amassed. The manor would have to be demolished and a more worthy building erected in its place. During his travels in Italy, Coke had been deeply impressed by the cool, classical lines favoured by the Renaissance architect Andrea Palladio. Working with his friend Lord Burlington - another fervent admirer of Palladio - and the architect William Kent, Coke's monumental project slowly took shape. Building began in 1734 but was not completed until 1762, three years after Coke's death.

The completed building, its classical balance and restraint emphasised by the pale honey local brick used throughout, has been described as 'the ultimate achievement of the English Palladian movement'. As you step into the stunning entrance hall, the tone is set for the rest of the house. Modelled on a Roman Temple of Justice, the lofty coved ceiling is supported by 18 huge fluted columns of pink Derbyshire alabaster, transported to nearby Wells by river and sea.

Each room reveals new treasures: Rubens and Van Dyck in the Saloon (the principal reception room), the Landscape Room with its incomparable collection of paintings by Lorrain, Poussin and other masters, the Brussels tapestries in the State Sitting Room and, on a more domestic note, the vast, high-ceilinged kitchen which remained in use until 1939 and still displays the original pots and pans.

Astonishingly, the interior of the house remains almost exactly as Thomas Coke planned it, his descendants having respected the integrity of his vision. They concentrated their reforming zeal on improving the enormous estate. It was Coke's great-nephew, Thomas William Coke (1754-1842), in particular who was responsible for the elegant layout of the 3,000-acre park visitors see today. Universally known as 'Coke of Norfolk', Thomas was a pioneer of the Agricultural Revolution, best known for introducing the idea of a four-crop rotation. As well as the Pottery in the former brickworks and its associated shop, Holkham's other attractions include an 18th century walled garden and a fascinating bygones museum

crammed with over 4,000 domestic and agricultural artefacts.

WELLS-NEXT-THE-SEA

17 miles E of Hunstanton, on the A149

There's no doubt about the appeal of the picturesque quayside, narrow streets and ancient houses of Wells. It has been a working port since at least the 13th century, but over the years the town's full name of Wells-next-the-Sea has become increasingly inapt – its harbour now stands more than a mile from the sea. In 1859, to prevent the harbour silting up altogether, Lord Leicester of Holkham Hall built an Embankment cutting off some 600 acres of marshland. This now provides a pleasant walk down to the sea.

The Embankment gave no protection, however, against the great floods of 1953 and 1978. On the 11th January 1978 the sea rose 16 feet 1 inch above high tide, a few inches less than the 16 feet 10 inches recorded on the 31st January 1953, when the floodwaters lifted a ship on to the quay. A silo on the harbour is marked with these abnormal levels.

Running alongside the Embankment in Wells-next-the-Sea is the Harbour Railway, which trundles from the small museum on the quay to the lifeboat station by the beach. This narrow-gauge railway is operated by the same company as the Wells to Walsingham Light Railway which carries passengers on a particularly lovely ride along the route of the former Great Eastern Railway to Little Walsingham. The four-mile journey takes about 20 minutes with stops at Warham St Mary and Wighton. Both the WWR and the Harbour Railway services are seasonal.

In a curious change of function, the former GER station at Wells is now home to the well-known Burnham Pottery, the former signal box is now the station, while the old station at Walsingham is now a church!

Holkham Hall

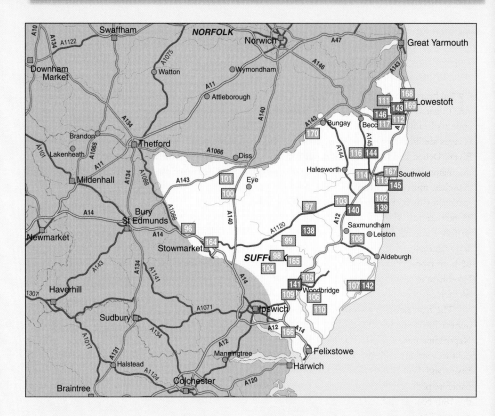

FOOD & DRINK

96 The Maypole Inn, Wetherden
97 The White Horse, Badingham
98 The White Hart, Otley
99 The Queens Head, Brandeston
100 Forge Café, Restaurant & Gift Shop, Thornham Magna
101 The Railway Tavern, Mellis
102 The Ship Inn at Dunwich, Dunwich
103 The Griffin Inn, Yoxford
104 The Moon & Mushroom, Swilland
105 The Horse & Groom, Melton
106 The Sutton Plough Inn, Sutton
107 The Kings Head Inn, Orford
108 The Old Chequers, Friston
109 The Bull Hotel, Woodbridge
110 The Sorrel Horse Inn, Shottisham
111 The Commodore, Oulton Broad
112 The George Borrow Hotel, Oulton Broad
113 The Anchor, Walberswick
114 The Star Inn, Wenhaston
116 The Racehorse, Westhall
117 The Swan Inn, Barnby

ACCOMMODATION

138 High House Farm, Framlingham
139 The Ship Inn at Dunwich, Dunwich
140 The Griffin Inn, Yoxford
141 The Bull Hotel, Woodbridge
142 Vesta Cottage, Orford
143 The George Borrow Hotel, Oulton Broad
144 Uggeshall Manor Farm, Uggeshall
145 The Anchor, Walberswick
146 The Swan Inn, Barnby

PLACES OF INTEREST

164 Museum of East Anglian Life, Stowmarket
165 Easton Farm Park, Easton
166 Sutton Hoo, Sutton Hoo
167 Southwold Pier, Southwold
168 Lowestoft Maritime Museum, Lowestoft
169 Somerleyton Hall & Gardens, Lowestoft
170 Norfolk & Suffolk Aviation Museum, Flixton

Central and Eastern Suffolk

The heart of Suffolk is *the* place in the county to get away from it all. Lying between the county's heathland and coastal area, many of its villages are little changed from olden days. The Rivers Deben and Gipping run through much of the region, which naturally has its fair share of churches, museums, fayres and festivals. The little market towns of Stowmarket and Needham Market are full of interest, and in this part of Suffolk some of the best-preserved windmills and watermills are to be found. Several examples of both types of mills survive, and the village of Pakenham is lucky in having a splendid example of each.

The sea brings its own dangers, even in human form, and it was against the threat of a Napoleonic invasion that Martello Towers were built in southeastern Suffolk, in the tradition of Saxon and Tudor forts and the precursors of concrete pillboxes. Starting just before the end of the 18th century, over 100 of these sturdy circular fortified towers were built along the coast from Suffolk to Sussex. Aldeburgh's at Slaughden is the most northerly (and the largest), while the tower at Shoreham in Sussex the southernmost.

The marshes by the coast have traditionally been a source of reeds, the raw material for the thatch that is such a pretty sight on so many Suffolk buildings. Reed-cutting happens between December and February, the beds being drained in preparation and reflooded after the crop has been gathered. Thatching itself is a highly skilled craft, but 10 weeks of work can give a thatched roof 50 years of life. Organised walks of the reed beds take place from time to time – wellies essential.

While inland Suffolk has few peers in terms of picturesque countryside and villages, Suffolk is also very much a maritime county, with over 50 miles of coastline. The whole coast is a conservation area, which the 50-mile Suffolk Coastal Path makes walkable throughout. With all the miles of meandering rivers and superb stretches of coastline, it is only natural that watery pursuits are a popular pastime, and everything from sailing to scuba diving, angling to powerboat racing, is available. Many of the local museums also have a nautical theme, and the Suffolk coast has been a source of inspiration for many of the nation's most distinguished artists, writers and composers.

Aldeburgh

69

• *Pakenham's current unique claim to fame is in being the last parish in England to have a working watermill and windmill, a fact proclaimed on the village sign. The Watermill was built around 1814 on a site mentioned in the Domesday Book (the Roman excavations suggest that there could have been a mill here as far back as the 1st century AD). The mill, which is fed from Pakenham fen, has many interesting features, including the Blackstone oil engine, dating from around 1900, and the Tattersall Midget rollermill from 1913, a brave but ultimately unsuccessful attempt to compete with the larger roller mills in the production of flour. The mill and the neighbouring recreation park are well worth a visit.*

No less remarkable is the Windmill, one of the most famous in Suffolk. The black-tarred tower was built in 1831 and was in regular use until the 1950s. One of the best preserved mills in the county, it survived a lightning strike in 1971. Both mills lie on the village's circular walks, and fresh flour is available from both.

•

NORTH AND EAST OF BURY ST EDMUNDS

PAKENHAM

4 mile NE of Bury St Edmunds off the A143

On a side road just off the A143 (turn right just north of Great Barton) lies the village of Pakenham, whose long history has been unearthed in the shape of a Bronze Age barrow and kiln, and another kiln from Roman times.

Elsewhere in Pakenham are the 17th century **Nether Hall**, from whose lake in the park the village stream flows through the fen into the millpond. From the same period dates **Newe House**, a handsome Jacobean building with Dutch gables and a two-storey porch. Pakenham's Church of St Mary has an impressive carved Perpendicular font, and in its adjacent vicarage is the famous Whistler Window - a painting by Rex Whistler of an 18th century parish priest. The fens were an important source of reeds, and many of Pakenham's buildings show off the thatcher's art.

IXWORTH

5 miles NE of Bury St Edmunds on the A143

Ixworth played its part as one of the Iceni tribe's major settlements, with important Roman connections and, in the 12th century, the site of an Augustinian priory. The remains of the priory were incorporated into a Georgian house known as Ixworth Abbey, which stands

among trees by the River Blackbourne. The village has many 14th century timber-framed dwellings, and the Church of St Mary dates from the same period, though with many later additions.

A variety of circular walks take in lovely parts of Ixworth, which is also the starting point of the Miller's Trail cycle route.

A little way north of the village, on the A1088, are a nature trail and bird reserve at Ixworth Thorpe Farm. At this point a brief diversion northwards up the A1088 is very worth while.

BARDWELL

7 miles NE of Bury St Edmunds just off the A1088

Bardwell offers another tower windmill. This one dates from the 1820s and was worked by wind for 100 years, then by an oil engine until 1941. It was restored in the 1980s, only to suffer severe damage in the great storm of October 1987, when its sails were torn off. Stoneground flour is still produced by an auxiliary engine, and there's an on-site bakery. Also in this delightful village are a 16th century inn and the Church of St Peter and St Paul, known particularly for its medieval stained glass.

HONINGTON

7 miles NE of Bury St Edmunds on the A1088

Back on the A1088, the little village of Honington was the birthplace of the pastoral poet Robert Bloomfield (1766-1823), whose best known work is *The Farmer's Boy*. The house where he was born is now divided, one part called Bloomfield Cottage, the other Bloomfield Farmhouse. A brass plaque to his memory can be seen in All Saints Church, in the graveyard of which his parents are buried.

EUSTON

9 miles N of Bury St Edmunds on the A1088

Euston Hall, on the A1088, has been the seat of the Dukes of Grafton for 300 years. It's open to the public on Thursday afternoons and is well worth a visit, not least for its portraits of Charles II and its paintings by Van Dyck, Lely and Stubbs. In the colourful landscaped grounds is an ice-house disguised as an Italianate temple, the distinguished work of John Evelyn and William Kent.

Euston's church, in the grounds of the Hall, is the only one in the county dedicated to St Genevieve. It's also one of only two Classical designs in the county, being rebuilt in 1676 on part of the original structure. The interior is richly decorated, with beautiful carving on the hexagonal pulpit, panelling around the walls and a carved panel of the Last Supper. Parts of this lovely wood carving are attributed by some to Grinling Gibbons. Behind the family pew is a marble memorial to Lord Arlington, who built the church.

Euston's watermill was built in the 1670s and rebuilt in 1730 as a Gothic church.

STANTON

7 miles NE of Bury St Edmunds on the A143

Stanton is mentioned in the *Domesday Book*; before that, the Romans were here. A double ration

of medieval churches - All Saints and St John the Baptist - will satisfy the ecclesiastical scholar, while for more worldly indulgences **Wyken Vineyards** will have a strong appeal. The four acres of grounds around the Elizabethan Wyken Hall include herb, knot, rose, kitchen, edible and woodland gardens, a water garden, a nuttery, a gazebo and a hornbeam maze planted in 1991. The gardens are open from April to September.

BARNINGHAM

8 miles NE of Bury St Edmunds on the B1111

Near the Norfolk border, Barningham was the first home of the firm of Fisons, which started in the late 18th century. Starting with a couple of windmills, they later installed one of the earliest steam mills in existence. The engine saw service for nearly 100 years and is now in an American museum; the mill building exists to this day, supplying animal feed.

WALSHAM-LE-WILLOWS

9 miles NE of Bury St Edmunds off the A143

A pretty name for a pretty village, with weather-boarded and timber-framed cottages along the willow-banked river which flows throughout its length. **St Mary's** church is no less pleasing to the eye, with its sturdy western tower and handsome windows in the Perpendicular style. Of particular interest inside is the superb tie and hammerbeam roof of the nave, and (unique in Suffolk, and very rare elsewhere) a tiny circular medallion which hangs suspended from the

•

The area around Barningham is marvellous walking country, and Knettishall Heath Country Park, on 400 acres of prime Breckland terrain, is the official starting place of the Peddars Way National Trail to Holme-next-Sea and of the Angles Way Regional Path that stretches 77 miles to Great Yarmouth by way of the Little Ouse and Waveney valleys.

•

Cotton's Mechanical Music Museum & Bygones has an extensive collection that includes gramophones, music boxes, street pianos, fairground organs and polyphons, as well as the marvellous Wurlitzer Theatre pipe organ. Open on Sunday afternoons from the Whitsun Bank Holiday to the end of September. Tel: 01449 613876

nave wall, known as a 'Maiden's Garland' or 'Virgin's Crant'. These marked the pew seats of unmarried girls who had passed away, and the old custom was for the young men of the village to hang garlands of flowers from them on the anniversary of a girl's death. This particular example celebrates the virginity of one Mary Boyce, who died (so the inscription says) of a broken heart in 1685, just 20 years old. There is also a carving on the rood screen which looks rather like the face of a wolf: this may well be a reference to the benevolent creature that plays such an important role in the legend of St Edmund. A museum by the church has changing exhibitions of local history.

RICKINGHALL

12 miles NE of Bury St Edmunds on the A143

More timber-framed buildings, some thatched, are dotted along the streets of the two villages, Superior and Inferior, which follow an underground stream running right through them. Each has a church dedicated to St Mary and featuring fine flintwork and tracery. The upper church, now closed, was used as a school for London evacuees during the Second World War.

REDGRAVE

13 miles NE of Bury St Edmunds on the B1113

Arachnophobes beware! Redgrave and Lopham Fens form a 360-acre reserve of reed and sedge beds where one of the most interesting inhabitants is the Great Raft Spider.

The village is the source of the Little Ouse and Waveney rivers, which rise on either side of the B1113 and set off on their seaward journeys in opposite directions.

THELNETHAM

12 miles NE of Bury St Edmunds off the B111

West of Redgrave between the B1113 and the B1111 lies Thelnetham – which boasts a windmill of its own. This one is a tower mill, built in 1819 to replace a post mill on the same site, and worked for 100 years. It has now been lovingly restored. Stoneground flour is produced and sold at the mill.

COTTON

16 miles E of Bury St Edmunds off the B1113

South of Finningham, where Yew Tree House displays some fine pargeting, and just by Bacton, a lovely village originally built round seven greens, lies the village of Cotton, which should be visited for several reasons, one of which is to see the splendid 14th century flint church of St Andrew, impressive in its dimensions and notable for its double hammerbeam roof with carved angels.

HESSETT

4 miles E of Bury St Edmunds off the A14

Dedicated to St Ethelbert, King of East Anglia, Hessett's church has many remarkable features, particularly some beautiful 16th century glass and wall paintings, both of which somehow escaped the Puritan wave of destruction. Ethelbert was unlucky enough to get on the wrong side of the mighty Offa, King of the Mercians, and was killed by him at Hereford in AD 794.

WOOLPIT

6 miles E of Bury St Edmunds on the A14

The church of St Mary the Virgin is Woolpit's crowning glory, with a marvellous porch and one of the most magnificent double hammerbeam roofs in the county. Voted winner of Suffolk Village of the Year in 2000, the village was long famous for its brick industry, and the majority of the old buildings are faced with 'Woolpit Whites'. This yellowish-white brick looked very much like more expensive stone, and for several centuries was widely exported. Some was used in the building of the Senate wing of the Capitol Building in Washington DC. Red bricks were also produced, and the village **Museum**, open in summer, has a brick-making display and also tells the story of the evolution of the village. Woolpit also hosts an annual music festival.

Nearby is a moated site known as **Lady's Well**, a place of pilgrimage in the Middle Ages. The water from the spring was reputed to have healing properties, most efficacious in curing eye troubles.

ELMSWELL

7 miles E of Bury St Edmunds off the A14

Clearly visible from the A14, the impressive church of St John the Baptist with its massive flint tower stands at the entrance to the village, facing Woolpit across the valley. A

short drive north of Elmswell lies **Great Ashfield**, an unspoilt village whose now disused airfield played a key role in both World Wars. In the churchyard of the 13th century All Saints is a memorial to the Americans who died during the Second World War, as attested to by the commemorative altar. Some accounts say that Edmund was buried here in AD 903 after dying at the hands of the Danes; a cross was put up in his memory. The cross was replaced in the 19th century and now stands in the garden of Ashfield House.

HAUGHLEY

12 miles E of Bury St Edmunds off the A14

On the run into Stowmarket, Haughley once had the largest motte-and-bailey castle in Suffolk. All that now remains is a mound behind the church. **Haughley Park** is a handsome Jacobean redbrick manor house set in gardens, parkland and surrounding woodland featuring ancient oaks and splendid magnolias. Woodland paths take the visitor past a half-mile stretch of rhododendrons, and in springtime the bluebells and lilies of the valley are a magical sight. The gardens are open on Tuesdays between May and September, the house by appointment only.

HARLESTON

9 miles E of Bury St Edmunds off the A14

The churches of Shelland and Harleston lie in close proximity on a minor road between Woolpit and Haughley picnic site. At Shelland, the tiny church of King Charles the

•

A favourite Woolpit legend concerns the Green Children, a brother and sister with green complexions who appeared one day in a field, apparently attracted by the church bells. Though hungry, they would eat nothing until some green beans were produced. Given shelter by the lord of the manor, they learned to speak English and said that they came from a place called St Martin. The boy survived for only a short time, but the girl thrived, lost her green colour, was baptised and married a man from King's Lynn – no doubt leaving many a Suffolk man green with envy!

•

164 MUSEUM OF EAST
ANGLIAN LIFE

Stowmarket

A former Dutch river barge
has been converted into a
floating restaurant.

 see page 298

Martyr is one of only four in
England to be dedicated to King
Charles I. The brick floor is laid in
a herringbone pattern, there are
high box pews and a triple-decker
pulpit, but the most unusual feature
is a working barrel organ dating
from the early 19th century.

The church of St Augustine at
Harleston stands all alone among
pine trees and is reached by a track
across a field. It has a thatched
roof, Early English windows and a
tower with a single bell.

STOWMARKET

The largest town in the heart of
Suffolk, Stowmarket enjoyed a
period of rapid growth when the
River Gipping was still navigable to
Ipswich and when the railway
arrived.

Much of the town's history and
legacy are brought vividly to life in
the splendid **Museum of East
Anglian Life**, situated in the centre
of town to the west of the
marketplace (where markets are held
twice a week), in a 70-acre
meadowland site on the old Abbot's
Hall Estate (the aisled original barn
dates from the 13th century). Part
of the open-air section features
several historic buildings that have
been moved from elsewhere in the
region and carefully re-erected on
site. These include an engineering
workshop from the 1870s, part of a
14th century farmhouse, a watermill
from Alton and a wind pump which
was rescued in a collapsed state at
Minsmere in 1977. There's also a
collection of working steam engines,

farm animals and year-round
demonstrations of all manner of
local arts and crafts, from coopering
to chandlery, from sheep shearing to
saddlery.

Stowmarket's church of St Peter
and St Mary acquired a new spire in
1994, replacing the 1715 version
(itself a replacement) which was
dismantled on safety grounds in
1975.

The town certainly merits a
leisurely stroll, while for a peaceful
picnic the riverbank beckons.
Serious scenic walkers should make
for the **Gipping Valley River Park**
walk, which follows the former
towpath all the way to Ipswich.

AROUND STOWMARKET

BUXHALL

3 miles W of Stowmarket just off the B1115

The village church here is notable
for its six heavy bells, but the best-
known landmark in this quiet
village is undoubtedly the majestic
tower mill, without sails since a gale
removed them in 1929 but still
standing as a silent, sturdy reminder
of its working days. This is good
walking country, with an ancient
wood and many signposted
footpaths.

NEEDHAM MARKET

4 miles SE of Stowmarket off the A14

A thriving village whose greatest
glory is the wonderful carvings on
the ceiling of the church of **St
John the Baptist**. The church's
ornate double hammerbeam roof is
nothing short of remarkable,

especially when bathed in light from the strategically placed skylight. The roof is massive, as high as the walls of the church itself; the renowned authority on Suffolk churches, H Munro Cautley, described the work at Needham as 'the culminating achievement of the English carpenter'. The village also boasts some excellent examples of Tudor architecture.

The River Gipping flows to the east of the High Street and its banks provide miles of walks: the towpath is a public right of way walkable all the way from Stowmarket to Ipswich. On the riverbank at Needham is a 25-acre picnic site and a nature reserve.

Monthly farmers' markets are held at Alder Carr Farm, where there is also a pottery, crafts centre and farm shop.

Barking, on the B1018 south of Needham, was once more important than its neighbour, being described in 1874 as 'a pleasant village … including the hamlet of Needham Market'. This explains the fact that Barking's church is exceptionally large for a village house of worship: it was the mother church to Needham Market and was used for Needham's burials when Needham had no burial ground of its own.

EARL STONHAM
6 miles E of Stowmarket on the A1120

A scattered village set around three greens in farming land, Earl Stonham's church of St Mary the Virgin boasts one of Suffolk's finest single hammerbeam roofs,

and is also notable for its Bible scene murals, the 'Doom' (Last Judgement scene) over the chancel arch and a triple hour-glass, presumably to record just how protracted were some of the sermons.

STONHAM ASPAL
7 miles E of Stowmarket on the A1120

On the other side of the A140 lies Stonham Aspal, where in 1962 the remains of a Roman bath-house were unearthed. The parish church has an unusual wooden top to its tower, a necessary addition to house the ten bells that a keen campanologist insisted on installing.

EARL SOHAM
12 miles E of Stowmarket on the A1120

Earl Soham comprises a long, winding street that was once part of a Roman road. It lies in a valley, and on the largest of its three greens the village sign is a carved wooden statue of a falconer given as a gift by the Women's Institute in 1953. The 13th century church of St Mary is well worth a visit.

SAXTEAD GREEN
14 miles E of Stowmarket off the A1120

One of the prettiest sights in Suffolk is the white **18th century mill** that stands on the marshy green in Saxtead. This is a wonderful example of a post mill, perhaps the best in the world, dating back to 1796 and first renovated in the 19th century. It worked until 1947 and has since been kept in working order, with

At Stonham Barns, the British Birds of Prey and Nature Centre is home to every British owl, together with raptors from Britain and around the world. These wonderful birds flap their wings in regular flying displays, and in the Pets Paradise area children can meet and greet hamsters and horses, mice and meerkats, parrots and piglets.

the sails turning even though the mill no longer grinds. In summer, visitors can climb into the buck (body) of this elegant weatherboarded construction and explore its machinery.

FRAMLINGHAM

18 miles NE of Stowmarket on the B1119

The marvellous **Castle**, brooding on a hilltop, dominates this agreeable market town, as it has since Roger Bigod, 2nd Earl of Norfolk, built it in the 12th century (his grandfather built the first a century earlier, but this wooden construction was soon demolished). The Earls and Dukes of Norfolk, the Howards, were here for many generations before moving to Arundel in 1635. The castle is in remarkably good condition, partly because it was rarely attacked – though King John put it under siege in 1215. Its most famous occupant was Mary Tudor, who was in residence when proclaimed Queen in 1553. During the reign of Elizabeth I it was used as a prison for defiant priests and, in the 17th century after being bequeathed to Pembroke College, Cambridge, it saw service as a home and school for local paupers. Nine of the castle's 13 towers are accessible - the climb up the spiral staircase and walk round the battlements are well worth the effort. On one side the view is of the Meres, a bird sanctuary. In the north wing is the **Lanman Museum**, devoted to agricultural, craftsman's tools and domestic memorabilia.

The castle brought considerable prestige and prosperity to Framlingham, evidence of which can be found in the splendid church of **St Michael**, which has two wonderful works of art. One is the tomb of Henry Fitzroy, bastard son of Henry VIII, beautifully adorned with scenes from Genesis and Exodus and in a superb state of repair. The other is the tomb of the 3rd Duke, with carvings of the apostles in shell niches. Also of note is the Carolean organ of 1674, a gift of Sir Robert Hitcham, to whom the Howards sold the estate. Cromwell and the Puritans were not in favour of organs in churches, so this instrument was lucky to have escaped the mass destruction of organs at the time of the Commonwealth. Sir Robert is buried in the church.

DENNINGTON

2 miles N of Framlingham on the B1116

The pretty little village of Dennington boasts one of the oldest post offices in the country, this one having occupied the same site since 1830. The village church has some very unusual features, none more so than the hanging 'pyx' canopy above the altar. A pyx served as a receptacle for the Reserved Sacrament, which would be kept under a canopy attached to weights and pulleys so that the whole thing could be lowered when the sacrament was required for the sick and the dying. In the chapel at the top of the south aisle stands the tomb of Lord Bardolph, who fought at Agincourt, and of his wife, their effigies carved in alabaster.

CHARSFIELD

5 miles S of Framlingham off the B1078

A minor road runs from Framlingham through picturesque Kettleburgh and Hoo to Charsfield, best known as the inspiration for Ronald Blyth's book *Akenfield*, later memorably filmed by Sir Peter Hall. A cottage garden in the village displays the Akenfield village sign and is open to visitors in the summer.

OTLEY

7 miles SW of Framlingham on the B1079

The 15th century **Moated Hall** in Otley is open to the public at certain times of the year. Standing in ten acres of gardens that include a canal, a nuttery and a knot garden, the hall was long associated with the Gosnold family, whose coat of arms is also that of the village. The best-known member of that family was Bartholomew Gosnold, who sailed to the New World, coined the named 'Martha's Vineyard' for the island off the coast of Massachusetts, discovered Cape Cod and founded the settlement of Jamestown, Virginia. The 13th century church of St Mary has a remarkable baptistry font measuring 6 feet in length and 2 feet 8 inches in depth. Though filled with water, the font is not used and was only discovered in 1950 when the vestry floor was raised. It may have been used for adult baptisms.

FRAMSDEN

7 miles SW of Framlingham on the B1077

The scenery in these parts is real picture-postcard stuff, and in the village of Framsden the picture is completed by a fine **Post Mill**, built high on a hill in 1760, refitted and raised in 1836 and in commercial use until 1934. The milling machinery is still in place and the mill is open for visits (at weekends, by appointment only).

CRETINGHAM

4 miles SW of Framlingham off the A1120

The village sign is the unusual item here, in that it has two different panels: one shows an everyday Anglo-Saxon farming scene, the other a group (of Danes?) sailing up the River Deben, with the locals fleeing. The signs are made from mosaic tiles.

BRANDESTON

3 miles SW of Framlingham off the A1120

A further mile to the east, through some charming countryside, Brandeston is another delightful spot, with a row of beautiful thatched cottages and the parish **Church of All Saints** with its 13th century font. The best-known vicar of Brandeston was John Lowes (1572-1646) who was accused of witchcraft by the villagers, interrogated by Witchfinder General Matthew Hopkins and hanged at Bury St Edmunds. His sad end was made even sadder by the fact that before being strung up he had to read out the burial service of a condemned witch

•

The church at Dennington also has many interesting carvings, the most remarkable being that of a skiapod, the only known representation in this county of a mythical creature of the African desert, humanoid but with a huge boat-shaped foot with which it could cover itself against the sun. This curious beast was 'known' to Herodotus and to Pliny, who remarked that it had 'great pertinacity in leaping'.

•

98 THE WHITE HART

Otley, nr Ipswich

The White Hart is a very pleasant country inn serving ale from a local brewery and good-value home cooking.

🍴 *see page 275*

99 THE QUEENS HEAD

The Street, Brandeston

A smart redbrick pub serving some of the best food in the area, with Adnams ales to accompany.

🍴 *see page 275*

100 THE FORGE CAFÉ, RESTAURANT & GIFT SHOP

Thornham Magna, nr Eye

Excellent home-cooked snacks and meals are served at **The Forge Café-Restaurant**, which also has a gift shop.

❚❚ *see page 275*

101 THE RAILWAY TAVERN

Yaxley Road, Mellis nr Eye

The Railway Tavern is a friendly, welcoming inn serving real ales and traditional pub dishes. Three letting bedrooms.

❚❚ *see page 275*

himself, as no priest was allowed to conduct the service. Hopkins made a handsome living out of this bizarre business, preying on the superstitions of the times and using the foulest means to obtain confessions. One account of Hopkins' end is that he himself was accused of being a witch and hanged. The less satisfactory alternative is that he died of tuberculosis.

DEBENHAM

10 miles E of Stowmarket on the B1077

Debenham is a sizable village of architectural distinction, with a profusion of attractive timber-framed buildings dating from the 14th to the 17th centuries. The River Deben flows beside and beneath the main street and, near one of the little bridges, weavers still practise their craft. There is also a pottery centre. St Mary's Church is unusual in having an original Saxon tower, and the roof alternates hammerbeams with crested tie beams.

MENDLESHAM

6 miles NE of Stowmarket off the A140

On the green in Old Market Street, Mendlesham, lies an enormous stone which is said to have been used as a preaching stone, mounted by itinerant Wesleyan preachers. In the Church of St Mary there is a collection of parish armour assembled some 400 years ago, and also some fine carvings. The least hidden local landmark is a 1,000-feet TV mast put up by the IBA in 1959. The 34th Bomb Group

operated from Mendlesham airfield, and an impressive memorial to personnel lost over the airfield was built in 1949.

WETHERINGSETT

7 miles NE of Stowmarket off the A140

On the other side of the A140, Wetheringsett is where visitors will find **Mid-Suffolk Light Railway Museum**, open on Sundays and Bank Holidays from Easter to September. Tel: 01449 766899

Wetheringsett has had two well-known rectors, famous for very different reasons. Richard Hakluyt, incumbent from 1590 to 1616, is remembered for his major work *Voyages* (full title *Principal Navigation, Voiages, Traffiques and Discoveries of the English Nation*). The rector between 1858 and 1883 was a certain George Wilfrid Ellis, sometime tailor and butler, and finally a bogus clergyman. After he was unmasked as a sham, a special Act of Parliament was needed to validate the marriage ceremonies he had illegally performed, and to legitimise the issue of those marriages.

THORNHAM MAGNA & PARVA

10 miles N of Stowmarket off the A140

The **Thornham Walks and Field Centre**, with 12 miles of walks and a herb garden and nursery, cater admirably for hikers, horticulturists and lovers of the countryside. The tiny thatched church of St Mary at Thornham Parva houses a considerable treasure in the shape of an exquisite medieval altar painting, known as a *retable*, with a central panel depicting the Crucifixion and four saints on each side panel. Its origins are uncertain, but it was possibly the work of the Royal Workshops at Westminster Abbey and made for Thetford Priory, or for a nearby Dominican monastery. When conservation work was urgently needed, the villagers of Thornham Parva managed to raise the money needed to save this national treasure; their successful efforts were rewarded when the work, carried out by the Hamilton Kerr Institute, part of the Fitzwilliam Museum in Cambridge, earned an allocation of funds from the Heritage Lottery Fund. Also to be admired is the 14th century octagonal font and a series of fascinating wall paintings. In the churchyard are the grave and monument of Sir Basil Spence (1907-76), architect of Coventry Cathedral.

YAXLEY
12 miles N of Stowmarket on the A140

Yaxley's church of **St Mary** offers up more treasures. One is an extremely rare sexton's wheel, which hangs above the south door and was used in medieval times to select fast days in honour of the Virgin. When a pair of iron wheels were spun on their axle, strings attached to the outer wheel would catch on the inner, stopping both and indicating the chosen day. The 17th century pulpit is one of the finest in the country, with the most glorious, sumptuous carvings.

EYE
13 miles NE of Stowmarket on the B1117

The name of this excellent little town is derived from the Saxon for an island, as Eye was once surrounded by water and marshes. The church of **St Peter and St Paul** stands in the shadow of a mound on which a castle once stood (the remains are worth a look and the mound offers a panoramic view of the town – almost a bird's eye view, in fact). The church's 100-feet tower was described by Pevsner as 'one of the wonders of Suffolk' and the interior is a masterpiece of restoration, with all the essential medieval features in place. The rood screen, with painted panels depicting St Edmund, St Ursula, Edward the Confessor and Henry VI, is particularly fine.

HOXNE
4 miles NE of Eye on the B1118

Palaeolithic remains indicate the exceptionally long history of Hoxne (pronounced Hoxon), which stands along the banks of the River Waveney near the Norfolk border. It is best known for its links with King Edmund, who was reputedly killed here, though Bradfield St Clare and Shottisham have rival claims to this distinction. The Hoxne legend is that Edmund was betrayed to the Danes by a newlywed couple who were crossing the Goldbrook bridge and spotted his golden spurs reflected from his hiding place below the bridge. Edmund put a curse on all

•

Other interesting Eye sights are the ornate redbrick Town Hall; the timbered Guildhall, with the archangel Gabriel carved on a corner post; a 'crinkle-crankle' (serpentine) wall fronting Chandos Lodge, where Sir Frederick Ashton once lived; and a thriving theatre, one of the smallest professional theatres in the country.

•

On a famous day during the Second World War, Glenn Miller brought his band to Horham to celebrate the 200th flying mission to set out from the American aerodrome. The 95th Bomb Group Hospital Museum contains some wonderful wartime paintings, and a memorial in Horham Church remembers the airfield's personnel.

Wingfield's Church of St Andrew was built as the collegiate church and has an extra-large chancel to accommodate the college choir. The church contains three really fine monuments: to Sir John (in stone); to Michael de la Pole, 2nd Earl of Suffolk (in wood); and to John de la Pole, Duke of Suffolk (in alabaster). In the churchyard there is a 'hudd' – a shelter for the priest for use at the graveside in bad weather.

newlyweds crossing the bridge, and to this day some brides take care to avoid it.

The story continues that Edmund was tied to an oak tree and killed with arrows. That same oak mysteriously fell down in 1848 while apparently in good health, and a monument at the site is a popular tourist attraction. In the church of St Peter and St Paul an oak screen (perhaps that very same oak?) depicts scenes from the martyr's life. A more cheerful event is the Harvest Breakfast on the village green that follows the annual service. The East Anglian bishops once had their seat at Hoxne, and the moated vicarage beside the church may have been the original location of the Bishops Palace.

HORHAM

6 miles E of Eye on the B1117

Three distinct musical connections distinguish this dapper little village. The Norman church has had its tower strengthened for the rehanging of the peal of eight bells, which is believed to be the oldest in the world. Benjamin Britten, later associated with the Aldeburgh Festival, lived and composed in Horham for a time.

WORLINGWORTH

8 miles SE of Eye off the B1118

It's well worth taking the country road to Worlingworth, a long, straggling village whose church of St Mary has a remarkable font cover reaching up about 30 feet. It is brilliantly coloured and intricately

carved, and near the top is an inscription in Greek which translates as 'wash my sin and not my body only.' Note, too, the Carolean box pews, the carved pulpit and an oil painting of Worlingworth's Great Feast of 1810 to celebrate George III's jubilee.

WINGFIELD

6 miles E of Eye off the B1118

Wingfield College is one of the country's most historic seats of learning, founded in 1362 as a college for priests with a bequest from Sir John de Wingfield, Chief Staff Officer to the Black Prince. Sir John's wealth came from ransoming a French nobleman at the Battle of Poitiers in 1356. Surrendered to Henry VIII at the time of the Dissolution, the college became a farmhouse and is now in private hands. The façade is now Georgian, but the original medieval Great Hall still stands, and the college and its three acres of gardens are open to the public at weekends in summer. Attractions include regular artistic events and printing demonstrations.

On a hill outside the village are the imposing remains of a castle built by the 1st Earl.

FRESSINGFIELD

10 miles E of Eye on the B1116

Fressingfield's first spiritual centre was the **Church of St Peter and St Paul**. It has a superb hammerbeam roof and a lovely stone bell tower that was built in the 14th century. On one of the pews the initials A P are carved. These are believed to be the work of Alice de la Pole, Duchess of Norfolk and grand-daughter of Geoffrey Chaucer. Was this a work of art or a bout of vandalism brought on by a dull sermon?

The village sign is a pilgrim and a donkey, recording that Fressingfield was a stopping place on the pilgrim route from Dunwich to Bury St Edmunds.

LAXFIELD

12 miles E of Eye on the B1117

Laxfield & District Museum, in the 16th century Guildhall, gives a fine insight into bygone ages with geology and natural history exhibits, agricultural and domestic tools, a Victorian kitchen, a village shop and a costume room. The museum is open on Saturday and Sunday afternoons in summer.

All Saints Church is distinguished by some wonderful flint 'flushwork' (stonework) on its tower, roof and nave. In the 1808 Baptist church is a plaque remembering John Noyes, burnt at the stake in 1557 for refusing to take Catholic vows. History relates that the villagers - with a single exception - dowsed their fires in protest. The one remaining fire, however, was all that was needed to light the stake.

A couple of miles east of Laxfield, **Heveningham Hall** is a fine Georgian mansion, a model of classical elegance designed by James Wyatt with lovely grounds by Capability Brown. As it runs through the grounds, the River Blyth widens into a lake.

ALONG THE COAST

DUNWICH

4 miles SW of Southwold off the B1105

Surely the hidden place of all hidden places, Dunwich was once the capital of East Anglia, founded by the Burgundian Christian missionary St Felix and for several centuries a major trading port (wool and grain out; wine, timber and cloth in) and a centre of fishing and shipbuilding. The records show that in 1241 no fewer than 80 ships were built here for the king. By the middle of the next century, however, the sea attacked from the east and a vast bank of sand and shingle silted up the harbour. The course of the river was diverted, the town was cut off from the sea and the town's trade was effectively

●

Close to Fressingfield at nearby Ufford Hall lived the Sancroft family, one of whom became Archbishop of Canterbury. He led the revolt of the bishops against James II and was imprisoned in the Tower of London. Released by William IV and sacked for refusing to swear the oath of allegiance, he returned home and is entombed by the south porch of the church.

●

102/139 THE SHIP INN AT DUNWICH

Dunwich, nr Saxmundham

The Ship Inn is one of East Anglia's best-known pubs, offering fine food, real ales and well-appointed letting bedrooms.

see pages 276 and 288

Dunwich Heath (National Trust)

81

•

Dunwich Forest, immediately inland from the village, is one of three – the others are further south at Tunstall and Rendlesham – named by the Forestry Commission as Aldewood Forest. Work started on these in 1920 with the planting of Scots pine, Corsican pine and some Douglas fir; oak and poplar were tried but did not thrive in the sandy soil. The three forests, which between them cover nearly 9,000 acres, were almost completely devastated in the hurricane of October 1987, Rendlesham alone losing more than a million trees. Replanting will take many years to be established.

•

103/140 THE GRIFFIN INN
High Street, Yoxford
Period character abounds at **The Griffin Inn**, which offers real ales, traditional cooking and comfortable accommodation.

⏸ ⊨ see pages 276 and 288

killed off. For the next 700 years the relentless forces of nature continued to take their toll, and of the six churches, monasteries, mills and hospitals all that remains now of ancient Dunwich are the ruins of the Norman leper hospital of St James, the ruins of a clifftop friary that was home to the Greyfriars, and a buttress of one of the nine churches which once served the community. The last church succumbed to the waves in 1920, but local legend says that the church bells can be heard beneath the waves on stormy nights. Other tales tell of strange lights in the ruined priory and the eerie chanting of long-dead monks.

Today's village comprises a 19th century church and a row of Victorian cottages, one of which houses the **Dunwich Museum**. Local residents set up the museum in 1972 to tell the Dunwich story; the historical section has displays and exhibits from Roman, Saxon and medieval times, the centrepiece being a large model of the town at its 12th century peak. There are also sections devoted to natural history, social history and the arts.

South of the village lies **Dunwich Heath**, one of Suffolk's most important conservation areas, comprising the beach, splendid heather, a field study centre, a public hide and an information centre and restaurant in converted coastguard cottages.

Around Dunwich Heath are the attractive villages of Westleton, Middleton, Theberton and Eastbridge. During the First World War, German airships were used to spy on and bomb England. In the porch of Theberton church are remains of a Zeppelin that crashed in a nearby field in 1917.

In **Westleton**, the 14th century thatched church of St Peter, built by the monks of Sibton Abbey, has twice seen the collapse of its tower. The first fell down in a hurricane in 1776; its smaller wooden replacement collapsed when a bomb fell during the Second World War. The village is also the main route of access to the RSPB-managed **Minsmere Bird Sanctuary**, the most important sanctuary for wading birds in eastern England. The marshland was flooded during the Second World War, and nature and this wartime emergency measure created the perfect habitat for innumerable birds. More than 100 species nest here, and a similar number of birds visit throughout the year, making it a birdwatcher's paradise. Minsmere is rich in other kinds of wildlife, and one of the best ways of discovering more is to join one of the guided walks. The **Suffolk Coastal Path** runs along the foreshore.

A little way inland from Westleton lies **Darsham**, where another nature reserve is home to many varieties of birds and flowers.

YOXFORD

10 miles SW of Southwold on the A12

Once an important stop on the London-to-Yarmouth coaching route, Yoxford now attracts visitors with its pink-washed cottages and its arts and crafts, antiques and food shops. Look for the cast-iron signpost outside the church, with hands pointing to London, Yarmouth and Framlingham set high enough to be seen by the driver of a stagecoach.

SAXMUNDHAM

12 miles SW of Southwold off the A12

A little town that was granted its market charter in 1272. On the font of the church in Saxmundham is the carving of a 'woodwose' - a tree spirit or green man. He, and others like him, have given their name to a large number of pubs in Suffolk and elsewhere. A major attraction was added in 2004 in the shape of **Saxmundham Museum**, housed in a former bakehouse. Among the many fascinating displays are a scale model of Saxmundham railway station as it was in the 1930s, complete with working trains; a re-creation of Saxmundham Playhouse; replicas of shops; costumes and dolls; and various memorabilia relating to the town. The museum is open Wednesday to Saturday from April to September.

BRUISYARD

4 miles NW of Saxmundham off the B1119

Just west of this village is the **Bruisyard Vineyard, Winery and Herb Centre**, a complex of a 10-acre vineyard with 13,000 Müller Thurgau grape vines, a wine-production centre, herb and water gardens, a tea shop and a picnic site.

PEASENHALL

6 miles NW of Saxmundham on the A1120

A little stream runs along the side of the main street in Peasenhall, whose buildings present several styles and ages. Most distinguished is the old timbered **Woolhall**, splendidly restored to its 15th century grandeur.

LEISTON

4 miles E of Saxmundham off the B1119

The first **Leiston Abbey** was built on Nunsmere marshes in 1182, but in 1363 the Earl of Suffolk rebuilt it on its present site away from the frequent floods. It became one of the largest and most prestigious monasteries in the country, and its wealth probably spelled its ruin, as it fell within Henry VIII's plan for the Dissolution of the Monasteries. The visible ruins are of a chapel built on the site of the monastic church. A new abbey was built using stone from the first abbey site, and the restored old hall is used as a base for PROCORDA, a group promoting musical excellence.

For 200 years the biggest name in Leiston was that of Richard Garrett, who founded an engineering works here in 1778 after starting a business in Woodbridge. In the early years ploughs, threshers, seed drills and other agricultural machinery were the main products, but the company later started one of the country's first production lines for steam machines. The Garrett works are now the **Long Shop Museum**, the factory buildings having been

•

The oddest building in Peasenhall is certainly a hall in the style of a Swiss chalet, built for his workers by James Josiah Smyth, grandson of the founder of James Smyth & Sons. This company, renowned for its agricultural drills, was for more than two centuries the dominant industrial presence in Peasenhall. On the south side of St Michael's churchyard stands the 1805 drill-mill where James Smyth manufactured his Nonpareil seed drills, one of which is on display in Stowmarket's museum.

•

Every August, in the week following the Aldeburgh Carnival, a regatta is held on the Meare at Thorpeness, culminating in a splendid fireworks show.

lovingly restored, and many of the Garrett machines are now on display, including traction engines, a steam-driven tractor and a road roller. There's also a section where the history and workings of steam engines are explained. A small area of the museum recalls the USAAF's 357th fighter group, who flew from an airfield outside Leiston during the Second World War. One of their number, a Captain Chuck Yeager, was the first man to fly faster than the speed of sound.

The Garrett works closed in 1980, but what could have been a disastrous unemployment situation was alleviated to some extent by the nuclear power station at **Sizewell**. The coast road in the centre of Leiston leads to this establishment, where visitors can take tours - on foot with access to buildings at

Sizewell A or by minibus, with a guide and videos, round Sizewell B.

ALDRINGHAM

4 miles E of Saxmundham on the B1122

Aldringham's church is notable for its superb 15th century font, and the village inn was once a haunt of smugglers. It now helps to refresh the visitors who flock to the **Aldringham Craft Market**, founded in 1958 and extending over three galleries, with a serious selection of arts and crafts, clothes and gifts, pottery, basketry, books and cards.

THORPENESS

6 miles E of Saxmundham on the B1353

Thorpeness is a unique holiday village with mock-Tudor houses and the general look of a series of eccentric film sets. Buying up a considerable packet of land called the Sizewell estate in 1910, the architect, barrister and playwright Glencairn Stuart Ogilvie created what he hoped would be a fashionable resort with cottages, some larger houses and a 65-acre shallow boating and pleasure lake called the Meare. The 85-feet water tower, built to aid in the lake's construction, looked out of place, so Ogilvie disguised it as a house. Known ever since as the **House in the Clouds**, it is now available to rent as a holiday home. The neighbouring mill, moved lock, stock and millstones from Aldringham, stopped pumping in 1940 but has been restored and now houses a visitor centre. Thorpeness is very much a one-

The House in the Clouds, Thorpeness

Aldeburgh

off, not at all typical Suffolk but with a droll charm that is all its own.

ALDEBURGH

6 miles SE of Saxmundham on the A1094

And so down the coast road to Aldeburgh, another coastal town that once prospered as a port with major fishing and shipbuilding industries.

Suffolk's best-known poet, George Crabbe, was born at Slaughden in 1754 and lived through the village's hard times. He reflected the melancholy of those days when he wrote of his fellow townsmen:

Here joyless roam a wild amphibious race,
With sullen woe displayed in every face;
Who far from civil arts and social fly,
And scowl at strangers with suspicious eye.

He was equally evocative concerning the sea and the river, and the following lines written about the River Alde could apply to several others in the county:

With ceaseless motion comes and goes the tide
Flowing, it fills the channel vast and wide;
Then back to sea, with strong majestic sweep
It- rolls, in ebb yet terrible and deep;
Here samphire-banks and salt-wort bound the flood
There stakes and seaweed withering on the mud;
And higher up, a ridge of all things base,
Which some strong tide has rolled upon the place.

It was Crabbe who created the character of the solitary fisherman Peter Grimes, later the subject of an opera composed by another Aldeburgh resident, Benjamin Britten.

Aldeburgh's role gradually changed into that of a holiday

•

Drake's Greyhound and Pelican were built at Slaughden, now taken by the sea, and during the 16th century some 1,500 people were engaged in fishing. Both industries declined as shipbuilding moved elsewhere and the fishing boats became too large to be hauled up the shingle.

•

85

•

The Martello Towers were named after the Torre della Mortella on the island of Corsica, which the English army saw in the war in 1793. Aldeburgh's tower was completed in 1810, and never saw action, although it had four guns at the ready and was manned until the middle of Queen Victoria's reign.

•

resort, and the Marquess of Salisbury, visiting early in the 19th century, was one of the first to be attracted by the idea of sea-bathing without the crowds. By the middle of the century the grand houses that had sprung up were joined by smaller residences, the railway had arrived, a handsome water tower was put up (1860) and Aldeburgh prospered once more. There were even plans for a pier, and construction started in 1878, but the project proved too difficult or too expensive and was halted, the rusting girders being removed some time later.

One of the town's major benefactors was Newson Garrett, a wealthy businessman who was the first mayor under the charter of the Local Government Act of 1875. This colourful character also developed the **Maltings at Snape,** but is perhaps best remembered through his remarkable daughter Elizabeth, who was the first woman doctor in England (having qualified in Paris at a time when women could not qualify here) and the first woman mayor (of Aldeburgh, in 1908). This lady married the shipowner James Skelton Anderson, who established the golf club in 1884.

If Crabbe were alive today he would have a rather less cantankerous opinion of his fellows, especially at carnival time on a Monday in August when the town celebrates with a colourful procession of floats and marchers, a fireworks display and numerous other events. As for the arts, there

is, of course, the **Aldeburgh Festival**, started in 1948 by Britten and others; the festival's main venue is Snape Maltings, but many performances take place in Aldeburgh itself.

The town's maritime connections remain very strong. There has been a lifeboat here since 1851, and down the years many acts of great heroism have been recorded. The very modern lifeboat station is one of the town's chief attractions for visitors, and there are regular practice launches from the shingle beach. A handful of fishermen still put out to sea from the beach, selling their catch from their little wooden huts, while a thriving yacht club is the base for sailing on the Orde and, sometimes, on the sea.

At the very southern tip of the town, the **Martello Tower** serves as a reminder of the power of the sea: old pictures show it standing well back from the waves, but now the seaward side of the moat has disappeared and the shingle is constantly being shored up to protect it. This squat tower is the most northerly of 75 erected on the coast between Sussex and Suffolk as a defence against a possible attack by Napoleon's forces. Beyond the tower, a long strip of marsh and shingle stretches right down to the mouth of the river at Shingle Street.

Back in town there are several interesting buildings, notably the **Moot Hall** and the parish church of **St Peter and St Paul**. The Moot Hall is a 16th century timber-framed building that was built in what was once the centre of town. It hasn't moved, but the sea long ago took away several houses and streets. Inside the Hall is a museum of town history and finds from the nearby Snape burial ship. The museum also recounts the story of the Aldeburgh lifeboat's rescue on the second Sunday of the Second World War of sailors from the SS *Magdapur*. Benjamin Britten set the first scene of Peter Grimes in the Moot Hall. A sundial on the south face of the Hall proclaims, in Latin, that it only tells the time when the sun shines.

The church, which stands above the town as a very visible landmark for mariners, contains a memorial to George Crabbe and a beautiful stained-glass window, the work of John Piper, depicting three Britten parables: *Curlew River*, *The Burning Fiery Furnace* and *The Prodigal Son*. Britten, his companion Peter Pears and the musician Imogen Holst are buried in the churchyard, part of which is set aside for the benefit of wildlife. The latest of the many tributes in Aldeburgh to Britten is a giant metal clam shell designed by Maggie Hambling. It stands on the beach at the north end of town. Elizabeth Garrett Anderson (see above) is also buried in the churchyard.

FRISTON

3 miles SE of Saxmundham off the A1094

Friston's **Post Mill**, the tallest in England, is a prominent sight on the Aldeburgh-Snape road, moved from Woodbridge in 1812 just after its construction. It worked by wind until 1956, then by engine until 1972.

SNAPE

3 miles S of Saxmundham on the A1094

This 'boggy place' has a long and interesting history. In 1862 the remains of an Anglo-Saxon ship were discovered here, and since that time regular finds have been made, with some remarkable cases of almost perfect preservation. Snape, like Aldeburgh, has benefited over the years from the philanthropy of the Garrett family, one of whose members built the primary school and set up the Maltings, centre of the Aldeburgh Music Festival.

108 THE OLD CHEQUERS

Friston, nr Aldeburgh

A distinguished country inn serving real ales and fresh local produce in the restaurant.

see page 277

Snape Maltings

87

•

A short distance west of Snape, off the B1069, lies Blaxhall, famed for its growing stone. The Blaxhall Stone, which lies in the yard of Stone Farm, is reputed to have grown to its present size (5 tons) from a comparative pebble the size of a football, when it first came to local attention 100 years ago. Could there be more 'Blarney' than Blaxhall at work here?

•

165 EASTON FARM PARK

Easton, Woodbridge

A family attraction with animals on show, including rare breeds and Suffolk Punch horses, as well as local crafts.

 see *page 298*

The last 30-odd years have seen the development of the **Snape Maltings Riverside Centre**, a group of shops and galleries located in a complex of restored Victorian granaries and malthouses that is also the setting for the renowned Aldeburgh festival. The Maltings began their designated task of converting grain into malt in the 1840s, and continued thus until 1965, when the pressure of modern techniques brought them to a halt. There was a real risk of the buildings being demolished, but George Gooderham, a local farmer, bought the site to expand his animal feeds business and soon saw the potential of the redundant buildings.

The Concert Hall came first, in 1967, and in 1971 the Craft Shop was established as the first conversion of the old buildings for retail premises. Conversion and expansion continue to this day, and in the numerous outlets visitors can buy anything from fudge to country-style clothing, from herbs to household furniture, silver buttons to top hats. Plants and garden accessories are also sold, and art galleries feature the work of local painters, potters and sculptors. The Centre hosts regular painting, craft and decorative art courses, and more recent expansion saw the creation of an impressive country-style store.

CAMPSEA ASHE

6 miles NE of Woodbridge on the B1078

On towards Wickham Market the road passes through Campsea Ashe

in the parish of Campsey Ashe. The 14th century church of St John the Baptist has an interesting brass showing one of its first rectors in full priestly garb.

WICKHAM MARKET

5 miles N of Woodbridge off the A12

Places to see in this straggling village are the picturesque watermill by the River Deben and All Saints Church, whose 137-feet octagonal tower has a little roof to shelter the bell. At Boulge, a couple of miles southwest of Wickham Market, is the grave of Edward Fitzgerald, whose free translation of *The Rubaiyat of Omar Khayyam* is an English masterpiece. Tradition has it that on his grave is a rose bush grown from one found on Omar Khayyam's grave in Iran.

EASTON

5 miles N of Woodbridge off the B1078

A scenic drive leads to the lovely village of Easton, one of the most colourful, flower-bedecked places in the county. A remarkable sight to the west of the village is the two-mile-long **Crinkle-Crankle Wall** that surrounds Easton Park. This extraordinary type of wall, also known as a ribbon wall, weaves snake-like in and out and is much stronger than if it were straight. This particular wall, said to be the world's longest, was built by Lord of the Manor, the Earl of Rochford, in the 1820s.

Tucked away three miles off the A12 in the beautiful Deben Valley, **Easton Park Farm** is one of Suffolk's greatest attractions. Since it opened in 1973, more than a million visitors have passed through the gates to have a great day out; they leave knowing a lot more about the ways of the countryside than when they arrived. It's a marvellous place to bring the family, as the children can have endless fun feeding and making friends with the animals in Pets Paddock, riding ponies, seeing the Suffolk Punches or simply running around in the adventure playground. The showpiece of the park is the Victorian dairy, an ornate octagonal building, while the Dairy Centre is contrastingly modern, with walkways over the top of the stalls and a viewing gallery over the milking parlour.

Open Day, Easton Park Farm

PARHAM

8 miles N of Woodbridge on the B1116

Parham Airfield is now agricultural land, but in the museum in the control tower and an adjacent hut can be found memorabilia of the 390th Bomb Group of the USAAF. The airfield was built in 1942 for the RAF, but it was taken over by the USAAF in 1943. From here they flew Flying Fortresses on many successful missions, and the museum is a memorial to all the airmen who flew from here.

UFFORD

4 miles N of Woodbridge off the A12

Pride of place in a village that takes its name from Uffa (or Wuffa), the founder of the leading Anglo-Saxon dynasty, goes to the 13th century **Church of the Assumption**. The font cover,

which telescopes from 5 feet to 18 feet in height, is a masterpiece of craftsmanship, its elaborate carving crowned by a pelican. Many 15th century benches have survived, but Dowsing smashed the organ and most of the stained glass – what's there now is mainly Victorian, some of it a copy of 15th century work at All Souls College, Oxford. Ufford is where the Suffolk Punch originated, Crisp's 404 being, in 1768, the progenitor of this distinguished breed of horses.

BREDFIELD

3 miles N of Woodbridge off the A12

There's a plaque on the wall of the village pub in Bredfield commemorating a day in 1742 on which nothing at all happened. On a day in 1809, however, something *did* happen: Edward Fitzgerald was

104 THE MOON &
MUSHROOM

High Road, Swilland

The attractions here include
superb real ales and hearty
home cooking.

🍴 see page 276

109/141 THE BULL
HOTEL

Market Hill, Woodbridge

With a tradition of
hospitality dating back to the
16th century, **The Bull** is a
fine hotel, restaurant and bar
in historic Woodbridge.

🛏 🍴 see pages 278 and
288

born. Something else happened in
1953: a wrought-iron canopy with a
golden crown, made at the village
forge, was put on the crossroads
pump to celebrate Queen Elizabeth
II's coronation.

WOODBRIDGE

Udebyge, Wiebryge, Wodebryge,
Wudebrige … just some of the
ways of spelling this splendid old
market town since it was first
mentioned in writing back in AD
970. As to what the name means, it
could simply be 'wooden bridge' or
'bridge by the wood', but the most
likely and most interesting
explanation is that it is derived
from Anglo-Saxon words meaning
'Woden's (or Odin's) town'.
Standing at the head of the Deben
estuary, it is a place of considerable
charm with a wealth of handsome,
often historic buildings and a
considerable sense of history, as
both a market town and a port.

The shipbuilding and allied
industries flourished here, as at most
towns on the Suffolk coast, and it is
recorded that both Edward III, in the
14th century, and Drake in the 16th
sailed in Woodbridge ships. There's
still plenty of activity on and by the
river, though nowadays it is all
leisure-orientated. The town's greatest
benefactor was Thomas Seckford,
who rebuilt the abbey, paid for the
chapel in the north aisle of St Mary's
Church and founded the original
almshouses in Seckford Street. In
1575 he gave the town the splendid
Shire Hall on Market Hill. Originally
used as a corn exchange, it now
houses the **Suffolk Punch Heavy
Horse Museum**, with an exhibition
devoted to the Suffolk Punch breed
of heavy working horse, the oldest
such breed in the world. The breed
dates from the 16th century, but all
animals alive today trace the male line
back to one stallion called Crisp's
Horse of Ufford, foaled in 1768. The
history of the breed and its rescue
from near-extinction in the
1960s is covered in
fascinating detail, and a small
section relates to other
famous Suffolk breeds – the
Red Poll cattle, the Suffolk
sheep and the Large Black
pigs. Tel: 01394 380643.
Opposite the Shire Hall is
Woodbridge Museum, a
treasure trove of
information on the history
of the town and its more
notable residents; from here
it is a short stroll down the
cobbled alleyway to the
magnificent parish church

Tide Mill and Harbour, Woodbridge

of St Mary, where Seckford was buried in 1587.

Seckford naturally features prominently in the museum, along with the painter Thomas Churchyard, the map-maker Isaac Johnson and the poet Edward Fitzgerald. 'Old Fitz' was something of an eccentric and, for the most part, fairly reclusive. He loved Woodbridge and particularly the River Deben, where he often sailed in his little boat *Scandal*.

Woodbridge is lucky enough to have two marvellous mills, both in working order, and both great attractions for the visitor. The **Tide Mill**, on the quayside close to the town centre, dates from the late 18th century (though the site was mentioned 600 years previously) and worked by the power of the tide until 1957. It has been meticulously restored and the waterwheel still turns, fed by a recently created pond which replaced the original huge mill pond when it was turned into a marina. **Buttrum's Mill**, named after the last miller, is a tower mill standing just off the A12 bypass a mile west of the town centre. A marvellous sight, its six storeys make it the tallest surviving tower mill in Suffolk. There is a ground-floor display of the history and workings of the mill.

Many of the town's streets are traffic-free, so shopping is a real pleasure. If you should catch the Fitzgerald mood and feel like 'a jug of wine and a loaf of bread', Woodbridge can oblige with a good variety of pubs and restaurants.

AROUND WOODBRIDGE

SUTTON HOO

1 mile E of Woodbridge off the B1083

A mile or so east of Woodbridge on the opposite bank of the Deben is the **Sutton Hoo Burial Site**, a group of a dozen grassy barrows which hit the headlines in 1939 and are sometimes known as 'page one of the history of England'. Excavations, which initially unearthed ship's rivets, brought to light the outline of an 80-feet long Anglo-Saxon ship, filled with one of the greatest hoards of treasure ever discovered in Britain. The priceless find, which eluded grave robbers and lay undisturbed for over 1,300 years, includes gold coins and ornaments, silverware, weapons and armoury, drinking horns and leather cups; it is housed in the British Museum in London, but there are exhibitions, replicas and plenty of other items of interest at the site, along with special events throughout the year. Research continues, and it is now believed that the ship was the burial place of Raedwald, of the Wuffinga dynasty, King of East Anglia from about AD 610 to AD 625. Access to the site is on foot from the B1083.

RENDLESHAM

5 miles NE of Woodbridge on the A1152

The church of **St Gregory the Great** dates from the 14th century, but there is evidence (not physical,

91

•

Rendlesham Forest, part of the Forest of Aldewood, was ravaged by the great hurricane of October 1987, when two-thirds of the trees, planted in the 1920s, were destroyed. Seven years before that, on Christmas night, another visitation had occurred. Security guards at RAF Woodbridge, at that time a front line NATO base, spotted strange lights in the forest and went to investigate. They came upon a nine-foot high triangular object with a series of lights around it. As they approached, it did what all good UFOs do and flew off before it could be photographed. The next day the guards returned to the spot where it had landed and found three depressions in the ground. The UFO was apparently sighted again two days later, and security in the area was heightened. No explanation has ever been forthcoming about the incident, but interest in it continues and from time to time guided walks to the landing site are arranged.

•

unfortunately) of an earlier Christian presence in the shape of Raedwald's palace.

The only part still standing of Rendlesham Hall, built in 1871 and demolished in 1949, is the Gothic folly of Woodbridge Lodge, a remarkable edifice which loses little in comparison with some of the more extraordinary buildings designed by Gaudi in Barcelona.

BUTLEY

5 miles NE of Woodbridge on the B1084

At the northern edge of Rendlesham Forest, the village of Butley has a splendid 14th century gatehouse, all that remains of **Butley Priory**, an Augustinian priory founded by Ranulf de Glanville in 1171. The gatehouse is, by itself, a fairly imposing building, with some interesting flintwork on the north façade (1320) and baronial carvings. Butley still has a working mill, remarkable for its fine Regency porch, and the parish church is Norman, with a 14th century tower.

There are some splendid country walks around Butley, notably by **Staverton Thicks**, which has a deer park and woods of oak and holly. The oldest trees date back more than 400 years. Butley Clumps is an avenue of beech trees planted in fours, with a pine tree at the centre of each clump – the technical term for such an arrangement is a *quincunx*. Butley has long been renowned for its oysters, and the beds have recently been revived.

CHILLESFORD

6 miles E of Woodbridge on the B1084

Brick was once big business here, and while digging for clay the locals made many finds, including hundreds of varieties of molluscs and the skeleton of an enormous whale. Chillesford supplies some of the clay for Aldeburgh brickworks.

ORFORD

12 miles E of Woodbridge at the end of the B1084

Without doubt one of the most charming and interesting of all the places in Suffolk, Orford has something to please everyone. The ruins of the **Castle**, one of the most important in medieval England, are a most impressive sight, even though the keep is all that remains of the original building commissioned by Henry II in 1165. The walls of the keep are 90 feet high and 10 feet deep, and behind them are many rooms and passages in a remarkable state of preservation. A climb up the spiral staircase to the top provides splendid views over the surrounding countryside and to the sea.

St Bartholomew's Church was built at the same time, though the present church dates from the 14th century. A wonderful sight at night when floodlit, the church is regularly used for the performance of concerts and recitals, and many of Benjamin Britten's works were first heard here. At the east end lie the still-splendid Norman remains, all that is left of the original chancel.

These two grand buildings indicate that Orford was a very important town at one time. Indeed it was once a thriving port, but the steadily growing shingle bank of Orford Ness gradually cut it off from the sea, and down the years its appeal has changed. The sea may have gone from Orford but the river is still there, and in summer the quayside is alive with yachts and pleasure craft. On the other side of the river is **Orford Ness**, the largest vegetated shingle spit in England which is home to a variety of rare flora and fauna. The lighthouse marks the most easterly point (jointly with Lowestoft) in Britain.

Access to the 10-mile spit, which is in the hands of the National Trust, is by ferry from Orford Quay. For many years the Ness was out of bounds to the public, being used for various military purposes, including pre-war radar research under Sir Robert Watson-Watt. Trails pass through the varied habitats found on the Ness, as well as areas and buildings of historic interest such as the First World War airfield site, firing ranges and the lighthouse. Boat trips also leave Orford Quay for the RSPB reserve at **Havergate Island**, haunt of avocet and tern (the former returned in 1947 after being long absent).

The Dunwich Underwater Exploration Exhibition in Front Street features exhibits on marine archaeology, coastal erosion and

St Barthlomew's Church, Orford

more, gleaned from the exploration of the ruins of the former town of Dunwich, now largely claimed by the sea.

Back in the market square are a handsome town hall, two pubs with a fair quota of smuggling tales, a well-loved restaurant serving Butley oysters and a smokehouse where kippers, salmon, trout, ham, sausages, chicken and even garlic are smoked over Suffolk oak.

BAWDSEY

7 miles SE of Woodbridge on the B1083

The B1083 runs from Woodbridge through farming country and several attractive villages (Sutton, Shottisham, Alderton) to Bawdsey, beyond which lies the mouth of the River Deben, the end of the Sussex

---

107 THE KINGS HEAD INN

Front Street, Orford

The Kings Head is an ancient inn with well-kept ales, food and B&B.

see page 276

---

142 VESTA COTTAGE

Orford, nr Woodbridge

In a quiet street a short walk from the village centre, **Vesta Cottage** provides a comfortable self-catering base for up to 4 guests.

see page 289

110 THE SORREL HORSE INN

Shottisham, southeast of Woodbridge

Local produce features strongly on the menu at **The Sorrel Horse Inn**, which lies close to the mouth of the River Deben.

🍽 see page 278

Coastal Path, and the ferry to Felixstowe. The late-Victorian Bawdsey Manor was taken over by the Government and became the centre for radar development when Orford Ness was deemed unsuitable. By the beginning of the Second World War there were two dozen secret radar stations in Britain, and radar HQ moved from Bawdsey to Dundee. The manor is now a leisure centre.

RAMSHOLT

7 miles SE of Woodbridge off the B1083

Ramsholt is a tiny community on the north bank of the Deben a little way up from Bawdsey. The pub is a popular port of call for yachtsmen, and half a mile from the quay, in quiet isolation, stands the Church of All Saints with its round tower. Road access to Ramsholt is from the B1083 just south of Shottisham.

HOLLESLEY

5 miles SE of Woodbridge off the B1083

The Deben and the Ore turn this part of Suffolk almost into a peninsula, and on the seaward side lie Hollesley and Shingle Street. The latter stands upon a shingle bank at the entrance to the Ore and comprises a row of little houses, a coastguard cottage and a Martello tower. Its very isolation is an attraction, and the sight of the sea rushing into and out of the river is worth the journey.

Brendan Behan did not enjoy his visit. Brought here on a swimming outing from the Borstal at Hollesley, he declared that the waves had 'no limit but the rim of the world'. Looking out to the bleak North Sea, it is easy to see what he meant.

LOWESTOFT

The most easterly town in Britain had its heyday as a major fishing port during the late 19th and early 20th centuries, when it was a mighty rival to Great Yarmouth in the herring industry. That industry has been in major decline since the First World War, but Lowestoft is still a fishing port and the trawlers still chug into the harbour in the early morning with the catches of the night. Guided tours of the **Fish Market** and the **Harbour** are available.

Lowestoft Beach

Lowestoft is also a popular holiday resort, the star attraction being the lovely South Beach with its golden sands, safe swimming, two piers and all the expected seaside amusements and entertainments. **Claremont Pier**, over 600 feet in length, was built in 1902, ready to receive day-trippers on the famous Belle steamers. The buildings near the pier were developed in mid-Victorian times by the company of Sir Samuel Morton Peto, also responsible for Nelson's Column, the statues in the Houses of Parliament, the Reform Club and Somerleyton Hall.

Fishing Boats, Lowestoft

At the heart of the town is the old harbour, home to the **Royal Norfolk & Suffolk Yacht Club** and the **Lifeboat Station**. Further upriver is the commercial part of the port, used chiefly by ships carrying grain and timber. The history of Lowestoft is naturally tied up with the sea, and much of that history is recorded in fascinating detail in the **Lowestoft & East Suffolk Maritime Museum** with model boats, fishing gear, a lifeboat cockpit, paintings and shipwrights' tools. The setting is a flint-built fisherman's cottage in Sparrow's Nest Gardens. The **Royal Naval Patrol Museum** nearby remembers the minesweeping service in models, photographs, documents and uniforms.

St Margaret's Church, notable for its decorated ceiling and copper-covered spire, is a memorial to seafarers, and the north aisle has panels recording the names of fishermen lost at sea from 1865 to 1923.

Lowestoft also has some interesting literary and musical connections. The Elizabethan playwright, poet and pamphleteer Thomas Nash was born here in 1567. His last work, *Lenten Stuffe*, was a eulogy to the herring trade and specifically to Great Yarmouth. Joseph Conrad (Jozef Teodor Konrad Korzeniowski), working as a deckhand on a British freighter bound for Constantinople, jumped ship here in 1878, speaking only a few words of the language in which he was to become one of the modern masters. Benjamin Britten, the greatest English composer of the 20th century, is associated with several places in Suffolk, but Lowestoft has the earliest claim, for it is here that he was born in 1913.

Just north of town, with access from the B1385, **Pleasurewood Hill** is the largest theme park in East Anglia.

Oulton Broad, on the western

Lowestoft had England's first lighthouse, installed in 1609. The present one dates from 1874. Also in Sparrow's Nest Gardens is the War Memorial Museum, dedicated to those who served during the Second World War. There's a chronological photographic collection of the bombing of the town, aircraft models and a chapel of remembrance.

111 THE COMMODORE

Oulton Broad, nr Lowestoft

River views are a bonus at **The Commodore**, which is open for pub food and real ales throughout the day.

 see page 279

112/143 THE GEORGE BORROW HOTEL

Oulton Broad, nr Lowestoft

The George Borrow Hotel provides a variety of accommodation and traditional pub food and drink for tourists and travellers.

 see pages 279 and 289

168 LOWESTOFT MARITIME MUSEUM

Whapload Road, Lowestoft

Lowestoft Maritime Museum relates the history of the Lowestoft fishing fleet from early sail to the modern day.

 see page 299

•

Blundeston has another notable literary connection: Blundeston Lodge was once the home of Norton Nichols, whose friend the poet Gray is reputed to have taken his inspiration for An Elegy Written in a Country Church Yard while staying there.

•

edge of Lowestoft, is a major centre of amusements afloat, with boats for hire and cruises on the Waveney. It also attracts visitors to Nicholas Everitt Park to look around **Lowestoft Museum**, housed in historic Broad House. Opened by the Queen and Prince Philip in 1985, the museum displays archaeological finds from local sites, some now lost to the sea, costumes, toys, domestic bygones and a fine collection of Lowestoft porcelain. (The porcelain industry lasted from about 1760 to 1800, using clay from the nearby Gunton Hall Estate. The soft-paste ware, resembling Bow porcelain, was usually decorated in white and blue.)

Lowestoft's **Maritime Museum** specialises in the history of the Lowestoft fishing fleet, from early sail to steam and through to the modern diesel-powered vessels. Methods of fishing are recorded, including trawling and the no longer practised driftnet fishing for herring, and other displays depict the evolution of lifeboats and the town's association with the Royal Navy.

AROUND LOWESTOFT

CARLTON COLVILLE

3 miles SW of Lowestoft on the B1384

Many a transport enthusiast has enjoyed a grand day out at the **East Anglia Transport Museum**, where children young and old (and even very old!) can climb aboard

wide-eyed to enjoy rides on buses, trams and trolleybuses (one of the resident trolleybuses was built at the Garrett works in Leiston). The East Suffolk narrow-gauge railway winds its way around the site, and there's a 1930s street with all the authentic accessories, plus lorries, vans and steamrollers.

Carlton Marshes is Oulton Broad's nature reserve, with grazing marsh and fen, reached by the Waveney Way footpath.

BLUNDESTON

4 miles N of Lowestoft off the A12

Known chiefly as the village used by Charles Dickens as the birthplace of that writer's 'favourite child', David Copperfield, the morning light shining on the sundial of Blundeston's church – which has the tallest, narrowest Saxon round tower of any in East Anglia – greeted young David as he looked out of his bedroom window in the nearby Rookery. He said of the churchyard: *"There is nothing half so green that I know anywhere, as the grass of that churchyard, nothing half so shady as its trees; nothing half so quiet as its tombstones."*

LOUND

5 miles N of Lowestoft off the A12

Lound's parish church of **St John the Baptist**, in the very north of the county, is sometimes known as the 'golden church'. This epithet is the result of the handiwork of designer/architect Sir Ninian Comper, seen most memorably in the gilded organ-case with two trumpeting angels, the font cover and the rood screen. The last is a very elaborate affair, with several heraldic arms displayed. The surprise package here is the modern St Christopher mural on the north wall. It includes Sir Ninian at the wheel of his Rolls Royce – and in 1976 an aeroplane was added to the scene!

SOMERLEYTON

5 miles NW of Lowestoft on the B1074

Somerleyton Hall, one of the grandest and most distinctive of stately homes, is a splendid Victorian mansion built in Anglo-Italian style by Samuel Morton Peto. The Oak Room, with 17th century panelling from the original Jacobean house, some outstanding wood carvings and an exquisite silver and gilt mirror made for the Doge's Palace in Venice, is one of several superb rooms in this most magnificent of houses; others include the elegant Library, its walls lined with over 3,500 books, the Dining Room and the sumptuous Ballroom. The grounds include a renowned yew-hedge maze, where people have been going round in circles since 1846, walled and sunken gardens, and a 300-feet pergola. There's also a sweet little miniature railway, and **Fritton Lake Countryworld**, part of the Somerleyton Estate, is a 10-minute drive away. The Hall is open to the public on most days in summer.

Samuel Morton Peto learned his skills as a civil engineer and businessman from his uncle, and was still a young man when he put the Reform Club and Nelson's

Somerleyton Hall

Column into his CV. The Somerleyton Hall he bought in 1843 was a Tudor and Jacobean mansion. He and his architect virtually rebuilt the place, and also built Somerleyton village, a cluster of thatched redbrick cottages. Nor was this the limit of Peto's achievements, for he ran a company which laid railways all over the world and was a Liberal MP, first for Norwich, then for Finsbury and finally for Bristol. His company foundered in 1863 and Somerleyton Hall was sold to Sir Francis Crossley, one of three brothers who made a fortune in mass-producing carpets. Crossley's son became Baron Somerleyton in 1916, and the Baron's grandson is the present Lord Somerleyton.

HERRINGFLEET

5 miles NW of Lowestoft on the B1074

Standing above the River Waveney, the parish church of St Margaret is a charming sight with its Saxon round tower, thatched roof and

169 SOMERLEYTON HALL & GARDENS

Lowestoft

The home of Lord and Lady Somerleyton, this splendid Victorian mansion has superb rooms and magnificent gardens.

 see page 299

Most of Kessingland's maritime trappings have now disappeared: the lighthouse on the cliffs was scrapped 100 years ago, the lifeboat lasted until 1936 (having saved 144 lives), and one of the several former coastguard stations was purchased by the writer Rider Haggard as a holiday home.

lovely glass. **Herringfleet Windmill** is a beautiful black-tarred smock mill in working order, the last survivor of the Broadland wind pump, whose job was to assist in draining the marshes. This example was built in 1820 and worked regularly until the 1950s. It contains a fireplace and a wooden bench, providing a modicum of comfort for a millman on a cold night shift. To arrange a visit call 01473 583352.

KESSINGLAND

3 miles S of Lowestoft off the A12

A small resort with a big history, Palaeolithic and Neolithic remains have come to light in Kessingland, and traces of an ancient forest have been unearthed on the sea bed. At the time of William the Conqueror, Kessingland prospered with its herring industry and was a major fishing port rivalled only by Dunwich. The estuary gradually silted up, sealing off the river with a shingle bank and cutting off the village's major source of wealth. The tower of the church of St Edmund reaches up almost 100 feet – not unusual on the coast - where it provides a conspicuous landmark for sailors and fishermen.

The village's major tourist attraction is the **Suffolk Wildlife Park**, 100 acres of coastal parkland that are home to a wide range of wild animals, from aardvarks to zebras by way of bats, flamingos, giraffes, meerkats and sitatunga. The flamingos have their own enclosure. Burmese pythons are used for snake-handling sessions – an experience that's definitely not for everyone!

COVEHITHE

7 miles S of Lowestoft off the A12

Leave the A12 at Wrentham and head for the tiny coastal village of Covehithe, remarkable for its 'church within a church'. The massive church of **St Andrew**, partly funded by the Benedictine monks at Cluniac, was left to decline after being laid waste by Dowsing's men. The villagers could not afford a replacement on the same grand scale, so in 1672 it was decided to remove the roof and sell off some of the material. From what was left a small new church was built within the old walls. The original tower still stands, spared by Cromwell for use as a landmark for sailors.

Southwold Beach

SOUTHWOLD

A town full of character and interest for the holidaymaker and for the historian. Though one of the most popular resorts on the east coast, Southwold has very little of the kiss-me-quick commercialism that spoils so many seaside towns. It's practically an island, bounded by creeks and marshes, the River Blyth and the North Sea, and has managed to retain the genteel atmosphere of the 19th century. There are some attractive buildings, from pink-washed cottages to elegant Georgian town houses, many of them ranged around a series of greens which were left undeveloped to act as firebreaks after much of the town was lost in the great fire of 1659.

In a seaside town whose buildings present a wide variety of styles, shapes and sizes, William Denny's **Buckenham House** is among the most elegant and interesting. On the face of it a classic Georgian town house, it's actually much older, dating probably from the middle of the 16th century. Richard Buckenham, a wealthy Tudor merchant, was the man who had it built and it was truly impressive in size, as can be deduced from the dimensions of the cellar (now the Coffee House). Many fine features survive, including moulded cornices, carefully restored sash windows, Tudor brickwork and heavy timbers in the ceilings.

The town, which was granted its charter by Henry VII in 1489, once prospered, like many of its neighbours, through herring fishing, and the few remaining fishermen share the harbour on the River Blyth with pleasure craft. Also adding to the period atmosphere is the pier, though as a result of storm damage this is much shorter than in the days when steamers from London called in on their way up the east coast.

There are also bathing huts, and a brilliant white **Lighthouse** that's over 100 years old. It stands 100 feet tall and its light can be seen 17 miles out to sea. Guided tours of the lighthouse culminate in

167 SOUTHWOLD PIER

North Parade, Southwold

Shops, amusements, dining and many other attractions are to be found on this award-winning pier.

 see page 298

Southwold

99

The Sole Bay Inn is one of several owned by the local brewery Adnams. One of the best known is the Lord Nelson, where traces can be seen of a smugglers' passageway leading to the cliffs. Where there were smugglers, there are usually ghosts, and here it's a man in a frock coat who disappears into the cliff face. Adnams still use horse-drawn drays for local beer deliveries.

144 UGGESHALL MANOR FARM

Uggeshall, nr Southwold

Uggeshall Manor Farm offers a choice of B&B and self-catering accommodation 3 miles from the coast.

see page 289

unrivalled views over the town and out to sea. Beneath the lighthouse stands a little Victorian pub, the Sole Bay Inn, whose name recalls a battle fought off Southwold in 1672 between the British and French fleets and the Dutch. This was an episode in the Third Anglo-Dutch War, when the Duke of York, Lord High Admiral of England and later to be crowned James II, used Sutherland House in Southwold as his headquarters and launched his fleet (along with that of the French) from here. One distinguished victim of this battle was Edward Montagu, 1st Earl of Sandwich, great-grandfather of the man whose gambling mania did not allow him time for a formal meal. By inserting slices of meat between slices of bread, the 4th Earl ensured that his name would live on.

Southwold's maritime past is recorded in the **Museum** set in a Dutch-style cottage in Victoria Street. Open daily in the summer months, it records the famous battle and also features exhibits on local archaeology, geology and natural history, and the history of the Southwold railway. The **Southwold Sailors' Reading Room** contains pictures, ship models and other items, and at Gun Hill the **Southwold Lifeboat Museum** has a small collection of RNLI-related material with particular reference to Southwold. The main attraction at Gun Hill is a set of six 18-pounder guns, captured in 1746 at the Battle of Culloden and presented to the town (hitherto more or less undefended)

by the Duke of Cumberland. Amber has been found on the beaches of Southwold for many years, and at the back of the Amber Shop in the market place is an **Amber Museum** with a large number of amber pieces, some in original form, others carved into beautiful pieces of jewellery.

No visitor to Southwold should leave without spending some time in the splendid church of **St Edmund King and Martyr**, which emerged relatively unscathed from the ravages of the Commonwealth. The lovely painted roof and wide screen are the chief glories, but the slim-stemmed 15th century pulpit and the Elizabethan Holy Table must also be seen. Inside the church there's also a splendid 'Jack o' the Clock' – a little wooden man in War of the Roses armour, holding a bell. A rope is pulled to sound the bell to mark the start of church services.

AROUND SOUTHWOLD

WANGFORD

2 miles NW of Southwold off the A12

There's some great walking in the country around Southwold, both along the coast and inland. At Wangford, a mile or so inland, **Henham Walks** are waymarked paths through Repton Park, lake and woods. A splendid place for a ramble or a picnic, or to see the wildlife, rare-breed sheep and Highland cattle, the paths are open only on specific dates, and there's an entry fee.

Also at Wangford is the Perpendicular church of St Peter and St Paul, built on the site of a Benedictine priory. Even closer to Southwold is Reydon Wood Nature Reserve.

BLYTHBURGH

2 miles SW of Southwold, A1095 then A12

Blythburgh's church of **Holy Trinity** is one of the wonders of Suffolk, a stirring sight as it rises from the reed beds, visible for miles around and floodlit at night to spectacular effect. This 'Cathedral of the Marshes' reflects the days when Blythburgh was a prosperous port with a bustling quayside wool trade. With the silting up of the river, trade rapidly fell off and the church fell into decay. In 1577 the steeple of the 14th century tower was struck by lightning in a severe storm; it fell into the nave, shattering the font and taking two lives. The scorch marks visible to this day on the north door are said to be the claw marks of the Devil in the guise of hellhound Black Shuck, left as he sped towards Bungay to terrify the congregation of St Mary's.

Disaster struck again in 1644, when Dowsing and his men smashed windows, ornaments and statues, blasted the wooden angels in the roof with hundreds of bullets and used the nave as a stable, with tethering rings screwed into the pillars of the nave. Luckily, the bench-end carvings escaped the desecration, not being labelled idolatrous. These depict the Labours of the Months, and the Seven Deadly Sins. Blythburgh also has a Jack o'the Clock, a brother of the figure at Southwold, and the priest's chamber over the south porch has been lovingly restored complete with an altar made with wood from *HMS Victory*. The angels may have survived, but the font was defaced to remove the signs of the sacraments.

A mile south of Blythburgh, at the junction of the A12 and the Walberswick road, **Toby's Walks** is an ideal place for a picnic and, like so many places in Suffolk, has its own ghost story. This concerns Tobias Gill, a dragoon drummer who murdered a local girl and was hanged here after a trial at Ipswich. His ghost is said to haunt the heath, but this should not deter picnickers. The **Norman Gwatkin Nature Reserve** is an area of marsh and fen with two hides, walkways and a willow coppice.

WENHASTON

5 miles W of Southwold off the A12

The church of **St Peter** is well worth a detour. Saxon stones are embedded in its walls, but the most remarkable feature is the Doom (Last Judgement scene), said to have been painted around 1500 by a monk from Blythburgh.

WALBERSWICK

1 mile SW of Southwold on the B1387

The story is familiar: flourishing fishing port; grand church; changing of the coastline due to erosion and silting; decline of fishing and trading; no money to maintain the church; church falls

114 THE STAR INN

Wenhaston, between Halesworth and Blythburgh

Steaks from home-reared beef cattle are the speciality at **The Star Inn**, a delightful, traditional country pub.

see page 279

113/145 THE ANCHOR

Walberswick

The Anchor is a pub of wide appeal, with fine food, beers and wines and excellent accommodation.

  see pages 279 and 289

116 THE RACEHORSE

Westhall, nr Halesworth

The Racehorse is a hot favourite in the hospitality, food and drink stakes.

see page 279

into disrepair. Towards the end of the 16th century, a smaller church was built within the original St Andrew's, by then in ruins through neglect. The situation in Walberswick had also been exacerbated by the seizing of church lands and revenues by the King, and by a severe fire.

Fishing hardly exists today, and boating in Walberswick is almost entirely a weekend and holiday activity. The tiny 'church within a church' is still in use, its churchyard a nature reserve. South of the village is the bird sanctuary of **Walberswick & Westleton Heaths**.

For more than two centuries, Walberswick has been a magnet for painters, with the religious ruins, the beach and the sea being favourite subjects for visiting artists. The tradition continues unabated, and many academics have also made their homes here.

HALESWORTH

16 miles SW of Lowestoft on the A144

Granted a market in 1222, Halesworth reached the peak of its trading importance when the River Blyth was made navigable as far as the town in 1756. A stroll around the streets reveals several buildings of architectural interest. The Market Place has a handsome Elizabethan timber-framed house, but the chief attraction for the visitor is the **Halesworth and District Museum** at the railway station, in Station Road, where exhibits feature local geology and archaeology, with various fossils and flints on display, and there's also a fascinating account of the Halesworth witchcraft trials of 1645.

Halesworth Gallery, at Steeple End, holds a collection of contemporary paintings, sculpture and other artwork in a converted row of 17th century almshouses.

BRAMFIELD

3 miles S of Halesworth on the A144

The massive Norman round tower of **St Andrew's** Church is separate from the main building and was built as a defensive structure, with walls over 3 feet thick. Dowsing ran riot here in 1643, destroying 24 superstitious pictures, one crucifix, a picture of Christ and 12 angels on the roof. The most important monument is one to Sir Arthur Coke, sometime

The River Blyth at Walberswick

Lord Chief Justice, who died in 1629, and his wife Elizabeth. Arthur is kneeling, resplendent in full armour, while Elizabeth is lying on her bed with a baby in her arms. This monument is the work of Nicholas Stone, the most important English mason and sculptor of his day. The Cokes at one time occupied Bramfield Hall, and another family, in residence for 300 years, were the Rabetts, whose coat of arms in the church punningly depicts rabbits on its shield.

BUNGAY

9 miles N of Halesworth on the A144

An ancient fortress town on the River Waveney, the river played an important part in Bungay's fortunes until well into the 18th century, with barges laden with coal, corn, malt and timber plying the route to the coast. The river is no longer navigable above Geldeston, but is a great attraction for anglers and yachtsmen.

Bungay is best known for its **Castle**, built in its original form by Hugh Bigod, 1st Earl of Norfolk, as a rival to Henry II's castle at Orford. In 1173 Hugh took the side of the rebellious sons of Henry, but this insurrection ended with the surrender of the castle to the King. Hugh was killed not long after this episode while on the Third Crusade; his son Roger inherited the title and the castle, but it was another Roger Bigod who came to Bungay in 1294 and built the round tower and mighty outer walls that stand today.

To the north of the castle are Bungay's two surviving churches of note (the *Domesday Book* records five). The Saxon round tower of **Holy Trinity Church** is the oldest complete structure in the town, and a brass plate on the door commemorates the church's narrow escape from the fire of 1688 that destroyed much of the town (similar disasters overtook many other towns with close-set timber-and-thatch buildings). The **Church of St Mary** - now deconsecrated - was not so lucky, being more or less completely gutted. The tower survives to dominate the townscape, and points of interest in the church itself include a woodcarving of the Resurrection presented by Rider Haggard, and a monument to General Robert Kelso, who fought in the American War of Independence.

A century before the fire, the church received a visit, during a storm, from the devilish Black Shuck, a retriever-like hound, who, hot from causing severe damage at Blythburgh, raced down the nave and killed two worshippers. A weather vane in the market place puts the legend into verse:

All down the church in midst of fire
The Hellish Monster Flew
And Passing onwards to the Quire
He many people slew.

EARSHAM

1 mile SW of Bungay off the A143

All Saints Church and Earsham Hall are well worth a visit, but what brings most people here is the **Otter Trust**, on the banks of the Waveney, where the largest

Near Bungay's church is the famous octagonal Butter Cross, rebuilt after the great fire of 1688 and topped by Justice with her scales and sword. This building was once used as a prison, with a dungeon below.

170 NORFOLK &
SUFFOLK AVIATION
MUSEUM

The Street, Flixton

Undercover exhibitions of
military and civil aviation set
in picturesque surroundings

 see page 299

collection of otters in natural
enclosures is bred for re-
introduction into the wild. The
British otter tends to be shy and
retiring, but his cousins the Asian
short-clawed otters are playful and
extrovert and always delighted to
welcome visitors. There are some
lovely walks by the river and the
lakes teeming with waterfowl and
other wetland wildlife. The flock of
free-flying Barnacle geese is
probably the largest in the country.
Also at home in the grounds are
Muntjac and fallow deer.

FLIXTON

2 miles SW of Bungay on the B1062

Javelin, Meteor, Sea Vixen, Avro
Anson C19, Dassault Mystère IVA,
Westland Whirlwind: names that
evoke earlier days of flying, and
just four of more than 25 aircraft
on show at The **Norfolk and
Suffolk Aviation Museum**, on the
site of a USAAF Liberator base
during the Second World War.
There's a lot of associated material,
both civil and military, covering the
period from the First World War to
the present day. The museum
incorporates the Royal Observer
Corps Museum, RAF Bomber
Command Museum, and the
Museum and Memorial of the
446th Bomb Group - the Bungay
Buckeroos. Tel: 01986 896644.
American airmen presented the
gates into Flixton churchyard.

MENDHAM

6 miles SW of Bungay off the A143

This pretty little village on the
Waveney was the birthplace of Sir

Alfred Munnings RA, who was
born at Mendham Mill, where his
father was the miller. Sir Alfred's
painting *Charlotte and her Pony* was
the inspiration for the village sign,
which was unveiled by his niece
Kathleen Hadingham.

BECCLES

9 miles W of Lowestoft on the A146

The largest town in the Waveney
district at the southernmost point
of the Broads, Beccles has in its
time been home to Saxons and
Vikings, and at one time the market
here was a major supplier of
herring (up to 60,000 a year) to the
Abbey at Bury St Edmunds. At the
height of its trading importance
Beccles must have painted a
splendidly animated picture, with
wherries constantly on the move
transporting goods from seaports
to inland towns. The same stretch
of river is still alive, but now with
the yachts and pleasure boats of
the holidaymakers and weekenders
who fill the town in summer. The
regatta in July and August is a
particularly busy time.

Fire, sadly such a common part
of small-town history, ravaged
Beccles at various times in the 16th
and 17th centuries, destroying
much of the old town. For that
reason the dwellings extant today
are largely Georgian in origin, with
handsome redbrick facades. One
that is not is **Roos Hall**, a gabled
building dating from 1583. Just
outside the town, far enough away
to escape the great fire of 1586, it
was built to a Dutch design,
underlining the links between East

Anglia and the Low Countries forged by the wool and weaving trades. Elizabeth I stayed at the Hall just after it was completed, when she visited Beccles to present the town's charter; the occasion is depicted in the town sign. One of the hall's owners was Sir John Suckling (later to become Controller of the Household to James I), one of whose descendants was Lord Nelson. Any old hall worth its salt has a ghost, and the Roos representative is a headless coachman who is said to appear on Christmas Eve.

The parish church of **St Michael** was built in the second half of the 14th century by the Abbot of Bury. Its tower stands separate, built in the 16th century, rising almost 100 feet and containing a peal of bells. An unusual feature at the north façade is an outside pulpit taking the form of a small balcony. The priest could enter the pulpit from inside the church and preach to lepers, who were not allowed inside. Nelson's parents, the Reverend Edmund Nelson and Catherine Suckling, were married in St Michael's, as was the great Suffolk poet George Crabbe.

A fine building with Dutch-style gables houses the **Beccles and District Museum**, whose contents include 19th century toys and costume, farm implements, items from the old town gaol and memorabilia from the sailing wherries, including a wealth of old photographs.

RINGSFIELD

2 miles SW of Beccles off the A146

In a wooded valley away from the main village, Ringfield's parish church of All Saints has a dual appeal: the marvellous array of spring flowers in the churchyard and the story of the robins. A pair nested in the lectern 50 years ago and raised a family, an event recalled in carvings on the new lectern and on the porch gates. The original nest, in the old lectern, can still be found in the church.

117/146 THE SWAN INN

Barnby

Regulars come from far and wide to enjoy the superb fish dishes that are the speciality of **The Swan Inn**. Self-catering accommodation is available.

see pages 280 and 289

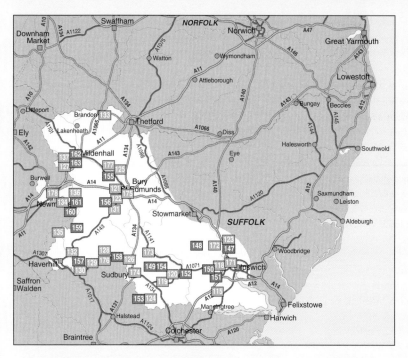

South and West Suffolk

John Constable, England's greatest landscape painter, was born at East Bergholt in 1776 and remained at heart a Suffolk man throughout his life. He was later to declare *'I associate my careless boyhood with all that lies on the banks of the Stour. Those scenes made me a painter and I am grateful.'* He painted the occasional portrait and even attempted a couple of religious works, but he concentrated almost entirely on the scenes that he knew and loved as a boy. The Suffolk tradition of painting continues to this day, with many artists drawn particularly to Walberswick and what is known as 'Constable Country'. Its beauty is not always that easy to appreciate when crowds throng the Stour Valley on summer weekends, but at other times the peace and beauty are much as they were in Constable's day.

Much of Suffolk's character comes from its rivers, and in the part of the county surrounding Ipswich, the Orwell and the Stour mark the boundaries of the Shotley Peninsula. The countryside here is largely unspoilt, with wide-open spaces between scattered villages. The relative flatness of Suffolk gives every encouragement for motorists to leave their machines, and the peninsula, still relatively peaceful, is ideal for a spot of walking or cycling, or even boating. Southeast of Ipswich, the peninsula created by the River Deben and the River Orwell is one of the prettiest areas in Suffolk, its winding lanes leading through a delightful series of quiet rural villages and colourful riverside communities.

Cambridgeshire, Norfolk, the A134 and the A14 frame the northern part of West Suffolk, which includes Bury St Edmunds, a pivotal player in the country's religious history, and Newmarket, one of the major centres of the horseracing world. Between and above them are picturesque villages, bustling market towns, rich farming countryside, the fens, and the expanse of sandy heath and pine forest that is Breckland. Many of the remains of the Anglo-Saxon period are on display, notably at West Stow and in Bury St Edmunds (Abbey ruins and Moyse's Hall), in Blythburgh, Sutton Hoo and Snape, and in museums in Ipswich and Woodbridge.

The area south and west of Bury towards the Essex border contains some of Suffolk's most attractive and peaceful countryside. The visitor will come upon a succession of picturesque villages, historic churches, remarkable stately homes, heritage centres and nature reserves. In the south, along the River Stour, stand the historic wool towns of Long Melford, Cavendish and Clare.

St James' Cathedral Precinct, Bury St Edmunds

107

Ipswich Museum is in a Victorian building in the High Street. Displays include a natural history gallery, a wildlife gallery complete with a model of a mammoth, a reconstruction of a Roman villa, replicas of Sutton Hoo treasures and a display of elaborately carved timbers from the homes of wealthy 17th century merchants. There is also a rolling programme of exciting temporary exhibitions, events and displays.

IPSWICH

History highlights Ipswich as the birthplace of Cardinal Wolsey, but the story of Suffolk's county town starts very much earlier than that. It has been a port since the time of the Roman occupation, and by the 7th century the Anglo-Saxons had expanded it into the largest port in the country. King John granted a civic charter in 1200, confirming the townspeople's right to their own laws and administration, and for several centuries the town prospered as a port, exporting wool, textiles and agricultural products.

Thomas Wolsey arrived on the scene in 1475, the son of a wealthy butcher. Educated at Magdalen College, Oxford, he was ordained a priest in 1498 and rose quickly in influence, becoming chaplain to Henry VII and then Archbishop of York, a cardinal, and Lord

Chancellor under Henry VIII. He was quite indispensable to the king and had charge of foreign policy as well as powerful sway over judicial institutions. He also managed to amass enormous wealth, enabling him to found a grammar school in Ipswich and Cardinal's College (later Christ Church) in Oxford. Wolsey had long been hated by certain nobles for his low birth and arrogance, and they were easily able to turn Henry against him when his attempts to secure an annulment from the Pope of the king's marriage to Catherine of Aragon met with failure. Stripped of most of his offices following a charge of overstepping his authority as a legate, he was later charged with treason, but died while travelling from York to London to face the king. His death put an end to his plans for the grammar school - all that remains now is a redbrick gateway.

When the cloth market fell into decline in the 17th century, a respite followed in the following century, when the town was a food-distribution port during the Napoleonic Wars. At the beginning of the 19th century the risk from silting was becoming acute at a time when trade was improving and industries were springing up. The Wet Dock, constructed in 1842, solved the silting problem and, with the railway arriving shortly after, Ipswich could once more

Christchurch Mansion, Ipswich

look forward to a safe future. The Victorians were responsible for considerable development: symbols of their civic pride include the handsome **Old Custom House** by the Wet Dock, the Town Hall, and the splendid **Tolly Cobbold** brewery, rebuilt at the end of the 19th century, 150 years after brewing started on the site. Victorian enterprise depleted some of the older buildings, but a number survive, notably the house where Wolsey was born, and the Ancient House (also called Sparrowe's House) with its wonderful pargeting and Royal Arms of Charles II – perhaps painted after the King hid here after the Battle of Worcester. Fine former Tudor merchants' houses grace the town's historic waterfront, such as Isaac Lord's and The Neptune (the latter was once home of Thomas Eldred, who circumnavigated the world with Thomas Cavendish shortly after Drake). A dozen medieval churches remain, of which St Margaret's is the finest, boasting some very splendid flintwork and a double hammerbeam roof. Another, St Stephen's, today houses the town's Tourist Information Centre.

Christchurch Mansion is a beautiful Tudor home standing in 65 acres of attractive parkland a short walk from the town centre. Furnished as an English country house, it contains a major collection of works by Constable and Gainsborough, as well as many other paintings, prints and sculptures by Suffolk artists from the 17th century onwards.

Wolsey Art Gallery is a purpose-built space entered through Christchurch Mansion which features changing displays including touring and national exhibitions.

In a former trolleybus depot on Cobham Road is the **Ipswich Transport Museum**, a fascinating collection dedicated to preserving the transport and engineering

171 IPSWICH TRANSPORT MUSEUM

Cobham Road, Ipswich

A large collection of exhibits and memorabilia covering all types of transport from the Ipswich area.

🏛 *see page 299*

The Ancient House, Ipswich

109

On the outskirts of Ipswich, signposted from Nacton Road, is Orwell Country Park, a 150-acre site of wood, heath and reed beds by the Orwell estuary. At this point the river is crossed by the imposing Orwell Bridge, a graceful construction in pre-stressed concrete that was completed in 1982 and is not far short of a mile in length.

123/147 THE SORREL HORSE INN

Old Norwich Road, Barham

A 17th c. inn offering real ales, home cooking and accommodation in a converted barn.

 see pages 281 and 290

172 BAYLHAM HOUSE RARE BREEDS FARM

Baylham

Popular family attraction at a rare breeds farm, set within a significant Roman site

 see page 299

heritage of the Ipswich area. Among the more unusual exhibits are a monorail for transporting spoil, a road sweeper converted from a Morris car, a horse-drawn tower wagon for maintaining overhead wires, and what is thought to be the oldest trolleybus in the world (Ipswich no.2, built by Railless in 1923). Ipswich's position at the head of the River Orwell has always influenced the town's fortunes; today, a stroll along the waterfront should be included in any visit. Tudor houses and medieval churches stand alongside stylish new apartments which overlook the new marinas. An art gallery and choice of eateries enhance the experience, and there are regular pub cruises, leaving the Ipswich waterfront and travelling the pretty River Orwell as far as Felixstowe harbour.

Notables from the world of the arts with Ipswich connections include Thomas Gainsborough, who got his first major commissions here to paint portraits of local people; David Garrick, the renowned actor-manager, who made his debut here in 1741 as Aboan in Thomas Southerne's *Oroonoko*; and the peripatetic Charles Dickens, who stayed at the Great White Horse while still a young reporter with the *Morning Chronicle*. Soon afterwards, he featured the tavern in *The Pickwick Papers* as the place where Mr Pickwick wanders inadvertently into a lady's bedroom. Sir V S Pritchett was born in Ipswich, while Enid Blyton trained as a kindergarten teacher at Ipswich High School.

AROUND IPSWICH

BRAMFORD
2 miles NW of Ipswich off the A14

Bramford has a pretty little church, St Mary's, with a 13th century stone screen. It was once an important spot on the river route, when barges from Ipswich stopped to unload corn; the walls of the old lock are still visible. In the vicinity is **Suffolk Water Park**, where the lake welcomes canoeists and windsurfers.

BAYLHAM
5 miles NW of Ipswich off the B11130

The Roman site of Combretrovium is home to **Baylham House Rare Breeds Farm**, and visitors (April-early October) will find displays and information relating to both Rome and rare animals. The farm's chief concern is the survival of rare breeds, and there are breeding groups of cattle, sheep, pigs, goats and poultry.

NACTON
4 miles SE of Ipswich off the A14

South of Nacton's medieval church lies **Orwell Park House**, which was built in the 18th century by Admiral Edward Vernon, sometime Member of Parliament for Ipswich. The admiral, who had won an important victory over the Spanish in the War of Jenkins Ear, was known to his men as 'Old Grog' because of his habit of wearing a cloak of coarse grogram cloth. His nickname passed into the language when he ordered that the rum ration dished out daily to sailors should be diluted with water to combat the drunkenness that was rife in the service. That was in 1740, but this allotted ration of 'grog' was officially issued to sailors right up until 1970.

George Tomline bought Orwell Park House in 1857 and made it even more splendid, adding a conservatory, a ballroom and towers. He also changed the façade along handsome Georgian lines. The house became the setting for some of the grandest shooting parties ever seen in this part of the world, and such was the power of the Tomlines that they were able to move the village away from the house to its present site. **Nacton Picnic Site** in Shore Lane (signposted from the village) commands wonderful views of the Orwell and is a prime spot in winter for birdwatchers. The birds feed very well off the mud flats.

LEVINGTON

5 miles SE of Ipswich off the A14

A pretty village on the banks of the Orwell. Fisons established a factory here in 1956, and developed the now famous Levington Compost. On the foreshore below the village is an extensive marina which has brought a bustling air to the area. The coastal footpath along the bank of the Orwell leads across the nature reserve of **Trimley Marshes** and on to Felixstowe.

TRIMLEY ST MARY & TRIMLEY ST MARTIN

6 miles SE of Ipswich off the A14

Twin villages with two churches in the same churchyard, famous Trimley residents have included the Cavendish family, whose best-known member was the adventurer Thomas Cavendish. In 1590 he became the second man to sail round the world. Two years later he died while embarked on another voyage. He is depicted on the village sign.

NEWBOURNE

7 miles E of Ipswich off the A12

A small miracle occurred here on the night of the hurricane of October 1987. One wall of the ancient St Mary's Church was blown out, and with it the stained glass, which shattered into fragments. One piece, showing the face of Christ, was found undamaged and was later incorporated into the rebuilt wall.

Two remarkable inhabitants of Newbourne were the Page brothers, who both stood over 7 feet tall; they enjoyed a career touring the fairs, and are buried in Newbourne churchyard.

WALDRINGFIELD

7 miles E of Ipswich off the A12

Waldringfield lies on a particularly beautiful stretch of the Deben estuary, and the waterfront is largely given over to leisure boating and cruising. The quay was once busy with barges, many of them laden with coprolite. This fossilised

148 RIVERSIDE COTTAGE & STUDIO

Great Bricett, nr Ipswich

Two thatched cottages and an adjoining studio provide a choice of quiet B&B and self-catering accommodation.

see page 291

118 THE WILD MAN INN

Sproughton, just east of Ipswich

The carvery available every session is a popular attraction at **The Wild Man Inn** on the eastern edge of Ipswich.

see page 280

Trimley Marshes were created from farmland and comprise grazing marsh, reed beds and wetland that's home to an abundance of interesting plant life and many species of wildfowl, waders and migrant birds. Access is on foot from Trimley St Mary.

149 JASMINE COTTAGE

Great Waldingfield, Sudbury

Two self-contained properties provide quiet, comfortable B&B accommodation.

see page 291

A walk from Felixstowe Ferry takes in a boatyard, Falkenham Marshes, St Ethelbert's Church, and an inlet where Edward III assembled a fleet of ships ready to sail to France. A ferry takes foot passengers (plus bicycles) across to Bawdsey.

dung, the forerunner of today's fertilisers, was found in great abundance in and around Waldringfield, and a number of exhausted pits can still be seen.

FELIXSTOWE

12 miles SE of Ipswich off the A14

Until the early 17th century, Felixstowe was a little-known village - but it was the good Colonel Tomline of Orwell Park who put it on the map by creating a port to rival its near neighbour Harwich. He also started work on the Ipswich-Felixstowe railway (with a stop at Nacton for the guests of his grand parties), and 1887 saw the completion of both projects. Tomline also developed the resort aspects of Felixstowe, rivalling the amenities of Dovercourt, and when he died in 1887 most of his dreams had become reality. (He was, incidentally, cremated, one of the first in the county to be so disposed of in the modern era.) The town has suffered a number of ups and downs since that time, but continues to thrive as one of England's busiest ports, having been much extended in the 1960s. The resort is strung out round a wide, gently curving bay, where the long seafront road is made even prettier with trim lawns and gardens.

The Martello tower is a noted landmark, as is the **Pier**, which was once long enough to merit an electric tramway. It was shortened as a security measure during the Second World War. All kinds of

attractions are provided for holidaymakers, including one very unusual one. This is the **Felixstowe Water Clock**, a curious piece assembled from dozens of industrial bits and pieces.

The original fishing hamlet from which the Victorian resort of Felixstowe was developed lies beyond a golf course north of the town. This is **Felixstowe Ferry**, a cluster of holiday homes, an inn, a boatyard, fishing sheds and two Martello towers. The sailing club is involved mainly with dinghy racing, and the whole place becomes a hive of activity during the class meetings.

At the southernmost tip of the peninsula is **Landguard Point**, where a nature reserve supports rare plants and migrating birds.

Just north on this shingle bank is **Landguard Fort**, built in 1718 to protect Harwich harbour and replacing an earlier construction ordered by Henry VIII. It is now home to **Felixstowe Museum**. The museum is actually housed in the Ravelin Block (1878), which was used as a mine storage depot by the army when a mine barrier was laid across the Orwell during the First World War. A fascinating variety of exhibits includes local history, model aircraft and model paddle steamers, Roman coins and the history of the fort itself, which was the scene of the last invasion of English soil. In 1667 Captain Nathaniel Darell and 500 men defeated Admiral de Ruyter's Dutch force. The fort is open daily from May to October. Beyond the fort is an excellent viewing point for watching the comings and goings of ships.

FRESTON

3 miles S of Ipswich off the B1080

Freston is an ancient village on the south bank of the Orwell, worth visiting for some fine old buildings and some curiosities. The most curious and best known of these buildings is the six-storey Tudor tower by the river in **Freston Park** (it's actually best viewed from across the river). This redbrick house, built around 1570, has just six rooms, one per storey. It might be a folly, but it was probably put up as a lookout tower to warn of enemies sailing up the river. The nicest theory is that it was built for Ellen, daughter of Lord Freston, to study a different subject each day, progressing floor by floor up the tower (and with Sundays off, presumably). Studies started with charity at 7 am, and continued onwards and upwards with tapestry, music, painting, literature and astronomy.

WOOLVERSTONE

4 miles S of Ipswich on the B1456

Dating back to the Bronze Age, Woolverstone has a large marina along the banks of the Orwell. One of the buildings in the complex is **Cat House**, where it is said that a stuffed white cat placed in the window would be the all-clear sign for smugglers. **Woolverstone House** was originally St Peter's Home for 'Fallen Women', run by nuns. It was designed by Sir Edwin Lutyens and has its own chapel and bell tower.

TATTINGSTONE

4 miles S of Ipswich off the A137

The Tattingstone Wonder, on the road between Tattingstone and Stutton, looks like a church from the front, but it isn't. It was built by a local landowner to provide accommodation for estate workers. He presumably preferred to look at a church from his mansion than some plain little cottages. Tattingstone lies at the western edge of Alton Water, a vast man-made lake created as a reservoir in the late 1970s. A footpath runs round the perimeter, and there's a wildlife sanctuary. On the water itself all sorts of leisure activities are on offer, including angling, sailing and windsurfing.

STUTTON

6 miles S of Ipswich on the B1080

The elongated village of Stutton lies on the southern edge of Alton Water. The *Domesday Book* records six manor houses standing here, and there are still some grand properties down by the Stour. St Peter's Church stands isolated overlooking Holbrook Bay, and a footpath from the church leads all the way along the river to Shotley Gate. A little way north, on the B1080, Holbrook is a large village with a brook at the bottom of the hill. Water from the brook once powered Alton Mill, a weather-boarded edifice on a site occupied by watermills for more than 900 years. The mill is now a restaurant.

115 THE CASE IS ALTERED

Bentley, south of Ipswich

Dishes of worldwide inspiration bring locals and visitors to **The Case Is Altered**.

 see page 279

The local hostelry In Chelmondiston is the 17th century Butt & Oyster, much visited, much painted and one of the best-known pubs in the county. To the east of the Quay is Cliff Plantation, an ancient coppiced wood of alder and oak.

150 COLLEGE FARM

Hintlesham, west of Ipswich

College Farm offers quiet, spacious Bed & Breakfast accommodation in an early-Tudor house on a working farm.

see page 291

151 THE GRANARY & STABLE COTTAGES

Chattisham, Ipswich

Converted farm buildings provide excellent self-catering accommodation with the bonus of a pool and tennis court.

see page 291

CHELMONDISTON

5 miles SE of Ipswich on the B1456

The church here is modern, but incorporates some parts of the original, which was destroyed by a flying bomb in 1944. In the same parish is the tiny riverside community of **Pin Mill**, a well-known beauty spot and sailing centre. The river views are particularly lovely at this point, and it's also a favourite place for woodland and heathland walks. Pin Mill was once a major manufacturer of barges, and those imposing craft can still be seen, sharing the river with sailing boats and pleasure craft. Each year veteran barges gather for a race that starts here, at Buttermans Bay, and ends at Harwich. Arthur Ransome, author of *Swallows and Amazons*, stayed here and had boats built to his specifications. His *We Didn't Mean to Go to Sea* starts aboard a yacht mooring here.

ERWARTON

6 miles SE of Ipswich off the B1456

An impressive redbrick Jacobean gatehouse with a rounded arch, buttresses and pinnacles is part of **Erwarton Hall**, the family home of the Calthorpes. Anne Boleyn was the niece of Philip Calthorpe, and visited as a child and as queen. Just before her execution Anne apparently requested that her heart be buried in the family vault at St Mary's Church. A casket in the shape of a heart was found there in 1836, but when opened contained only dust that could not be positively identified. The casket was resealed and laid in the Lady Chapel.

SHOTLEY

8 miles SE of Ipswich on the B1456

Right at the end of the peninsula, with the Orwell on one side and the Stour on the other, Shotley was the home of *HMS Ganges*, where generations of sailors received their training. A small museum records the history of the establishment from 1905 to 1976, when it became a police academy. At the very tip of the Shotley Peninsula is a large marina where a classic boat festival is an annual occasion.

HINTLESHAM

7 miles W of Ipswich on the A1071

Hintlesham's glory is a magnificent hall dating from the 1570s, when it was the home of the Timperley family. It was considerably altered during the 18th century, when it acquired its splendid Georgian façade. For some years the hall was owned by the celebrated chef Robert Carrier, who developed it into the county's leading restaurant. It still functions as a high-class hotel and restaurant.

HADLEIGH

10 miles W of Ipswich on the A1071

The old and not-so-old blend harmoniously in a variety of architectural styles in Hadleigh. Timber-framed buildings, often with elaborate plasterwork, stand in the long main street as a reminder of the prosperity generated by the wool trade in the 14th to 16th centuries, and there are also some fine houses from the Regency and Victorian periods. The 15th century **Guildhall** has two overhanging storeys, and together with the Deanery Tower and the church makes for a magnificent trio of huge appeal and contrasting construction – timber for the Guildhall, brick for the tower and flint for the church.

Guthrun, the Danish leader who was captured by Alfred and pardoned on condition that he became a Christian, made Hadleigh his HQ and lived here for 12 years. He was buried in the church, then a wooden construction but subsequently twice rebuilt. In the south chapel of the present church is a 14th century bench-end carving depicting the legendary scene of the wolf guarding the head of St Edmund. The wolf is wearing a monk's habit, indicating a satirical sense of humour in the carpenter. Also of interest is the **Clock Bell**, which stands outside the tower.

There are two good walks from Hadleigh, the first being along the Brett with access over medieval **Toppesfield Bridge**. The other is a walk along the disused railway line between Hadleigh and Raydon through peaceful, picturesque countryside. At Raydon a few buildings survive from the wartime base of the 353rd, 357th and 358th Fighter Groups of the USAAF.

Two miles east of Hadleigh is **Wolves Wood**, an RSPB reserve with woodland nature trails - and no wolves!

KERSEY

12 miles W of Ipswich off the A1141

The ultimate Suffolk picture-postcard village, Kersey boasts a wonderful collection of timbered merchants' houses and weavers' cottages with paint and thatch. The main street has a **Water Splash**, which, along with the 700-year-old Bell Inn, has featured in many films and travelogues. The Church of St Mary, which overlooks the village from its hilltop position, is of massive proportions, testimony to the wealth that came with the wool and cloth industry. Kersey's speciality was a coarse twill broadcloth much favoured for greatcoats and army uniforms. Headless angels and mutilated carvings are reminders of the Puritans' visit to the church, though some treasures survive, including the ornate flintwork of the 15th century south porch.

152 EDGE HALL HOTEL

High Street, Hadleigh

Edge Hall is a distinguished family-run hotel with comfortable, characterful rooms and a budget alternative.

see page 292

•

A famous resident of Hadleigh was the rector Dr Rowland Taylor, who was burnt at the stake on Aldham Common for refusing to hold a mass. A large stone, inscribed and dated 1555, marks the spot.

•

Kersey

Traditional craftsman-ship can still be seen in practice at the Kersey Pottery, which sells many items of stoneware plus paintings by Suffolk artists.

173 THE GUILDHALL, LAVENHAM

Market Place, Lavenham,

A fine example of a close-studded timber framed building, now housing a museum of local history

 see page 299

CHELSWORTH

14 miles W of Ipswich off the A1141

Chelsworth is an unspoilt delight in the lovely valley of the River Brett, which is crossed by a little double hump-backed bridge. The timbered houses and thatched cottages look much the same as when they were built, and every year the villagers open their gardens to the public.

MONKS ELEIGH

16 miles W of Ipswich on the A1141

The setting of thatched cottages, a 14th century church and a pump on the village green is so traditional that Monks Eleigh was regularly used on railway posters as a lure to this wonderful part of the country.

BILDESTON

14 miles W of Ipswich on the B1115

More fine old buildings here, including timber-framed cottages with overhanging upper floors. The Church of St Mary has a superb

Monks Eleigh Church

carved door and a splendid hammerbeam roof. A tablet inside the church commemorates Captain Edward Rotherham, Commander of the *Royal Sovereign* at the Battle of Trafalgar. He died in Bildeston while staying with a friend, and is buried in the churchyard. The local manor was once a royal estate owned by Queen Edith, consort of Edward the Confessor. The only trace of the manor is an ancient manorial wood, enclosed by a deep ditch.

BRENT ELEIGH

17 miles W of Ipswich off the A1141

The church at Brent Eleigh, on a side road off the A1141, is remarkable for a number of quite beautiful ancient wall paintings, discovered during maintenance work as recently as 1960. The most striking and moving of the paintings is one of the Crucifixion.

Chelsworth

LAVENHAM

18 miles W of Ipswich on the A1141

An absolute gem of a town, the most complete and original of the medieval 'wool towns', with crooked timbered and whitewashed buildings lining the narrow streets, from the 14th to the 16th centuries Lavenham flourished as one of the leading wool and cloth-making centres in the land. With the decline of that industry, however, the prosperous times soon came to an end. It is largely due to the fact that Lavenham found no replacement industry that so much of its medieval character remains: there was simply not enough money for the rebuilding and development programmes that changed many other towns, often for the worse. The medieval street pattern still exists, complete with market place and market cross.

More than 300 of Lavenham's buildings are officially listed as being of architectural and historical interest, and none of them is finer than the **Guildhall**. This superb 16th century timbered building was originally the meeting place of the Guild of Corpus Christi, an organisation that regulated the production of wool. It now houses exhibitions of local history and the wool trade, and has a walled garden with a special area devoted to dye plants. **Little Hall** is hardly less

remarkable, a 15th century hall house with a superb crown post roof. It was restored by the Gayer Anderson brothers, and has a fine collection of their furniture. The Church of St Peter and St Paul dominates the town from its elevated position. It's a building of great distinction, perhaps the greatest of all the 'wool churches', and declared by the 19th century architect August Pugin to be the finest example of late-Perpendicular style in the world. It was built, with generous help from wealthy local families (notably the Spryngs and the de Veres) in the late 15th and early 16th centuries to celebrate the end of the Wars of the Roses. Its flint tower is a mighty 140 feet in height, and it's possible to climb to the top to take in the glorious views over Lavenham and the surrounding countryside. Richly carved screens and fine (Victorian) stained glass are eye-catching features within.

•

The Priory originated in the 13th century as a farm for Benedictine monks; the beautiful timber-framed house on the site dates from about 1600. In the original hall, at the centre of the building, is an important collection of paintings and stained glass. The extensive grounds include a kitchen garden, a herb garden and a pond. John Constable went to school in Lavenham, where one of his friends was Jane Taylor, who wrote the words to 'Twinkle Twinkle Little Star'.

•

Lavenham

117

St Peter and St Paul Church, Lavenham

174 GAINSBOROUGH'S HOUSE

The Street, Brandeston

A smart redbrick pub serving some of the best food in the area, with Adnams and Fullers ales to accompany.

 see page 300

SUDBURY

Sudbury is another wonderful town, the largest of the 'wool towns' and still home to a number of weaving concerns.

Sudbury boasts three medieval churches, but what most visitors make a beeline for is **Gainsborough's House** on Gainsborough Street. The painter Thomas Gainsborough was born here in 1727 in the house built by his father John. Around 25 oil paintings are on show, including a magnificent landscape of 1782 and a touching miniature of his wife, and among the memorabilia to be seen in the house are the artist's studio cabinet, his swordstick and his pocket watch. A changing programme of contemporary art exhibitions includes fine art, photography and sculpture, highlighting East Anglian artists in particular, and the print workshop hosts evening classes and summer courses in the techniques of etching, screenprinting, stone lithography and relief printing. A bronze statue of Gainsborough stands in the square.

About those churches: All Saints dates from the 15th century and has a glorious carved tracery pulpit and screens; 14th century St Gregory's is notable for a wonderful medieval font; and St Peter's has some marvellous painted screen panels and a piece of 15th century embroidered velvet.

Other buildings of interest are the **Victorian Corn Exchange**, now a library; **Salter's Hall**, a 15th century timbered house; and the **Quay Theatre**, a thriving centre for the arts.

Unlike Lavenham, Sudbury kept its weaving industry because it was a port, and the result is a much more varied architectural picture. The surrounding countryside is some of the loveliest in Suffolk, and the River Stour is a further plus, with launch trips and fishing available.

CONSTABLE COUNTRY

England's greatest landscape painter was born at East Bergholt in 1776

Gainsborough Statue, Sudbury

match his powers of observation. He painted the occasional portrait and even attempted a couple of religious works, but he concentrated almost entirely on the scenes that he knew and loved as a boy.

The most significant works of the earlier years were the numerous sketches in oil which were forerunners of the major paintings of Constable's mature years. He had exhibited at the Royal Academy every year since 1802, but it was not until 1817 that the first of his important canvases, *Flatford Mill on the River Stour*, was hung. This was succeeded by the six large paintings which became his best-known works. These were all set on a short stretch of the Stour, and all except *The Hay Wain* show barges at work. These broad, flat-bottomed craft were displayed in scenes remarkable for the realism of the colours, the effects of light and water and, above all, the beautiful depiction of clouds. His fellow-artist Fuseli declared that whenever he saw a Constable painting he felt the need to reach for his coat and umbrella. Though more realistic than anything that preceded them, Constable's paintings were never lacking soul, and his work was much admired by the painters of the French Romantic School.

and remained at heart a Suffolk man throughout his life. His father, Golding Constable, was a wealthy man who owned both Flatford Mill and Dedham Mill, the latter on the Essex side of the Stour. The river was a major source of inspiration to the young John Constable, and his constant involvement in country matters gave him an expert knowledge of the elements and a keen eye for the details of nature. He was later to declare *'I associate my careless boyhood with all that lies on the banks of the Stour. Those scenes made me a painter and I am grateful.'* His interest in painting developed early and was fostered by his friendship with John Dunthorne, a local plumber and amateur artist. Constable became a probationer at the Royal Academy Schools in 1799, and over the following years developed the technical skills to

The Suffolk tradition of painting continues to this day, with many artists drawn to this part of the county. While nowadays crowds congregate throughout the Stour valley at summer weekends, at other times the tranquillity and loveliness are just as unmatched as they were in Constable's day.

•

Two quotations from Constable himself reveal much about his aims and philosophy:

'In a landscape I want to give one brief moment caught from fleeting time a lasting and sober existence.'

'I never saw any ugly thing in my life; in fact, whatever may be the shape of an object, light, shade or perspective can always make it beautiful.'

•

At the time of his death in 1837, Constable's reputation at home was relatively modest, though he had many followers and admirers in France. Awareness and understanding of his unique talent grew only in the ensuing years, so that, today, his place as England's foremost landscape painter is rarely disputed.

Suffolk has produced many other painters of distinction. Thomas Gainsborough, born in Sudbury in 1727, was an artist of great versatility, innovative and instinctive, and equally at home with portraits and landscapes. He earned his living for a while from portrait painting in Ipswich before making a real name for himself in Bath. His relations with the Royal Academy were often stormy, however, culminating in 1784 in a major dispute over the height at which a painting should be hung. He withdrew his intended hangings from the exhibition and never again showed at the Royal Academy.

A man of equally indomitable spirit was Sir Alfred Munnings, born at Mendham in the north of Suffolk in 1878. The last of the great sporting painters in the tradition of Stubbs and Marshall, Munnings was outspoken in his opinions on modern art. In 1949, as outgoing President of the Royal Academy, he launched an animated attack on modern art as 'silly daubs' and 'violent blows at nothing'. The occasion was broadcast on the radio; in response many listeners complained about the 'strong language' Munnings had used. In

1956, Munnings jolted the art world again by describing that year's Summer Exhibition as 'bits of nonsense' hung on the wall.

Mary Beale, born at Barrow in 1633, was a noted portrait painter and copyist; some of her work has been attributed to Lely and Kneller, and it was rumoured that Lely was in love with her.

Philip Wilson Steer (1860-1942) was among the most distinguished of the many painters who were attracted to Walberswick. He studied in Paris and acquired the reputation of being the best of the English impressionist painters.

BRANTHAM

8 miles SW of Ipswich on the A137

Also known as 'Burnt Village' – possibly because it was sacked during a Danish invasion 1,000 years ago – Brantham's Church of St Michael owns one of the only two known religious paintings by Constable, *Christ Blessing the Children*, which he executed in the style of the American painter Benjamin West. It is kept in safety in Ipswich Museum.

EAST BERGHOLT

8 miles SW of Ipswich on the B1070

Narrow lanes lead to this picturesque and much-visited little village. The **Constable Country Trail** starts here, where the painter was born, and passes through Flatford Mill and on to Dedham in Essex. The actual house where he was born no longer stands, but the site is marked by a plaque on the fence of its successor, a private house called Constables. A little further along Church Street is Moss Cottage, which Constable once used as his studio. **St Mary's** is one of the many grand churches built with the wealth brought by the wool trade. This one should have been even grander, with a tower to rival that of Dedham across the river. The story goes that Cardinal Wolsey pledged the money to build the tower, but fell from grace before the funds were forthcoming. The tower got no further than did his college in Ipswich, and a bellcage constructed in the churchyard as a temporary house for the bells became their permanent home, which it remains to this day. In this unique timber-framed structure the massive bells hang upside down and are rung by hand by pulling on the wooden shoulder stocks - an arduous task,

as the five bells are among the heaviest in England.

The church is naturally something of a shrine to Constable, his family and his friends. There are memorial windows to the artist and to his beloved wife Maria Bicknell, who bore him seven children and whose early death was an enormous blow to him. His parents, to whom he was clearly devoted, and his old friend Willy Lott, whose cottage is featured famously in *The Hay Wain*, are buried in the churchyard.

East Bergholt has an interesting mix of houses, some dating back as far as the 14th century. One of the grandest is **Stour House**, once the home of Randolph Churchill. Its gardens are open to the public, as is **East Bergholt Place Garden** on the B1070.

A leafy lane leads south from the village to the Stour, where two

Just off the junction of the A137 and the B1070 is Cattawade picnic site, a small area on the edge of the Stour estuary. It's a good spot for birdwatching, and redshanks, lapwings and oystercatchers all breed on the well-known Cattawade Marshes. Fishing and canoeing are available, and there are public footpaths to Flatford Mill.

Boating on the River Stour, East Bergholt

Constable's Mill Reflection, Flatford

Bridge Cottage at Flatford is a restored 16th century building housing a Constable display, a tea room and a shop. There's also a restored dry dock, and the whole area is a delight for walkers; it is easy to see how Constable drew constant inspiration from the wonderful riverside setting.

of Constable's favourite subjects, **Flatford Mill** and **Willy Lott's Cottage**, both looking much as they did when he painted them, are to be found. Neither is open to the public, and the brick watermill is run as a residential field study centre.

STRATFORD ST MARY

10 miles SW of Ipswich off the A12

Another of Constable's favourite locations, Stratford St Mary is the most southerly village in Suffolk. *The Young Waltonians* and *A House in Water Lane* (the house still stands today) are the best known of his works set in this picturesque spot. The village church is typically large and imposing, with parts dating back to 1200. At the top of the village are two splendid half-timbered cottages called the

Ancient House and the **Priest's House**. Stratford was once on the main coaching route to London, and the largest of the four pubs had stabling for 200 horses. It is claimed that Henry Williamson, author of *Tarka the Otter*, saw his first otter here.

NAYLAND

14 miles SW of Ipswich on the B1087

On a particularly beautiful stretch of the Stour in Dedham Vale, Nayland has charming colour-washed cottages in narrow, winding streets, as well as two very fine 15th century buildings in Alston Court and the Guildhall. Abels Bridge, originally built of wood in the 15th century by wealthy merchant John Abel, divides Suffolk from Essex. In the 16th century a hump bridge replaced it, allowing barges to pass beneath. The current bridge carries the original keystone, bearing the initial A. In the Church of St James stands an altarpiece by Constable entitled *Christ Blessing the Bread and Wine*.

One mile west of Nayland, at the end of a track off the Bures road, stands the Norman Church of St Mary at Wissington. The church has a number of remarkable features, including several 13th century wall paintings, a finely carved 12th century doorway and a tiebeam and crown post roof.

STOKE BY NAYLAND

12 miles SW of Ipswich on the B1087

The drive from Nayland reveals quite stunning views, and the village itself has a large number of listed buildings. The magnificent **Church of St Mary**, with its 120-feet tower, dominates the scene from its hilltop position. This church also dominates more than one Constable painting, the most famous showing the church lit up by a rainbow. William Dowsing destroyed 100 'superstitious pictures' here in his Puritan purges, but plenty of fine work is still to be seen, including several monumental brasses.

The Guildhall is another very fine building, now privately occupied but in the 16th century a busy centre of trade and commerce. When the wool trade declined, so did the importance of the Guildhall, and for a time this noble building saw service as a workhouse.

St Mary's Church, Stoke by Nayland

POLSTEAD

11 miles SW of Ipswich off the B1068

Polstead is a very pretty village set in wooded, hilly countryside, with thatched, colour-washed cottages around the green and a wide duck pond at the bottom of the hill. Standing on a rise above the pond are Polstead Hall, a handsome Georgian mansion, and the 12th century Church of St Mary. The church has two features not found elsewhere in Suffolk – a stone spire and the very early bricks used in its construction. The builders used not only these bricks, but also tiles and tufa, a soft, porous stone much used in Italy. In the grounds of the hall stand the remains of a 'Gospel Oak' said to have been 1,300 years old when it collapsed in 1953. Legend has it that Saxon missionaries preached beneath it in the 7th century; an open-air service is still held here annually.

Polstead has two other claims to fame. One is for Polstead Blacks, a particularly tasty variety of cherry which was cultivated in orchards around the village and which used to be honoured with an annual fair. The other is much less agreeable, for it was here that the notorious Red Barn murder hit the headlines in 1827. A young girl called Maria Marten, daughter of the local molecatcher, disappeared with William Corder, a farmer's son who was the girl's lover and father of her child. It was at first thought that they had eloped, but Maria's stepmother dreamt three times that

The decline of the cloth trade in East Anglia had several causes. Fierce competition came from the northern and western weaving industries, which generally had easier access to water supplies for fulling; the wars on the continent of Europe led to the closure of some trading routes and markets; and East Anglia had no supplies of the coal that was used to drive the new steam-powered machinery. In some cases, as at Sudbury, weaving or silk took over as smaller industries.

119 THE FLEECE

Boxford, nr Sudbury

Fine home cooking is served at **The Fleece**, a former coaching inn at the heart of Boxford.

 see page 280

120 THE FOX & HOUNDS

Groton, north of Boxford, east of Sudbury

The Fox & Hounds is a traditional village inn serving real ales, snacks and hearty pub classics.

see page 280

124/153 THE LAMARSH LION

Bures Road, Lamarsh

Daily specials add to the choice of home cooking at **The Lamarsh Lion**, which also has 3 rooms for B&B.

 see pages 282 and 292

154 GROVE COTTAGES

Edwardstone

Grove Cottages provide idyllic self-catering retreats in the countryside, combining old-world charm with modern comforts.

 see page 293

she had been murdered and buried in a red barn. A search of the barn soon revealed this to be true. Corder was tracked down to Middlesex, tried and found guilty of Maria's murder and hanged. (Until August 2004 his skeleton was kept at the Royal College of Surgeons of England's Hunterian Museum in London, where it was taken in 1949. After a long campaign by a descendant of Corder, the skeleton was released and was cremated at London's Streatham crematorium.) The murder aroused a great deal of interest at the time, and today's visitors to the village will still find reminders of the ghastly deed: the thatched cottage where Maria lived stands, in what is now called Marten's Lane, and the farm where the murderer lived, now called Corder's Farm. Maria is buried in St Mary's Church in Polstead.

BOXFORD

12 miles W of Ipswich on the A1071

A gloriously unspoilt weaving village, downhill from anywhere, surrounded by the peaceful water meadows of the River Box, Boxford's St Mary's Church dates back to the 14th century. Its wooden north porch is one of the oldest of its kind in the country. In the church is a touching brass in memory of David Byrde, son of the rector, who died a baby in 1606. At the other end of the continuum is Elizabeth Hyam, four times a widow, who died in her 113th year.

BURES

17 miles W of Ipswich on the B1508

At this point the River Stour turns sharply to the east, creating a natural boundary between Suffolk and Essex. The little village of Bures straddles the river, lying partly in each county. Bures St Mary in Suffolk is where the church is, overlooked by houses of brick and half-timbering.

Bures wrote itself very early into the history books when on Christmas Day AD 855 it is thought that our old friend Edmund the Martyr, the Saxon king, was crowned at the age of 15 in the Chapel of St Stephen. For some time after that momentous occasion, Bures was the capital seat of the East Anglian kings.

Bures has a long connection with the Waldegrave family, possibly from as far back as Chaucer's day. One of the Waldegrave memorials shows graphically the results of a visitation by Dowsing and the Puritan iconoclasts: all the figures of the kneeling children have had their hands cut off.

EDWARDSTONE

14 miles W of Ipswich off the A1071

Just to the north of Boxford and close to Edwardstone Hall and the Temple Bar Gate House, Edwardstone is now a 700-acre estate originally home to the Winthrop family. Winthrop was born in Edwardstone and emigrated to the New World, eventually becoming Governor of Massachusetts.

BURY ST EDMUNDS

A gem among Suffolk towns, rich in archaeological treasures and places of religious and historical interest, Bury St Edmunds takes its name from St Edmund, who was born in Nuremberg in AD 841 and came here as a teenager to become the last King of East Anglia. He was a staunch Christian, and his refusal to deny his faith caused him to be tortured and killed by the Danes in AD 870. Legend has it that although his body was recovered, his head (cut off by the Danes) could not be found. His men searched for it for 40 days, then heard his voice directing them to it from the depths of a wood, where they discovered it lying protected between the paws of a wolf. The head and the body were seamlessly united and, to commemorate the wolf's deed, the crest of the town's armorial bearings depicts a wolf with a man's head.

Edmund was possibly buried first at Hoxne, the site of his murder, but when he was canonised in about AD 910 his remains were moved to the monastery at Beodricsworth, which changed its name to St Edmundsbury. A shrine was built in his honour, later incorporated into the Norman Abbey Church after the monastery was granted abbey status by King Canute in 1032. The town soon became a place of pilgrimage, and for many years St Edmund was the patron saint of England, until replaced by St George. Growing rapidly around the great abbey, which became one of the largest and most influential in the land, Bury prospered as a centre of trade and commerce, thanks notably to the cloth industry.

The next historical landmark was reached in 1214, when on St Edmund's Feast Day the then Archbishop of Canterbury, Simon Langton, met with the Barons of England at the high altar of the Abbey and swore that they would force King John to honour the proposals of the Magna Carta. The twin elements of Edmund's canonisation and the resolution of the Barons explain the motto on the town's crest: *sacrarium regis,*

121 THE LINDEN TREE

Outnorthgate, Bury St Edmunds

An across-the-board menu of home-cooked dishes and a lovely leafy garden are two of the chief assets of **The Linden Tree**.

see page 280

The Theatre Royal in Bury St Edmunds, now in the care of the National Trust, was built in 1819 by William Wilkins, who was also responsible for the National Gallery in London. It once staged the premiere of Charley's Aunt, and still operates as a working theatre; it is currently closed for restoration until the autumn of 2006.

House in Bury St Edmunds

cunabula legis – 'shrine of a king, cradle of the law'.

Rebuilt in the 15th century, the Abbey was largely dismantled after its Dissolution by Henry VIII, but imposing ruins remain in the colourful Abbey Gardens beyond the splendid Abbey Gate and Norman Tower. **St Edmundsbury Cathedral** was originally the Church of St James, built in the 15th/16th century and accorded cathedral status (alone in Suffolk) in 1914. The original building has been much extended over the years (notably when being adapted for its role as a cathedral) and outstanding features include a magnificent hammerbeam roof, whose 38 beams are decorated with angels bearing the emblems of St James, St Edmund and St George. The monumental Bishop's throne depicts wolves guarding the crowned head of St Edmund, and there's a fascinating collection of 1,000 embroidered kneelers. The Cathedral Centre houses the Song School, refectory and meeting rooms.

St Mary's Church, in the same complex, is also well worth a visit: an equally impressive hammerbeam roof, the detached tower standing much as Abbot Anselm built it in the 12th century, and several interesting monuments, the most important commemorating Mary Tudor, sister of Henry VIII, Queen of France and Duchess of Suffolk. Her remains were moved here when the Abbey was suppressed; a window in the Lady Chapel recording this fact was the gift of Queen Victoria.

The **Abbey Gardens**, laid out in 1831, have as their central feature a great circle of flower beds following the pattern of the Royal Botanical Gardens in Brussels. Some of the original ornamental trees can still be seen, and other - later - features include an Old English rose garden, a water garden and a garden for the blind where fragrance counts for all. Ducks and geese live by the little River Lark, and there are tennis courts, putting and bowls greens and children's play equipment.

Bury is full of fine non-ecclesiastical buildings, many with

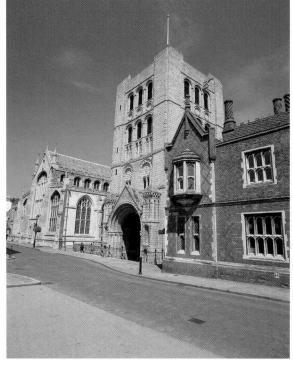

St James' Cathedral

Georgian frontages concealing medieval interiors. Among the most interesting are the handsome **Manor House Museum** with its collection of clocks, paintings, furniture, costumes and objets d'art; the **Victorian Corn Exchange** with its imposing colonnade; the Athenaeum, hub of social life since Regency times and scene of Charles Dickens's public readings; **Cupola House**, where Daniel Defoe once stayed; the **Angel Hotel**, where Dickens and his marvellous creation Mr Pickwick stayed; and the **Nutshell**, owned by Greene King Brewery and probably the smallest pub in the country.

One of Bury's oldest residents and newest attractions is the **Greene King Brewery Museum and Shop**. Greene King has been brewed here in Bury since 1799; the museum's informative storyboards, artefacts, illustrations and audio displays bring the history and art of brewing to life. Brewery tours include a look round the museum and beer-tasting (and the best view of Bury from the brewhouse roof). The shop sells a variety of memorabilia, souvenirs, gifts and clothing – as well, of course, as bottles and cans of the frothy stuff.

The **Bury St Edmunds Art Gallery** is housed in one of Bury's noblest buildings, built to a Robert Adam design in 1774. It has filled many roles down the years, and was rescued from decline in the 1960s to be restored to Adam's original plans. It is now one of the county's premier art galleries, with eight

The Nutshell, Bury St Edmunds

exhibitions each year and a thriving craft shop.

Perhaps the most fascinating building of all is **Moyse's Hall Museum**, located at one end of the Buttermarket. Built of flint and limestone about 1180, it has claims to being the oldest stone domestic building in England. Originally a rich man's residence, it later saw service as a tavern, gaol, police station and railway parcels office, but since 1899 it has been a museum, and has recently undergone total refurbishment. It houses some 10,000 items,

127 RED LODGE INN

Red Lodge, nr Newmarket, Mildenhall and Bury St Edmunds

The family-friendly **Red Lodge Inn** is open all day, every day serving a good selection of home-cooked dishes.

❚ *see page 283*

127

Bury's disciplined network of streets (the layout was devised in the 11th century) provides long, alluring views. A great fire destroyed much of Bury in 1608, but it was rebuilt using traditional timber-framing techniques.

including many important archaeological collections, from a Bronze Age hoard, Roman pottery and Anglo-Saxon jewellery to a 19th century doll's house and relics of the notorious Red Barn murder. One wing contains the Suffolk Regiment collection and education room.

Outside the Spread Eagle pub on the western edge of town is a horse trough erected to the memory of the Victorian romantic novelist 'Ouida' (Maria Louisa Ramee, 1839-1908).

Steeped though it is in history, Bury also moves with the times, and its sporting, entertainment and leisure facilities are impressive. A mile and a half outside town on the

A14 (just off the East Exit) is **Nowton Park**, 172 acres of countryside landscaped in Victorian style and supporting a wealth of flora and fauna; the avenue of limes, carpeted with daffodils in the spring, is a particular delight. There's also a play area and a ranger centre.

Arriving in Bury in 1698, Celia Fiennes, the inveterate traveller and stern architecture critic, was uncharacteristically favourable in her remarks about Cupola House, which had just been completed at the time of her visit. William Cobbett (1763-1835), a visitor when chronicling his Rural Rides, did not disagree with the view that Bury St Edmunds was 'the nicest town in the world' - a view which would be endorsed by many of today's inhabitants and by many of the millions of visitors who have been charmed by this jewel in Suffolk's crown.

AROUND BURY ST EDMUNDS

HENGRAVE

3 miles NW of Bury St Edmunds on the A1101

A captivating old-world village of flint and thatch, excavations and aerial photography indicate that there has been a settlement at Hengrave since Neolithic times.

Those parts of the village that are of archaeological interest are now protected. The chief attraction is **Hengrave Hall**, a rambling Tudor mansion built partly of Northamptonshire limestone and

Ruins in the Abbey Gardens

partly of yellow brick by Sir Thomas Kytson, a wool merchant. A notable visitor in the early days was Elizabeth I, who brought her court here in 1578. Several generations of the Gage family were later the owners of Hengrave Hall - one of them, with a particular interest in horticulture, imported various kinds of plum trees from France. Most of the bundles were properly labelled with their names, but one had lost its label. When it produced its first crop of luscious green fruit, someone had the bright idea of calling it the green Gage. The name stuck, and the descendants of these trees, planted in 1724, are still at the Hall, which may be visited by appointment. In the grounds stands a lovely little church with a round Saxon tower and a wealth of interesting monuments. The church was for some time a family mausoleum; restored by Sir John Wood, it became a private chapel and now hosts services of various denominations.

FLEMPTON

4 miles NW of Bury St Edmunds on the A1101

An interesting walk from this village just north of the A1101 follows the **Lark Valley Park** through Culford Park, providing a good view of Culford Hall, which has been a school since 1935. A handsome cast-iron bridge dating from the early 19th century - and recently brought to light from amongst the reeds - crosses a lake in the park.

WEST STOW

4 miles NW of Bury St Edmunds off the A1101

The villages of West Stow, Culford, Ingham, Timworth and Wordwell were for several centuries part of a single estate covering almost 10,000 acres. Half the estate was sold to the Forestry Commission in 1935 and was renamed the King's Forest in honour of King George V's Jubilee in that year.

An Anglo-Saxon cemetery was discovered in the village in 1849; subsequent years have revealed traces of Roman settlements and the actual layout of the original **Anglo-Saxon Village**. A trust was established to investigate further the Anglo-Saxon way of life and their building and farming techniques. Several buildings were constructed using, as accurately as could be achieved, the tools and methods of the 5th century. The undertaking has become a major tourist attraction, with assistance from guides both human (in Anglo-Saxon costume) and in the form of taped cassettes. There are pigs and hens, growing crops, craft courses, a Saxon market at Easter, a festival in August and special events all year round. This fascinating village, which is entered through the Visitor Centre, is part of the 125-acre **West Stow Country Park**, a large part of which is designated a Site of Special Scientific Interest (SSSI). Over 120 species of birds and 25 species of animals have been sighted in this Breckland setting, and a well-marked 5-mile nature trail links this nature reserve

125/155 GREYHOUND INN

Flempton, north of Bury St Edmunds

The Greyhound offers a convivial ambience and good honest cooking in a pleasant setting overlooking the village green.

 see pages 282 and 293

177 WEST STOW ANGLO-SAXON VILLAGE

Icklingham Road, West Stow

Reconstruction of an Anglo-Saxon village, as part of an ongoing experiment, with displays illustrating how the local inhabitants would have lived.

see page 300

Bradfield Combust, where the pretty River Lark rises, probably takes it curious name from the fact that the local hall was burnt to the ground during the 14th century riots against the Abbot of St Edmundsbury's crippling tax demands.

with the woods, a large lake and the River Lark. The Park is open daily all year.

ICKLINGHAM

8 miles NW of Bury St Edmunds on the A1101

The village of Icklingham boasts not one but two churches - the parish church of St James (mentioned in the *Domesday Book*) and the deconsecrated thatched-roofed **All Saints**, with medieval tiles on the chancels and beautiful east windows in the south aisle. At the point where the Icknield Way crosses the River Lark, Icklingham has a long history, brought to light in frequent archaeological finds, from pagan bronzes to Roman coins. The place abounds in tales of the supernatural, notably of the white rabbit who is seen at dusk in the company of a witch, causing – it is said - horses to bolt and men to die.

GREAT WELNETHAM

2 miles S of Bury St Edmunds off the A134

One of the many surviving Suffolk windmills is to be found here, just south of the village. The sails were lost in a gale 80 years ago, but the tower and a neighbouring old barn make an attractive sight.

THE BRADFIELDS

7 miles SE of Bury St Edmunds off the A134

The Bradfields - St George, St Clare and Combust - and Cockfield thread their way through a delightful part of the countryside and are well worth a little exploration, not only to see the picturesque villages themselves but for a stroll in the historic **Bradfield Woods**. These woods stand on the eastern edge of the parish of Bradfield St George and have been turned into an outstanding nature reserve, tended and coppiced in the same way for more than 700 years, and home to a wide variety of flora and fauna. They once belonged to the Abbey of St Edmundsbury, and one area is still today called Monk's Park Wood.

Coppicing involves cutting a tree back down to the ground every ten years or so. Woodlands were managed in this way to provide an annual crop of timber for local use and fast regrowth. After coppicing, as the root is already strongly established, regrowth is quick. Willow and hazel are the trees most commonly coppiced. Willow is often also pollarded, a less drastic form of coppicing where the trees are cut far enough from the ground to stop grazing animals having a free lunch.

Bradfield St Clare, the central of the three Bradfields, has a rival claim to that of Hoxne as the site of the martyrdom of St Edmund. The St Clare family arrived with the Normans and added their name to the village, and to the church, which was originally All Saints but was then rededicated to St Clare; it is the only church in England dedicated to her.

COCKFIELD

8 miles SE of Bury St Edmunds off the A1141

Cockfield is perhaps the most widely spread village in all Suffolk, its little thatched cottages scattered around and between no fewer than nine greens. Great Green is the largest, with two football pitches and other recreation areas, while Parsonage Green has a literary connection: the **Old Rectory** was once home to a Dr Babbington, whose nephew Robert Louis Stephenson was a frequent visitor and who is said to have written *Treasure Island* while staying there. Cockfield also shelters one of the last windmills to have been built in Suffolk (1891). Its working life was very short but the tower still stands, now in use as a private residence.

THORPE MORIEUX

9 miles SE of Bury St Edmunds off the B1071

St Mary's Church in Thorpe Morieux is situated in as pleasant a setting as anyone could wish to find. With water meadows, ponds, a stream and a fine Tudor farmhouse to set it off, this 14th century church presents a memorable picture of old England. Look at the church, then take the time to wander round the peaceful churchyard with its profusion of springtime aconites, followed by the colourful flowering of limes and chestnuts in summer.

LAWSHALL

8 miles S of Bury St Edmunds off the A134

A spread-out village first documented in AD 972 but regularly giving up evidence of earlier occupation, Lawshall was the site where a Bronze Age sword dated at around 600 BC was found (the sword is now in Bury Museum). The Church of All Saints, Perpendicular with some Early English features, stands on one of the highest points in Suffolk. Next to it is Lawshall Hall, whose owners once entertained Queen Elizabeth I.

ALPHETON

10 miles S of Bury St Edmunds on the A134

There are several points of interest in this little village straddling the main road. It was first settled in AD 991 and its name means 'the farm of Aefflaed'. That lady was the wife of Ealdorman Beorhtnoth of Essex, who was killed resisting the Danes at the Battle of Maldon and is buried in Ely Minster.

The hall, the farm and the church stand in a quiet location away from the main road and about a mile from the village. This remoteness is not unusual: some attribute it to the villagers moving during times of plague, but the more likely explanation is simply that the scattered cottages, originally in several tiny hamlets, centred on a more convenient site than that of the church. Equally possible is that the church was located here to suit the local landed family (who desired to have the church next door to their home). The main features at the church of **St Peter and St Paul** are the flintwork around the parapet (the exterior is otherwise fairly undistinguished), the carefully restored 15th century porch and some traces of an ancient wall painting of St Christopher with the Christ Child. All in all, it's a typical country church of unpretentious dignity and well worth a short detour from the busy main roads.

An interesting site in Lawshall is the Wishing Well, a well-cover on the green put up in memory of Charles Tyrwhitt Drake, who worked for the Royal Geographic Society and was killed in Jerusalem.

From 1789 until the 1930s, Hartest staged a St George's Day Fair, an annual event celebrating King George III's recovery from one of his spells of illness.

During the last century several factories in Glemsford produced matting from coconut fibres, and in 1906 the town was responsible for the largest carpet in the world, used to cover the floor at London's Olympia. To this day one factory processes horse hair for use in judges' wigs, sporrans and busbies.

Back in the village, two oak trees were planted and a pump installed in 1887, to commemorate Queen Victoria's 50th year on the throne. Another of the village's claims to fame is that its American airfield was used as the setting for the classic film *Twelve o'Clock High*, in which Gregory Peck memorably plays a Second World War flight commander cracking under the strain of countless missions. Incidentally, one of the reasons for constructing the A134 was to help in the development of the airfield. The A134 continues south to Long Melford. An alternative road from Bury to Long Melford is the B1066, quieter and more scenic, with a number of pleasant places to visit en route.

HARTEST

9 miles S of Bury St Edmunds on the B1066

Hartest, which has a history as long as Alpheton's, celebrated its millennium in 1990 with the erection of a village sign (the hart, or stag). It's an agreeable spot in the valley, with colour-washed houses and chestnut trees on the green. Also on the green are All Saints Church (mentioned in the *Domesday Book*) and a large glacial stone, the **Hartest Stone**, which was dragged by a team of 45 horses from where it was found in a field in neighbouring Somerton. Just outside the village is **Gifford's Hall**, a smallholding which includes 14 acres of nearly 12,000 grapevines, as well as a winery producing white and rosé wines and fruit liqueurs. There are also

organic vegetable gardens, wildflower meadows, black St Kilda sheep, black Berkshire pigs, goats and free-range fowl, together with a trailer ride ('The Grape Express') and children's play area. The Hall is particularly famous for its sweet peas and roses, and an annual festival is held on the last weekend in June. Open from Easter to the end of October.

SHIMPLING

9 miles S of Bury St Edmunds off the B1066

Shimpling is a peaceful farming community whose church, St George's, is approached by a lime avenue. It is notable for Victorian stained glass and a Norman font, and in the churchyard is the **Faint House**, a small stone building where ladies overcome by the tightness of their stays could decently retreat from the service. The banker Thomas Hallifax built many of Shimpling's cottages, as well as the village school and Chadacre Hall, which Lord Iveagh later turned into an agricultural college (a role it ceased to hold in 1989 - the Hall is today again in private hands).

GLEMSFORD

12 miles S of Bury St Edmunds off the B1066

Driving in from the north on the B1066, the old Church of St Mary makes an impressive sight on what, for Suffolk, is quite a considerable hill. Textiles and weaving have long played a prominent part in Glemsford's history, and thread from the silk factory, which opened in 1824 and is still going strong, has been woven into dresses and robes for various members of the royal family, including Princess Diana's wedding dress.

LONG MELFORD

13 miles S of Bury St Edmunds off the A134

The heart of this atmospheric wool town is its very long and, in stretches, fairly broad main street, set on an ancient Roman site in a particularly beautiful part of south Suffolk. In Roman times the Stour was a navigable river, and trade flourished. Various Roman finds have been unearthed, notably a blue glass vase which is now on display in the British Museum in London. The street is filled with antique shops, book shops and art galleries, and is a favourite place for collectors and browsers. Some of the houses are washed in the characteristic Suffolk pink, which might originally have been achieved by mixing ox blood or sloe juice into the plaster.

Holy Trinity Church, on a 14-acre green at the north end of Hall Street, is a typically exuberant manifestation of the wealth of the wool and textile trade. It's big enough to be a cathedral, but served (and still serves) comparatively few parishioners. John Clopton, grown rich in the woollen business, was largely responsible for this magnificent Perpendicular-style edifice, which has a 180-feet nave and chancel and half timbers, flint 'flushwork' (stonework) of the highest quality, and 100 large windows to give a marvellous sense of light and

space. Medieval glass in the north aisle depicts religious scenes and the womenfolk of the Clopton family. There are many interesting monuments and brasses, and in the chantry entrance is a bas relief of the Three Wise Men, the Virgin and Child, and St Joseph. In the Lady Chapel, reached by way of the churchyard, a children's multiplication table written on one wall is a reminder that the chapel

Long Melford is a great place for leisurely strolls, and for the slightly more energetic there's a scenic 3-mile walk along a disused railway track and farm tracks that leads straight into Lavenham.

Long Melford

133

served as the village school for a long period after the Reformation.

John Clopton's largesse is recorded rather modestly in inscriptions on the roof parapets. His tower was struck by lightning in the early 18th century; the present brick construction dates from around 1900. The detail of this great church is of endless fascination, but it's the overall impression that stays in the memory, and the sight of the building floodlit at night is truly spectacular. The distinguished 20th century poet Edmund Blunden spent his last years at Hall Mill in Long Melford and is buried in the churchyard. The inscription on his gravestone reads *'I live still to love still things quiet and unconcerned.'*

Melford Hall, east of town beyond an imposing 16th century gateway, was built around 1570 by Sir William Cordell on the site of an earlier hall that served as a country retreat, before the Dissolution of the Monasteries, for the monks of St Edmundsbury Abbey. There exists an account of Cordell entertaining Queen Elizabeth I at the Hall in 1578, when she was welcomed by '200 young gentlemen in white velvet, 300 in black and 1,500 serving men'. Much of the fine work of Sir William (whose body lies in Holy Trinity Church) has been altered in restoration, but the pepperpot chimneys are original, as is the panelled banqueting hall. The rooms are in various styles, some with ornate walnut furniture, and there's a notable collection of Chinese porcelain on show. Most delightful of all is the Beatrix Potter room, with some of her watercolours, first editions of her books and, among the toys, the original of Jemima Puddleduck. She was a frequent visitor here (her cousins, the Hyde Parkers, were then the owners), bringing small animals to draw. The Jeremy Fisher illustrations were mostly drawn at Melford Hall's fishponds, and the book is dedicated to Stephanie Hyde Parker. The Hall, which is a

Kentwell Hall, Long Melford

National Trust property, stands in a lovely garden with some distinguished clipped box hedges. On the green near the hall is a vast brick conduit built to supply water to the hall and the village. William Cordell was also responsible for the red-brick almshouses, built in 1593 for '12 poor men', which stand near Holy Trinity.

Kentwell Hall is a red-brick Tudor moated mansion approached by a long avenue of limes. Its grounds include a unique Tudor rose maze, and are set out to illustrate and re-create Tudor times, with a walled garden, a bakery, a dairy and several varieties of rare-breed farm animals. The buildings include a handsome 14th century aisle barn. The Hall was the setting for a film version of *Toad of Toad Hall*.

CAVENDISH

3 miles W of Long Melford on the A1092

A most attractive village, where the Romans stayed awhile - the odd remains have been unearthed - and the Saxons settled, Cavendish is splendidly traditional, with its church, thatched cottages, almshouses, Nether Hall and the **Sue Ryder Foundation Museum** spread around the green. The last, in a 16th century rectory by the pond, illustrates the work of the Sue Ryder Foundation, and was formally opened by Queen Elizabeth II in 1979. Once a refuge for concentration camp victims, it houses abundant war

photographs and memorabilia. Nether Hall is a well-restored 16th century building and the headquarters of **Cavendish Vineyards**.

In the church of **St Mary**, whose tower has a pointed bellcote and a room inside complete with fireplace and shuttered windows, look for the two handsome lecterns, one with a brass eagle (15th century), the other with two chained books; and for the Flemish and Italian statues. In 1381 Wat Tyler, leader of the Peasants' Revolt, was killed at Smithfield, in London, by John Cavendish, son of Sir John Cavendish, then lord of the manor and Chief Justice of England. Sir John was then hounded by the peasants, who caught him and killed him near Bury St Edmunds. He managed en route to hide some valuables in the belfry of St Mary's here in Cavendish, and bequeathed to the church £40, sufficient to restore the chancel. A later Cavendish –

128 THE FIVE BELLS

The Green, Cavendish
The Five Bells provides character and home cooking overlooking the village green.

see page 284

158 EMBLETON HOUSE

Cavendish, Sudbury
Luxury Bed & Breakfast Accommodation in peaceful surroundings.

see page 294

Cavendish

135

•

A mile or so west of Clare on the A1092 lies Stoke-by-Clare, a pretty village on one of the region's most picturesque routes. It once housed a Benedictine priory, whose remains are now in the grounds of a school. There's a fine 15th century church and a vineyard: Boyton Vineyards at Hill Farm, Boyton End, is open early April to the end of October for a tour, a talk and a taste.

•

Thomas – sailed round the world in the 1580s and perished on a later voyage. In the shadow of the church, on the edge of the village green, is a cluster of immaculate thatched cottages at a spot known as Hyde Park Corner. Pink-washed and pretty as a picture, they look almost too good to be true – and they almost are, having been rebuilt twice since the Second World War due to unhappy forces that included fires and dilapidation.

CLARE

6 miles W of Long Melford on the A1092

A medieval wool town of great importance, Clare repays a visit today with its fine old buildings and some distinguished old ruins. Perhaps the most renowned tourist attraction is **Ancient House**, a timber-framed building dated 1473 and remarkable for its pargeting. This is the decorative treatment of external plasterwork, usually by dividing the surface into rectangles and decorating each panel. It was very much a Suffolk speciality, particularly in the 16th and 17th centuries, with some examples also being found in Cambridgeshire and Essex. The decoration could be simple brushes of a comb, scrolls or squiggles, or more elaborate, with religious motifs, guild signs or family crests. Some pargeting is incised, but the best is in relief – pressing moulds into wet plaster or shaping it by hand. Ancient House sports some splendid entwined flowers and branches, and a representation of two figures holding a shield. The best-known

workers in the unique skill of pargeting had their own distinctive styles, and the expert eye could spot the particular 'trademarks' of each man (the same is the case with the master thatchers). Ancient House is now a museum, open during the summer months and housing an exhibition on local history.

Another place of historical significance is **Nethergate House**, once the workplace of dyers, weavers and spinners. The Swan Inn, in the High Street, has a sign which lays claim to being the oldest in the land. Ten feet in length and carved from a solid piece of wood, it portrays the arms of England and France. **Clare Castle** was a motte-and-bailey fortress that sheltered a household of 250. **Clare Castle Country Park**, with a visitor centre in the goods shed of a disused railway line, contains the remains of the castle and the moat, the latter now a series of ponds and home to varied wild life. At the Prior's House, the original cellar and infirmary are still in use. Established in 1248 by Augustine friars and used by them until the Dissolution of 1538, the priory was handed back to that order in 1953 and remains their property.

HORRINGER

3 miles SW of Bury St Edmunds on the A143

Rejoining the A143 by Chedburgh, the motorist will soon arrive at Horringer, whose village green is dominated by the flintstone Church of St Leonard. Beside the church are the gates of one of the country's most extraordinary and fascinating houses, now run by the National Trust. **Ickworth House** was the brainchild of the eccentric 4th Earl of Bristol and Bishop of Derry, a collector of art treasures and an inveterate traveller (witness the many Bristol Hotels scattered around Europe). His inspiration was Belle Isle, a house built on an island in Lake Windermere, and the massive structure is a central rotunda linking two semi-circular wings. It was designed as a treasure house for his art collection, and work started in 1795. Sadly, the first collection of the Earl's treasures was seized by Napoleon in 1798, so never reached England.

Derry died in 1803 and his son, after some hesitation, saw the work through to completion in 1829. Its chief glories are some marvellous paintings by Titian, Gainsborough, Hogarth, Velasquez,

Reynolds and Kauffman, but there's a great deal more to enthral the visitor: late Regency and 18th century French furniture, a notable collection of Georgian silver, friezes and sculptures by John Flaxman, frescoes copied from wall paintings discovered at the Villa Negroni in Rome in 1777. The Italian garden, where Mediterranean species have been bred to withstand a distinctly non-Mediterranean climate, should not be missed, with its hidden glades, orangery and temple rose garden, and in the park landscaped by Capability Brown there are designated walks and cycle routes, bird hides, a deer enclosure and play areas. More recent attractions include the vineyard and plant centre.

Arable land surrounds Horringer, with a large annual crop of sugar beet grown for processing at the factory in Bury, the largest of its kind in Europe.

130 THE LION

Stoke by Clare, nr Haverhill

The Lion is a welcoming, traditional village pub with home-cooked food and a secluded beer garden.

see page 284

131/156 THE SIX BELLS

Horringer, nr Bury St Edmunds

The Six Bells provides home-cooked food, real ales and B&B accommodation a short drive from Bury St Edmunds.

see pages 284 and 293

Ickworth House, Horringer

132/157 THE WHITE HORSE

Kedington, on the edge of Haverhill

The White Horse is a good place for a drink, a meal or an overnight stay in a village setting.

see pages 285 amd 293

HAVERHILL

18 miles SW of Bury St Edmunds on the A604

Notable for its fine Victorian architecture, Haverhill also boasts one fine Tudor gem. Although many of Haverhill's buildings were destroyed by fire in 1665, the **Anne of Cleves House** was restored and is well worth a visit. Anne was the fourth wife of Henry VIII and, after a brief political marriage, she was given an allowance and spent the remainder of her days at Haverhill and Richmond. **Haverhill Local History Centre**, in the Town Hall, has an interesting collection of memorabilia, photographs and archive material.

East Town Park is an attractive and relatively new country park on the east side of Haverhill.

KEDINGTON

2 miles N of Haverhill on the B1061

Haverhill intrudes somewhat, but the heart of the old village of Kedington gains in appeal by the presence of the River Stour. Known to many as the 'Cathedral of West Suffolk', the church of **St Peter and St Paul** is the village's chief attraction. Almost 150 feet in length, it stands on a ridge overlooking the Stour Valley. It has several interesting features, including a 15th century font, a Saxon cross in the chancel window, a triple-decker pulpit (with a clerk's desk and a reading desk) and a sermon-timer, looking rather like a grand egg-timer. The foundations of a Roman building have been found beneath the floorboards.

The Bardiston family, one of the oldest in Suffolk, had strong links with the village and many of the family tombs are in the church. In the church grounds is a row of ten elm trees, each, the legend says, with a knight buried beneath its roots.

Following the Stour along the B1061, the visitor will find a number of interesting little villages. In Little Wratting, Holy Trinity Church has a shingled oak-framed steeple (a feature more usually associated with Essex churches). John Sainsbury was a local resident, while in Great Wratting another magnate, W H Smith, financed the restoration of St Mary's Church in 1887. This church boasts some diverting topiary in the shape of a church, a cross and – somewhat comically - an armchair.

GREAT AND LITTLE THURLOW

3 miles N of Haverhill on the B1061

Great and Little Thurlow form a continuous village on the west bank of the River Stour a few miles north of Haverhill. Largely undamaged thanks to being in a conservation area, together they boast many 17th century cottages and a Georgian manor house. In the main street is a schoolhouse built in 1614 by Sir Stephen Soame, one-time Lord Mayor of London, whose family are commemorated in the village church.

A short distance further up the B1061 stands the village of **Great Bradley**, divided in two by the River Stour, which rises just outside the village boundary. Chief points of note in the tranquil parish church are a fine Norman doorway sheltering a Tudor brick porch and some beautiful stained glass poignantly depicting a soldier in the trenches during the First World War. The three bells in the tower include one cast in the 14th century, among the oldest in Suffolk.

DENSTON

6 miles NE of Haverhill just off the A143

Denston lies just east of the A143 on the River Glem, and is notable chiefly for its magnificent Perpendicular church, one of 18 dedicated to St Nicholas, patron saint of sailors. Stop and admire the fan vaulting in the roof (a comparative rarity in Suffolk), the outstanding brasses and the wide variety of carved animals.

HAWKEDON

7 miles NE of Haverhill off the A143

Hawkedon is designated a place of outstanding natural beauty. Here the Church of St Mary is located atypically in the middle of the village green. The pews and intricately carved bench-ends take the eye here, along with a canopied stoup (a recess for holding holy water) and a Norman font. There is a wide variety of carved animals, many on the bench-ends but some also on the roof cornice. One of the stalls is decorated with the carving of a crane holding a stone in its claw: legend has it that if

the crane were on watch and should fall asleep, the stone would drop and the noise would wake it.

WICKHAMBROOK

8 miles NE of Haverhill on the B1063

Wickhambrook is a series of tiny hamlets with no fewer than 11 greens and three manor houses. The greens have unusual names - Genesis, Nunnery, Meeting, Coltsfoot - whose origins keep local historians busy. One of the two pubs has the distinction of being officially half in Wickhambrook and half in Denston.

NEWMARKET

On the western edge of Suffolk, Newmarket is home to some 17,000 human and 4,000 equine inhabitants. The historic centre of British racing lives and breathes horses, with 73 training establishments, 70 stud farms, the top annual thoroughbred sales and two racecourses (the only two in Suffolk). Thousands of the

Also on the River Glem is Denston's neighbour Stansfield, where stand the ruins of another mill, this one a tower mill but sadly dilapidated and lacking its cap.

Horse Racing at Newmarket

139

159 THRIFT FARM

Cowlinge, nr Newmarket

Thrift Farm is a homely, family-run B&B in a pleasant secluded setting not far from Newmarket.

 see *page 295*

178 NATIONAL HORSERACING MUSEUM

High Street, Newmarket

The story of horseracing is told through a series of collections and exhibitions.

 see *page 300*

population are involved in the trade, and racing art and artefacts fill the shops, galleries and museums; one of the oldest established saddlers even has a preserved horse on display - 'Robert the Devil', runner-up in the Derby in 1880.

History records that Queen Boudica of the Iceni, to whom the six-mile Devil's Dyke stands as a memorial, thundered around these parts in her lethal chariot behind her shaggy-haired horses. She is said to have established the first stud here. In medieval times the chalk heathland was a popular arena for riders to display their skills. In 1605, James I paused on a journey northwards to enjoy a spot of hare coursing. He enjoyed the place and said he would be back. By moving the royal court to his Newmarket headquarters, he began the royal patronage which has remained strong throughout the years. James' son, Charles I, maintained the royal connection, but it was Charles II who really put the place on the map when he, too, moved the Royal court here in the spring and autumn of each year. He initiated the Town Plate, a race which he himself won twice as a rider and which, in a modified form, still exists.

One of the racecourses, the **Rowley Mile**, takes its name from Old Rowley, a favourite horse of the Merry Monarch. Here the first two classics of the season, the 1,000 and 2,000 Guineas, are run, together with important autumn events including the

Cambridgeshire and the Cesarewich. There are some 18 race days at this track, while on the leafy July course, with its delightful garden-party atmosphere, a similar number of race days take in all the important summer fixtures.

The visitor to Newmarket can learn almost all there is to know about flat racing and racehorses by making the grand tour of the several establishments open to the public (sometimes by appointment only). **The Jockey Club**, which was the first governing body of the sport and, until recently, its ultimate authority, was formed in the mid-18th century and occupies an imposing building which was restored and rebuilt in Georgian style in the 1930s. Originally a social club for rich gentlemen with an interest in the turf, it soon became the all-powerful regulator of British racing, owning all the racing and training land. When holding an enquiry the stewards sit round a horseshoe-shaped table while the jockey or trainer under scrutiny faces them on a strip of carpet by the door - hence the expression 'on the mat'.

Next to the Jockey Club in the High Street is the **National Horseracing Museum**. Opened by Her Majesty the Queen in 1983, its five galleries chronicle the history of the Sport of Kings from its royal beginnings through to the top trainers and jockeys of today. Highlights include the head of Persimmon, who won the Derby in 1896, a special display about Fred

Archer, and items associated with Red Rum, Lester Piggott, Frankie Dettori and other heroes of the turf. Visitors can ride a mechanical horse, try on racing silks, record a race commentary, ask questions and enjoy a snack in the café, whose walls are hung with murals of racing personalities.

A few steps away is **Palace House**, which contains the remains of Charles II's palace and which, as funds allow, has

Horse Racing at Newmarket

been restored over the years for use as a visitor centre and museum. In the same street is **Nell Gwynn's House**, which some say was connected by an underground passage beneath the street to the palace. The diarist John Evelyn spent a night in (or on?) the town during a royal visit, and declared the occasion to be 'more resembling a luxurious and abandoned rout than a Christian court'.

Other must-sees on the racing enthusiast's tour are **Tattersalls**, where leading thoroughbred sales take place from February to December; the **British Racing School**, where top jockeys are taught the ropes; the **National Stud**, open from March till the end of September (plus race days in October - booking essential); and the **Animal Health Trust** based at Lanwades Hall, where there's an

informative Visitor Centre. The National Stud at one time housed no fewer than 3 Derby winners - Blakeney, Mill Reef, and Grundy.

Horses aren't all about racing, however. One type of horse you won't see in Newmarket is the wonderful Suffolk Punch, a massive yet elegant working horse which can still be seen at work at Rede Hall Park Farm near Bury St Edmunds and at Kentwell Hall in Long Melford. All Punches descend from Crisp's horse, foaled in 1768. The Punch is part of the Hallowed Trinity of animals at the very centre of Suffolk's agricultural history; the others being the Suffolk Sheep and the Red Poll Cow. It is entirely appropriate that the last railway station to employ a horse for shunting wagons should have been at Newmarket. That hardworking one-horse-power shunter retired in 1967.

134/160 THE REINDEER

Saxon Street, south of Newmarket

The Reindeer attracts a far-flung clientele with its excellent cooking. Also B&B accommodation.

see pages 285 and 295

●

Newmarket also has things to offer the tourist outside the equine world, including the churches of St Mary and All Saints, and St Agnes, and a landmark at each end of the High Street - a Memorial Fountain in honour of Sir Daniel Cooper and the Jubilee Clock Tower commemorating Queen Victoria's Golden Jubilee.

●

AROUND NEWMARKET

EXNING

2 miles NW of Newmarket on the A14

A pause is certainly in order at this ancient village, whether on your way from Newmarket or arriving from Cambridgeshire on the A14. Anglo-Saxons, Romans, the Iceni and the Normans were all here, and the *Domesday Book* records the village under the name of Esselinga. The village was stricken by plague during the Iceni occupation, so its market was moved to the next village along - thus Newmarket acquired its name.

Exning's written history begins when Henry II granted the manor to the Count of Boulogne, who divided it between four of his knights. References to them and to subsequent Lords of the Manor are to be found in the little church of **St Martin**, which might well have been founded by the Burgundian Christian missionary monk St Felix in the 7th century. Water from the well used by that saint to baptise members of the Saxon royal family is still used for baptisms by the current vicar.

KENTFORD

5 miles E of Newmarket by the A14

At the old junction of the Newmarket-to-Bury road stands the grave of a young boy who hanged himself after being accused of sheep-stealing. It was a well-established superstition that suicides should be buried at a crossroads to prevent their spirits from wandering. Flowers are still sometimes laid at the **Gypsy Boy's Grave**, sometimes by punters hoping for good luck at Newmarket races.

MOULTON

4 miles E of Newmarket on the B1085

This most delightful village lies in wonderful countryside on chalky downland in farming country; its proximity to Newmarket is apparent from the racehorses which are often to be seen on the large green. The River Kennett flows through the green before running north to the Lark, a tributary of the Ouse. Flint walls are a feature of many of the buildings, but the main point of interest is the 15th century **Four-arch Packhorse Bridge** on the way to the church.

DALHAM

5 miles E of Newmarket on the B1063

Eighty per cent of the buildings in Dalham are thatched (the highest proportion in Suffolk) and there are many other attractions in this pretty village. Above the village on one of the county's highest spots stands **St Mary's** church, which dates from the 14th century. Its spire toppled over during the gales which swept the land on the night that Cromwell died, and was replaced by a tower in 1627. Sir Martin Stutteville was the leading light behind this reconstruction; an inscription at the back of the church notes that the cost was £400. That worthy's grandfather was Thomas Stutteville, whose memorial near the altar declares that 'he saw the New World with Francis Drake.' (Drake did not survive that journey - his third to South America.) Thomas' grandson died in the fullness of his years (62 wasn't bad for those times) while hosting a jolly evening at The Angel Hotel in Bury St Edmunds.

Dalham Hall was constructed in the first years of the 18th century at the order of the Bishop of Ely, who decreed that it should be built up until Ely Cathedral could be seen across the fens on a clear day. That view was sadly cut off in 1957 when a fire shortened the hall to only two storeys high. Wellington lived here for some years, and much later it was bought by Cecil Rhodes, who unfortunately died before taking up residence. His brother Francis erected the village hall in the adventurer's memory, and he himself is buried in the churchyard.

MILDENHALL
8 miles NE of Newmarket off the A11

On the edge of the Fens and Breckland, Mildenhall is a town which has many links with the past. It was once a port for the hinterlands of West Suffolk, though the River Lark has long ceased to be a trade route. Most of the town's heritage is recorded in the excellent **Mildenhall & District Museum** in King Street. Here will be found exhibits of local history (including the distinguished RAF and USAAF base), crafts and domestic skills, the natural history of the Fens and Breckland and,

perhaps most famously, the chronicle of the 'Mildenhall Treasure'. This was a cache of 34 pieces of 4th century Roman silverware - dishes, goblets and spoons - found by a ploughman in 1946 at Thistley Green and now on display in the British Museum in London, while a replica makes its home here where it was found. There is evidence of much earlier occupation than the Roman era, with flint tools and other artefacts being unearthed in 1988 on the site of an ancient lake.

The parish of Mildenhall is the largest in Suffolk, so it is perhaps fitting that it should boast so magnificent a parish church as **St Mary's**, built of Barnack stone; it dominates the heart of the town and indeed its west tower commands the flat surrounding countryside. Above the splendid north porch (the largest in Suffolk) are the arms of Edward the Confessor and of St Edmund. The chancel, dating back to the 13th century, is a marvellous work of architecture, but pride of place goes to the east window, divided into seven vertical lights. Off the south aisle is the Chapel of St Margaret, whose altar, itself modern, contains a medieval altar stone. At the west end, the font, dating from the 15th century, bears the arms of Sir Henry Barton, who was twice Lord Mayor of London and whose tomb is located on the south side of the tower. Above the nave and aisles is a particularly fine hammerbeam roof whose outstanding feature is the carved

Dalham is a place of charm and interest - clearly no longer resembling the place described in The Times in the 1880s as full of ruffians and drunks, where the vicar felt obliged to give all the village children boxing lessons to increase their chances of survival.

Sir Henry Edward Bunbury was the man chosen to let Napoleon Bonaparte know of his exile to St Helena, but the best-known member of the family is Sir Thomas, who in 1780 tossed a coin with Lord Derby to see whose name should be borne by a race to be inaugurated at Epsom. Lord Derby won, but Sir Thomas had the satisfaction of winning the first running of the race with his colt, Diomed.

137/163 WORLINGTON HALL COUNTRY HOUSE HOTEL

Worlington, nr Mildenhall

Worlington Hall is an elegant family-run country house hotel set in 5 acres of grounds.

see pages 286 and 297

angels. Efforts of the Puritans to destroy the angels failed, though traces of buckshot and arrowheads remain and have been found embedded in the woodwork.

Sir Henry North built a manor house on the north side of the church in the 17th century. His successors included a dynasty of the Bunbury family, who were Lords of the Manor from 1747 to 1933.

The other focal point in Mildenhall is the Market Place, with its 16th century timbered cross.

BARTON MILLS

1 mile S of Mildenhall off the A11

Known as Barton Parva (Little Barton) in Saxon times, this village changed its name during the 18th century. St Mary's Church can trace its origins back to at least 1150, and one of its early rectors had the Pope as his patron. Sir Alexander Fleming had a country house in the village of Barton Mills, and it is possible that he worked on the invention of penicillin in a shed in the garden.

WORLINGTON

2 miles W of Mildenhall on the B1102

Worlington is a small village near the River Lark, known chiefly as the location of **Wamil Hall**, an Elizabethan mansion which stands on the riverbank. Popular lore has it that a person called Lady Rainbow haunts the place, though the spot she once favoured for appearances, a flight of stairs, was destroyed in one of the many fires the mansion

has suffered. Cricket is very much part of the village scene (there's a splendid village green), and has been since the early days of the 19th century.

BRANDON

9 miles NE of Mildenhall on the A1065

On the edge of **Thetford Forest** by the Little Ouse, Brandon was long ago a thriving port, but flint is what really put it on the map. The town itself is built mainly of flint, and flint was mined from early Neolithic times to make arrowheads and other implements and weapons of war. The gun flint industry brought with it substantial wealth, and a good flint-knapper could produce up to 300 gun flints in an hour. The invention of the percussion cap killed off much of the need for this type of work, however, so they turned to shaping flints for church buildings and ornamental purposes. **Brandon Heritage Centre**, in a former fire station in George Street, provides visitors with a splendid insight into this industry, while for an even more tangible feel, a visit to **Grime's Graves**, just over the Norfolk border, reveals an amazing site covering 35 acres and 300 pits (one of the shafts is open to visitors). With the close proximity of numerous warrens and their rabbit population, the fur trade also flourished here, and that, too, along with forestry, is brought to life in the Heritage Centre.

The whole of this northwestern corner of Suffolk,

know as **Breckland**, offers almost unlimited opportunities for touring by car, cycling or walking. A mile south of town on the B1106 is **Brandon Country Park**, a 30-acre landscaped site with a tree trail, forest walks, a walled garden and a visitor centre. There's also an orienteering route leading on into Thetford Forest, Britain's largest lowland pine forest. The **High Lodge Forest Centre**, near Santon Downham (off the B1107), also attracts with walks, cycle trails and adventure facilities.

ELVEDEN

5 miles S of Brandon on the A11

The road from Brandon leads south through the forest to a historic estate village with some unusual architectural features. Where the three parishes of Elveden, Eriswell and Icklingham meet, a tall war memorial in the form of a Corinthian column is a landmark.

Elveden Hall became more remarkable than its builders intended when Prince Duleep Singh, the last Maharajah of Punjab and a noted sportsman, crack shot and the man who handed over the Koh-I-Noor diamond to Queen Victoria, arrived on the scene. Exiled to England with a handsome pension, he bought the Georgian house in 1863 and commissioned John Norton to transform it into a palace modelled on those in Lahore and Delhi. Although it is stated that in private Duleep Singh referred to Queen Victoria as 'Mrs Fagin … receiver of stolen goods', he kept close contact with the royal household and the Queen became his son's godmother. The Guinness family (Lord Iveagh) later took the Hall over and joined in the fun, adding even more exotic adornments including a replica Taj Mahal, while at the same time creating the largest arable farm in the whole of the country. In recent times, Stanley Kubrick's last film, *Eyes Wide Shut*, was shot here, as was *Tomb Raider*.

133 THE WHITE HORSE

White Horse Street, Brandon

Major plans by the new tenants at **The White Horse** have included a complete refurbishment and a new kitchen for a day-long selection of pub food and snacks.

see page 285

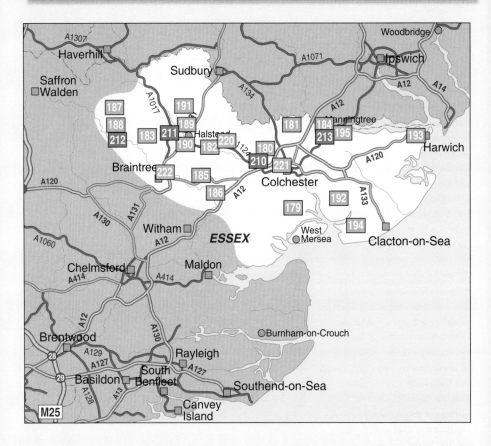

Colchester and North East Essex

Northeast Essex has the true feel of East Anglia, particularly around the outstanding villages of the Stour Valley - which has come to be known as "Constable Country" along with its near neighbour, southern Suffolk. The inland villages and small towns here are notably historic and picturesque, offering very good touring and walking opportunities.

A plethora of half-timbered medieval buildings, farms and churches mark this region out as of particular historical interest. Monuments to engineering feats past and present include Hedingham Castle, Chappel Viaduct and the postmill at Bocking Church Street. Truly lovely villages such as Finchingfield abound, rewarding any journey to this part of the county. There are also many lovely gardens to visit, and this region's principal town, Colchester, is a mine of interesting sights and experiences.

The North Essex coastal region is redolent with distinguished history and a strong maritime heritage, as exemplified in towns like Harwich, Manningtree and Mistley. Further examples are the fine Martello Towers - circular brick edifices built to provide a coastal defence against Napoleon's armies - along the Tendring coast at Walton and Clacton. Dating from 1808 to 1812, each is mounted with a gun on the roof.

The Tendring Peninsula, which takes its name from the old Tendring Hundred (a name coming from the county divisions of Saxon times, of which Tendring was a centre), has a rich and varied heritage ranging from prehistoric remains to medieval churches and elegant Victorian villas. It was settled by successive waves of invading Romans, Angles, Saxons and Vikings. Place names include the Danish ending 'by', meaning a settlement, and the Old English 'ea' and 'ey' for an island. Among the many attractive villages in the district are Thorpe-le-Soken, Kirby-le-Soken and Great Bentley - the last reputed to have the largest village green in England. The Tendring Coast contains an interesting mix of extensive tidal inlets, sandy beaches and low cliffs.

The Stour Estuary and Colne Estuary are renowned for seabirds and other wildlife, and many areas are protected nature reserves. The Manningtree-to-Ramsey road passes through some of the best coastal scenery in Essex, with some outstanding views of the Suffolk shore.

This is, of course, also the part of the county known as 'the sunshine holiday coast'. Resorts, both boisterous and more sedate, dot the coastline here (Clacton-on-Sea, Frinton-on-Sea and Walton-on-the-Naze to name but three) and offer many opportunities for relaxation and recreation.

Dutch Quarter, Colchester

147

COLCHESTER

Today, Colchester is presided over by its lofty town hall and enormous Victorian Water Tower, nicknamed 'Jumbo' after London Zoo's first African elephant, an animal sold to P T Barnum (causing some controversy) in 1882. The tower has four massive pillars made up of one-and-a-quarter million bricks, 369 tons of stone and 142 tons of iron, all working to support the 230,000-gallon tank.

This ancient market town and garrison stands in the midst of rolling East Anglian countryside. England's oldest recorded town, it has over 2,000 years of history, there to be discovered by visitors. First established during the 7th century BC, west of town there are the remains of the massive earthworks built to protect Colchester in pre-Roman times. During the 1st century, Colchester's prime location made it an obvious target for invading Romans. The Roman Emperor Claudius accepted the surrender of 11 British Kings in Colchester. In AD 60, Queen Boudica helped to establish her place in history by taking revenge on the Romans and burning the town to the ground, before going on to destroy London and St Albans. Here in this town that was once capital of Roman Britain, Roman walls - the oldest in Britain - still surround the oldest part of town. Balkerne Gate, west gate of the original Roman town, is the largest surviving Roman gateway in the country, and remains magnificent to this day.

The town affords plenty to see and explore. There are many guided town walks available, as well as bus tours. The local Visitor Information Centre on Queen Street has details of the many places to visit. Market days in this thriving town are Friday and Saturday.

A good place to start any exploration of the town is **Colchester Castle** and its museum. When the Normans arrived, Colchester (a name given the town by the Saxons) was an important borough. The Normans built their castle on the foundations of the Roman temple of Claudius. Having used many of the Roman bricks in its construction, it boasts the largest Norman keep ever built in Europe - the only part still left standing. The keep houses the **Castle Museum**, one of the most exciting hands-on historical attractions in the country. Its fascinating collection of Iron

Colchester

Age, Roman and medieval relics is one of the most important in the country. Among the numerous attractions are a Roman bronze statue of Mercury; the original charter granted to Colchester in 1413; the Colchester Vase, one of the most important examples of Roman pottery found in Britain; the Colchester Sphinx, once part of a Roman tomb; gold coins of King Cunobelin; and a new interactive gallery affording a walk through virtual Colchester. Visitors can try on a toga and medieval hats and shoes, feel the weight of Roman armour and experience the town's murkier past by visiting the Castle prisons, where witches were interrogated by the notorious Witchfinder General Matthew Hopkins.

Hollytrees Museum in the High Street is located in a fine Georgian home dating back to 1718. This award-winning museum, found on the edge of Castle Park, houses a wonderful collection of toys, costumes, curios and antiquities from the last two centuries. Purchased for the town by Viscount Cowdray it first opened as a museum in 1920. Also nearby, housed in the former All Saints' Church, is the **Natural History Museum**, with many hands-on displays illustrating the natural history of Essex from the Ice Age right up to the present day.

Housed in the Minories Art Gallery, **First Site** is a recent addition to Colchester's fine choice of art institutes, and features changing exhibitions of contemporary visual art, housed in a converted Georgian town house

with beautiful walled garden. An arch in Trinity Street leads to **Tymperleys Clock Museum**, the 15th century timber-framed home of William Gilberd, who entertained Elizabeth I with experiments in electricity. Today this fine example of architectural splendour houses a magnificent collection of 18th and 19th century Colchester-made clocks. The **Colchester Arts Centre**, not far from Balkerne Gate, features a regular programme of visual arts, drama, music, poetry and dance; the **Mercury Theatre** is the town's premier site for stage dramas, comedies and musical theatre.

Dutch Protestants arrived in Colchester in the 16th century, fleeing Spanish rule in the Netherlands, and revitalised the local cloth industry. The houses of these Flemish weavers in the **Dutch Quarter** to the west of the castle, and the Civil War scars on the walls of Siege House in East Street, bear testimony to their place in the town's history. The Dutch Quarter west of the castle remains a charming and relatively quiet corner of this bustling town.

Close to the railway station are the ruins of **St Botolph's Priory**, the oldest Augustinian priory in the country. Its remains are a potent reminder of the bitterness of Civil War times, as it was here that Royalists held out for 11 weeks during the siege of Colchester, before finally being starved into submission.

Colchester Zoo, just off the A12 outside the town, stands in the

On Bourne Road, south of the town centre just off the B1025, there's a striking stepped-and-curved gabled building known as Bourne Mill, now owned by the National Trust. Built in 1591 from stone taken from the nearby St John's Abbeygate, this delightful restored building near a lovely millpond was originally a fishing lodge, later converted (in the 19th century) into a mill - and still in working order.

221 COLCHESTER CASTLE

Colchester

A building of major historic importance, now home to a museum with hands on displays to explain Colchester's history.

🏛 *see page 323*

149

St Botolph's Priory Ruins

lion pool with a viewing tunnel.

Colchester has been famous in its time for both oysters and roses. Colchester oysters are still cultivated on beds in the lower reaches of the River Colne, which skirts the northern edge of town. A visit to the **Oyster Fisheries** on Mersea Island is a fascinating experience, and the tour includes complimentary fresh oysters and a glass of wine.

Just north of the centre of town, **High Woods Country Park** offers 330 acres of woodland, grassland, scrub and farmland. A central lake is fed by a small tributary of the River Colne. The land originated as three ancient farms, and forms part of a Royal hunting forest. Large numbers of musket balls dating from the Civil War period have been unearthed, indicating that the woods served as a base for the Roundheads.

AROUND COLCHESTER

ABBERTON

3 miles S of Colchester off the B1026

Abberton Reservoir Nature Reserve is a 1,200-acre reservoir and wildlife centre, ideal for birdwatching. Designated a Site of Special Scientific Interest, it is home to hundreds of goldeneye, wigeon, gadwall and shovellers, as well as a resting colony of cormorants; the site has a conservation room, shop, toilets and hides.

180/210 THE WHITE HART INN

West Bergholt, Colchester

Hearty home cooking brings visitors to **The White Hart Inn**, which is soon to add B&B rooms to its facilities.

see pages 303 and 316

40-acre park of Stanway Hall, with its 16th century mansion and church dating from the 14th century. Founded in 1963, the Zoo has a wide and exciting variety of attractions. The Zoo has gained a well-deserved reputation as one of the best in Europe. Its award-winning enclosures allow visitors closer to the animals and provide naturalistic environments for upwards of 200. The daily displays include the chance to help feed elephants and giraffes, and watch the free-flying birds of prey. Other attractions include the African Zone, the Penguin Parade, the Tiger Taiga enclosure and the sea

GREAT WIGBOROUGH

6 miles S of Colchester off the B1026 or B1025

This area had a number of experiences with Zeppelins during the First World War. In September 1916 Zeppelin L33, which had been hit over Bromley, crashed near here. The event is commemorated in an account in St Stephen's Church, framed by metal from the wreck. Another part of L33 can be seen in the Church of St Nicholas in neighbouring Little Wigborough.

COPFORD GREEN & COPFORD

3½ miles SW of Colchester off the B1022

Copford is home to the wonderful Norman church of **St Michael and All Angels**, with its magnificent, well-restored medieval wall paintings, while Copford Green, a lovely and peaceful village, is home to **Springfields at Copford** with 17 acres of gardens and parkland. Here visitors will find old established south gardens with roses and shrubbery, as well as a parterre planted in 1997 with 330 rose bushes. Other attractions include a rare Maidenhair Gingko tree, ancient mulberry, woodland walks, spring-fed water gardens and lake, and croquet and putting greens. The church of **St Mary the Virgin** also repays a visit.

LAYER BRETON

5½ miles SW of Colchester off the B1026

On the right side of Layer Breton Heath there's **Stamps and Crows**, a must for gardening enthusiasts. Two and a half acres of moated garden surrounding a 15th century farmhouse boast herbaceous borders, mixed shrubs, old roses and good ground cover. There is also a bog garden and dovecote.

LAYER MARNEY

6 miles SW of Colchester off the B1022

The mansion, which was planned to rival Hampton Court, was never completed, but its massive 8-storey Tudor gatehouse, known as **Layer Marney Tower**, is very impressive. Built between 1515 and 1525, it is one of the most striking examples of 16th century architecture in Britain. Its magnificent four red brick towers, covered in 16th century Italianate design, were built by Lord Marney, Henry VIII's Lord Privy Seal. As well as spectacular views from the top of the towers, they are surrounded by formal gardens designed at the turn of the century, with lovely roses, yew hedges and herbaceous borders. There is also on site a rare breeds farm, farm shop and tea room.

TIPTREE

7 miles SW of Colchester on the B1023

As all true jam-lovers will know, Tiptree is famed as the home of the **Wilkin and Son Ltd** jam factory, a Victorian establishment which now boasts a fascinating visitors' centre in the grounds of the original factory.

CHAPPEL

5 miles W of Colchester off the A604

Here, on an open-air site with beautiful valley views beside Chappel and Wakes Colne Station,

---

181 THE WIG & FIDGETT

Boxted, north of Colchester

Country lanes lead to **The Wig & Fidgett**, where an across-the-board menu is served lunchtime and evening.

🍴 *see page 303*

---

179 THE LION

Langenhoe, near Colchester

The Lion is a cheerful local and a top destination restaurant with an amazing variety of meat and seafood dishes.

🍴 *see page 302*

---

220 EAST ANGLIAN RAILWAY MUSEUM

Chappel Station

A fascinating collection of period railway architecture, engineering and memorabilia.

🏛 *see page 322*

151

182 THE CASTLE

Earls Colne, nr Colchester

The Castle welcomes visitors with warm hospitality, an old-world ambience and well-kept cask ales.

 see page 304

184 THE ROSE & CROWN

Dedham, northeast of Colchester

In the centre of Dedham, **The Rose & Crown** keeps visitors happy with splendid home cooking served throughout the day.

 see page 304

•

Dedham Vale Family Farm on Mill Street is a nicely undeveloped 16-acre farm boasting a comprehensive collection of British farm animals, including many different breeds of livestock such as pigs, sheep, cattle, Suffolk horses, goats and poultry. Children may enter certain of the paddocks to stroke and feed the animals (bags of feed provided).

•

is the **East Anglian Railway Museum**, a comprehensive collection spanning 150 years of railway history, with period railway architecture, engineering and memorabilia in beautifully restored station buildings. For every railway buff, young or old, this is the place to try your hand at being a signalman and admire the handsome restored engines and carriages. Easy to find on the A1124 (off the A12), the Museum is open daily from 10 to 5.

Chappel Galleries (free entry) is a commercial gallery with a programme of changing exhibits of fine art.

The dramatic 32-arched **Chappel Viaduct** standing 75 feet above the Colne Valley, a designated European Monument, was begun in 1846 and opened in 1849.

EARLS COLNE
7 miles W of Colchester off the A604

The de Veres, Earls of Oxford, and the River Colne bestowed this village with its name. Aubery de Vere founded a Benedictine priory here in the 12th century, and both he and his wife, sister of William the Conqueror, were buried there. Today the site is marked by a redbrick Gothic mansion. Though the commuter culture has spread modern housing around the village, the cluster of timbered cottages hearkens back to this village's distinguished past. At Pound Green, on the Coggeshall road, stands a pump erected in 1853 by benefactor Mary Gee in thanks for the absence of cholera in the village.

DEDHAM
6 miles NE of Colchester off the A14

This is true Constable country, along the border with Suffolk, the county's prettiest area. The village has several fine old buildings, especially the 15th century flint church, its pinnacled tower familiar from so many Constable paintings. There's also the school Constable went to, and good walks through the protected riverside meadows of Dedham Vale to **Flatford**, where **Bridge Cottage** is a restored thatched 16th century building housing a display about Constable, who featured this cottage in several of his paintings (his father's mill is across the river lock in Dedham).

The **Art & Craft Centre** on Dedham's High Street is well worth a visit. **Marlborough Head**, a wool merchant's house dating back to 1475, is now a pub. The **Toy Museum** has a fascinating collection of dolls, teddy bears, toys, games, doll houses and other artefacts of childhoods past.

At Castle House, approximately three-quarters of a mile from the village centre on the corner of East Lane and Castle Hill, The **Sir Alfred Munnings Art Museum** is housed in the former home, studios and grounds of the famous painter, who lived here between 1898 and 1920. The museum prides itself on the diversity of paintings and sculptures on view. The house itself is a mixture of Tudor and Georgian periods, carefully restored. Munnings' original furniture is still in place. The spacious grounds boast well-maintained gardens.

Dedham Vale

East of Wivenhoe quay, the public footpath takes visitors to the Tidal Surge Barrier, one of only two in the country. Volunteers run a ferry service operating across the River Colne between the Quay at Wivenhoe, Fingringhoe and Rowhedge. Nearby Wivenhoe Park has been the site of the campus for the University of Essex since 1962. Visitors are welcome to stroll around the grounds.

WIVENHOE

4 miles SE of Colchester off the A133

This riverside town on the banks of the River Colne was once renowned as a smugglers' haunt, and there is a very pretty quayside that is steeped in maritime history. There are still strong connections with the sea, with boat-building having replaced fishing as the main industry. The pretty church, with its distinctive cupola atop a sturdy tower, stands on the site of the former Saxon church and retains some impressive 16th century brasses.

The small streets lead into each other and end at the picturesque waterfront, where fishing boats and small sailing craft bob at their moorings. On the Quay visitors will find the **Nottage Institute**, the River Colne's nautical academy; classes here teach students about knots, skippering and even how to build a boat! It is open to visitors on Sundays in summer. The Wivenhoe Trail, by the river, is an interesting cycle track starting at the railway station and continuing along the river to Colchester Hythe. Wivenhoe Woods is dotted with grassy glades set with tables, the perfect place for a picnic.

BRAINTREE

This town and its close neighbour Bocking are sited at the crossing of two Roman roads and were brought

153

183 THE BULL AT BLACKMORE END

Blackmore End, nr Braintree

The Bull at Blackmore End invites visitors with a friendly ambience, real ales and home-cooked food.

 see page 304

222 BRAINTREE DISTRICT MUSEUM

Market Place, Braintree

An award-winning museum whose main displays feature the history of the wool trade, when Braintree was an important medieval centre.

 see page 323

together by the cloth industry in the 16th century. Flemish weavers settled here, followed by many Huguenots. One, Samuel Courtauld, set up a silk mill in 1816 and, by 1866, employed over 3,000 Essex inhabitants.

The magnificent former Town Hall is one of the many Courtauld legacies in the town. It was built in 1928 with panelled walls, murals by Grieffenhagen showing stirring scenes of local history, and a grand central tower with a five-belled striking clock. A smaller but no less fascinating reminder of Courtauld's generosity is the 1930s bronze fountain, with bay, shell and fish, near St Michael's Church.

Huguenot names such as Courtauld are connected with international enterprises to this day. Their reason for coming to Britain is a fascinating and poignant tale. Formed in France in 1559 as an organised Protestant group taking direction from Calvin and the Calvinistic Reformation in Geneva, the Huguenots were at first allowed to live and worship freely. However, as political and religious rivalries grew in France, the Catholic majority started to persecute them; a century of war, massacre and bloodshed followed. Finally in 1685 all their rights were stripped. In the chaos that ensued, many died and thousands fled. It was to turn out to be France's loss, for the Huguenots were among the most industrious and economically advanced elements in French society. Others gained at France's expense; Huguenots poured into

England, and especially East Anglia, where their skills soon made them welcome and valued members of the community.

The **Braintree District Museum**, housed in a converted Victorian school in the historic market square tells the story of Braintree's diverse industrial heritage and traditions; exhibits include a re-created Victorian classroom, the wool and silk industries and various country crafts. The **Town Hall Centre** is a Grade II listed building housing the Tourist Information Centre and the Art Gallery, which boasts a continuous changing programme of exhibitions and works.

AROUND BRAINTREE

COGGESHALL

5 miles E of Braintree on the A120

This medieval hamlet, a pleasant old cloth and lace town, has some very fine timbered buildings. **Paycocke's House** on West Street, a delightful timber-framed medieval merchant's home dating from about 1500, boasts unusually rich panelling and wood carvings, and is owned by the National Trust. Inside there's a superb carved ceiling and a display of Coggeshall lace. Outdoors there's a lovely garden. The village also has some good antique shops and a working pottery.

Located in Stoneham Street, **Coggeshall Heritage Centre** displays items of local interest and features changing exhibitions on themes relating to the past of this historic wool town.

The National Trust also owns the restored **Coggeshall Grange Barn**, which dates from around 1140 and is the oldest surviving timber-framed barn in Europe. Built for the monks of the nearby Cistercian Abbey, it is a magnificent example of this type of architecture.

Marks Hall is a historic estate and arboretum that began life in Saxon times, and is mentioned in the *Domesday Book*. In the 15th century, then-owner Sir Thomas Honywood was a leading Parliamentarian who commanded the Essex Regiment during the Civil War. Local legend has it that the two artificial lakes on the grounds were dug by Parliamentary troops during the siege of Colchester in 1648. One of his successors, General Philip Honywood, in 1758 forbade (under the terms of his will) any of his successors to fell timber - thus his lasting legacy of avenues of mature oaks, limes and horse chestnuts, surrounded by one of the largest continuous areas of ancient woodland in the county.

The estate fell on hard times in the 19th and early 20th century, but owner Thomas Phillips Price began an association with Kew Gardens and left the estate to be held and used for 'advancement in the National interest of Agriculture, Aboriculture and Forestry'. The Thomas Phillips Price Trust was formed and registered as a charity in 1971, and a major programme of revitalisation and restoration began. The estate now flourishes with native plants and wildlife, ornamental lakes, a 17th

century walled garden, cascades, Coach House and Information Centre. This last is housed in a painstakingly refurbished 15th century barn, and features informative displays as well as a gift shop and tea room.

Plans for the on-site arboretum were first drawn up in the late 1980s, to cover 120 acres. Still being established, it will contain a collection of trees from all over the world, laid out in geographical themes - Europe, Asia, America, and the southern hemisphere.

CRESSING
4 miles E of Braintree off the B1018

Cressing Temple Barns, set in the centre of an ancient farmstead, are two splendid medieval timber barns commissioned in the 12th century by the Knights Templar. They contain the timber of over 1,000 oak trees; an interpretive exhibition explains to visitors how the barns were made, as a special viewing platform brings visitors up into the roof of the magnificent Wheat Barn for a closer look. There's also a beautiful walled garden re-creating the Tudor style, with an arbour, fount and physic garden. Special events are held throughout the year.

FEERING
6 miles E of Braintree off the A12

Feeringbury Manor near Feering has a fine, extensive riverside garden with ponds, streams, a little waterwheel, old-fashioned plants and bog gardens, and fascinating sculpture by artist Ben Coode-Adams.

185 THE WOOLPACK INN

Church Street, Coggeshall
The Woolpack Inn scores on old-world charm, excellent hospitality and fine home cooking.

see page 305

186 THE BELL INN

Feering, southwest of Colchester
Overlooking the village green at Feering, **The Bell** serves well-kept ales and tasty home-cooked food.

see page 305

Blake House Craft Centre comprises carefully preserved farm buildings centred round a courtyard. Visitors will find a fine array of craft shops and a restaurant serving breakfast and morning coffee, lunch and afternoon tea.

KELVEDON

6 miles SE of Braintree off the A12

This village alongside the River Blackwater houses the **Feering and Kelvedon Museum**, which is dedicated to manorial history and houses artefacts from the Roman settlement of Canonium, agricultural tools through the ages and other interesting exhibits.

FAIRSTEAD

4 miles S of Braintree off the A131

Fairstead (or Fairsted) is an undulating parish about three miles east of the A131. The **Church of St Mary and St Peter** is an ancient building of flint, in the Norman style, consisting of chancel, nave, north porch and a western tower with a lofty shingled spire with four bells, one of which dates back to before the Reformation. During restoration in the late 1800s various handsome mural paintings were discovered, including, over the chancel arch, those entitled *Our Lord's Triumphal Entry into Jerusalem, The Last Supper, The Betrayal, Our Lord being crowned with thorns, and Incidents on the way to Calvary.*

BLAKE END

3 miles W of Braintree off the A120

The Great Maze at Blake End is one of the most challenging in the world. Set in over 10 acres of lovely North Essex farmland, it is grown every year from over half a million individual maize and sunflower seeds, and is open every summer. Continuing innovations bring with them extra twists and turns, making this wonderful maze, with more than five miles of pathways, even more of a brain teaser. A viewing platform makes it easy to help anyone hopelessly lost! Ten per cent of all profits go to the Essex Air Ambulance service.

GREAT SALING

4 miles NW of Braintree off the A120

Saling Hall Garden is a 12-acre garden including a walled garden dating from 1698. The small park boasts a collection of fine trees, and there are ponds, a water garden and an extensive collection of unusual plants with an emphasis on rare trees.

WETHERSFIELD

5 miles NW of Braintree on the B1053

Boydells Dairy Farm is a working farm where visitors are welcome to join in with tasks such as milking, feeding and more. A guided tour mixes fun with education, and all questions are most welcome. From bees to llamas, just about every kind of farm animal can be found here

GREAT BARDFIELD

6 miles NW of Braintree off the B1053

This old market town on a hill above the River Pant is a pleasant mixture of cottages and shops, nicely complemented by the 14th century church of **St Mary the Virgin**. Perhaps Great Bardfield's most notable feature is, however, a restored windmill that goes by the strange name of Gibraltar.

Here in one of the prettiest villages in all of Essex, the **Great**

Bardfield Museum occupies a 16th century charity cottage and 19th century village lockup (the Cage), and features exhibits of mainly 19th and 20th century domestic and agricultural artefacts and some fine examples of rural crafts such as corn dollies and straw-plaiting.

FINCHINGFIELD

6 miles NW of Braintree off the B1053

This charming village is graced with thatched cottages spread generously around a sloping village green that dips to a stream and duck pond at the centre of the village. Nearby stands an attractive small 18th century Post Mill with one pair of stones and tailpole winding. Extensively restored, today's visitors can climb up the first two floors.

Just up the hill, visitors will find the Norman church of **St John the Baptist**, the **Guildhall** (mentioned in the *Domesday Book*), which has a small museum open Sundays and also houses a local heritage centre with displays of artwork, paintings, pottery, sewing and weaving.

Finchingfield is easily one of the most picturesque and most photographed villages in Essex, featured in many television programmes and the home of the series *Lovejoy*. Here visitors will also find the privately owned Tudor stately home, **Spains Hall**,

which has a lovely flower garden containing a huge Cedar of Lebanon planted in 1670 and an Adams sundial. Many good roses surround the kitchen garden, which contains an ancient Paulonia tree and a bougainvillea in the greenhouse. Dodie Smith, author of *101 Dalmatians*, lived for many years in a 17th century cottage in the village.

GOSFIELD

4 miles N of Braintree off the A1017

Gosfield Lake Leisure Resort, the county's largest freshwater lake, lies in the grounds of Gosfield Hall. This Tudor mansion was remodelled in the 19th century by its owner Samuel Courtauld. He also built the attractive mock-Tudor houses in the village.

188/212 THE RED LION

Finchingfield

Traditional English Inn with restaurant and three guest bedrooms

🍴 🛏 see pages 306 and 317

187 THE HORSE & GROOM

Cornish Hall End, nr Finchingfield

The Horse & Groom is a cheerful family-run country pub of wide appeal serving a wide range of snacks and meals.

🍴 see page 305

Finchingfield

High Street, Halstead

Traditional English teas and superb cooking of dishes both sweet and savoury make **The White House** a perfect choice for daytime eating.

see pages 307 and 316

Butler Road, Halstead

Locals and visitors steam along to **The Locomotive** to enjoy great hospitality, well-kept beer and good home cooking.

see page 307

Halstead's most famous product was once mechanical elephants. Life-sized and weighing half a ton, they were built by W Hunwicks. Each one consisted of 9,000 parts and could carry a load of eight adults and four children at speeds of up to 12 miles per hour.

HALSTEAD

The name 'Halstead' comes from the Anglo-Saxon for *healthy place*. Like Braintree and Coggeshall, Halstead was an important weaving centre. **Townsford Mill** is certainly the most picturesque reminder of Halstead's industrial heritage. Built in the 1700s, it remains one of the most handsome buildings in a town with a number of historic buildings. This white, weather-boarded three-storey mill across the River Colne at the Causeway was once a landmark site for the Courtauld empire, producing both the famous funerary crepe and rayon. Today the Mill is an antiques centre, one of the largest in Essex, with thousands of items of furniture, porcelain, collectibles, stamps, coins, books, dolls, postcards, costume, paintings, glass and ceramics, old lace and clocks.

There are several historic buildings in the shopping centre of Halstead, which is part of a designated conservation area. Markets are held every Friday and Saturday.

AROUND HALSTEAD

CASTLE HEDINGHAM

3 miles NW of Halstead off the B1058

This town is named for its Norman **Castle**, which dominates the landscape. One of England's strongest fortresses in the 11th century, even now it is impossible not to sense its power and strength. The impressive stone keep is one of the tallest in Europe, with four floors and rising over 100 feet, with 12-feet thick walls. The banqueting hall and minstrels' gallery can still be seen. It was owned by the Earls of Oxford, the powerful de Vere family, one of whom was among the barons who forced King John to accept the Magna Carta. Among those entertained at the castle were Henry VII and Elizabeth I.

The village itself is a maze of narrow streets radiating from Falcon Square, named after the half-timbered Falcon Inn. Attractive buildings include many Georgian and 15th century houses comfortably vying for space, and the **Church of St Nicholas**, built by the de Veres, which avoided Victorian 'restoration' and is virtually completely Norman, with grand masonry and interestingly carved choir seats. There is a working pottery in St James' Street.

At the **Colne Valley Railway and Museum**, on the A1017 between Sible Hedingham and Great Yeldham, a mile of the Colne Valley and Halstead line between Castle Hedingham and Great Yeldham has been restored and now runs steam and heritage diesel trains operated by enthusiasts. These lovingly restored Victorian railway buildings feature a collection of vintage engines and carriages; short steam train trips are available. **Colne Valley Farm Park**, set in 30 acres of traditional river meadows, is home to sheep,

Castle Hedingham

191 THE VICTORY INN & WICKHAM SHIP RESTAURANT

Wickham St Pauls, nr Halstead

The Victory Inn is an absolute winner in terms of setting, ambience, food and drink.

see page 308

pigs, poultry, cattle and natural flora and fauna.

SIBLE HEDINGHAM
3 miles NW of Halstead off the A1017

Mentioned in the *Domesday Book* as the largest parish in England, Sible Hedingham was the birthplace of Sir John Hawkwood, one of the 14th century's most famous soldiers of fortune. He led a band of mercenaries to Italy, where he was paid to defend Florence and where he married the daughter of the Duke of Milan. He died in Italy and was buried in Florence Cathedral, where a commemorative fresco was painted by Uccello. His body was returned to Essex and was reputedly buried in the south aisle of Sible Hedingham's Church of St Peter. A monument to him in the church is decorated with hawks and various other beasts.

Swan Street is the main artery of this charming village, boasting several delightful establishments devoted to providing visitors and natives of the town with places to shop, dine, enjoy a quiet drink and even stay for the night.

GESTINGTHORPE
5 miles N of Halstead off the A131

The Church of **St Mary the Virgin** in Gestingthorpe is distinctive in many respects. Witness to centuries of Christian worship, the *Domesday Book* of 1086 tells that 'Ghestingetorp' was held by Ledmer the priest before 1066. The oldest part extant of the existing building is the blocked-up lancet window in the north wall of the chancel, which dates back to the 1200s. Apart from this, most of the chancel, nave and south aisle dates from the 14th century. The

Jousting at Castle Hedingham

• *One of the handsome memorials in Gestingthorpe's Church of St Mary the Virgin commemorates Captain L E G Oates, who died in an attempt to save the lives of his companions on an ill-fated expedition to the Antarctic in 1912.* •

tower, constructed in about 1500, is 66 feet high. Of the six bells hung in the tower, four were cast in 1658-9 by Miles Gray, a Colchester bellfounder. The 16th century fifth and sixth bells were cast in Bury St Edmunds, and recast in 1901. The west door, set in a stepped brick arch, is the original. The unusual tracery in the East window consists of arches placed atop the apexes of the arches beneath them. The late 15th century/early 16th century nave roof is of the double hammer-beam type, and one of the finest in Essex. The font is late 14th century.

LITTLE MAPLESTEAD

3 miles NE of Halstead off the A131

Little Maplestead has an unusual round church, dedicated to **St**

John the Baptist, modelled on the Holy Sepulchre in Jerusalem, and used as a stopping-point for pilgrims on their way there. Built more than 600 years ago by the military order of the Knights Hospitallers, their 'Perceptory' at Little Maplestead was suppressed more than 400 years ago by Henry VIII.

THE NORTH ESSEX COAST

CLACTON-ON-SEA

16 miles SE of Colchester on the A133

Clacton is a traditional sun-and-sand family resort with a south-facing, long sandy beach, lovely gardens on the seafront and a wide variety of shops and places to explore. It also boasts a wide variety of special events and entertainment taking place throughout the year.

Settled by hunters during the Stone Age - which is borne witness to by the wealth of flint implements and the fossilised bones of the cave lion, straight-tusked elephant and wild ox unearthed on the Clacton foreshore and at Lion Point - the town grew over the centuries from a small village into a prosperous seaside resort in the 1800s, when the craze for the health benefits of coastal air and bathing was at its peak. The Pier was constructed in 1871; at first paddle steamers provided the only mode of transport to the resort, the railway arriving in 1882. **The Pier** was

Clacton-on-Sea

widened from 30 to over 300 feet in the 1930s. On the pier, apart from the marvellous traditional sideshows, big wheel, restaurants and fairground rides, there is the fascinating **Seaquarium and Reptile Safari**.

Amusement centres include the arcades and **Clacton Pavilion**. The two theatres, Princes Theatre and West Cliff, are open all year. Clacton Pavilion boasts a range of attractions, including crazy golf, dodgems and a rock & roll Fun House. The **Clifftop Public Gardens** also repay a visit.

Great Clacton is the oldest part of town, comprising an attractive grouping of shops, pubs and restaurants within the shadow of the 12th century parish church.

A walk round the town rewards the visitor with some very handsome sights. There are three Martello Towers along this part of the Essex coast.

HOLLAND-ON-SEA

1½ miles NE of Clacton off the B1032

This attractive community is home to **Holland Haven Country Park**, 100 acres of open space near the seashore, ideal for watching the marine birds and other wildlife of the region. Throughout the area there are a number of attractive walks which take full advantage of the varied coastal scenery.

FRINTON-ON-SEA

3 miles NE of Clacton off the B1032

Once a quiet fishing village, this town was developed as a select resort by Sir Richard Cooper, and expanded in the 1880s to the genteel family resort it is today. Situated on a long stretch of sandy beach, Frinton remains peaceful and unspoilt. The tree-lined residential avenues sweep elegantly down to the Esplanade and extensive clifftop greensward.

Frinton-on-Sea

•

The Church of Old St Mary in Frinton contains some panels of stained glass in the East window designed by the Pre-Raphaelite artist Burne-Jones. A good example of 20th century English vernacular architecture is The Homestead at the corner of Second Avenue and Holland Road, built in 1905 by C F Voysey.

•

Along its main shopping street in Connaught Avenue, the 'Bond Street' of the East Coast, shopkeepers maintain a tradition of friendly and courteous service. Summer theatre and other open-air events take place throughout the season, and there are also some excellent tennis and golf clubs in the town. The grace and elegance of this sophisticated resort is evidenced all round, as are hints of its distinguished past: Victorian beach huts still dot the extensive beach.

The area south of **Frinton Gates** has a unique local character, being laid out with detached houses set along broad tree-lined avenues.

WEELEY

5 miles NW of Clacton off the A133

St Andrew's is the handsome parish church just south of the centre of this picturesque village. There is a lovely tree-lined path that passes Weeleyhall Wood and Weeley Lodge, with its beautifully kept gardens. Here visitors will also pass a navigational beacon that

forms part of Aircraft Flight Operations for both civil and military flights.

A mile south, off the B1411, Weeley Heath is a small and attractive community boasting a lovely village green and stunning surrounding countryside.

LITTLE CLACTON

3 miles NW of Clacton off the A133

Though it shares its name with its near neighbour, this is a town apart. Quiet and secluded, multiple-winner of the Best Kept Village award, Little Clacton features a lovely Jubilee Oak, planted to celebrate Victoria's 50th year on the throne.

The fine church of **St James** has been described as one of the most beautiful medieval churches in Essex, and sits at the heart of the village.

Oakwood Crafts Resource Centre in Little Clacton provides an environment for people with learning disabilities to learn and develop work skills, motivation, responsibility, team spirit, self-esteem and confidence through horticulture, woodwork, ceramics, crafts and catering. As a horticultural centre, it sells a wide range of bedding plants, shrubs and hanging baskets seasonally, along with a selection of wooden garden implements, furnishings and other items, and ceramics.

TENDRING

7 miles NW of Clacton off the A133

This village that gives its name to both the peninsula and the district council contains the handsome church of **St Edmund**, whose elegant spire can be seen for miles around. The church is dedicated to the last King of independent East Anglia, martyred by the Danes in the 9th century.

WALTON-ON-THE-NAZE

8 miles NE of Clacton on the B1034

Walton is all the fun of the fair. It is a traditional, singular and cheerful resort which focuses on the pier and all its attractions, including a ten-pin bowling alley. The gardens at the seafront are colourful and the beach has good sand. The Backwaters to the rear of Walton are made up of a series of small harbours and saltings, which lead into Harwich harbour.

Walton has an outstanding sandy beach. The town's seafront was developed in 1825 and provides a fine insight into the character of an early Victorian seaside resort. The charming narrow streets of the town contain numerous shops, restaurants and pubs overlooking the second longest pier in the country. **Marine Parade**, originally called The Crescent, was built in 1832. **The Pier**, first built in 1830, was originally constructed of wood and measured 330 feet long. It was extended to its present length of 2,610 feet in 1898, at the same time as the electric train service began.

The wind-blown expanse of **The Naze** just north of Walton is an extensive coastal recreation and picnic area, pleasant for walking, especially out of season when the visitor is likely to have all 150

The Old Lifeboat House Museum at East Terrace, in a building over 100 years old, houses an interpretive museum of local history and development, rural and maritime, covering Walton, Frinton and the Sokens

Walton-on-the-Naze

The 13th century Jacobes Hall in centre of Brightlingsea is one of the oldest occupied buildings in Essex. It is timber-framed with an undulating tile roof and an external staircase. Used as a meeting hall during the reign of Henry III, its name originates from its first owner, Edmund, Vicar of Brightlingsea, who was known locally as Jacob le Clerk.

Brightlingsea Museum in Duke Street offers an insight into the lives, customs and traditions of the area, housing a collection of exhibits relating to the town's maritime connections and the oyster industry.

192 THE RED LION

Thorrington, southeast of Colchester

Traditional and modern elements combine well in both the décor and the cooking at **The Red Lion**.

see page 309

acres virtually to him or herself, with great views out over the water. The shape of the Naze is constantly changing, eroded by wind, water and tide.

The year 1796 saw the demise of the medieval church, and somewhere beyond the 800-feet pier lies medieval Walton. The sandstone cliffs are internationally important for their shell fossil deposits. Inhabitants have been enjoying the bracing sea air at Walton since before Neolithic times: flint-shaping instruments have been found here, and the fossil teeth and the ears of sharks and whales have been discovered in the Naze's red crag cliffs. The **Naze Tower** is brick built and octagonal in shape, originally built as a beacon in 1720 to warn seamen of the West Rocks off shore. A nature trail has been created nearby, and the Essex Skipper butterfly and Emperor moth can be seen here.

BRIGHTLINGSEA

7 miles W of Clacton on the B1029

Brightlingsea enjoys a long tradition of shipbuilding and seafaring. In 1347, 51 men and five ships were sent to the siege of Calais. Among the crew members of Sir Francis Drake's fleet which vanquished the Spanish Armada was one 'William of Brightlingsea'. Brightlingsea has the distinction of being the only limb of the Cinque Ports outside Kent and Sussex.

All Saints Church, which occupies the highest point of the town on a hill about a mile from the centre, is mainly 13th century. Here are to be found some Roman brickwork and a frieze of ceramic tiles commemorating local residents whose lives were lost at sea. Its 97-feet tower can be seen from 17 miles out to sea. A light was once placed in the tower to guide the town's fishermen home

The **Town Hard** is where you can see all the waterfront comings and goings, including the activities of the Colne Smack Preservation Society, which maintains a seagoing link with the past.

There are plenty of superb walks along Brightlingsea Creek and the River Colne, which offer a chance to watch the birdlife on the saltings and the plethora of boats on the water. Today the town is a haven for the yachting fraternity and is the home of national and international sailing championships, with one of the best stretches of sailing on the East Coast. Day and half-day sailing and canoeing sessions are held at the **Brightlingsea Outdoor Education Centre**.

ELMSTEAD MARKET

6 miles N of Brightlingsea off the A120

The Church of **St Anne and St Lawrence** to the north of this village has a rare carved oak recumbent effigy of a knight in armour.

Elmstead Market is perhaps best known as the location of **Beth Chatto Gardens**, at White Barn House. Here visitors will find six acres of gravel, water and woodland gardens, five large ponds, shady walks and a Mediterranean-style garden where aromatic drought-loving plants thrive. The adjoining nursery contains a wide variety of plants for sale. Close by is the **Rolts Nursery Butterfly Farm**.

THORRINGTON

3 miles NW of Brightlingsea off the B1027

Thorrington Tide Mill, built in the early 19th century, is the only remaining Tide Mill in Essex, and one of very few left in East Anglia. It has been fully restored, and although no longer in use, the Wheel can be run for guided groups. There is a public footpath which runs along the creek here.

POINT CLEAR

2 miles SE of Brightlingsea off the B1027

The **East Essex Aviation Society & Museum**, located in the Martello Tower at Point Clear, not only retains its original flooring and roof, but today contains interesting displays of wartime aviation, military and naval photographs, uniforms and other memorabilia with local and US Air Force connections. There are artefacts on show from the crash sites of wartime aircraft in the Tendring area, including the engine and fuselage section of a recovered P51D Mustang fighter. The museum also explores civil and military history from both World Wars. There are very good views from the tower over the Colne Estuary and Brightlingsea.

ST OSYTH

3 miles SE of Brightlingsea off the B1027

This pretty little village has a fascinating history and centres around its Norman church and the ancient ruins of **St Osyth Priory**, founded in the 12th century. The village and Priory were named by Augustinian Canons after St Osytha, martyred daughter of Frithenwald, first Christian King of the East Angles, who was beheaded by Diceian pirates AD 653. Little of the original Priory remains, except for the magnificent late-15th century flint gatehouse, complete with battlements.

MERSEA ISLAND

2 miles SW of Brightlingsea off the B1025

Much of this island is a National Nature Reserve, home to its teeming shorelife. The island is linked to the mainland by a narrow causeway which is covered over at high tide. The towns of both East and West Mersea have excellent facilities for sailing enthusiasts, and East Mersea is also a haven for birdwatchers. **Mersea Island Museum** contains exhibits on Mersea's social and natural history, archaeology and the fishing industry, including a fisherman's cottage. Tel: 01206 385191. Visitors to Mersea Island Vineyard can enjoy tours and tastings. Tel: 01206 385900.

Cudmore Grove Country Park on Bromans Lane, East Mersea, boasts fine views across the Colne and Blackwater estuaries.

The village of St Osyth is centred on a crossroads and contains an attractive group of shops and restaurants. The Church of St Peter and St Paul in the village centre has unusual internal red brick piers and arches. The nearby creek has a small boatyard.

194 THE WHITE HART

St Osyth, on the road to Point Clear

The White Hart is a family-friendly pub serving well-kept real ales and classic pub dishes.

see page 309

193 THE NEW BELL INN

Outpart Eastward, Harwich

Real ales from local brewers and freshly made snacks are popular offerings at **The New Bell Inn**.

see page 309

Grassland adjoining a sandy beach, it's an ideal spot for shore walks and picnics. There's also a pathway on the sea wall and a birdwatching hide.

HARWICH

Harwich's name probably originates from the time of King Alfred, when 'hare' meant army, and 'wic' a camp. This attractive old town was built in the 13th century by the Earls of Norfolk to exploit its strategic position on the Stour and Orwell estuary; the town has an important and fascinating maritime history, the legacy of which continues into the present.

During the 14th and 15th century French campaigns, Harwich was an important naval base. The famous Elizabethan seafarers Hawkins, Frobisher and Drake sailed from Harwich on various expeditions; in 1561 Queen Elizabeth I visited the town, describing it *'a pretty place and want[ing] for nothing'*. Christopher Newport, leader of the *Goodspeed* expedition which founded Jamestown, Virginia, in 1607, and Christopher Jones, master of the Pilgrim ship *The Mayflower*, lived in Harwich (the latter just off the quay in King's Head Street), as did Jones' kinsman John Alden, who sailed to America in 1620. The famous diarist Samuel Pepys was MP for the town in the 1660s, thus it was also during this time headquarters for the King's Navy. Charles II took the first pleasure cruise from Harwich's shores. Other notable visitors included Lord Nelson and Lady Hamilton, who are reputed to have stayed at The Three Cups in Church Street.

Harwich remains popular as a vantage point for watching incoming and outgoing shipping in the harbour and across the waters to Felixstowe. Nowadays, lightships, buoys and miles of strong chain are stored along the front, and passengers arriving on North Sea ferries at Harwich International Port see the 90-feet

High Lighthouse, Harwich

high, six-sided **High Lighthouse** as the first landmark. Now housing the **National Vintage Wireless and Television Museum**, it was built in 1818 along with the **Low Lighthouse**. When the two lighthouses were in line they could indicate a safe shipping channel into the harbour. Each had replaced earlier wooden structures, and were themselves replaced by cast iron structures (both of which still stand on the front in nearby Dovercourt) in 1863 when the shifting sandbanks altered the channel. Shipping now relies on light buoys to find its way. The Low lighthouse is now the town's **Maritime Museum**, with specialist displays on the Royal Navy and commercial shipping.

Two other worthwhile museums in the town are the **Lifeboat Museum** off Wellington Road, which contains the last Clacton offshore 34-feet lifeboat and a history of the lifeboat service in Harwich, and the **Ha'penny Pier Visitor Centre** on the Quay, with information on everything in Harwich and a small heritage exhibition.

The **Treadwell Crane** now stands on Harwich Green, but for over 250 years it was sited in the Naval Shipyard. It is worked by two people walking in two 16-feet diameter wheels, and is the only known British example of its kind. Amazingly, it was operational up until the 1920s.

The importance of Harwich's port during the 19th century is confirmed by **The Redoubt**, a huge grey fort built between 1808 and 1810. Its design is an enlarged version of the Martello towers which dotted the English coast, awaiting a Napoleonic invasion that never came (some of these towers, of course, still exist). Today the Harwich Society has largely restored it and opened it as a small museum.

The old town also contains many ancient buildings, including the **Guildhall**, which was rebuilt in 1769 and is located in Church Street. The Council chamber, Mayor's Parlour and other rooms may be viewed. The former gaol contains unique graffiti of ships, probably carved by prisoners, and is well worth putting aside a morning to explore (by appointment only). Documents on show include those detailing the connection of Harwich with Pepys, the Pilgrim Fathers, and the Virginia settlement.

AROUND HARWICH

DOVERCOURT

1 mile S of Harwich off the A120

This residential and holiday suburb of Harwich has Market Day on Fridays. With its attractive cliffs and beach, it also boasts the **Iron Lighthouse** or 'Leading Lights' located just off lower Marine Parade. The town has been settled from prehistoric times, as attested to by the late-Bronze Age axe-heads found here (now in Colchester Museum). The Romans found the town a useful source of the stone 'Septaria', taken from the

A fascinating piece of Harwich's history is the Electric Palace Cinema, built in 1911 and now the oldest unaltered purpose-built cinema in Britain. It was restored by a trust and re-opened in 1981.

A curiosity in Dovercourt's All Saints Church is a stained-glass window presented by the German Kaiser as a memorial to the thousands of British troops killed in an aborted expedition to Walcheren in Holland, sent to secure the area and prevent the French navy from operating from Antwerp – Britain and Germany were both at war with Napoleon's France at the time.

195/213 THE RED LION

South Street, Manningtree

The Red Lion is a popular pub offering fine home cooking, real ales, excellent wines and two B&B guest rooms.

 see pages 309 and 318

cliffs and used in building. The town that visitors see today developed primarily in Victorian times as a fashionable resort.

MISTLEY

7 miles W of Harwich off the B1352

Here at the gateway to Constable Country, local 18th century landowner and MP Richard Rigby had grand designs to develop Mistley into a fashionable spa to rival Harrogate and Bath, adopting the swan as its symbol. Sadly, all that remains of Rigby's ambitious scheme is the Swan Fountain, a small number of attractive Georgian houses and **Mistley Towers**, the remains of a church (otherwise demolished in 1870) designed by the flamboyant architect Robert Adams. From the waterfront, noted for its colony of swans, there are very pleasant views across the estuary to Suffolk.

Mistley Quay Workshops in the High Street feature a pottery workshop, lute/cello maker, harpsichord maker, wood worker, bookbinder, and stained-glass window maker and restorer. There is also a tea shop on the premises.

Mistley Place Park Environmental & Animal Rescue Centre is set in 25 acres of parkland with country walks, wildlife habitats, lake, farm animals and great views across the Stour Estuary. Over 2,000 rescued animals including rabbits, Vietnamese pigs and horses roam free.

MANNINGTREE

9 miles W of Harwich off the B1352

The Walls, on the approach to Manningtree along the B1352, offer unrivalled views of the Stour estuary and the Suffolk coast, and the swans for which the area is famous. Lying on the River Stour amid beautiful rolling countryside, the scene has oft been depicted by artists over the centuries.

Back in Tudor times, Manningtree was the centre of the cloth trade, and later a port filled with barges carrying their various cargoes along the coast to London. Water still dominates today and the town is a centre of leisure sailing.

Manningtree has been a market town since 1238, and is still a busy shopping centre. It is the smallest town in Britain, and a stroll through the streets reveals the diversity of its past.

There are still traditional (and mainly Georgian) restaurants, pubs and shops, as well as handcraft and specialist outlets. The views over the river are well known to birdspotters, sailors and ramblers. The town has an intriguing past - as a river crossing, market, smugglers' haven and home of Matthew Hopkins, the reviled and self-styled Witchfinder General who struck terror into the local community during the 17th century. Some of his victims were hanged on Manningtree's small village green.

It is believed that the reference in Shakespeare's *Henry IV* to Falstaff as 'that roasted

Manningtree ox' relates to the practice of roasting an entire ox, as was known at that time to be done at the town's annual fair.

Manningtree Museum in the High Street opened in the late 1980s and mounts two exhibitions a year, together with permanent photographs and pieces relating to the heritage of Manningtree, Lawford, Mistley and the district.

ARDLEIGH

10 miles W of Harwich off the A137

Tendring's westernmost village comprises an attractive group of 16th and 17th century cottages grouped around the fine 15th century **Butterfield Church**. **Spring Valley Mill**, a now privately owned 18th century timber-framed and weather-boarded edifice, was once a working watermill, later adapted to steam. Day and half-day canoeing and sailing lessons can be taken at the **Ardleigh Outdoor Education Centre**.

Nearby is **Ardleigh Reservoir**, offering up many opportunities for water sports and trout fishing.

Manningtree railway station is an alternative to Dedham as a start point of a walk to Constable Country, taking in Cattawade Marshes (SSSI), Willy Lot's Cottage and Flatford Mill. In the station itself is a buffet serving a range of excellent traditional English dishes.

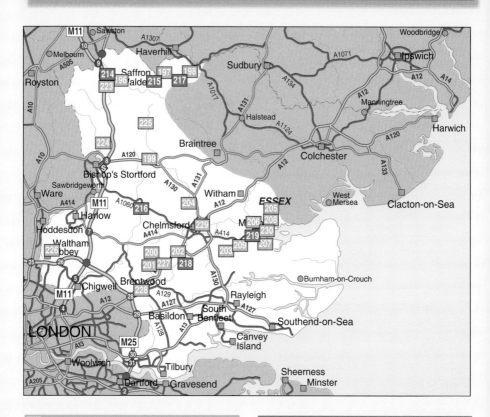

South and West Essex

The small northwest Essex towns of Saffron Walden, Thaxted, Great Dunmow and Stansted Mountfichet are among the most beautiful and interesting in the country. This area is also home to a wealth of picturesque villages, many of them boasting weather-boarded houses and pargeting. The quiet country lanes are perfect for walking, cycling or just exploring. This area also retains three beautiful and historic windmills, at Stansted Mountfichet, Aythorpe Roding and Thaxted.

Visitors to southwest Essex and the Epping Forest may associate it solely with its larger towns, some of the most populous in the county, including Harlow and Brentwood. All offer excellent shopping and a variety of very good entertainment venues, but to focus on these towns is to overlook the region's wealth of woodland, nature reserves, superb gardens and rural delights.

Epping Forest dominates much of the far western corner, but all this part of Essex is rich in countryside, forests and parks, including the magnificent Lee (Lea) Valley Regional Park, Thorndon Country Park at Brentwood, and Weald Country Park at South Weald. Many of these parks arrange special events during the year. Southwest Essex is also home to Waltham Abbey.

Bordering the north bank of the Thames, the southern Essex borough of Thurrock also boasts a good number of fine towns and villages, with attractions ranging from superb heritage sites and museums to family-run specialist shops as these communities continue to go from strength to strength. Henry VIII built riverside Block Houses at East and West Tilbury, which later became Coalhouse Fort and Tilbury Fort. It was at West Tilbury that Queen Elizabeth I gave her famous speech to her troops, gathered to meet the Spanish Armada threat. Both forts also played an important defensive role during the two World Wars.

At the extreme southeast of the county, Southend is a popular seaside resort with a wealth of sites and amenities. There are also smaller seaside communities that repay a visit.

In the area surrounding the Blackwater and Crouch estuaries is the county's principal town, Chelmsford, and also a wealth of ancient woodland and other natural beauties, particularly along the estuaries and the Chelmer and Blackwater Canal. This corner of Essex is ideal for those who enjoy any kind of watersports activities. The island of Northey near Maldon is owned by the National Trust and is a haven for wildlife.

This is also the region of Essex dominated by hundreds of acres of ancient woodland, much of it coppiced - the traditional woodland management technique which encourages a vast array of natural flora and fauna.

Saffron Walden

171

SAFFRON WALDEN

Named after the Saffron crocus - grown in the area to make dyestuffs and fulfil a variety of other uses in the Middle Ages - Saffron Walden has retained much of its original street plan, as well as hundreds of fine old buildings, many of which are timbered and have overhanging upper floors and decorative plastering (also known as pargeting). Gog and Magog (or, in some versions, folk-hero Tom Hickathrift and the Wisbech Giant) battle forever in plaster on the gable of the **Old Sun Inn**, where, legend has it, Oliver Cromwell and General Fairfax both lodged during the Civil War.

A typical market town, Saffron Walden's centrepiece is its magnificent church. At the **Saffron Walden Museum**, as well as a glove reputedly worn by Mary Queen of Scots on the day she died is what was once believed to be a piece of human skin which coated the church door at Hadstock, although now known to be leather hide. The museum first opened to the public at its present location in 1835, and was founded 'to gratify the inclination of all who value natural history'. It remains faithful to this credo, while widening the museum's scope in the ensuing years. The museum has won numerous awards, including joint winner of the Museum of the Year Award for best museum of Industrial or Social History in 1997. At this friendly, family-sized museum visitors can try their hand at corn grinding with a Romano-British quern, see how a medieval timber house would have been built, admire the displays of Native American and West African embroidery, and come face to face with Wallace the Lion, the museum's faithful guardian. Over two floors, exhibits focus on town and country, with furniture and woodwork, costumes, ancient Egyptian artefacts, geology exhibits, and ceramics and glass. In the 'ages of man' gallery, the history of northwest Essex is traced from the Ice Age to the Middle Ages, while the Discovery Centre offers a personal encounter with natural history. The ruins of historic Walden Castle are also on-site.

View to Saffron Walden

On the local **Common**, once known as Castle Green, is the largest surviving Turf Maze in England. Only eight ancient turf mazes survive in England: though there were many more in the Middle Ages, if they are not looked after they soon become overgrown and are lost. This one is believed to be some 800 years old, a circular labyrinth of medieval Christian design.

Henry Winstanley - inventor, engineer and engraver, and builder of the first Eddystone Lighthouse at Plymouth - was born in the town in 1644. His design for the lighthouse drew heavily on his previously constructed wooden 'lantern' which then crowned the 16th century parish church. The Lighthouse, and Winstanley with it, were swept away in a fierce storm in 1703.

To the north of the town are the **Bridge End Gardens**, a wonderfully restored example of early Victorian gardens, complete with the wonderful Hedge Maze, which was planted in 1840 in the Italian Renaissance style and has 610 metres of paths.

Next to the gardens is the **Fry Public Art Gallery**, with a unique collection of work by 20th century artists and designers such as Edward Bawden, Michael Rothenstein, Eric Ravilious, John Aldridge and Sheila Robinson. It also exhibits work by contemporary artists working in Essex today, demonstrating the area's continuing artistic tradition. The gallery was purpose-designed and opened in

River Cam, Saffron Walden

1856 to house the collection of Francis Gibson. The gallery also houses the Lewis George Fry RBA, RWA (1860-1933) Collection, which is exhibited each summer, along with works by Robert Fry (1866-1934) and Anthony Fry.

Audley End House was built by the first Earl of Suffolk, and was at one time owned by Charles II. The original early 17th century house, with its two large courtyards, had a magnificence claimed to match that of Hampton Court. Remodelled in the 18th century by

•

Close to Bridge End is the Anglo-American War Memorial dedicated by Field Marshal the Viscount Montgomery of Alamein in 1953 to the memory of all the American flyers of the 65th Fighter Wing who lost their lives in the Second World War.

•

173

223 AUDLEY END STEAM RAILWAY

Wendens Ambo, Saffron Walden

A narrow guage miniature steam railway running through woodland on the Audley End Estate.

 see page 324

197 THE THREE HORSESHOES

Helions Bumpstead, nr Saffron Walden

The Three Horseshoes is a pleasant old village pub serving traditional dishes and very good wines.

 see page 309

198/217 THE RED LION

Steeple Bumpstead

The Red Lion is a stylishly modernised pub that's going places – a new dining area and accommodation planned for 2006.

 see pages 310 and 319

215 HOLLINGATE BED & BREAKFAST

Radwinter End, nr Saffron Walden

Peace, comfort and a lovely rural setting await guests at **Hollingate B&B**.

 see page 318

174

Robert Adam, unfortunately the subsequent earls lacked their forebears' financial resources, and much of the house was demolished as it fell into disrepair. Nevertheless it remains today one of England's most impressive Jacobean mansions; its distinguished stone façade set off perfectly by Capability Brown's lake. The remaining state rooms retain their palatial magnificence and the exquisite state bed in the Howard Room is hung with the original embroidered drapes. The silver, the Jacobean Screen and Robert Adam painted Drawing Room are among the many sights to marvel at. The natural history collection features more than 1,000 stuffed animals and birds. To complement this, there are paintings by Holbein, Lely and Canaletto. Fascinating introductory talks help visitors get the most from any visit to this, one of the most magnificent houses in England. This jewel also has a kitchen garden and grounds landscaped by Capability Brown, including the 'Temple of Concord' dedicated to George III. There is a lovely parterre, lake and Pond Garden. Circular walks help visitors make the most of all there is to see. The organic kitchen garden was recently opened to the public for the first time in 250 years. The gardens are managed by the Henry Doubleday Research Association, who grow and sell a wide range of organic produce in the shop. Within the rolling parkland of the grounds there are several elegant outbuildings, some of which were designed by Robert Adam. Among these are an icehouse, a circular temple and a Springwood Column.

The Audley End Miniature Railway is 1.5 miles long and takes visitors along Lord Braybrooke's private 10¼-inch gauge railway through beautiful private woods.

AROUND SAFFRON WALDEN

RADWINTER

4 miles E of Saffron Walden off the B1053

Radwinter boasts a fine church, which was largely renovated and rebuilt in the 19th century by architect William Eden Nesfield and has a fine Tudor porch with a room above. The village also has cottages and almshouses designed by Nesfield.

HEMPSTEAD

5 miles E of Saffron Walden off the B1054

The highwayman, Dick Turpin, was born here in 1705. His parents kept the Bell Inn, later renamed the Bluebell and more recently known as 'Turpin's Tavern'. Gilt letters announce that *'It is the Landlord's great desire that no one stands before the fire'* over the wide hearth where logs still burn; pictures all around celebrate the infamy of the former innkeeper's son.

Inside the 14th to 15th century village church, an impressively life-like bust carved by Edward Marshall recalls the town's rather worthier son, William Harvey (1578-1657), who is buried in a white marble sarcophagus in the crypt. Harvey was chief physician to Charles I and the discoverer of the circulation of blood, as recorded in his *De Motu Cordis* of 1628.

WIDDINGTON

4 miles S of Saffron Walden off the B1383

Covering over 20 acres, **Mole Hall Wildlife Park** offers visitors the chance to come close to a range of wild and domesticated animals. With the private fully-moated 13th century manor house as a backdrop, the wide variety of animals in this excellent park include South American llamas, flamingos, Formosa Sika deer (which are extinct in the wild), chimpanzees, muntjac, Arctic fox, wallabies, red squirrels and much more. Mole Hall is also home to two species of otters: Short-clawed and North American. Domesticated animals such as guinea pigs, rabbits, goats, pigs and sheep can also be seen. The Butterfly Pavilion offers a tropical experience where brilliantly coloured butterflies flit about freely. Within the tropical pavilion you can also find lovebirds and small monkeys, along with a variety of snakes, spiders and insects (safe behind glass). The pools are home to goldfish, toads and terrapins.

Widdington is also home to **Priors Hall Barn**, one of the finest surviving medieval 'aisled' barns in all of southeast England, and owned by English Heritage.

STANSTED MOUNTFICHET

8 miles SW of Saffron Walden off the B1383

Pilots approaching the airport may be surprised at the sight of a **Norman Village**, complete with domestic animals, and the reconstructed motte-and-bailey **Mountfichet Castle**, standing just two miles from the runway. The original castle was built after 1066 by the Duke of Boulogne, a cousin of the Conqueror. Siege weapons on show include two giant catapults. The Castle was voted Essex attraction of the year in 2002 by the Good Britain Guide, and visitors can take a trip to the top of the siege tower and tiptoe into the baron's bed chamber while he sleeps!

Next door to the castle is **The House on the Hill Museum Adventure**, where there are three museums for the price of one. The Toy Museum is the largest of its kind in the world, and here children of every age are treated to a unique and nostalgic trip back to their childhood. There is every toy imaginable here, many of them now highly prized collectors' items. There is a shop selling new toys and a collectors' shop with many old toys and books to choose from. The Rock 'n' Roll, Film and Theatre Experience and the End-of-the-pier Amusement machine displays also contribute to a grand day out here in Stansted Mountfichet.

Stansted Windmill is one of the best-preserved tower mills in

Dick Turpin trained as a butcher before turning to cattle and deer stealing, smuggling and robbery. Narrowly avoiding capture, he fled to Yorkshire and carried on his nefarious ways as John Palmer. He was captured while horse-stealing and hanged in York in 1739.

Like many other villages, Hempstead once boasted a village cockpit; its faint outline can still be traced, though the steep banks are now crowned with trees.

224 MOUNTFITCHET CASTLE & NORMAN VILLAGE

Stansted

Reconstruction of a Norman village, together with a motte and bailey castle. A fascinating day out for all the family, it offers a rare insight into life as it was 900 years ago.

 see page 324

175

Linton Zoo near Hadstock village is a privately owned collection of wild animals set in 10½ acres of gardens. A free car park, children's play area, picnic areas and a café are on site.

the country. Dating back to 1787 and in use until 1910, most of the original machinery has survived. It is open on the first Sunday of each month from April to October and on Bank Holiday Mondays.

HADSTOCK

6 miles N of Saffron Walden off the B1052

As well as claiming to have the oldest church door in England, at the parish **Church of St Botolph**, Hadstock also has a macabre tale to tell. The church's north door was once covered with a piece of skin, now to be seen in Saffron Walden Museum. Local legend says it is a 'Daneskin', from a Viking flayed alive, but recent DNA analysis has disproved this legend. Lining doors with animal leather was common in the Middle Ages, and many so-called 'Daneskins'

are just that. The door itself is Saxon, as are the 11th century carvings, windows and arches, rare survivors that predate the Norman Conquest.

BARTLOW

5 miles NE of Saffron Walden off the B1052

Bartlow Hills are reputed to be the largest burial mounds in Europe dating from Roman times, one 15 metres high. They date back to the 2nd century.

THAXTED

7 miles SE of Saffron Walden on the B184

This small country town has a recorded history that dates back to before the *Domesday Book*. Originally a Saxon settlement, it developed around a Roman road. The town's many beautiful old buildings contribute to its unique character and charm. To its credit Thaxted has no need of artificial tourist attractions, and is today what it has been for the last ten centuries: a thriving and beautiful town.

Thaxted has numerous attractively pargeted and timber-framed houses, and a magnificent **Guildhall**, built as a meeting-place for cutlers around 1390. The demise of the cutlery industry in this part of Essex in the 1500s led it to becoming the administrative centre of the town. Restored in Georgian times, it became the town's Grammar School, as well as remaining a centre of administration. Once more

Morris Dancers, Thaxted

restored in 1975, the Parish council still holds its meetings here.

The town's famous **Tower Windmill** was built in 1804 by John Webb. In working order until 1907, it had fallen into disuse and disrepair but work is in progress to restore it to full working order. It contains a rural life museum, well worth a visit. Close to the windmill are the town's **Almshouses**, which continued to provide homes for the elderly even 250 years after they were built for that purpose.

Thaxted Church stands on a hill and soars cathedral-like over the town's streets. It has been described as the finest Parish church in the country and, though many towns may protest long and loud at this claim, it certainly is magnificent. It was also the somewhat unlikely setting for a pitched battle in 1921. The rather colourful vicar and secretary of the Church Socialist League, the Revd Conrad Noel, displayed the red flag of communism and the Sinn Fein flag in the church. Incensed Cambridge students tore them down and substituted the Union Jack; Noel in turn ripped that down, and his friends are said to have slashed the tyres of the students' cars and motorbikes. A fine bronze in the church celebrates this adventurous man of the cloth.

Conrad Noel's wife is remembered for encouraging Morris dancing in the town. Today, the famous Morris Ring is held annually in early June, attracting over 300 dancers from all over the country, who dance through the streets. Dancing can also be seen around the town on most Bank Holiday Mondays, usually in the vicinity of a pub!

In Park Street, at Aldborough Lodge, the **Thaxted Garden for Butterflies** is an ordinary garden that has been developed with a view to pleasing birds, butterflies and other wildlife species - including humans. Displays depict the 22 native wild butterfly species that have visited the garden since its inception in 1988.

GREAT EASTON

3 miles S of Thaxted off the B184

Great Easton boasts a wealth of cottages and farmhouses with ornamental plasterwork, clustered Tudor chimneys and half-timbering. Great Easton's well-known and very popular Green Man pub occupies a handsome building dating back to the 15th century.

LITTLE EASTON

5 miles S of Thaxted off the B184

The charming 12th century **Church** in this small village is rich in historic features. Its Maynard Chapel features some outstanding marble monuments of the family that gives the chapel its name, as well as some famous brasses. The church's oldest treasures are, however, a well-preserved and priceless 12th century wall painting and several 15th century frescoes. Two more recent additions, a pair of stained glass windows, were unveiled in 1990. The 'Window of the Crusaders' and the 'Window of Friendship and Peace' are a lasting

225 THE THAXTED GARDEN FOR BUTTERFLIES

Thaxted

A conservation project which has proved very successful, attracting many species of Native British butterflies, as well as a wide variety of wildlife.

 see page 325

•

Gustav Holst, composer of, among other pieces, the renowned 'Planets' Suite', lived in Thaxted from 1914-1925, and often played the church organ. To celebrate his connection with the town there is a music festival in late June/early July which attracts performers of international repute.

•

The Barn Theatre at Little Easton Manor is situated in one of the finest and oldest tithe barns in the country, with magnificent oak timbers and ancient tiled roof. It was visited by some of the most distinguished actors and impresarios of the early 20th century, including Ellen Terry, Hermione Baddeley, Charlie Chaplin, George Formby, Basil Dean (who married Daisy's daughter) and George Bernard Shaw

199 THE CRICKETERS

Beaumont Hill, Great Dunmow

The Cricketers is a very convivial inn serving real ales and popular pub dishes; naturally, the decorative theme is cricket.

see page 311

memorial to the American 386th Bomb Group. Known as 'The Crusaders', they were stationed nearby for 13 months and lost over 200 of their number in battle overseas during that short time. They flew from an airstrip created in the park of **Easton Lodge**, the favourite home of Frances, Countess of Warwick – Edward VII's 'Darling Daisy'. Harold Peto designed the gardens for her in 1902. The house was demolished in 1950 but the pavilions were restored in 1996 and much other restoration has taken place in the garden, including the sunken Italian garden; the Glade, formerly Peto's Japanese garden; and the living sundial with a border featuring every plant mentioned in Shakespeare's plays and sonnets. The 17th century dovecote houses an exhibition of photography, prints and writings on the history of the Lodge since 1950.

BROXTED

3 miles SW of Thaxted off the B1051

The parish **Church of St Mary the Virgin** here in the handsome village of Broxted has two remarkably lovely stained glass windows commemorating the captivity and release of John McCarthy and the other Beirut hostages, dedicated in January 1993. Though just a few minutes drive from Stansted Airport off the M11, it is a welcoming haven of rural tranquillity.

GREAT DUNMOW

13 miles SE of Saffron Walden on the A120

The town is famous for the 'Flitch of Bacon', an ancient ceremony which dates back as far as the early 12th century. A prize of a flitch, or side, of bacon was awarded to the local man who *'does not repent of his marriage nor quarrel, differ or dispute with his wife within a year and a day after the marriage'*.

Amidst great ceremony, the winning couple would be seated and presented with their prize. The custom, lapsed on the Dissolution of the Monasteries, was briefly revived in the 18th century, and became established again after 1885. 'Trials' to test the truth are all in good fun, and carried out every leap year. The successful couple are carried through the streets on chairs and then presented with the Flitch. The original 'bacon chair' can be seen in Little Dunmow parish church.

Other places of historical interest include the parish church of St Mary at Church End, Great Dunmow, dating back to 1322. The Clock House, a private residence built in 1589, was the home of St Anne Line, martyred for sheltering a Jesuit priest. Clock House was subsequently occupied by Sir George Beaumont. He used it to store and display his extensive art collection, which he bequeathed to the nation and which forms the nucleus of the National Gallery collection in London.

The **Great Dunmow Maltings**, opened to the public in 2000 after restoration costing £750,000, is the most complete example of a medieval timber-framed building of its type in the

United Kingdom, and a focal point for local history in the shape of Great Dunmow Museum, with changing displays illustrating the history of the town from Roman times to the present day.

The Flitch Way is a 15-mile country walk along the former Bishop's Stortford-to-Braintree railway, taking in Victorian stations, impressive views, and a wealth of woodland wildlife.

TAKELEY

4 miles W of Great Dunmow off the A120

The village is built on the line of the old Roman **Stane Street**. There are plenty of pretty 17th century timbered houses and barns to be seen in the village, and the church still has many of its original Norman features along with some Roman masonry. Rather unusually, it has a modern font that is surmounted by a six-feet-high medieval cover.

HATFIELD BROAD OAK

3 miles SW of Great Dunmow off the B184

This very pretty village has many notable buildings for visitors to enjoy, including a church dating from Norman times, some delightful 18th century almshouses and several distinctive Georgian houses.

Nearby **Hatfield Forest** is a rare surviving example of a medieval Royal hunting forest. It has wonderful 400-year-old pollard trees, two ornamental lakes and an 18th century shell house. Once covering a great deal more land,

the remaining 400 hectares are now protected by the National Trust and offer splendid woodland walks along with good chases and rides.

AYTHORPE RODING

4 miles SW of Great Dunmow off the B184

Aythorpe Roding Windmill is the largest remaining post mill in Essex. Four storeys high, it was built around 1760 and remained in use up until 1935. It was fitted in the 1800s with a fantail which kept the sails pointing into the wind.

PLESHEY

5 miles SE of Great Dunmow off the A130

Pleshey, midway between Chelmsford and Great Dunmow, is surrounded by a mile-long earthen rampart, protecting its castle, of which only the motte with its moat and two baileys survive. There are good views from the mound, which although only 60 feet high, is nonetheless one of the highest points in Essex. The village is truly delightful, with a number of thatched cottages, and the area is excellent for walkers and ramblers.

SAWBRIDGEWORTH

6 miles SW of Great Dunmow off the A1184

Quite a number of fine old buildings, many of which are Georgian, survive in this small town. To the south is **Pishiobury**, built by James Wyatt in 1782, now a school. In St Mary's Church there are 15 wonderful ancient and beautifully preserved brasses.

H G Wells lived at Brick House in Great Dunmow, overlooking the Doctor's Pond, where in 1784 Lionel Lukin is reputed to have tested the first unsinkable lifeboat.

WALTHAM ABBEY

Along the Cornhill Stream, crossed by the impressive stone bridge, Waltham Abbey's Dragonfly Sanctuary is home to over half the native British species of dragonflies and damselflies. It is noted as the best single site for seeing these species in Greater London, Essex and Hertfordshire.

Sun Street is Waltham Abbey's main thoroughfare, and it is pedestrianised. It contains many buildings from the 16th century onwards. The Greenwich Meridian (0 degrees longitude) runs through the street, marked out on the pavement and through the Abbey Gardens.

The town of Waltham began as a small Roman settlement on the site of the present-day Market Square. The early Saxon kings maintained a hunting lodge here; a town formed round this, and the first church was built in the 6th century. By the 8th, during the reign of Cnut, the town had a stone minster church with a great stone crucifix that had been brought from Somerset, where it had been found buried in land owned by Tovi, a trusted servant of the king. This cross became the focus of pilgrims seeking healing. One of those cured of a serious illness, Harold Godwinsson, built a new church, the third on the site, which was dedicated in 1060 - and it was this self-same Harold who became king and was killed in the battle of Hastings six years later. Harold's body was brought back to Waltham to be buried in his church. The church that exists today was built in the first quarter of the 12th century. It was once three times its present length, and incorporated an Augustinian Abbey, built in 1177 by Henry II. The town became known for the Abbey, which was one of the largest in the country and the last to be the victim of Henry VIII's Dissolution of the Monasteries, in 1540.

The Abbey's Crypt Centre houses an interesting exhibition explaining the history of both the Abbey and the town, highlighting the religious significance of the site. Some visible remains of the Augustinian Abbey include the chapter house and precinct walls, cloister entry and gateway in the surrounding Abbey Gardens. The Abbey Gardens are also host to a Sensory Trail exploring the highlights of hundreds of years of the site's history; there's also a delightful Rose Garden.

A Tudor timber-framed house forms part of the **Epping Forest District Museum** in Sun Street. The wide range of displays includes exhibits covering the history of the Epping Forest District from the Stone Age to the 20th century. Tudor and Victorian times are particularly well represented, with some magnificent oak panelling dating from the reign of Henry VIII, and re-creations of Victorian rooms and shops. There is also an archaeological display and temporary exhibitions covering such subjects as contemporary arts and crafts. The museum has several hands-on displays which help to bring history to life, and features special events and adult workshops throughout the year.

In spite of its proximity to London and more recent development, the town retains a peaceful, traditional character, with its timber-framed buildings and small traditional market which has been held here since the early 12th century (now every Tuesday and Saturday). The whole of the town centre has been designated a conservation area. The Market Square boasts many fine and interesting buildings such as the lych-gate and The Welsh Harp, dating from the 17th and 16th centuries respectively.

The **Town Hall** offers a fine example of Art Nouveau style design, and houses the Waltham Abbey Town Council Offices and Epping Forest District Council Information Desk. The Tourist Information Centre is in Highbridge Street, opposite the entrance to the Abbey Church.

Gunpowder production became established in Waltham as early as the 1660s, and in 1787 the **Royal Gunpowder Mills** were acquired by the Crown. They became the pre-eminent powder works in Britain, employing up to 500 workers; production did not cease until 1943, after which time the factory became a research facility. In the spring of 2000, however, all this changed and much of the site is open to the public; some of the rest is a Site of Scientific Interest and the largest heronry in Essex.

Lee Valley Regional Park is a leisure area stretching for 26 miles along the River Lea (sometimes also spelled Lee) from East India Dock Basin, on the north bank of the River Thames in East London, to Hertfordshire. There's a range of facilities ideal for anglers, walkers and birdwatchers. The Lee Valley is an important area of high biodiversity, sustaining a large range of wildlife and birds. Two hundred species of birds, including internationally important populations of Gadwall and Shoveler ducks, can be seen each year on the wetlands and water bodies along the Lea. Of national importance for over-wintering waterbirds including rare species of bittern and smew, this fine park makes an ideal place for a picnic. Guided tours by appointment.

At the southern end of Lee Valley Park, **The House Mill**, one of two tidal mills still standing at this site, has been restored by the River Lea Tidal Mill Trust. It was built in 1776 in the Dutch style, and was used to grind grain for gin distilling.

Lee Valley Park Farms, along Stubbins Hall Lane, boasts two farms on site: Hayes Hill and Holyfield Hall. At Hayes Hill Farm, visitors can interact with the animals and enjoy a picnic or the children's adventure playground. This traditional farm also boasts old-fashioned tools and equipment, an exhibition in the medieval barn and occasional craft demonstrations. At Holyfield Hall Farm, a working farm and dairy, visitors can see milking and learn about modern farming methods. Seasonal events such as sheep-shearing and harvesting are held, and there's an attractive farm tea room and a toy shop. A farm trail is another of the site's attractions, offering wonderful views of the Lee Valley, an expanse of open countryside dotted with lakes and

To the west of town, the Lee Navigation Canal offers opportunities for anglers, walkers, birdwatching and pleasure craft. Once used for transporting corn and other commercial goods to the growing City of London, and having associations with the town's important gunpowder industry for centuries, the canal remains a vital part of town life.

226 ROYAL GUNPOWDER MILLS

Waltham Abbey

The Royal Gunpowder Mills offers a fascinating day out for everyone. The 300 year old gunpowder production site has been regenerated and offers a mix of history, science and beautiful surroundings.

see page 325

Myddleton House Gardens within Lee Valley Park is the place to see the work of the famous plantsman who created them - E A Bowles, the greatest amateur gardener of his time. Breathtaking colours and interesting plantings - such as the National Collection of award-winning bearded iris, the Tulip Terrace and the Lunatic Asylum (home to unusual plants) - are offset by a beautiful carp lake, two conservatories and a rock garden.

wildflower meadows attracting a wide range of wildlife including otters, bats, dragonfly, kingfisher, great-crested grebe and little-ringed plover. The area is ideal for walking or fishing, and the bird hides are open to all at weekends; permits available for daily access. Guided tours by arrangement.

AROUND WALTHAM ABBEY

LOUGHTON

5 miles SE of Waltham Abbey off the A121

Corbett Theatre in Rectory Lane in Loughton is a beautiful Grade I listed converted medieval tithe barn, where classical, modern and musical theatre productions are performed. The theatre is set in a five-acre site with lovely gardens.

Loughton borders **Epping Forest**, a magnificent and expansive tract of ancient hornbeam coppice, mainly tucked between the M25 and London. There are miles of leafy walks and rides (horses can be hired locally), with some rough grazing and occasional distant views. Just off the A104 running through the forest, in the middle of a field called The Warren, stands an obelisk that is a memorial to the horse of General Thomas Grosvenor, who lived here and died at the Battle of Waterloo in 1815.

ABRIDGE

7 miles SE of Waltham Abbey off the A113

The **BBC Essex Garden** at Crowther Nurseries, Ongar Road, is a working garden consisting of a vegetable plot, two small greenhouses, lawns and herbaceous and shrub borders. The garden is also home to a range of farmyard animals which visitors are welcome

Little Monk Wood, Epping Forest

to see and interact with, and there's a delightful tea shop filled with homemade cakes.

CHIGWELL

8 miles SE of Waltham Abbey off the A113

Hainault Forest Country Park is an ancient woodland covering 600 acres, with a lake and rare breeds farm, managed by the London Borough of Redbridge and the Woodland Trust for Essex County Council.

CHINGFORD

6 miles S of Waltham Abbey off the A11

Queen Elizabeth Hunting Lodge in Rangers Road, Chingford, is a timber-framed hunting grandstand first built for Henry VIII. This unique Tudor-era survivor boasts exceptional carpentry, and is situated in a beautiful part of Epping Forest with ancient oaks and fine views. The Lodge and the countryside around once provided a day out for thousands of Londoners, with buses arriving every few minutes and huge (and orderly) queues waiting for the homeward journey in the early evening.

HODDESDON

6 miles NW of Waltham Abbey off the A10

Rye House Gatehouse in Rye Road was built by Sir Andre Ogard, a Danish nobleman, in 1443. It is a moated building and a fine example of early English brickwork. Now restored, visitors can climb up to the battlements. A permanent exhibition covers the architecture and history of the Rye House Plot

Queen Elizabeth Hunting Lodge

to assassinate Charles II in 1683. Guided tours by prior arrangement. The building lies adjacent to a Royal Society for the Protection of Birds reserve. Other features include an information centre, shop, and circular walks around the site.

HARLOW

The 'New Town' of Harlow sometimes gets short shrift, but it is in fact a lively and vibrant place with a great deal more than excellent shopping facilities. There are some very good museums and several sites of historic interest.

The **Gibberd Collection** in Harlow Town Hall offers a delightful collection of British watercolours featuring works by Blackadder, Sutherland, Frink,

•

Harlow Museum in Passmores House, Third Avenue, occupies a Georgian manor house set in picturesque gardens which includes a lovely pond and is home to several species of butterfly. The museum has extensive and important Roman, post-medieval and early 20th century collections, as well as a full programme of temporary exhibitions.

•

183

Parndon Wood Nature Reserve, Parndon Wood Road in Harlow, is an ancient woodland with a fine variety of birds, mammals and insects. Facilities include two nature trails with hides for observing wildlife, and a study centre.

The explorer David Livingstone was a pupil pastor Chipping Ongar's United Reform Church, and lived in what are now called Livingstone Cottages before his missionary work in Africa began.

A short drive to the north of Bobbingworth is the village of High Laver, where the philosopher John Locke (1632-1704)is buried in the churchyard of All Saints.

Nash and Sir Frederick Gibberd, Harlow's master planner and the founder of the collection.

Mark Hall Cycle Museum and Gardens in Muskham Road offers a unique collection of cycles and cycling accessories illustrating the history of the bicycle from 1818 to the present day, including one made of plastic, one that folds, and one where the seat tips forward and throws its rider over the handlebars if the brakes are applied too hard. The museum is housed in a converted stable block within Mark Hall manor. Adjacent to the museum are three period walled gardens.

Gibberd Gardens, on the eastern outskirts of Harlow in Marsh Lane, Gilden Way, is well worth a visit, reflecting as it does the taste of Sir Frederick Gibberd, the famous architect. This 7-acre garden was designed by Sir Frederick on the side of a small valley, with terraces, wild garden, landscaped vistas, pools and streams and some 80 sculptures. Marsh Lane is a turning off the B183.

Harlow Study and Visitors Centre in Netteswellbury Farm is set in a medieval tithe barn and 13th century church. The site has displays outlining the story of Harlow New Town.

AROUND HARLOW

ROYDON

3 miles W of Harlow off the A414

Preserved in this handsome village are the old parish cage, stocks and a whipping post. Just about 1 mile

southwest of Roydon are the ruins of Tudor **Nether Hall**, a manor house that once belonged to the Coates family. Here Thomas More came to woo and win the elder daughter of John Coates.

CHIPPING ONGAR

8 miles SE of Harlow on the A414

Today firmly gripped in the commuter belt of London, Chipping Ongar began as a Saxon market town protected beneath the walls of a Norman castle. The motte and bailey were built by Richard de Lucy in 1155. Indeed, the town's name comes from 'cheaping', meaning market. Only the mound and moat of the castle remain, but the contemporary **Church of St Martin of Tours** still stands. Built in 1080, it has fine Norman flint walls and an anchorite's recess.

BOBBINGWORTH

2 miles NW of Chipping Ongar off the A414

Blake Hall Gardens at Bobbingworth near Chipping Ongar incorporates a Tropical House, an Ice House, Bog garden, wild gardens, herbaceous borders, rose garden, sunken garden, duck pond and an ornamental wood. The south wing of Blake Hall itself houses the **Airscene Aviation Museum** run by local RAF enthusiasts.

WILLINGALE

3 miles NE of Chipping Ongar off the B184

St Christopher's and **St Andrew's**, churches of the respective parishes of Willingale Doe and Willingale

Spain, stand side by side in the same churchyard in the heart of this lovely village. St Andrew's is the older, dating back to the 12th century.

FYFIELD

2 miles N of Chipping Ongar off the B184

The name 'Fyfield' means five river meadows. Originally a Saxon enclave, the village church of St Nicholas is Norman. There's a beautiful mill house with flood gates in the village. **Fyfield Hall**, opposite the church, is said to be the oldest inhabited timber frame building in England (it dates from AD 870).

BEAUCHAMP RODING

3 miles NE of Chipping Ongar off the B184

One of the eight Rodings, it was at Beauchamp Roding that a local farm labourer, Isaac Mead, worked and saved enough to become a farmer himself in 1882. To show his gratitude to the land that made him his fortune, he had a corner of the field consecrated as an eternal resting place for himself and his family. Their graves can still be seen in the undergrowth.

GOOD EASTER AND HIGH EASTER

5 miles NE of Chipping Ongar off the B184

A quiet farming village, now in the commuter belt for London, Good Easter's claim to fame is the making of a world-record daisy chain (6,980 feet 7 inches) in 1985. The village's interesting name is probably derived from 'Easter', the Old English for 'sheepfolds' and

'Good' from a Saxon lady named Godiva.

Close to Good Easter, and thus named because it stands on higher ground than its neighbour, High Easter is a quiet and very picturesque village not far from the impressive **Aythorpe Post Mill**.

BLACKMORE

3 miles E of Chipping Ongar off the A414

The plague almost totally destroyed the village of Blackmore. Red Rose Lane was so-named because a red rose had to be given at the toll to indicate clear health from the dreaded disease. Henry VIII's mistress Bessie Blount lived in Jericho Priory in the village. Her son by Henry, the Earl of Rochford, also made his home here.

INGATESTONE

6 miles E of Chipping Ongar off the B1002

Ingatestone Hall on Hall Lane is a 16th century mansion set in 11 acres of grounds that include a fine walled garden and extensive lawns with specimen trees. It was built by Sir William Petre, Secretary of State to four monarchs, whose family continue to reside here. The Hall contains family portraits, furniture and memorabilia accumulated over the centuries. The Church of St Edmund and St Mary is notable for its magnificent redbrick tower and the many monuments to Sir William, who rebuilt the south chapel, and other members of the Petre family. Just north of Ingatestone, at **Fryerning**, the 16th century **Church of St Mary** contains a memorial to the MP

Beauchamp's Church of St Botolph stands alone in the fields, marked by a tall 15th century tower and reached by a track off the B184. Inside, the raised pews at the west end have clever space-saving wooden steps, pulled out of slots by means of iron rings.

227 INGATESTONE HALL

Ingatestone
Ingatestone Hall is a 16th century mansion and grounds, still retaining much of its original appearance and still occupied by the decendants of its original Tudor owner.

🏛 *see page 326*

200 THE VIPER

Mill Green, north of Ingatestone

The Viper enjoys a secluded rural setting, notable real ales and home-cooked lunches.

 see page 311

201 THE CRICKETERS

Mill Green, nr Ingatestone

The food is outstanding at **The Cricketers**, a fine village pub dating from the early 19th century.

 see page 311

202/218 THE WHITE HART

Margaretting Tye, south of Chelmsford

The White Hart is an outstanding family-friendly pub with fine food, lots of cask ales and two annual beer festivals.

 see pages 312 and 320

Airey Neave, a native of the parish who was killed by the IRA in 1979. The window was designed by his cousin Penelope and shows St Michael and St Christopher, with roundels depicting Colditz, where he was a prisoner of war, and the Houses of Parliament.

MARGARETTING TYE

6 miles E of Chipping Ongar off the A12/B1007

The nickname of this town is 'Tigers Island'. Legend has it that in bygone days, bare-knuckle fights known as 'Tigers' would take place on Fridays, and the 'island' part of its soubriquet derives from the fact that in ancient times the area was subject to flooding all round the village.

MOUNTNESSING

6 miles SE of Chipping Ongar off the A12

This village has a beautifully restored early-19th century windmill as its main landmark, though the isolated church also has a massive beamed belfry. **Mountnessing Post Mill** in Roman Road is open to the public. This traditional weather-boarded post mill was built in 1807 and restored to working order in 1983. Visitors can see the huge wooden and iron gears; one pair of stones have been opened up for viewing.

KELVEDON HATCH

4 miles S of Chipping Ongar off the A128

A simple bungalow in the rural Essex village of Kelvedon Hatch is the deceptively simple exterior for the **Kelvedon Secret Nuclear Bunker**. Built in 1952, 40,000 tons of concrete were used to create a base some 80 feet underground for up to 600 top Government and civilian personnel in the event of nuclear war. Visitors can explore room after room to see communications equipment, a BBC studio, sick bay, massive kitchens and dormitories, power and filtration plant, government administration room and the scientists' room, where nuclear fall-out patterns would have been measured.

GREENSTED

1½ miles SW of Chipping Ongar off the A414

St Andrew's in Greensted is almost certainly the world's oldest wooden church, dating from the 9th to 11th centuries, with a later Tudor chancel. It is famous as the only surviving example of a Saxon log church extant in the world, built from split oak logs from Epping Forest, held together with dowells. Over the centuries the church has been enlarged and restored; later additions include the simple weather-boarded tower, Norman flint walls, the Tudor tiled roof, Victorian stone coping, porch and stained glass windows. The body of King Edmund (later canonised a saint) is believed to have rested here in 1013.

The village also has associations with the Tolpuddle Martyrs - six Dorset farm labourers who were taken to court on a legal technicality because they agitated for better conditions and wages, and formed a Trades Union. After their conviction in 1834 they were condemned to transportation to Australia for seven years. There was a public outcry for their release, and their sentences were commuted in 1837. Unable to return to Dorset, they were granted tenancies in Greensted and High Laver. One of the martyrs, James Brine, of New House Farm (now Tudor Cottage, on Greensted Green), married Elizabeth Standfield, daughter of one of his fellow victims - the record of their marriage in 1839 can be seen in the parish register.

NORTH WEALD

3 miles W of Chipping Ongar off the A414

North Weald Airfield Museum and Memorial at Ad Astra House, Hurricane Way, North Weald Bassett is a small, meticulously detailed 'House of Memories' displaying the history of the famous airfield and all who served at RAF North Weald from 1916 to the present. Collections of photos and artefacts such as uniforms and the detailed records of all flying operations are on display. There is also a video exhibit recounting a day-to-day account of North Weald history. Guided tours of the airfield can be arranged for large groups.

BRENTWOOD

Brentwood is a very pleasant shopping and entertainment centre, with quite a distinguished past. The town was on the old pilgrim and coaching routes to and from London. Mainly post-war in character, the town is the setting for the UK headquarters of Ford Motors.

Brentwood Cathedral on Ingrave Road was built in 1991. This classically-styled church incorporates the original Victorian church that stood on this spot. It was designed by the much-admired architect Quinlan Terry, with roundels by Raphael Maklouf (who also created the relief of the Queen's head used on current coins).

Brentwood Centre on Doddinghurst Road is one of the top entertainment venues in the UK, with an extensive programme of concerts, shows, bands and top comedy names, and extensive sports and fitness facilities.

Brentwood Museum at Cemetery Lode in Lorne Road, in the Warley Hill area of Brentwood, is a small and picturesque cottage museum concentrating on local and social interests during the late 19th and early 20th centuries.

AROUND BRENTWOOD

BILLERICAY

6 miles E of Brentwood off the A129

There was a settlement here as far back as the Bronze Age, though there is to date no conclusive explanation of Billericay's name. There is no question about the attraction of the High Street,

•

Thorndon Country Park, on the outskirts of Brentwood, boasts historic parkland, lakes and woods. The site, formerly a Royal deer park, also features a wildlife exhibition and attractive gift shop. Fishing is also available.

•

228 KELVEDON HATCH SECRET NUCLEAR BUNKER

Brentwood

This bunker was built in 1952 as a base from which the government and military could have run operations in the event of a nuclear war.

 see page 326

•

The Peasants' Revolt of 1381 saw the massacre of hundreds of rebels just northeast of Billericay, at Norsey Wood. Today this area of ancient woodland is a country park, managed by coppicing (the traditional way of ensuring the timber supply), which also encourages plant and birdlife.

•

though, with its timber weather-boarding and Georgian brick. **The Chantry House**, built in 1510, was the home of Christopher Martin, treasurer to the Pilgrim Fathers.

Barleylands Farm Museum and Visitors' Centre features a glass-blowing studio, blacksmith's and other craft shops, a wealth of farm animals, chick hatchery, duck pond and one of the largest collections of vintage farm machinery in the country, together with a play area, picnic area and, on Sunday afternoons, a steam railway.

GREAT WARLEY

1 mile S of Brentwood on the B186

Warley Place was formerly home to one of the most famous female gardeners, Ellen Willmott, who died in 1934. She introduced to Warley - and to Britain - many exotic plants. A trail takes visitors through what is now Warley Place Nature Reserve, with 16 acres of what was once domesticated garden but has now reverted to woodland. A fascinating selection of trees, shrubs and wildlife makes this well worth a visit.

SOUTH WEALD

2 miles W of Brentwood off the A12

This very attractive village has, at its outskirts, **Weald Country Park**, a former estate with medieval deer park, partially landscaped in the 1700s. Featuring lake and woodland, visitors' centre, landscapes exhibition and gift shop, with facilities for fishing and horse-riding, there are guided events and activities programmes held

throughout the year.

Another good day out in the open air can be had at **Old Macdonald's Educational Farm Park**, where visitors can see the largest selection of pure-bred British farm animals and poultry in the southeast of England.

THE NORTH THAMES CORRIDOR

Bordering the north bank of the Thames, the borough of **Thurrock** has long been a gateway to London but also affords easy access to southwest Essex and to Kent. This thriving borough encompasses huge swathes of green belt country, and along its 18 miles of Thames frontage there are many important marshland wildlife habitats. This stretch of Essex affords some marvellous walking, cycling, birdwatching and other nature pursuits. The area has many bridleways, footpaths and country parks, including Davy Down within the Mardyke Valley. The river's flood plain is a broad tract of grassland which is an important feature of the landscape of the area.

GRAYS

4 miles S of Brentwood off the M25

Thurrock Museum is in the Thamesside Complex in Grays. It collects, conserves and displays items of archaeology and local history from prehistoric times to the end of the 20th century. The archaeological items include flint and metal tools of people who lived in prehistoric Thurrock and pottery, jewellery and coins from the Roman and Saxon period.

WEST THURROCK

1½ miles SW of Grays off the A13

Immortalised by the film *Four Weddings and a Funeral*, little **St Clement's Church** occupies a striking location and is one of a number of picturesque ancient churches in the borough. Although this 12th century church is now deconsecrated, it was in its day a stopping point for pilgrims; visitors can see the remains of its original round tower. There is also a mass grave to the boys of the reformatory ship *Cornwall* who were drowned in an accident off Purfleet.

PURFLEET

3 miles W of Grays off the M25/A13

Fans of Bram Stoker's novel *Dracula* will know that in this book the famous vampire buys a house called 'Carfax' in Purfleet. The town's esteemed **Royal Hotel**, by the Thames, is said to have played host to Edward VII, while still Prince of Wales in the 1880s and 1890s, at which time the hotel was called Wingrove's.

The **Purfleet Heritage and Military Centre** is a heritage and military museum featuring displays of many items of interest and memorabilia in the setting of the No 5 Gunpowder Magazine on Centurion Way. This remaining magazine was built in the 1770s for testing and issuing gun powder to the army and navy.

AVELEY

3 miles NW of Grays off the A13

Mardyke Valley is an important wildlife corridor running from Ship Lane in Aveley to Orsett Fen. Many pleasant views can be had along the seven-mile stretch of footpaths and bridleways. Davy Down within Mardyke Valley consists of riverside meadows, ponds and wetland. The Visitors' Centre is in the well-preserved water pumping station on the B186 near South Ockendon.

Aveley's 12th century **St Michael's Church** features many Flemish brasses and other items of historical interest.

SOUTH OCKENDON

3 miles N of Grays off the A13/A1306

Belhus Woods Country Park covers approximately 250 acres and contains an interesting variety of habitats, including woodland, two lakes and the remains of a pond designed by 'Capability' Brown. The Visitors' Centre to this superb park can be found at the main entrance off Romford Road. Belhus Park Golf Course is a well-established 18-hole course set within this beautiful parkland.

Grangewaters Country Park, also in South Ockendon, has two lakes. Managed by Thurrock Environmental and Outdoor Education Centre, it offers watersports such as windsurfing, sailing and canoeing, as well as off-road biking, climbing and other outdoor pursuits. **Brannetts Wood** is one of the oldest recorded

Purfleet Conservation Area includes several buildings which were part of a planned village built by the one-time owners of the chalk quarry, the Whitbread family.

South Ockenden's Church of St Nicholas has one of only six round church towers in Essex. This one was built in the 13th century and used to have a spire, which was sadly destroyed by lightning in the 17th century.

ancient woodlands in South Essex. It can be reached from the Mardyke Way, or from South Road here in South Ockendon.

HORNDON-ON-THE HILL

6 miles NE of Grays off the B1007/A13

Listed in the *Domesday Book* as *Horninduna*, a name which also appears on a Saxon coin of Edward the Confessor (1042-1066), it is said to have once been the site of a Royal Anglo-Saxon mint. The town's 16th century **Woolmarket** indicates the importance of the wool trade to the region, and is one of the area's historical treasures. The upper room served as Horndon's manor courtroom, while the lower, open area was used for trading in woollen cloth.

The main entrance and Visitors' Centre for **Langdon Hills Conservation Centre and Nature Reserve** are located off the Lower Dunton Road north of Horndon-on-the-Hill. A bridleway and footpaths lead visitors to meadows, a pond and outstanding ancient woods. Also within the reserve is the **Plotlands Museum**, housed in an original 1930s plotland bungalow known as the Haven.

LINFORD

3 miles NE of Grays off the A13/A1013

Walton Hall Museum on Walton Hall Road has a large collection of historic farm machinery in a 17th century barn. It affords visitors the opportunity to watch traditional craftsmen, such as a blacksmith, saddlemaker, printer and

wheelwright, together with a printing shop, baker's, dairy and nursery.

STANFORD-LE-HOPE

4 miles NE of Grays off the A1014

Stanford Marshes is an area to the south of Stanford-le-Hope, next to the Thames. The Marshes are home to a variety of wildlife and are an ideal location for birdwatching. **Grove House Wood** in Stanford-le-Hope is a nature reserve managed by Essex Wildlife Trust and the local Girl Guides. A footpath here leads to reed beds, a pond and a brook as well as an area of woodland.

The graveyard of St Margaret's Church has an unusual half-barrelled tomb, for one James Adams (d. 1765), that is decorated with a gruesome stone-carved symbol of death.

CANVEY ISLAND

10 miles NE of Grays off the A130

Canvey Island is a peaceful and picturesque stretch of land overlooking the Thames estuary with views to neighbouring Kent.

The island boasts two unusual museums: **Dutch Cottage Museum** is an early 17th century eight-sided cottage built by Dutch workmen for Dutch workmen and boasting many traditional Flemish features. **Castle Point Transport Museum** is housed in a 1930s bus garage. It houses an interesting collection of historic and modern buses and coaches, mainly of East Anglian origin.

The **Canvey Miniature**

Railway at the Waterside Farm Centre has two steam miniature railways guaranteed to delight the child in all of us.

WEST TILBURY

3 miles E of Grays off the A1089

West Tilbury was the site chosen for the Camp Royal in 1588, to prepare for the threatened Spanish invasion. Queen Elizabeth I visited the army here, and made her famous speech, *'I know I have the body but of a weak and feeble woman: but I have the heart and stomach of a king, and a king of England too.'*

Hidden away in rural tranquillity over-looking the Thames estuary, West Tilbury remains unspoilt in spite of its proximity to busy, industrial Tilbury.

EAST TILBURY

5 miles E of Grays off the A13

Coalhouse Fort is considered to be one of the best surviving examples of a Victorian Casement fortress in the country. As such it is a protected Scheduled Ancient Monument. Built between 1861 and 1874 as a first line of defence to protect the Thames area against invasion, it stands on the site of other defensive works and fortifications dating back to around 1400. Even before the Middle Ages, this was an important site.

Part of the construction work on the Fort was overseen by Gordon of Khartoum. It was constructed to be a dedicated Artillery casement fortress, which meant that the guns were housed in large vaulted rooms with armour-plated frontages. Beneath these rooms lies an extensive magazine tunnel system to service the artillery.

Over the years many alterations were made to the Fort to accommodate new artillery. The Fort was manned during both World Wars, and is now owned by Thurrock Borough Council and administered by The Coalhouse Fort Project, a registered charity manned entirely by volunteers. Open to the public, it contains reconstructions of period guns and other displays, and also houses the **Thamesside Aviation Museum**, with a large collection of local finds and other aviation material. In the two parade grounds visitors will find various artillery pieces and military vehicles. One recent addition to the many pieces of historical military equipment is a Bofor Anti-Aircraft Gun of the Second World War. The site also offers visitors the chance to handle period equipment or try on a period uniform.

During the year the Fort hosts a range of shows, including an historic artillery rally when various big guns are fired by crews in the uniforms of the period, including a Second World War crew firing a 1940 25-pounder field gun. A guided tour (included in the price of admission) allows visitors to see the magazine tunnels beneath the gun casements and offers a feel for the work and conditions of a Victorian gunner. The tour also takes in the roof of the Fort, from

The former local church (now a private dwelling) in West Tilbury is a nautical landmark used for navigation. The list of Rectors of the church, dating from 1279-1978, when the church was disestablished, can be seen in The Kings Head Pub.

The Bata Estate at East Tilbury is a conservation area of architectural and historical interest. Established in 1933, the British Bata Shoe Company was the creation of Czech-born Thomas Bata, who also developed a housing estate for his workforce. The uniform flat-roofed houses can still be seen on the site.

- *Tilbury Energy and Environment Centre at Tilbury Power Station provides a nature reserve and study centre for schools and community education. There is a flat two-mile nature trail leading to and from the Centre.*

which you will be able to judge for yourself the value of a fortification at this point along the Thames. The view from here is outstanding, taking in the two sister forts in Kent and, on a clear day, Southend.

The Fort is set in a lovely riverside park with walks and a children's play area, as well as other items of military history including a Quick Fire Battery and Minefield Control box. You can also follow the old railway tracks from the Fort to the side of the old jetty, where many of the armaments and supplies for the fort were shipped in.

TILBURY

3 miles SE of Grays off the A1089

Tilbury Fort is a well-preserved and unusual 17th century structure with double moat. The largest and best example of military engineering in England at that time, the fort also affords tremendous views of the Thames estuary. The most violent episode in the fort's history occurred in 1776, during a particularly vociferous cricket match which left three people dead. For a small fee visitors to the fort can fire a 1943 3.7mm anti-aircraft gun - a prospect most children and many adults find irresistible! Owned by English Heritage, the site was used for a military Block House during the reign of Henry VIII and was rebuilt in the 17th century. It remains one of Britain's finest examples of a star-shaped bastion fortress. Extensions were made in the 18th and 19th centuries, and the Fort was still being used in the Second World War.

Tilbury Festival is held every year in July in the field near the fort, and features arena events, craft and food stalls, and living history re-enactments.

SOUTHEND-ON-SEA

Beside the seaside in Southend-on-Sea there is always plenty to do and see, and many events are held throughout the year to ensure its continuing interest and popularity. The town is one of the best loved and most friendly resorts in Britain, featuring the very best ingredients for a break at the seaside. With seven miles of beaches, this treasure trove boasts **Adventure Island** theme park, **Cliffs Bandstand**, **Cliffs**

Sea Front, Southend-on-Sea

Pavilion, a distinguished art gallery and several interesting museums.

Southend Pier and Museum brings to life the fascinating past of the longest Pleasure Pier in the world. The Pier itself is well over a mile in length and visitors can either enjoy a leisurely walk along to the end or take advantage of the regular electric railway service that plies up and down the pier alongside the walkway.

Central Museum, Planetarium and Discovery Centre on Victoria Avenue is the only planetarium in the southeast outside London, and also features local history exhibits, archaeology and wildlife exhibits. **Beecroft Art Gallery** boasts the work of four centuries of artistic endeavour, with some 2,000 works on display.

Sealife Adventure employs the most advanced technology to bring visitors incredibly close to the wonders of British marine life, offering fun ways of exploring life under the waves, with concave bubble windows helping to make it seem you're actually part of the sea-creatures' environment. Another exhibit features a walk-through tunnel along a reconstructed seabed. The Shark Exhibition is not to be missed.

A floral trail guided tour around the parks and gardens will reveal why Southend has won the Britain in Bloom Awards so often, as well as winning medals at the Chelsea Flower Show.

Southend-on-Sea Beach

The Kursaal on the Eastern Esplanade is an indoor entertainment complex, one of the largest in the country, with indoor bowling, synthetic ice and roller rink, a fun casino, children's play area, snooker and pool, arts and crafts, retail units and theme restaurants.

Boat trips in summer include occasional outings on a vintage paddle steamer. Ferry trips to Felixstowe are also available from Southend.

The **Southchurch Hall Museum** in Park Lane is a delightful 13th to 14th century timber-framed manor house with various displays and landscaped gardens. Period room settings are among this museum's many delights.

•

Prittlewell Priory Museum, slightly north of Southend town centre in Priory Park, is a well-preserved 12th century Cluniac Priory set in lovely grounds and housing collections of the Priory's history, natural history and the Caten collection of radios and communications equipment.

•

Hadleigh Castle Country Park offers a variety of woodland and coastal walks in grounds overlooking the Thames estuary. A Guided Events programme runs throughout the year.

Rayleigh Windmill, in Bellingham Lane close to Rayleigh Mount, was built around 1809; the tower mill houses a fascinating collection of bygones mostly used in and around Rayleigh. Refreshments are available from the coffee shop adjacent to the mill.

AROUND SOUTHEND

OLD LEIGH

½ mile W of Southend off the A13

The unspoilt fishing village of Old Leigh has a long and distinguished history. It is picturesque, with seafront houses and narrow winding alleys. It has also earned its place in history: The pilgrim ship *The Mayflower* restocked here en route to the New World of America back in the mid-17th century, and the Dunkirk rescue embarked from here, as commemorated in a framed poem on the wall of the local pub, The Crooked Billet.

LEIGH-ON-SEA

2 miles W of Southend off the A13

Leigh-on-Sea has a quite different character from Southend, being more intimate and serene, with wood-clad buildings and shrimp boats in the working harbour. The shellfish stall on the harbourside is justly famous. The **Leigh Heritage Centre**, housed in a former ancient blacksmith's in the waterside High Street of the Old Town, now houses historical artefacts including a photographic display of the history of Leigh-on-Sea.

HADLEIGH

5 miles NW of Southend off the A13

Hadleigh Castle, built originally for Edward III, is owned by English Heritage and once belonged to Anne of Cleves, Catherine of Aragon and Katherine Parr. The ruins were also immortalised in a painting by Constable. The remains of this once impressive castle can still be seen. The curtain walls towers, which survive almost to their full height, overlook the Essex marshes and the Thames estuary.

HULLBRIDGE

8 miles NW of Southend off the A132

Jakapeni Rare Breed Farm at Burlington Gardens in Hullbridge is a pleasant small-holding set in 30 acres of rolling countryside. Specialising in sheep and pigs, with other pets and wildlife, there's also a fishing lake, country walk and pets corner. Snacks and light refreshments are available from the café, and there's an attractive shop.

HOCKLEY

6 miles NW of Southend off the A129

Hockley Woods is a 280-acre ancient woodland, managed for the benefit of wildlife and for the public. Traditional coppice management encourages a diverse array of flora and fauna, including the nationally rare Heath Fritillary butterfly.

RAYLEIGH

6 miles NW of Southend off the A1016

Dutch Cottage at Crown Hill in Rayleigh is a tiny traditional Flemish eight-sided cottage based on a 17th century design created by Dutch settlers.

Rayleigh Mount is a prominent landmark in this part of the county. Once a motte-and-bailey castle built in the 11th century, it was abandoned some 200 years later.

ROCHFORD

3 miles N of Southend off the B1013

The Old House, at 17 South Street, is an elegant, lovingly restored house originally built in 1270. The twisting corridors and handsome rooms of this fine structure offer a glimpse into the past; the building now houses some District Council offices, and is said to be haunted.

CHELMSFORD

Roman workmen cutting their great road linking London with Colchester built a fort at what is today called Chelmsford. Then called *Caesaromagus*, it stands at the confluence of the Rivers Chelmer and Can. The town has always been an important market centre and is now the bustling county town of Essex. It is also directly descended from a new town planned by the Bishop of London in 1199. At its centre are the principal inn, the **Royal Saracen's Head**, and the elegant **Shire Hall** of 1791. Three plaques situated high up on the eastern face of the Hall overlooking the High Street represent Wisdom, Justice and Mercy. The building now houses the town magistrates court.

Christianity came to Essex with the Romans and again, later, with St Cedd (AD 654); in 1914 the diocese of Chelmsford was created. **Chelmsford Cathedral** in New Street dates from the 15th century and is built on the site of a church constructed 800 years ago. The cathedral is noted for the harmony and unity of its perpendicular architecture. It was John Johnson, the distinguished local architect who designed both the Shire Hall and the 18th century **Stone Bridge** over the River Can, who also rebuilt the Parish Church of St Mary when most of its 15th century tower fell down. The church became a cathedral when the new diocese of Chelmsford was created. Since then it has been enlarged and re-organised inside. The cathedral boasts memorial windows dedicated to the USAAF airmen who were based in Essex from 1942 to 1945.

The Marconi Company, pioneers in the manufacture of wireless equipment, set up the first radio company in the world here in Chelmsford, in 1899. Exhibits of those pioneering days of wireless can be seen in the **Chelmsford Museum** in Oaklands Park, Moulsham Street, as can interesting displays of Roman remains and local history. Fine and decorative arts (ceramics, costume, glass), coins, natural history (live beehive, animals, geological exhibits) rub shoulders with displays exploring the history of the distinguished Essex Regiment. This section relates the history of the 44th and 56th Regiments from 1741 to the modern Royal Anglian Regiment. Exhibits include regimental colours and silver and four Victoria Crosses. The museum is set in a lovely park complete with children's play area.

Three modern technologies - electrical engineering, radio, and

229 CHELMSFORD MUSEUM & ESSEX REGIMENT MUSEUM

Moulsham Street, Chelmsford

A variety of displays illustrate the history of Chelsford and its people. The Essex Regiment museum is on the same site.

 see page 327

Also in Chelmsford, at Parkway, is Moulsham Mill Business & Craft Centre, set in an early 18th century water mill that has been renovated and now houses a variety of craft workshops and businesses. Crafts featured include jewellery, pottery, flowers, lace-making, dolls houses and bears, and decoupage work. There is a charming picnic area nearby, and a good café.

203 THE WHITE SWAN

Bicknacre, southeast of Chelmsford

The White Swan is a traditional village pub serving real ales, bar snacks and weekend restaurant meals.

 see page 313

204 THE WHITE HART

Little Waltham, north of Chelmsford

A friendly welcome awaits visitors to the **White Hart**, which offers real ales and menus for all tastes and appetites.

see page 313

216 GARNISH HALL

Margaret Roding, on the A1060 between Chelmsford and Bishops Stortford

Garnish Hall is a delightful, civilised rural retreat with three beautiful bedrooms and lovely gardens and grounds.

 see page 318

From a tucked-away corner of St John's Green in Writtle came Britain's first regular broadcasting service, an experimental 15-minute programme beamed out nightly by Marconi's engineers.

ball and roller bearings - began in Chelmsford. At the **Engine House Project** at Sandford Mill Waterworks, museum collections from the town's unique industrial story provide a fun and fascinating insight into the science of everyday things.

AROUND CHELMSFORD

GREAT BADDOW

1 mile S of Chelmsford off the A12/A130

Baddow Antiques Centre at The Bringy, Church Street, is one of the leading antiques centres in Essex. Here, 20 dealers offer a wide selection of silver, porcelain, glass, furniture, paintings and collectibles.

SANDON

2 miles SE of Chelmsford off the A414

The village green here in Sandon has produced a notable Spanish oak tree, the biggest in the country, planted in the centre of the village green. This oak tree is remarkable not so much for its height as for the tremendous horizontal spread of its branches. Around the green are a fine church and a number of attractive old houses, some dating back to the 16th century when Henry VIII's Lord Chancellor, Cardinal Wolsey, was Lord of the Manor of Sandon.

SOUTH HANNINGFIELD

6 miles S of Chelmsford off the A130

The placid waters of nearby **Hanningfield Reservoir** were created by damming Sandford

Brook, and transformed the scattered rural settlement of Hanningfield into a lakeside village. Now on the shores of the lake, the 12th century village church's belfry has been a local landmark in the flat Essex countryside for centuries. Some of the timbers in the belfry are said to have come from Spanish galleons, wrecked in the aftermath of Sir Francis Drake's defeat of the Armada.

The Visitor Centre at the Reservoir overlooks the 870-acre reservoir and the gateway to the 100-acre woodland beyond. The Centre also offers refreshments, a gift shop and toilet.

WRITTLE

2 miles W of Chelmsford off the A414

Hylands House was built in 1728; this beautiful neo-Classical Grade II listed villa is set in over 500 acres of parkland landscaped by Repton. Rooms that are open to the public include the Blue Room, Entrance Hall, Library, Saloon, Boudoir and Drawing Room. Host to many outdoor events, including the annual 'V' concerts and the Chelmsford Spectacular, **Hylands Park** features lawns, rhododendron bushes, woodland paths, ornamental ponds and Pleasure Gardens adjacent to the House.

Writtle's parish church of St John features a cross of charred timbers, a reminder of the fire which gutted the chancel in 1974. Ducks swim on the pond of the larger and quite idyllic main village green, which is surrounded by lovely Tudor and Georgian houses.

WITHAM

6 miles NE of Chelmsford off the A12/B1018

The River Brain flows through this delightful town; a continuous walk has been created along its length for a distance of about three miles. The settlement dates back to at least the 10th century; remains of a Roman temple have been found at Ivy Chimneys, off Hatfield Road. Blackwater Lane leads to Whetmead, a nature reserve of 25 acres between the rivers Blackwater and Brain.

The **Dorothy L Sayers Centre** in Newland Street houses a collection of books by and about Sayers, the theologian, Dante scholar and novelist/creator of the Lord Peter Wimsey mysteries, who lived in Witham for many years.

LITTLE BRAXTED

6 miles NE of Chelmsford off the A12/B1018

Little Braxted has been voted the best-kept village on a regular basis since 1973. The privately owned St Mary's chapel was built in 1888, and can accommodate only 12 people at a time. The village church of St Nicholas is mentioned in the *Domesday Book*, and is famous for its murals.

LITTLE BADDOW

5 miles E of Chelmsford off the A414

Blakes Wood is a designated Site of Special Scientific Interest, an ancient woodland of hornbeam and sweet chestnut renowned for its bluebells. There is a good circular way-marked one-and-a-half mile walk.

St Nicholas' Church , Little Braxted

DANBURY

5 miles E of Chelmsford off the A414

This village is said to take its name from the Danes who invaded this part of the country in the Dark Ages. In the fine church, under a rare 13th century carved effigy, a crusader knight was found when the tomb was opened in 1779, perfectly preserved in the pickle which filled his coffin. Fine carving is also a feature of the bench ends;

Cruising along the Chelmer and Blackwater Canal provides the visitor with a unique view of this part of rural Essex. Chelmer Cruises & Canal Centre at Paper Mill Lock in Little Baddow offers the barge Victoria for group hire.

206/219 THE BLUE BOAR HOTEL

Silver Street, Maldon

Continuing a tradition of hospitality dating back to the 14th century, **The Blue Boar** offers comfortable accommodation, home cooking and fine beers and car park.

 see pages 313 and 321

207 MALONES DINER

High Street, Maldon

Malones Diner provides a taste of America in relaxed surroundings on Maldon's historic High Street.

see page 314

205 MILL BEACH

Heybridge, nr Maldon

A warm welcome for all the family, summer lunches and a garden by the Blackwater Estuary are among the attractions at **Mill Beach**.

see page 313

the oldest among them have inspired modern craftsmen to continue the same style of carving on all the pews. In 1402, *'the devil appeared in the likeness of Firor Minor, who entered the church, raged insolently to the great terror of the parishioners ... the top of the steeple was broken down and half the chancel scattered abroad.'* And, in 1941, another harbinger of disaster, a 500-lb German bomb, reduced the east end to ruins.

At **Danbury Common**, acres of gorse flower in a blaze of golden colour for much of the year. Along with Lingwood Common, Danbury Common is at the highest point of the gravel ridge between Maldon and Chelmsford. There is evidence here of Napoleonic defences and old reservoirs. Circular nature trails make exploring the area easily accessible. To the west, Danbury Country Park offers another pleasant stretch of open country, boasting woodland, a lake and ornamental gardens.

WOODHAM WALTER

6 miles E of Chelmsford off the B1010

Woodham Walter is a small village which lies two and a half miles west of the ancient market town and coastal port of Maldon. It is rumoured that Henry VIII hunted in Woodham Walter during his reign. During the troubled times after Henry's death, Mary Tudor was concealed in Woodham Walter Hall, from where she was planning to escape from England in 1550. The church in Woodham Walter, **St Michael's**, was constructed in April 1563.

MALDON

10 miles E of Chelmsford on the A414

Maldon's High Street has existed since medieval times, and the alleys and mews leading from it are full of intriguing shops, welcoming old inns and good places to eat. One of the most distinctive features of the High Street is the **Moot Hall**. Built in the 14th century for the D'Arcy family, this building passed into the hands of the town corporation and was the seat of power in Maldon for over 400 years. The original brick spiral staircase (the best-preserved of its kind in England) and the 18th century courtroom are of particular interest. Guided tours are available on Saturdays in summer and by appointment with Maldon Town Council (01621 857373) at other times.

A colourful appliquéd embroidery made to commemorate the 1,000th anniversary of the crucial Battle of Maldon (see Northey Island, below) is on display at the **Maeldune Heritage Centre** (Maeldune being the Saxon name for Maldon). The Centre is housed in the Grade I listed St Peter's Building, erected in the 17th century by a local benefactor when the nave of the church that had once stood on this site collapsed. It can be found at the junction of the High Street and the steep and architecturally interesting Market Hill. The benefactor, one Thomas Plume, erected the building to house his collection of 6,000 books and a school; **The Plume Library**

Maldon Basin

208 CHIGBOROUGH LODGE RESTAURANT

Heybridge, nr Maldon

This restaurant is hidden amidst beautiful lakes. Enjoy the friendly atmosphere and fine dining. Evening a la carte, lunch and lighter lunch menus.

see page 314

209 HURDLEMAKERS ARMS

Woodham Mortimer, west of Maldon

The Hurdlemakers Arms is a cosy village pub serving real ales and a good choice of home-cooked dishes, plus weekend summer barbecues.

see page 314

•

Ruins are all that remain of the St Giles the Leper Hospital, founded by King Henry II in the 12th century. As with all monastic buildings, it fell into disuse after Henry VIII's Dissolution of the Monasteries, though it retained its roof and was used as a barn until the late 19th century. Many other buildings in Maldon, almost as old, fortunately remain - including two fine churches.

•

in St Peter's Building is open to the public.

A few minutes' walk down one of the small roads leading from the High Street brings you to the waterfront, where the old wharfs and quays are still active. Moored at **Hythe Quay** are several Thames Sailing Barges, all over 100 years old and still boasting their traditional rigging and distinctive tan sails. The barges and Quay are overlooked by two pubs, the Queen's Head and the Jolly Sailor. Maldon, famous for its sea salt, is the only place in England still making salt from sea water. Salt production in Maldon dates from Roman times, and from its current premises on the waterfront has continued uninterrupted since 1882.

Promenade Park lies adjacent to Hythe Quay. This attractive park next to the River Blackwater opened in 1895. The Edwardian-style gardens include a marine lake. Also in the park are an adventure playground, picnic site, amusement centre, tennis courts and mini-golf. A varied programme of events takes place in the park throughout the year, including the Mad Maldon Mud Race and the RNLI Rowing Race, both held annually over the Christmas and New Year holidays.

Housed in what was originally the park-keeper's lodge, by the park gates, **Maldon District Museum** looks back on the colourful history of the town through permanent and changing displays of exhibits and objects associated with the area and the people of Maldon.

LANGFORD

2 miles NW of Maldon on the B1019

The **Museum of Power**, Hatfield Road, covers all aspects of power, from domestic batteries to the massive machines that powered British industry. It includes the steam-powered pumping-station machinery of the redundant

230 MALDON DISTRICT MUSEUM

Mill Road, Maldon

Occupying an Edwardian Park keepers cottage, the collections tell the story of the social history and development of Maldon.

 see page 327

•

The sea walls of Northney Island make for an interesting walk, and were used as the camp base for the Viking army in AD 991, when Byrhtnoth led the Saxons against the invading army. A fierce three-day battle took place, with Byrhtnoth's head eventually being cut off and the Viking warriors retreating despite their victory, leaving the English King Ethelred the Unready to pay an annual tribute, 'danegold', to the Danes to prevent further incursions.

•

waterworks in which the museum is housed.

NORTHEY ISLAND

1 mile SE of Maldon off the B1018

This small island, comprising mainly salt-marsh, is owned by the National Trust. Access to this nature reserve is on foot via a causeway passable at low tide with prior arrangement with the warden. It is a Site of Special Scientific Interest, important to over-wintering birds.

GOLDHANGER

4 miles NE of Maldon off the B1026

Maldon District Agricultural & Domestic Museum, at 47 Church Street in Goldhanger, features a large collection of vintage farm tools and machinery manufactured locally, as well as printing machinery and domestic artefacts.

TOLLESBURY

9 miles NE of Maldon on the B1023

Located at the mouth of the River Blackwater is the marshland village of Tollesbury. **Tollesbury Marina** has been designed as a family leisure centre for the crews and passengers of visiting yachts. The Marina, with its tennis courts, heated covered swimming pool, bar and restaurant is ideally located for exploring the Blackwater and the neighbouring estuaries of the Crouch, Colne, Stour and Orwell.

MUNDON

3 miles S of Maldon off the B1018

Mundon and the surrounding area

boasts some excellent walking. The **St Peter's Way**, a long-distance path from Ongar to St Peter's Chapel, Bradwell-on-Sea, leads through the village and past the disused Church of St Mary. This 14th century church is maintained by the Friends of Friendless Churches and is open to the public. Tolstoy is known to have visited the village.

ALTHORNE

6 miles SE of Maldon on the B1012

The **Church of St Andrew**, some 600 years old, has a fine flint and stone tower, built in the perpendicular style. Inside the church there's a 15th century font which retains its original carvings of saints and angels. A brass plaque dated 1508 records that William Hyklott 'Paide for the werkemanship of the wall'; an inscription over the west door remembers John Wylson and John Hyll, who probably paid for the tower.

To the south, where Station Road meets Burnham Road, stands the villagers' own **War Memorial**. This solid structure of beams and tiles lends dignity and honour to the tragic roll-call of names listed on it.

To the north of the village is the golden-thatched and white-walled Huntsman and Hounds, an alehouse since around 1700.

STEEPLE AND ST LAWRENCE

8 miles SE of Maldon off the B1018

Public footpaths lead down to the water from the village of Steeple;

the houses of St Lawrence stand close to the water. Several sailing clubs and some waterside caravan and camping parks ensure that there is plenty of activity on the adjacent stretch of the River Blackwater. The **St Lawrence Rural Discovery Church**, on high ground further inland, overlooks the villages and the River Blackwater to the north; it also offers views over the River Crouch to the south. Exhibitions with local themes are held in the church during the summer months.

BURNHAM-ON-CROUCH

12 miles SE of Maldon on the B1012

Burnham-on-Crouch is attractively old-fashioned, and probably best known as a yachting venue. It is lively in summer, especially at the end of August when the town hosts one of England's premier regattas, Burnham Week. This week of racing and shore events attracts many visiting craft and landlubbers alike. In winter many yachts are left to ride at anchor offshore, and the sound of the wind in their rigging is ever-present.

Behind the gaily-coloured cottages along the Quay lie the High Street and the rest of the town, its streets lined with a delightful assortment of old cottages and Victorian and Georgian houses and shops.

In past times, working boats thronged the estuary where yachts now ply to and fro. Seafarers still come ashore to buy provisions, following a tradition that goes back to medieval times when Burnham

was the market centre for the isolated inhabitants of Wallasea and Foulness Islands in the estuary.

Burnham-on-Crouch & District Museum on The Quay features agricultural, maritime and social history exhibits relating to the Dengie Hundred. There is also a small archaeological collection. Special exhibitions are mounted periodically.

Mangapps Farm Railway Museum on the edge of town offers an extensive collection of railway relics of all kinds, including steam and diesel locos, carriages and wagons, relocated railway buildings, one of the largest collections of signalling equipment open to the public, a complete country station and items of East Anglian railway history.

St Mary's Church is constructed of Kentish ragstone that was transported to Burnham by sea. Construction was begun in the 12th century and was completed in the 14th, but since that time the nucleus of the town has moved closer to the waterfront. The arches and pillars are particularly fine examples of medieval craftsmanship, hence the church being known as 'The Cathedral of the Dengie'.

SOUTHMINSTER

3 miles N of Burnham on the B1021

The old market town of Southminster was important as the economic centre for the isolated marshland communities of the Dengie Peninsula.

A ferry still links Burnham with Wallasea at weekends during the summer, and a programme of boat trips to see the seals on Foulness Sands operates from Burnham Quay. Near the Yacht Harbour, west of the town and accessible along the sea-wall path is Burnham Country Park.

201

Bradwell Lodge, in the village centre, is a part-Tudor former rectory that has known some famous visitors. Gainsborough, the Suffolk artist, used rooms as a studio, while the Irish writer Erskine Childers, who was shot by the Irish Free State in 1920 because he fought for the IRA, wrote The Riddle of the Sands here.

BRADWELL-ON-SEA/ BRADWELL WATERSIDE

12 miles NE of Burnham off the B1021

A visit to Bradwell-on-Sea (the name derives from the Saxon words *brad pall*, meaning 'broad wall') is well worth the long drive for its sense of being right out on the edge of things – the timeless emptiness is, if anything, exaggerated by the distant views of buildings across the water on Mersea Island and the bulk of the nearby (now decommissioned) nuclear power station. A walk eastwards along the old Roman road across the marshes takes you to the site of their fort, 'Othona', on which the visitors of today will find the chapel of **St Peter's on the Wall**, built by St Cedd and his followers in AD 654 using rubble from the ruined fort. In the 14th century the chapel was abandoned as a place of worship, and over the following centuries used at various times as a barn and a shipping beacon. Restored and re-consecrated in 1920, it is well worth the half-mile walk from the car park to reach it. It

is the site of a pilgrimage each July. It has claims to be the oldest church in the land, with St Martin's in Canterbury and St Paul's in Jarrow as other contenders. St Cedd did not survive all that long after founding this chapel, dying of a fever in Yorkshire in AD 664.

An unusual war memorial marks the site of the Bradwell Bay Secret Airfield, used during the Second World War for aircraft unable to return to their original base.

At Bradwell Waterside, a large marina has berths for 300 boats. The now-decommissioned nuclear power station has a visitor centre with an exhibition and high-tech audio-visual displays about electricity production and the decommissioning process. A nature trail is waymarked within the grounds of the station.

To the south of the village lie the remote marshes of the **Dengie Peninsula**, parts of which are important nature reserves. The salty tang of sea air, brought inland on easterly winds, gives an exhilarating flavour to the marshlands. Like the Cambridgeshire and Lincolnshire fens, this once-waterlogged corner of Essex was reclaimed from the sea by 17th century Dutch engineers. The views across the marshes take in great sweeps of countryside inhabited only by wildfowl and seabirds.

PURLEIGH

5 miles SW of Maldon on the B1010

The first recorded vineyard in Purleigh was planted in the early

Thatched Cottage at Bradwell

12th century, only 400 yards from the site of New Hall Vineyards in Chelmsford Road. It covered three acres of land next to Purleigh Church, where first US president George Washington's great-great-grandfather was the rector - until the time he was removed from this office for sampling too much of the local brew! Purleigh Vineyard became Crown property in 1163; subsequently the wines produced were taken each year to London to be presented to the monarch.

SOUTH WOODHAM FERRERS

5 miles SW of Maldon off the B1012

The empty marshland of the Crouch estuary, a yachtsman's paradise, was chosen by Essex County Council as the site for one of its most attractive new towns schemes. At its centre, this successful 20th century new town boasts a traditional market square surrounded by pleasant arcades and terraces built in the old Essex style with brick, tile and weather-board.

RETTENDON

6 miles SW of Maldon off the A130

The **Royal Horticultural Society Garden** at Hyde Hall comprises 28 acres of year-round hillside colour, with a woodland garden, large rose garden, ornamental ponds with lilies and fish, herbaceous borders, shrubs, trees, and a National Collection of viburnums. 3,000 trees have recently been planted, and a new dry garden features huge boulders from Scotland.

BATTLESBRIDGE

7 miles SW of Maldon off the A132

Battlesbridge Antiques Centre at Hawk Hill in Battlesbridge is the largest in Essex. Housed in five period buildings, more than 70 dealers display and sell their wares. The heart of the Centre is Cromwell House, its ground floor dedicated to specialist dealers with individual units. They will advise, value and give an expert opinion free of charge. They offer a wide variety of old and interesting pieces and collectibles.

The Centre's Haybarn Cottages were constructed as dwellings, while, alongside, The Bridgebarn began life as a barn with thatched roof and dates from the 19th century, at which time there were lime kilns nearby. It was converted to its present tiled roof in the 1930s. The building retains some fine oak beam work, and houses a small 'penny arcade' with working model roundabout, fortune teller, and 'What the Butler Saw' as well as a large collection of antiques for sale.

There are superb views from the top floor of the River Crouch and the surrounding area.

This superb location is also the site of a **Classic Motor Cycle Museum**, with displays evoking the history of motorcycling through the ages and some interesting memorabilia. Open on Sundays or by appointment. Three classic vehicle events are held annually.

Marsh Farm Country Park in Marsh Farm Road, South Woodham Ferrers, is a working farm and country park adjoining the River Crouch. Sheep, pigs, cattle and hens roam; visitors can also partake of the adventure play area, farm trail, Visitors' Centre, gift shop and tea rooms. Guided tours are available by prior arrangement. Special events are held throughout the year

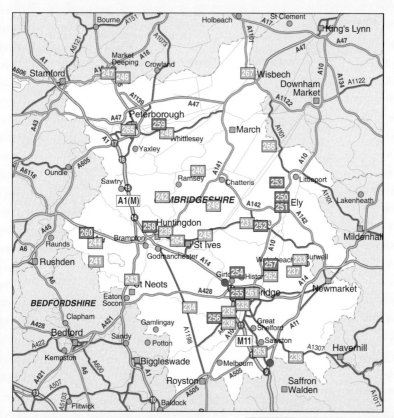

Cambridgeshire

Far removed from the hustle and bustle of modern life, the Fens are like a breath of fresh air. Extending over much of Cambridgeshire from the Wash, these flat, fenland fields contain some of the richest soil in England. Villages such as Fordham and small towns like Ely rise out of the landscape on low hills.

Before the Fens were drained, this was a land of mist, marshes and bogs, of small islands inhabited by independent folk, their livelihood the fish and waterfowl of this eerie, watery place. The region is full of legends of web-footed people, ghosts and witchcraft.

Today's landscape is the result of human ingenuity, with its constant desire to tame the wilderness and create farmland. This fascinating story spans the centuries from the earliest Roman and Anglo-Saxon times, when the first embankments and drains were constructed to lessen the frequency of flooding. Throughout the Middle Ages large areas were reclaimed, with much of the work being undertaken by the monasteries. The first straight cut bypassed the Great Ouse, allowing the water to run out to sea more quickly. After the Civil War, the New Bedford River was cut parallel to the first. These two still provide the basic drainage for much of Fenland.

The significant influence of the Dutch lives on in some of the architecture and place names of the Fens. Over the years it became necessary to pump rainwater from the fields up into the rivers and, as in the Netherlands, windmills took on this task. They could not always cope with the height of the lift required, but fortunately the steam engine came along, to be replaced eventually by the electric pumps that can raise thousands of gallons of water a second to protect the land from the ever-present threat of rain and tide.

The Fens offer unlimited opportunities for exploring on foot, by car, bicycle or by boat.

Anglers are well catered for, and visitors with an interest in wildlife will be in their element.

Southeastern Cambridgeshire covers the area around the city of Cambridge and is rich in history, with a host of archaeological sites and monuments to visit, as well as many important museums. The area is fairly flat, so it makes for great walking and cycling tours, and offers a surprising variety of landscapes. The Romans planted vines here, and to this day the region is among the main producers of British wines.

At the heart of it all is Cambridge itself, one of the leading academic centres in the world and a city which deserves plenty of time to explore - on foot, by bicycle or by the gentler, more romantic option of a punt.

The old county of Huntingdonshire is the heartland of the rural heritage of Cambridgeshire. Here, the home of Oliver Cromwell beckons with a wealth of history and pleasing landscapes. Many motorists follow the Cromwell Trail, which guides tourists around the legacy of buildings and places in the area associated with the man. The natural start of the Trail is Huntingdon itself, where he was born the son of a country gentleman.

The Ouse Valley Way (26 miles long) follows the course of the Great Ouse through pretty villages and a variety of natural attractions. A gentle cruise along this area can fill a lazy day to perfection, but for those who prefer something more energetic on the water there are excellent, versatile facilities at Grafham Water.

The Nene-Ouse Navigation Link, part of the Fenland Waterway, provides the opportunity for a relaxed look at a lovely part of the region. It travels from Stanground Lock near Peterborough to a lock at the small village of Salters Lode in the east, and the 28-mile journey passes through several Fenland towns and a rich variety of wildlife habitats.

ELY

Ely is the jewel in the crown of the Fens, in whose history the majestic **Cathedral** and the Fens themselves have played major roles. The Fens' influence is apparent even in the name: Ely was once known as Elge or Elig ('eel island') because of the large number of eels which lived in the surrounding fenland.

Ely owes its existence to St Etheldreda, Queen of Northumbria, who in AD 673 founded a monastery on the 'Isle of Ely', where she remained as abbess until her death in AD 679. It was not until 1081 that work started on the present Cathedral, and in 1189 this remarkable example of Romanesque architecture was completed. The most outstanding feature in terms of both scale and beauty is the Octagon, built to replace the original Norman tower, which collapsed in 1322.

Alan of Walsingham was the inspired architect of this massive work, which took 30 years to complete and whose framework weighs an estimated 400 tons. Many other notable components include the 14th century Lady Chapel, the largest in England, the Prior's Door, the painted nave ceiling and St Ovin's cross, the only piece of Saxon stonework in the building.

The Cathedral, sometimes known as the 'Ship of the Fens', is set within the walls of the monastery, and many of the ancient buildings still stand as a tribute to the incredible skill and craftsmanship of their designers and builders. Particularly worth visiting among these are the monastic buildings in the College, the Great Hall and Queens Hall.

Just beside the Cathedral is the Almonry, in whose 12th century vaulted undercroft visitors can take coffee, lunch or tea - outside in the garden if the weather permits. Two other attractions that should not be missed are the **Brass Rubbing Centre**, where visitors can make their own rubbings from replica brasses, and the **Stained Glass Museum**. The latter, housed in the south Triforium of the Cathedral, is the only museum of stained glass in the country and contains over 100 original panels from every period, tracing the complete history of stained glass.

Ely's **Tourist Information Centre** is

Oliver Cromwell's House, Ely

itself a tourist attraction, since it is housed in a pretty black-and-white timbered building that was once the home of Oliver Cromwell. It is the only remaining house, apart from Hampton Court, where Oliver Cromwell and his family are known to have lived; parts of it trace back to the 13th century, and its varied history includes periods when it was used as a public house and, more recently, a vicarage. There are eight period rooms, exhibitions and videos to enjoy.

Riverside Walk, Ely

The Old Gaol, in Market Street, houses **Ely Museum**, with

Ely Cathedral

nine galleries telling the Ely story from the Ice Age to modern times. The tableaux of the condemned and debtors' cells are particularly fascinating and poignant.

Ely is not just the past, and its fine architecture and sense of history blend well with the bustle of the streets and shops and the riverside. That bustle is at its most fervent on Thursdays, when the largest general market in the area is held. Every Saturday there's a craft and collectibles market, and on the second and fourth Saturdays of the month Ely hosts a Farmers' Market.

The Riverside Trail takes in the

The cannon on Palace Green opposite the Cathedral was captured from the Russians in Sebastopol and was given to the citizens of Ely by Queen Victoria after the Crimean War. The gift was made in recognition of the formation of the Ely Rifle Volunteers.

252 SHARPS FARM

Wilburton, nr Ely

Sharps Farm offers quality B&B bedrooms in an attractive rural setting.

 see page 337

253 BURY HOUSE

Little Downham, nr Ely

Bury House is a comfortable Bed & Breakfast guest house in homely, civilised surroundings.

 see page 338

Babylon Gallery in a converted 18th century brewery warehouse, where visitors will find an exciting collection of contemporary arts and crafts, in a programme of changing local and international exhibitions; the Jubilee Gardens; Ely Park, and the Quai d'Orsay, named after the twinning of East Cambridgeshire with the town of Orsay in France in 1981.

AROUND ELY

PRICKWILLOW

4 miles NE of Ely on the B1382

On the village's main street is the **Prickwillow Drainage Engine Museum**, which houses a unique collection of large engines associated with the drainage of the Fens. The site had been in continuous use as a pumping station since 1831, and apart from the engines there are displays charting the history of Fens drainage, the effects on land levels and the workings of the modern drainage system.

LITTLEPORT

6 miles N of Ely on the A10

St George's Church, with its very tall 15th century tower, is a notable landmark here in Littleport. Of particular interest are two stained-glass windows depicting St George slaying the dragon. Littleport was the scene of riots in 1861, when labourers from Ely and Littleport, faced with unemployment or low wages, and soaring food prices, attacked houses and people in this area, causing several deaths. Five of the rioters were hanged and buried in a common grave at St Mary's church. A plaque commemorating the event is attached to a wall at the back of the church.

LITTLE DOWNHAM

3 miles N of Ely off the A10

Little Downham's church of St Leonard shows the change from Norman to Gothic in church building at the turn of the 13th century. The oldest parts are the Norman tower and the elaborately carved south door. Interior treasures include what is probably the largest royal coat of arms in the country. At the other end of the village are the remains (mainly the gatehouse and kitchen) of a 15th century palace built by a Bishop of Ely.

COVENEY

3 miles W of Ely off the A10/A142

A Fenland hamlet on the Bedford Level just above West Fen, Coveney's church of St Peter-ad-Vincula has several interesting features, including a colourful German screen dating from around 1500 and a painted Danish pulpit. Unusual figures on the bench ends and a fine brass chandelier add to the opulent feel of this atmospheric little church.

SUTTON

6 miles W of Ely off the A142/B1381

A very splendid 'pepperpot' tower with octagons, pinnacles and spire tops marks out Sutton's grand church of St Andrew. Inside, take time to look at the 15th century font and a fine modern stained-glass window.

The reconstruction of the church was largely the work of two Bishops of Ely, whose arms appear on the roof bosses. One of the Bishops was Thomas Arundel, appointed at the age of 21.

A mile further west, there's a great family attraction in the **Mepal Outdoor Centre**, an outdoor leisure centre with a children's playpark, an adventure play area and boat hire.

HADDENHAM
5 miles SW of Ely on the A1123

More industrial splendour: **Haddenham Great Mill**, built in 1803 for a certain Daniel Cockle, is a glorious sight, and one definitely not to be missed. It has four sails and three sets of grinding stones, one of which is working. The mill last worked commercially in 1946 and was restored between 1992 and 1998. Open on the first Sunday of each month and by appointment.

STRETHAM
5 miles S of Ely off A10/A1123

The **Stretham Old Engine**, a fine example of a land-drainage steam engine, is housed in a restored, tall-chimneyed brick engine house. Dating from 1831, it is one of 90 steam pumping engines installed throughout the Fens to replace some 800 windmills. It is the last to survive, having worked until 1925 and still under restoration. During the great floods of 1919 it really earned its keep by working non-stop for 47 days and nights.

This unique insight into Fenland history and industrial archaeology is open to the public on summer weekends, and on certain dates the engine and its wooden scoop-wheel are rotated (by electricity, alas!). The adjacent stoker's cottage contains period furniture and photographs of fen drainage down the years.

WICKEN
9 miles S of Ely off the A1123

Owned by the National Trust, **Wicken Fen** is the oldest nature reserve in the country, 600 acres of undrained fenland famous for its rich plant, insect and bird life and a delight for both naturalists and ramblers. Features include boardwalk and nature trails, hides and watchtowers, a cottage with 1930s furnishings, a working wind pump (the oldest in the country), a visitor centre and a shop. Open daily, dawn to dusk. Wicken fen is also the new home of the **National Dragonfly Museum**.

St Lawrence's Church is well worth a visit, small and secluded among trees. In the churchyard are buried Oliver Cromwell and several members of his family. One of Cromwell's many nicknames was 'Lord of the Fens': he defended the rights of the Fenmen against those who wanted to drain the land without providing adequate compensation.

SOHAM
6 miles SE of Ely off the A142

Downfield Windmill was built in 1726 as a smock mill, destroyed by

231 THE THREE KINGS

Haddenham, nr Ely

The Three Kings provides excellent hospitality and fine food and drink in a village setting.

see page 330

The Church of St Andrew stands on a hillside in Haddenham. Look for the stained-glass window depicting two souls entering Heaven, and the memorial (perhaps the work of Grinling Gibbons) to Christopher Wren's sister, Anne Brunsell.

Wicken Windmill is a fine and impressive smock windmill restored back to working order. One of only four smock windmills making flour by windmill in the UK, it is open the first weekend of every month and every Bank Holiday (except Christmas and Good Friday) from 11 until 5, and also over the National Mills Weekend, the second week in May.

A plaque in Soham commemorates engine driver Ben Gimbert and fireman James Nightall, who were taking an ammunition train through the town when a wagon caught fire. They uncoupled it and began to haul it into open country. The wagon exploded, killing the fireman and a signalman.

gales and rebuilt in 1890 as an octagonal tower mill. It still grinds corn and produces a range of flours and breads for sale (open Sundays and Bank Holidays).

St Andrew's church is a fine example of the Perpendicular style of English Gothic architecture. Very grand and elaborate, it was built on the site of a 7th century cathedral founded by St Felix of Burgundy. The 15th century west tower has an ornate parapet and two medieval porches. Note, too, the chancel with its panelling and stained glass.

ISLEHAM

10 miles SE of Ely off the B1104

The remains of a Benedictine priory, with a lovely Norman chapel under the care of English Heritage, are a great draw here in Isleham. Also well worth a visit is the church of St Andrew, a 14th century cruciform building entered by a very fine lychgate. The 17th century eagle lectern is the original of a similar lectern in Ely Cathedral.

FORDHAM

10 miles SE of Ely off the A142

A small village on the **Newmarket Cycle Way**, the poet James Withers spent most of his life in Fordham and is buried in the churchyard. A stained-glass window in the church is inscribed in his memory.

SNAILWELL

12 miles SE of Ely off the A142

Snailwell's pretty, mainly 14th century church of St Peter on the banks of the River Snail boasts a 13th century chancel, a hammerbeam and tie beam nave roof, a 600-year-old font, pews with poppy heads and two medieval oak screens. The Norman round tower is unusual for Cambridgeshire.

CAMBRIDGE

There are many Cambridges spread around the globe, but this, the original, is the one that the whole world knows as one of the leading university cities. Cambridge was an important town many centuries before the scholars arrived, standing at the point where forest met fen, at the lowest fording point of the river. The Romans took over a site previously settled by an Iron Age Belgic tribe, to be followed in turn by the Saxons and the Normans. Soon after the Norman Conquest, William I built a wooden motte-and-bailey castle; Edward I built a stone replacement: a mound still marks the spot. The town flourished as a market and river trading centre, and in 1209 a group of students fleeing the Oxford riots arrived. These students made their own arrangements for accommodation, and it was not until 1284 that the first residential college was opened. This was **Peterhouse**, founded by the Bishop of Ely, and in the next century Clare, Pembroke, Gonville & Caius, Trinity Hall and Corpus Christi followed. One of the modern Colleges is **Robinson College**, the gift of self-made millionaire David Robinson. The

Colleges represent various architectural styles, the grandest and most beautiful being King's. Robinson has the look of a fortress; its concrete structure covered with a 'skin' of a million and a quarter hand-made red Dorset bricks.

The Colleges are all well worth a visit, but places that simply must not be missed include **King's College Chapel** with its breathtaking fan vaulting, glorious stained glass and Peter Paul Rubens' *Adoration of the Magi*; **Pepys Library**, including his diaries, in Magdalene College; and Trinity's wonderful **Great Court**. A trip by punt along the 'Backs' of the Cam brings a unique view of many of the Colleges and passes under six bridges, including the **Bridge of Sighs** (St John's) and the extraordinary wooden **Mathematical Bridge** at Queens'. It is not only the bricks and mortar and the treasures within that bring visitors to the colleges, as many of them have gardens of particular interest, some of them open to the public at various times. Notable among these is Christ's College, where the trees include an ancient mulberry and a cypress grown from seed from the tree on Shelley's grave in Rome. The **University Botanic Garden** in the south of the city covers 40 acres and has a triple role of research, education and amenity.

Cambridge has nurtured more Nobel Prize winners than most countries - 32 from Trinity alone - and the list of celebrated alumni covers every sphere of human endeavour and achievement: Byron, Tennyson, Milton and Wordsworth; Marlowe and Bacon; Samuel Pepys; Sir Isaac Newton and Charles Darwin; Charles Babbage, Bertrand Russell and Ludwig Wittgenstein; actors Sir Ian McKellen, Sir Derek Jacobi and Stephen Fry; Lord Burghley; Harold Abrahams, who ran for England in the Olympics; and Burgess, Maclean, Philby and Blunt, all Trinity men who spied for Russia.

The Colleges apart, Cambridge is packed with interest for the visitor, with a wealth of grand buildings both religious and secular, and some of the country's leading museums, many of them run by the University. The **Fitzwilliam Museum** is renowned for its art collection, which includes works by

255 AMBER LODGE

Newmarket Road, Cambridge

Amber Lodge is a quiet, comfortable B&B guest house on the eastern edge of the city.

see *page 338*

Kings College Chapel

211

232 THE PORTLAND ARMS

Chesterton Road, Cambridge

Locals and visitors are attracted to **The Portland Arms** with excellent real ales and fine home cooking.

see page 330

261 CAMBRIDGE & COUNTY FOLK MUSEUM

Castle Street, Cambridge

A smart redbrick pub serving some of the best food in the area, with Adnams and Fullers ales to accompany.

see page 341

Kings College Gatehouse

Titian, Rembrandt, Gainsborough, Hogarth, Turner, Renoir, Picasso and Cezanne, and for its antiquities from Egypt, Greece and Rome. **Kettle's Yard** has a permanent display of 20th century art in a house maintained just as it was when the Ede family donated it, with the collection, to the University in 1967. The **Museum of Classical Archaeology** has 500 plaster casts of Greek and Roman statues, and the **University Museum of Archaeology and Anthropology** covers worldwide prehistoric archaeology with special displays relating to Oceania and to the Cambridge area. The **Museum of Technology**, housed in a Victorian sewage pumping station, features an impressive collection of steam, gas and electric pumping engines and examples, great and small, of local industrial technology. Anyone with an interest in fossils should make tracks for the **Sedgwick Museum of Earth Sciences**, while in the same street (Downing) the **Museum of**

Zoology offers a comprehensive and spectacular survey of the animal kingdom. The **Whipple Museum of the History of Science** tells about science through instruments; and the **Scott Polar Research Institute** has fascinating, often poignant exhibits relating to Arctic and Antarctic exploration.

The work and life of the people of Cambridge and the surrounding area are the subject of the **Cambridge and County Folk Museum**, housed in a 15th century building that for 300 years was the White Horse Inn. Topics include Crafts & Trades, Town & Gown, and Skating & Eels, and throughout the year themed talks and exhibitions take place. One of the city's greatest treasures is the **University Library**, one of the world's great research libraries with 6 million books, a million maps and

University Botanic Garden

350,000 manuscripts. The Library was built between 1930 and 1934 to a design of Giles Gilbert Scott.

Cambridge also has many fine churches, some of them used by the Colleges before they built their own chapels. Among the most notable are **St Andrew the Great** (note the memorial to Captain Cook); **St Andrew the Less**; **St Benet's** (its 11th century tower is the oldest in the county); **St Mary the Great**, a marvellous example of Late Perpendicular Gothic; and **St Peter Castle Hill**. This last is one of the smallest churches in the country, with a nave measuring just 25 feet by 16 feet. Originally much larger, the church was largely demolished in 1781 and rebuilt in its present diminished state using the old materials, including flint rubble and Roman bricks. The Church of the Holy Sepulchre, always known as the **Round Church**, is one of only four surviving circular churches in England.

AROUND CAMBRIDGE

BOTTISHAM

5 miles E of Cambridge on the A1303

John Betjeman ventured that Bottisham's Holy Trinity Church was 'perhaps the best in the county', so time should certainly be made for a visit. Among the many interesting features are the 13th century porch, an 18th century monument to Sir Roger Jenyns and some exceptionally fine modern woodwork in Georgian style.

Bridge of Sighs, Cambridge

SWAFFHAM PRIOR

8 miles NE of Cambridge on the B1102.

Swaffham Prior gives double value to the visitor, with two churches in the same churchyard and two fine old windmills. The churches of St Mary and St Cyriac stand side by side, a remarkable and dramatic sight in the steeply rising churchyard. One of the mills, a restored 1850s tower mill, still produces flour and can be visited by appointment.

At **Swaffham Bulbeck**, a little way to the south, stands another church of St Mary, with a 13th century tower and 14th century arcades and chancel. Look for the fascinating carvings on the wooden benches and a 15th century cedarwood chest decorated with biblical scenes.

LODE

6 miles NE of Cambridge on the B1102

Anglesey Abbey dates from 1600 and was built on the site of an Augustinian priory, but the house

254 ROSE CORNER

Impington, 4 miles north of Cambridge

Rose Corner provides comfortable B&B accommodation in a spacious modern house.

see page 338

Lode Watermill at Anglesey Abbey

a history going back to Saxon times. **Burwell Museum** reflects many aspects of a village on the edge of the Fens up to the middle of the 20th century. A general store, model farm, local industries and children's toys are among the displays. Next to the museum is the famous **Stephens Windmill**, built in 1820 and extensively restored.

The man who designed parts of King's College Chapel, Reginald Ely, is thought to have been responsible for the beautiful **St Mary's Church**, which is built of locally quarried clunch stone and is one of the finest examples of the Perpendicular style. Notable internal features include a 15th century font, a medieval wall painting of St Christopher and roof carvings of elephants, while in the churchyard a gravestone marks the terrible night in 1727 when 78 Burwell folk died in a barn fire while watching a travelling Punch & Judy show.

Behind the church are the remains of Burwell Castle, started in the 12th century but never properly completed.

The Devil's Dyke runs through Burwell on its path from Reach to Woodditton. This amazing dyke, 30 yards wide, was built, it is thought, to halt Danish invaders.

---

233 THE FIVE BELLS

Burwell, northeast of Newmarket

The Five Bells rings out a welcome with affable hosts, snacks, meals, real ales and good wines.

see page 331

and the 100-acre garden came together as a unit thanks to the vision of the 1st Lord Fairhaven. The garden, created in its present form from the 1930s, is a wonderful place for a stroll, with 98 acres of landscaped gardens including wide grassy walks, open lawns, a riverside walk, a working water mill and one of the finest collections of garden statuary in the country. There's also a plant centre, shop and restaurant. In the house itself is Lord Fairhaven's magnificent collection of paintings, sumptuous furnishings, tapestries and clocks.

BURWELL

10 miles NE of Cambridge on the B1102

Burwell is a village of many attractions with

REACH

8 miles NE of Cambridge off the A4280

The charming village of Reach is home to the oldest fair in England, which celebrated its 800th anniversary on 1st May, 2000.

Burwell Windmill

WATERBEACH

5 miles N of Cambridge off the A10

Denny Abbey, easily accessible on the A10, is an English Heritage Grade I listed Abbey with ancient earthworks. On the same site, and run as a joint attraction, is the **Farmland Museum**. The history of Denny Abbey runs from the 12th century, when it was a Benedictine monastery. It was later home to the Knights Templar, Franciscan nuns and the Countess of Pembroke, and from the 16th century was a farmhouse. The old farm buildings have been splendidly renovated and converted to tell the story of village life and Cambridgeshire farming up to modern times. The museum is ideal for family outings, with plenty of hands-on activities for children and a play area, gift shop and weekend tearoom. Among the top displays are a village shop, agricultural machinery, a magnificent 17th century stone barn, a traditional farmworker's cottage and the workshops where various crafts are practised.

MILTON

3 miles N of Cambridge off the A10

Milton Country Park offers fine walking and exploring among acres of parkland, lakes and woods. There's a visitor centre, a picnic area and a place serving light refreshments.

COTTENHAM

5 miles NW of Cambridge on the B1049

At nearby Cottenham, All Saints Church has an unusual tower of yellow and pink Jacobean brick topped with four pinnacles that look like pineapples. The original tower fell down in a gale, and its replacement was partially funded by former US President Calvin Coolidge, one of whose ancestors had lived in the village at the time when the tower fell down.

RAMPTON

6 miles N of Cambridge off the B1050/B1049

A charming village in its own right, with a tree-fringed village green, Rampton is also the site of one of the many archaeological sites in the area. This is **Giant's Hill**, a motte castle with part of an earlier medieval settlement.

GIRTON

3 miles NW of Cambridge off the A14

The first Cambridge College for women was founded in 1869 in Hitchin, by Emily Davies. It moved here to Girton in 1873, to be *'near enough for male lecturers to visit but far enough away to discourage male students from doing the same'*. The problem went away when Girton became a mixed College in 1983.

MADINGLEY

4 miles W of Cambridge on the A428

The **American Cemetery** is one of the loveliest, most peaceful and most moving places in the region, a place of pilgrimage for the families of the American servicemen who operated from the many wartime bases in the county. The cemetery commemorates service personnel who lost their lives in World War II serving as crew members of British-based American aircraft.

237 DYKES END INN

Reach, nr Cambridge

Outstanding food brings visitors from near and far to the **Dykes End Inn** overlooking the village green in Reach.

 see page 332

257 GOOSE HALL FARM

Ely Road, Waterbeach

Midway between Cambridge and Ely, **Goose Hall Farm** offers a choice of B&B and self-catering accommodation.

 see page 339

262 FARMLAND MUSEUM & DENNY ABBEY

Ely Road, Waterbeach

A superbly restored Norman building, once part of a Benedictine Abbey. Also here is the Farmland Museum, which relates the rural history of Cambridgeshire.

 see page 341

235 THE BARN TEA ROOMS

New Road, Barton

Home-cooked meals, salads, cakes and Traditional afternoon tea are served in the delightful surroundings of **The Barn Tea Rooms**.

see page 331

236/256 THE WHITE HORSE INN

High Street, Barton

The White Horse is a fine traditional inn serving outstanding bar and restaurant food; also B&B rooms.

see pages 331 and 338

234 THE DUKE OF WELLINGTON

Bourn, Cambridgeshire

Fine wines and cask ales accompany a fine choice of dishes at **The Duke of Wellington**.

see page 331

The tablet of the missing records 5,126 missing in action, lost or buried at sea, and the graves area contains 3,812 headstones.

CAXTON

6 miles W of Cambridge off the A1219 & A428

Caxton is home to Britain's oldest surviving postmill, and at **Little Gransden**, a couple of miles further southwest on the B1046, another venerable mill has been restored. A scheduled ancient monument, it dates from the early 17th century and was worked well into the early years of the 20th century.

BARTON

3 miles SW of Cambridge off the A603/B1046

Looking south from this pleasant village you can see the impressive array of radio telescopes that are part of Cambridge University's Mullard Radio Astronomy Observatory.

GRANTCHESTER

2 miles SW of Cambridge off the A603

A pleasant walk by the Cam, or a punt on it, brings visitors from the bustle of Cambridge to the famous village of Grantchester, where Rupert Brooke lived and Byron swam. The walk passes through **Paradise Nature Reserve**.

*'Stands the church clock at ten to three
And is there honey still for tea?'*

The Orchard, with its Brooke connections, is known the world over. Brooke spent two happy years in Grantchester, and immortalised afternoon tea in The Orchard in a poem he wrote while homesick in Berlin. Time should also be allowed for a look at the church of St Andrew and St Mary, in which the remains of a Norman church have been incorporated into the 1870s main structure.

ARRINGTON

8 miles SW of Cambridge off the A603/A1198

Arrington's 18th century **Wimpole Hall**, owned by the National Trust, is probably the most spectacular country mansion in the whole county, and certainly the largest 18th century country house in Cambridgeshire. The lovely interiors are the work of several celebrated architects, and there's a fine collection of furniture and pictures. The mansion's state and private rooms show how the last owner Mrs Elsie Bambridge lived at Wimpole trying to restore the house and estate to its former glory. The magnificent formally laid-out grounds include a Victorian parterre (with some surprising modern sculptures), a rose garden and a walled garden. The park provides miles of wonderful walking and is perfect for anything from a gentle stroll to a strenuous hike.

A brilliant attraction for all the family is **Wimpole Home Farm**, a working farm that is the largest rare breeds centre in East Anglia. The animals include Bagot goats, Tamworth pigs, Soay sheep and Longhorn cattle, and there's also a pets corner and horse-drawn wagon ride. Children can spend hours with the animals or in the adventure playground.

SHEPRETH

8 miles S of Cambridge off A10

A paradise for lovers of nature and gardens and a great starting point for country walks, **Shepreth L Moor Nature Reserve** is an L-shaped area of wet meadowland - now a rarity - that is home to birds and many rare plants. The nearby **Shepreth Wildlife Park** started life as a refuge for injured and orphaned British birds and mammals. It now houses a collection of wild and domestic animals including wolves, monkeys, birds and reptiles. In the Water World and Bug City visitors can see insects and fish including the amazing leaf cutter ants.

DUXFORD

8 miles S of Cambridge off A505 by J10 of M11

Part of the **Imperial War Museum**, Duxford Aviation Museum is probably the leader in its field in Europe, with an outstanding collection of over 150 historic aircraft from biplanes through Spitfires, Concorde and Gulf War fighters. The American Air Museum, where aircraft are suspended as if in flight, is part of this terrific place, which was built on a former RAF and USAAF fighter base. Major air shows take place several times a year,

and among the permanent features are a reconstructed wartime operations room, a hands-on exhibition for children and a dramatic land warfare hall with tanks, military vehicles and artillery. Everyone should take time to see this marvellous show - and it should be much more than a flying visit! A free bus service operates from Cambridge City Centre.

At nearby **Hinxton**, a few miles further south, is another mill: a 17th century water mill that is grinding once more.

LINTON

10 miles SE of Cambridge on the B1052

The village is best known for its zoo, but visitors will also find many handsome old buildings and the church of St Mary the Virgin, built mainly in Early English style.

A world of wildlife set in 16 acres of spectacular gardens, **Linton Zoo** is a major wildlife breeding centre and part of the

---

•

Surrounding 18th century Docwra's Manor at Shepreth is a series of enclosed gardens with multifarious plants that is open for visits Wednesday and Friday all year and the first Sunday afternoons from April to October. Fowlmere, on the other side of the A10, is an 86-acre nature reserve designed as a Site of Special Scientific Interest, with hides and trails for bird-watching.

•

263 IMPERIAL WAR MUSEUM DUXFORD

Duxford

Europe's premier aviation museum with many military aircraft on display including Spitfires and bi-planes.

 see page 341

Duxford Aviation Museum

238 THE DOG & DUCK

High Street, Linton

The Dog & Duck is a thatched riverside pub, serving real ales and both traditional and contemporary cuisine.

 see page 333

•

Among Huntingdon's many fine former coaching inns is The George Hotel. Although badly damaged by fire in 1865, the north and west wings of the 17th century courtyard remain intact, as does its very rare wooden gallery. The inn was one of the most famous of all the posting houses on the old Great North Run. It is reputed that Dick Turpin used one of the rooms here. The medieval courtyard, gallery and open staircase are the scene of annual productions of Shakespeare.

•

inter-zoo breeding programme for endangered species. Among the rare and exotic creatures to be seen are Grevy's zebra, snow leopards, tigers, lions, tapirs, lemurs, binturongs, owls, parrots, giant tortoises and tarantulas. The gardens also include picnic areas, a children's play area and, in summer, pony rides and a bouncy castle.

Chilford Hall Vineyard, on the B1052 between Linton and Balsham, comprises 18 acres of vines, with tours and wine-tastings available.

Some two miles further off the A1307, **Bartlow Hills** are the site of the largest Roman burial site to be unearthed in Europe.

HUNTINGDON

The former county town of Huntingdonshire is an ancient place first settled by the Romans. It boasts many grand Georgian buildings, including the handsome three-storeyed Town Hall.

Oliver Cromwell was born in Huntingdon in 1599 and attended Huntingdon Grammar School. The schoolhouse was originally part of the Hospital of St John the Baptist, founded during the reign of Henry II by David, Earl of Huntingdon. Samuel Pepys was also a pupil here.

Cromwell was MP for Huntingdon in the Parliament of 1629, was made a JP in 1630 and moved to St Ives in the following year. Rising to power as an extremely able military commander in the Civil War, he raised troops

from the region and made his headquarters in the Falcon Inn.

Appointed Lord Protector in 1653, Cromwell was ruler of the country until his death in 1658. The school he attended is now the **Cromwell Museum**, located on Huntingdon High Street, housing the only public collection relating specifically to him, with exhibits that reflect many aspects of his political, social and religious life. The museum's exhibits include an extensive collection of Cromwell family portraits and personal objects, among them a hat and seal, contemporary coins and medals, an impressive Florentine cabinet - the gift of the Grand Duke of Tuscany - and a surgeon's chest made by Kolb of Augsburg. This fine collection helps visitors interpret the life and legacy of Cromwell and the Republican movement.

All Saints Church, opposite the Cromwell Museum, displays many architectural styles, from medieval to Victorian. One of the two surviving parish churches of Huntingdon (there were once 16), All Saints was considered to be the church of the Hinchingbrooke part of the Cromwell family, though no memorials survive to attest to this. The Cromwell family burial vault is contained within the church, however, and it is here that Oliver's father Robert and his grandfather Sir Henry are buried. The church has a fine chancel roof, a very lovely organ chamber, a truly impressive stained glass window and the font in which Cromwell was baptised, as it's the old font from the destroyed St John's church, discovered in a local garden in 1927!

Huntingdon's other church, **St Mary's**, dates from Norman times but was almost completely rebuilt in the 13th century. It boasts a fine Perpendicular west tower, which partially collapsed in 1607. The damage was extensive, and the tower was not completely repaired until 1621. Oliver Cromwell's father Robert was one of two bailiffs who contributed to the cost of the repairs, as recorded on the stone plaque fixed to the east wall on the nave, north of the chancel arch.

Cowper House (No 29 High Street) has an impressive early 18th century frontage. A plaque commemorates the fact that the poet William Cowper (pronounced 'Cooper') lived here between 1765 and 1767. "Huntingdon is one of the neatest towns in England" wrote Cowper, so it's not surprising that he made it his home.

Along the south side of the Market Square, the **Falcon Inn** dates back in parts to the 1500s. Oliver Cromwell is said to have used this as his headquarters during the Civil War.

Huntingdon is twinned with Salon de Provence in France, Wertheim am Main in Germany and Szentendre in Hungary.

About half a mile southwest of town stands **Hinchingbrooke House**, which today is a school but which has its origins in the Middle Ages, when it was a nunnery (ghostly nuns are said to haunt the building to this day). The remains of the Benedictine nunnery can still be seen. It was given to the Cromwell family by Henry VIII in 1538. Converted by the Cromwell family in the 16th century and later extended by the Earls of Sandwich, it displays examples of every period of English architecture from the 12th to early 20th centuries. King James I was a regular visitor, and Oliver Cromwell spent part of his childhood here. The 1st Earl of Sandwich was a central figure in the Civil War and subsequent Restoration, while the 4th Earl (inventor of the lunchtime favourite that bears his name) was one of the most flamboyant politicians of the 18th century. The House, now the Sixth Form Centre of Hinchingbrooke School, is open to the public every Sunday afternoon from the early May Bank Holiday to the late August Bank Holiday for guided tours, which end with a delicious cream tea served in the Tudor kitchens.

Hinchingbrooke Country Park covers 180 acres of grassy meadows, mature woodland, ponds and lakes. There is a wide variety of wildlife including woodpeckers, herons, kestrels, butterflies and foxes. The network of paths makes exploring the park easy, and battery-powered wheelchairs are provided for less able visitors. The Visitors Centre serves refreshments at peak times.

Half a mile north of Hinchingbrooke, Spring Common offers another chance to enjoy some marvellous Cambridgeshire countryside. Covering 13 acres, its name comes from the natural spring that runs constantly and has long been a gathering place. The town developed around rather than within this area of rural tranquillity, which boasts a range of diverse habitats including marsh, grassland, scrub and streams. Plant life abounds, providing food and shelter for a variety of animals, amphibians, birds and invertebrates.

AROUND HUNTINGDON

BRAMPTON

2 miles SW of Huntingdon off the A1

Brampton is where Huntingdon racecourse is situated. An average of 18 meetings (all jumping) are scheduled every year, including Bank Holiday fixtures (extra-special deals for families). In November, the Grade II Peterborough Chase is the feature race.

Brampton's less speculative attractions include the 13th century church of St Mary, and Pepys House, the home of Samuel's uncle, who was a cousin of Lord Sandwich and who got Samuel his job at the Admiralty.

HARTFORD

½ mile N of Huntington off the B1514

At just half a mile from Hartford Marina, this lovely village offers plenty of excellent riverside walks.

ALCONBURY

3 miles NW of Huntingdon off the A1

Fenland walks can be interspersed with pauses at the local inns and a look at the church of St Peter and St Paul, whose steeple and chancel are particularly noteworthy. This long village has a large green, an ancient village pump and a 15th century bridge crossing the brook that runs through Alconbury.

BARHAM

6 miles W of Huntingdon off the A1/A14

This delightful hamlet boasts 12 houses an ancient church with box pews, surrounded by undulating farmland. Nearby attractions include angling and sailing on Grafham Water, go-karting at Kimbolton and National Hunt racing at Huntingdon.

RAMSEY

9 miles NE of Huntingdon on the B1040

A pleasant market town with a broad main street down which a river once ran, Ramsey is home to the medieval **Ramsey Abbey**, founded in AD 969 by Earl Ailwyn as a Benedictine monastery. The Abbey became one of the most important in England in the 12th and 13th centuries, and as it prospered, so did Ramsey, so that by the 13th century it had become a town with a weekly market and an annual three-day festival at the time of the feast of St Benedict. After the Dissolution of the Monasteries in 1539, the Abbey and its lands were sold to Sir Richard Williams, great-grandfather of Oliver Cromwell. Most of the buildings were then demolished, the stones being used to build Caius, Kings and Trinity Colleges at Cambridge, the towers of Ramsey, Godmanchester and Holywell churches, the gate at Hinchingbrooke House and several local properties. In 1938 the house was converted for use as a school, which it remains to this day.

To the northwest are the ruins of the once magnificent stone gatehouse of the late 15th century - only the porter's lodge remains, but inside can be seen an unusual large carved effigy made of Purbeck marble and dating back to the 14th century. It is said to represent Earl

Ailwyn, founder of the Abbey. The gatehouse, now in the care of the National Trust, can be visited daily from April to October.

Most of **Ramsey Rural Museum** is housed in an 18th century farm building and several barns set in open countryside. Among the many fascinating things to see are a Victorian home and school, a village store, and restored farm equipment, machinery, carts and wagons. The wealth of traditional implements used by local craftsmen such as the farrier, wheelwright, thatcher, dairyman, animal husbandman and cobbler offer an insight into bygone days. The Museum is open Thursday, Sunday and Bank Holiday afternoons between April and September.

The unusual Ramsey War Memorial, standing almost at the end of Church Green, is a listed Grade II memorial consisting of a fine bronze statue of St George slaying the dragon atop a tall, octagonal pillar crafted of Portland stone.

UPWOOD

8 miles NE of Huntingdon off the B1040

Upwood is a pleasant, scattered village in a very tranquil and picturesque setting. **Woodwalton Fen** nature reserve is a couple of minutes' drive to the west.

SAWTRY

8 miles NW of Huntingdon on the A1

The main point of interest here has no point! All Saints Church, built in 1880, lacks both tower and steeple,

and is topped instead by a bellcote. Inside the church are marvellous brasses and pieces from ancient Sawtry Abbey.

Just south of Sawtry, **Aversley Wood** is a conservation area with abundant birdlife and plants.

HAMERTON

9 miles NW of Huntingdon off the A1

Hamerton Zoological Park has hundreds of animals from tortoises to tigers. Specially designed enclosures make for unrivalled views of the animals, and the park features meerkats, marmosets and mongooses, lemurs, gibbons, possums and sloths, snakes and even creepy-crawlies such as cockroaches!

GREAT GIDDING

10 miles NW of Huntingdon off the B660

Stained-glass windows are a notable feature of **St Michael's** church in this, the largest of the three Giddings. A fire ravaged the village in the 1860s and the church was one of the few buildings to survive. Today the church is the atmospheric setting for concerts and plays.

STILTON

12 miles NW of Huntingdon off the A1

Stilton has an interesting main street with many fine buildings, and is a good choice for the hungry or thirsty visitor, as it has been since the heyday of horse-drawn travel. Journeys were a little more dangerous then, and Dick Turpin is said to have hidden at the Bell Inn. The famous cheese is still produced and sold here.

The church of St Thomas à Becket of Canterbury forms an impressive vista at the end of the Ramsey High Street. Dating back to 1180, it is thought to have been built as a hospital or guesthouse for the Abbey. It was converted, perhaps a century later, to a church to accommodate the many pilgrims who flocked to Ramsey. The church has what is reputed to be the finest nave in Huntingdonshire, dating back to the 12th century and consisting of seven bays. The church's other treasure is a 15th century carved oak lectern, thought to have come from the Abbey. Oliver Cromwell's uncle Sir Oliver is buried in the church.

242 THE CROSS KEYS

High Street, Upwood

Meat-eaters, fish-eaters and vegetarians will all find plenty of choice at the **Cross Keys**.

see page 334

244/260 THE
RACEHORSE
COUNTRY INN

Catworth, west of Huntingdon

The Racehorse Country Inn offers traditional hospitality, real ales, fine home cooking and comfortable accommodation in a village just off the A14 (J16).

 see pages 334 and 339

241 THE NEW SUN INN & RESTAURANT

High Street, Kimbolton

Food, ales and wines are all outstanding at the **New Sun Inn & Restaurant**.

 see page 333

ELLINGTON

4 miles W of Huntingdon off the A14

Ellington is a quiet village just south of the A14 and about a mile north of Grafham Water. Both Cromwell and Pepys visited, having relatives living in the village, and it was in Ellington that Pepys' sister Paulina found a husband, much to the relief of the diarist, who had written: '*We must find her one, for she grows old and ugly.*' All Saints Church at Ellington is magnificent, like so many in the area, and among its many fine features are the 15th century oak roof and the rich carvings in the nave and the aisles. The church and its tower were built independently.

SPALDWICK

6 miles W of Huntingdon off the A14

A sizable village that was once the site of the Bishop of Lincoln's manor house, Spaldwick boasts the grand church of St James, which dates from the 12th century and has seen restoration in most centuries, including the 20th, when the spire had to be partly rebuilt after being struck by lightning.

Two miles further west, **Catworth** is another charming village, regularly voted Best Kept Village in Cambridgeshire and well worth exploring.

KEYSTON

12 miles W of Huntingdon off the A14

A delightful village with a pedigree that can be traced back to the days of the Vikings, Keyston has major attractions both sacred and secular:

the **Church of St John the Baptist** is impressive in its almost cathedral-like proportions, with one of the most magnificent spires in the whole county.

GRAFHAM

5 miles SW of Huntingdon on the B661

Created in the mid-1960s as a reservoir, **Grafham Water** offers a wide range of outdoor activities for visitors of all ages, with 1,500 acres of beautiful countryside, including the lake itself. The ten-mile perimeter track is great for jogging or cycling, and there's excellent sailing, windsurfing and fly-fishing. The area is a Site of Special Scientific Interest, and an ample nature reserve at the western edge is run jointly by Anglian Water and the Wildlife Trust. There are nature trails, information boards, a wildlife garden and a dragonfly pond. Bird-watchers have the use of six hides, three of them accessible to wheelchairs. An exhibition centre has displays and video presentations of the reservoir's history, a gift shop and a café.

KIMBOLTON

8 miles SW of Huntingdon on the B645

History aplenty here, and a lengthy pause is in order to look at all the interesting buildings. St Andrew's Church would head the list were it not for **Kimbolton Castle** which, along with its gatehouse, dominates the village. Parts of the original Tudor building are still to be seen, but the appearance of the castle today owes much to the major remodelling carried out by

Vanbrugh and Nicholas Hawksmoor in the first decade of the 18th century. The gatehouse was added by Robert Adam in 1764. Henry VIII's first wife Catherine of Aragon spent the last 18 months of her life imprisoned here, where she died in 1536. She is buried in Peterborough Cathedral.

BUCKDEN

4 miles SW of Huntingdon on the A1

This historic village was an important coaching stop on the old Great North Road. It is known particularly as the site of **Buckden Towers**, the great palace built for the Bishops of Lincoln. In the splendid grounds are the 15th century gatehouse and the tower where Henry VIII imprisoned his first wife, Catherine of Aragon, in 1533 (open only on certain days of the year).

ST NEOTS

10 miles SW of Huntingdon off the A1

St Neots dates back to the founding of a Saxon Priory, built on the outskirts of Eynesbury in AD 974. Partially destroyed by the Danes in 1010, it was re-established as a Benedictine Priory in about 1081 by St Anselm, Abbot of Bec and later Archbishop of Canterbury. For the next two centuries the Priory flourished. Charters were granted by Henry I to hold fairs and markets.

The first bridge over the Great Ouse, comprising 73 timber arches, was built in 1180. The name of the town comes from the Cornish saint whose remains were interred in the Priory some time before the Norman Conquest. With the Dissolution of the Monasteries, the Priory was demolished. In the early 17th century the old bridge was replaced by a stone one. This was then the site of a battle between the Royalists and Roundheads in 1648 - an event sometimes re-enacted by Sealed Knot societies.

St Neots repays a visit on foot, since there are many interesting sites and old buildings tucked away. The famous Market Square is one of the largest and most ancient in the country. A market has been held here every Thursday since the 12th century. The magnificent parish church of St Mary the Virgin is a very fine edifice, known locally as the Cathedral of Huntingdonshire. It is an outstanding example of Late

St Neots Museum – opened in 1995 – tells the story of the town and the surrounding area. Housed in the former magistrates' court and police station, it still has the original cells. Eye-catching displays trace local history from prehistoric times to the present day. Open Tuesday to Saturday.

St Neots

223

243 THE ANCHOR INN

Little Paxton, nr St Neots

Traditional home cooking and well-kept real ales are spreading the reputation of **The Anchor Inn**.

see page 334

Wood Green Animal Shelter at Kings Bush Farm, Godmanchester is a purpose-built, 50-acre centre open to the public all year round. Cats, dogs, horses, donkeys, farm animals, guinea pigs, rabbits, llamas, red deer and ferrets are among the many creatures for visitors to see, and there is a specially adapted nature trail and restaurant.

Medieval architecture. The gracious interior complements the 130-feet Somerset-style tower, with a finely carved oak altar, excellent Victorian stained glass and a Holdich organ, built in 1855.

LITTLE PAXTON

2½ miles N of St Neots off the A1/A428

Fewer than three miles north of St Neots at Little Paxton is **Paxton Pits Nature Reserve**. Created alongside gravel workings, the Reserve attracts thousands of water birds for visitors to observe from hides. The wealth of wildlife means that the area is an SSSI (Site of Special Scientific Interest) and ensures a plethora of colour and activity all year round. The site also features nature trails and a visitors' centre. It has thousands of visiting waterfowl, including one of the largest colonies of cormorants, and is particularly noted for its wintering wildfowl, nightingales in late spring and kingfishers. There are about four miles of walks, some suitable for wheelchairs. Spring and summer also bring a feast of wildflowers, butterflies and dragonflies.

EYNESBURY

1 mile S of St Neots on the A428

Eynesbury is actually part of St Neots, with only a little stream separating the two. Note the 12th century church of St Mary with its Norman tower. Rebuilt in the Early English period, it retains some well-preserved locally sculpted 14th century oak benches.

History has touched this quiet and lovely village from time to time: it was the home of the famous giant James Toller, who died in 1818 and is buried in the middle aisle of the church. Only 21 when he died, he measured some 8 feet tall - it is said he was buried here to escape the attention of body-snatchers, whose activities were widespread at the time. Eynesbury was also the birthplace of the Miles' Quads, the first-ever surviving quadruplets in Britain.

BUSHMEAD

4 miles W of St Neots off the B660

The remains of **Bushmead Abbey**, once a thriving Augustinian community, are well worth a detour. The garden setting is delightful, and the surviving artefacts include some interesting stained glass. Open weekends in July and August.

GODMANCHESTER

2 miles SW of Huntingdon off the A1

Godmanchester is linked to Huntingdon by a 14th century bridge across the River Ouse. It was a Roman settlement and one that continued in importance down the years, as the number of handsome buildings testifies. One such is **Island Hall**, a mid-18th century mansion built for John Jackson, the Receiver General for Huntingdon; it contains many interesting pieces. This family home has lovely Georgian rooms, with fine period detail and fascinating possessions relating to the owners' ancestors since their first occupation of the house in 1800. The tranquil riverside setting and formal gardens add to the peace and splendour - the house takes its name from the ornamental island that forms part of the grounds. Octavia Hill was sometimes a guest, and wrote effusively to her sister that Island Hall was 'the loveliest, dearest old house, I never was in such a one before.' Open only to pre-booked groups.

A footpath leads from the famous Chinese Bridge (1827) to **Port Holme Meadow**, at 225 acres one of the largest in England and the site of Roman remains. It is a Site of Special Scientific Interest, with a huge diversity of botanical and bird species. Huntingdon racecourse was once situated here, and it was a training airfield during the First World War. Another site of considerable natural activity is **Godmanchester Pits**, accessed along the Ouse Valley Way and home to a great diversity of flora and fauna.

PAPWORTH EVERARD

6 miles S of Huntingdon on the A1198

One of the most recent of the region's churches, St Peter's dates mainly from the mid-19th century. Neighbouring **Papworth St Agnes** has an older church in St John's, though parts of that, too, are Victorian. Just up the road at **Hilton** is the famous **Hilton Turf Maze**, cut in 1660 to a popular medieval design.

BOXWORTH

7 miles SE of Huntingdon off the A14

A village almost equidistant from Huntingdon and Cambridge, and a pleasant base for touring the area,

River Ouse, Hemingford Grey

Boxworth's church of St Peter is unusual in being constructed of pebble rubble.

A mile south of Boxworth is **Overhall Grove**, one of the largest elm woods in the country and home to a variety of wildlife.

THE GREAT OUSE VALLEY

HEMINGFORD ABBOTS

3 miles SE of Huntingdon off the A14

Once part of the Ramsey Abbey Estate, Hemingford Abbots is set around the 13th century church of St Margaret, along the banks of the Great Ouse. Opportunities for angling and boating facilities, including rowing boats for hire, as well as swimming, country walks, golf and a recreation centre are all within a couple of miles. The village hosts a flower festival every two years.

•

Just to the east of Hemingford Abbots is Hemingford Grey, with its church on the banks of the Ouse. The manor at Hemingford Grey is reputedly the oldest continuously inhabited house in England, built around 1130. One of the owners was the author Lucy Boston, who used it as the house of Green Knowe in her children's books. This remarkable lady made a collection of exquisite patchworks, most of which are on display, and she also designed the garden, including topiary in the form of chess pieces in the garden. The garden is open daily, the house by appointment.

•

225

Houghton, Huntingdon

A five-storey, brick and clapboard mill dating from the 18th century, one of last and most complete. It has recently been restored and on certain days visitors can see the mill in action.

 see page 342

FENSTANTON

7 miles SE of Huntingdon off the A14 bypass

Capability Brown was Lord of the Manor from 1768, and he, his wife and his son are buried in the medieval church. Lancelot Brown (1716-1783) acquired his nickname from assuring innumerable clients that he could see the capabilities in their lands. He became head gardener and clerk of works at Stowe in 1741, where he helped in executing the designs of William Kent. He branched out on his own as an 'improver of gardens' in 1751, creating more than 140 splendid parks: Blenheim, Burghley and Badminton are among his many masterpieces – and that's just a few of the Bs! Any visit here should also take in the 17th century manor house and the red-brick Clock Tower.

SWAVESEY

10 miles SE of Huntingdon off the A14

Look for the large 14th century church and the windmill a little way west, on the way to Fen Drayton, whose church is built of pebble rubble.

WYTON

2 miles E of Huntington off the A1123

Wyton is mentioned in the *Domesday Book*, and is thought to have been founded in the 8th century. It is a popular tourist destination thanks to its proximity to **Houghton Mill** and opportunities for riverside walks, as well as its charming thatched buildings and shops. The large, impressive, timber-built water mill dates from the 17th century and is owned by the National Trust. Potto Brown, a Quaker merchant and non-conformist, was one of its famous millers. Milling days are held on Sundays and Bank Holidays. Tel: 01480 301494

HOUGHTON

5 miles E of Huntingdon on the A1123

Houghton Meadows is a Site of Special Scientific Interest with an abundance of hay meadow species.

Houghton Mill

One of the most popular walks in the whole area links Houghton with St Ives.

ST IVES

6 miles E of Huntingdon off the A1123

This is an ancient town on the banks of the Great Ouse which once held a huge annual fair and is named after St Ivo, said to be a Persian bishop who came here in the Dark Ages to spread a little light. In the Middle Ages, kings bought cloth for their households at the village's great wool fairs and markets, and a market is still held every Monday. The Bank Holiday Monday markets are particularly lively affairs, and the Michaelmas fair fills the town centre for three days.

Seagoing barges once navigated up to the famous six-arched **River Bridge** that was built in the 15th century and has a most unusual chapel in its middle: the two-storey Chapel of St Leger is one of only four surviving bridge chapels in the country. Oliver Cromwell lived in St Ives in the 1630s; the statue of him on Market Hill, with its splendid hat, is one of the village's most familiar landmarks. It was made in bronze, with a Portland stone base, and was erected in 1901. It was originally designed for Huntingdon, but they wouldn't accept it!

The beautiful **All Saints Church** in its yard beside the river is well worth a visit. The quayside provides a tranquil mooring for holidaymakers and there are wonderful walks by the riverside.

Clive Sinclair developed his tiny TVs and pocket calculators in the town, and another famous son of St Ives was the great Victorian rower John Goldie, whose name is remembered each year by the second Cambridge boat in the Boat Race.

The **Norris Museum**, founded in 1933 by the St Ives historian Herbert Norris in a delightful setting by the river, tells the story of Huntingdonshire from the age of the dinosaurs to flint tools, Roman artefacts and Civil War armour, lace-making and ice-skating displays, and contemporary works of art. Exhibitions include a life-size replica of a 160-million-year-old ichthyosaur. There are remains of woolly mammoths from the Ice Ages, tools and pottery from the Stone Age to Roman times and relics from the medieval castles and abbeys. Also on show are toys and models made by prisoners of the Napoleonic Wars. Open all year; free admission.

Just outside St Ives are **Wilthorn Meadow**, a Site of Natural History Interest where Canada geese are often to be seen, and **Holt Island Nature Reserve**, where high-quality willow is being grown to reintroduce the traditional craft of basket-making. Take some time for spotting the butterflies, dragonflies and kingfishers.

EARITH

4 miles E of St Ives on the A1123

The **Ouse Washes**, a special protection area, runs northeast from the village to Earith Pits, a well-known

•

*As I was going to St Ives
I met a man with seven wives.
Each wife had seven sacks,
each sack had seven cats,
each cat had seven kits.
Kits, cats, sacks and wives,
how many were there going to
St Ives?'*

Just the story teller, of course, but today's visitors are certain to have a good time while they are here.

•

245 THE QUEEN'S HEAD

Needingworth, nr St Ives

Lovers of real ales and good food make for **The Queen's Head**, a welcoming inn on the main street of Needingworth.

see page 335

249 THE BLACK BULL

Somersham, nr Huntingdon

The Black Bull combines the best qualities of a friendly local, a place to pause on a journey and a first-rate restaurant.

see page 336

habitat for birds and crawling creatures; some of the pits are used for fishing. The Washes are a wetland of major international importance supporting such birds as ruffs, Bewick and Whooper swans, and hen harriers. The average bird population is around 20,000. Some of the meadows flood in winter, and ice-skating is popular when the temperature really drops. There's a great tradition of ice-skating in the Fens, and Fenmen were the national champions until the 1930s.

WOODHURST

2 miles NE of St Ives off the B1040

The **Raptor Foundation** is a bird of prey rescue centre set in 20 acres of woodland and home to 300 birds of prey, mostly injured, orphaned or unwanted. Attractions include regular falconry displays, a flower garden, tea room, art gallery, craft village and picnic area. Nearby **Somersham** once had a palace for the Bishops of Ely, and its splendid church of St John would have done them proud.

PETERBOROUGH

The second city of Cambridgeshire has a long and interesting history that can be traced back to the Bronze Age, as can be seen in the archaeological site at Flag Fen. Although a cathedral city, it is also a New Town (designated in 1967), so modern development and expansion have vastly increased its facilities while retaining the quality of its historic heart.

Peterborough's crowning glory is, of course, the Norman **Cathedral**, built in the 12th and 13th centuries on a site that had seen Christian worship since AD 655. Henry VIII made the church a cathedral, and his first queen, Catherine of Aragon, is buried here, as for a while was Mary Queen of Scots after her execution at Fotheringay. Features to note are the huge (85-feet) arches of the West Front, the unique painted wooden nave ceiling, some exquisite late 15th century fan vaulting, and the tomb of

Peterborough Cathedral

Catherine, who died at Kimbolton Castle.

Though the best-known of the city's landmarks, the Cathedral is by no means the only one. The **Peterborough Museum and Art Gallery** covers all aspects of the history of Peterborough from the Jurassic period to Victorian times.

The Gildenburgh Gallery at 44 Broadway boasts a good collection of fine art from the 20th and 21st centuries and a design-led craft shop. The views of Peterborough to be had from the gallery are panoramic and impressive.

Just outside the city, by the river Nene, is **Thorpe Meadows Sculpture Park**, one of several open spaces in and around the city with absorbing collections of modern sculpture.

Bishops Palace, Peterborough

AROUND PETERBOROUGH

LONGTHORPE

2 miles W of Peterborough off the A47

Longthorpe Tower, part of a fortified manor house, is graced by some of the very finest 14th century domestic wall paintings in Europe, featuring scenes both sacred and secular: the Nativity, the Wheel of Life, King David, the Labours of the Months. The paintings were discovered during renovations after the Second World War.

ELTON

6 miles SW of Peterborough on the B671

Elton is a lovely village on the river Nene, with stone-built houses and thatched roofs. **Elton Hall** is a mixture of styles, with a 15th century tower and chapel, and a major Gothic influence. The grandeur is slightly deceptive, as some of the battlements and turrets were built of wood to save money. The hall's sumptuous rooms are filled with art treasures (Gainsborough, Reynolds, Constable) and the library has a wonderful collection of antique tomes.

THORNHAUGH

8 miles NW of Peterborough off the A1/A47

Hidden away in a quiet valley is **Sacrewell Farm and Country Centre**, whose centrepiece is a working watermill. All kinds of farming equipment are on display, and there's a collection of farm

•

There are twin attractions for railway enthusiasts in Peterborough in the shape of Railworld, a hands-on exhibition dealing with modern rail travel, and the wonderful Nene Valley Railway, which operates 15-mile steam-hauled trips between Peterborough and its HQ and museum at Wansford. A feature on the main railway line at Peterborough is the historic Iron Bridge, part of the old Great Northern Railway and still virtually as built by Lewis Cubitt in 1852.

•

229

246 THE GOAT

Deeping St James, nr Peterborough

Real ales, malt whiskies and excellent home cooking have built up a loyal clientele at **The Goat**.

🍴 *see page 335*

247 DEEPING COFFEE HOUSE

Market Deeping, nr Peterborough

Hot and cold snacks, both sweet and savoury, are served throughout the day at the smart modern **Deeping Coffee House**.

🍴 *see page 335*

The Thorney Heritage Museum at Thorney is a small, independently-run museum of great fascination, describing the development of the village from a Saxon monastery, via Benedictine Abbey to a model village built in the 19th century by the Dukes of Bedford. The main innovation was a 10,000-gallon water tank that supplied the whole village; other villages had to use unfiltered river water.

248/259 THE BOAT INN

Whittlesey, nr Peterborough

A fine variety of well-kept real ales is on tap at the 11th century **Boat Inn**, which has five letting bedrooms.

🍴 🛏 *see pages 335 and 339*

animals, along with gardens, nature trails and general interest trails, play areas, a gift shop and a restaurant serving light refreshments.

PEAKIRK

7 miles N of Peterborough off the A15

Peakirk boasts a village church of Norman origin that is the only one in the country dedicated to St Pega, the remains of whose hermit cell can still be seen.

CROWLAND

10 miles NE of Peterborough off the A1073

It is hard to imagine that this whole area was once entirely wetland and marshland, dotted with inhospitable islands. Crowland was one such island, then known as Croyland, and on it was established a small church and hermitage back in the 7th century, which was later to become one of the nation's most important monasteries. The town's impressive parish church was just part of the great edifice which once stood on the site. A wonderful exhibition can be found in the **Abbey** at Crowland, open all year round. The remains cover a third of the Abbey's original extent.

Crowland's second gem is the unique **Trinity Bridge** - set in the centre of town on dry land! Built in the 14th century, it has three arches built over one over-arching structure. Before the draining of the Fens, this bridge crossed the point where the River Welland divided into two streams.

THORNEY

8 miles E of Peterborough on the A47

Thorney Abbey, the church of St Mary and St Botolph, is the dominating presence even though what now stands is but a small part of what was once one of the greatest of the Benedictine abbeys. Gravestones in the churchyard are evidence of a Huguenot colony that settled here after fleeing France in the wake of the St Bartholomew's Day massacre of 1572.

WHITTLESEY

5 miles E of Peterborough off the A605

The market town of Whittlesey lies close to the western edge of the Fens and is part of one of the last tracts to be drained. Brick-making was a local speciality, and 180-feet brick chimneys stand as a reminder of that once-flourishing industry. The church of **St Andrew** is mainly 14th century, with a 16th century tower; the chancel, chancel chapels and naves still have their original roofs.

A walk round this charming town reveals an interesting variety of buildings: brick, of course, and also some stone, thatch on timber frames, and rare thatched mud boundary walls.

The Whittlesey Museum, housed in the grand 19th century Town Hall in Market Street, features an archive of displays on local archaeology, agriculture, geology, brick-making and more. Reconstructions include a 1950s corner shop and post office, blacksmith's forge and wheelwright's bench.

A highlight of Whittlesey's year is the **Straw Bear Procession** that is part of a four-day January festival. A man clad in a suit of straw dances and prances through the streets, calling at houses and pubs to entertain the townspeople. The origins are obscure: perhaps it stems from pagan times when corn gods were invoked to produce a good harvest; perhaps it is linked with the wicker idols used by the Druids; perhaps it derives from the performing bears which toured the villages until the 17th century. What is certain is that at the end of the jollities the straw suit is ceremoniously burned.

Whittlesey was the birthplace of the writer L P Hartley (*The Go-Between*) and of General Sir Harry Smith, hero of many 19th century campaigns in India. He died in 1860, and the south chapel off **St Mary's** church (note the beautiful spire) was restored and named after him.

FLAG FEN

6 miles E of Peterborough signposted from the A47 and A1139

Flag Fen Bronze Age Centre comprises massive 3,000-year-old timbers that were part of a major settlement and have been preserved in peaty mud. The site includes a Roman road with its original surface, the oldest wheel in England, re-creations of a Bronze Age settlement, a museum of artefacts, rare breed animals, and a visitor

centre with a shop and restaurant. Ongoing excavations, open to the public, make this one of the most important and exciting sites of its kind.

MARCH

14 miles E of Peterborough off the A141

March once occupied the second-largest 'island' in the great level of Fens. As the land was drained the town grew as a trading and religious centre, and in more recent

265 FLAG FEN

Northey Road, Peterborough

An opportunity to see how people of the Bronze and Iron ages lived in their roundhouses. Artefacts found during excavation are on display.

 see page 342

St Wendeda's Church, March

266 THE WILDFOWL &
WETLAND TRUST
WELNEY

Welney, Wisbech

Wetland paradise where
hundreds of birds, including
swans, ducks and waders can
be seen. Perfect for walks on
boardwalks through the reeds.
Visitor Centre and gift shop

 see page 343

times as a market town and major
railway hub. **March and District
Museum**, in the High Street, tells
the story of the people and the
history of March and the
surrounding area, and includes a
working forge and a reconstruction
of a turn-of-the-century home.

The uniquely dedicated **Church
of St Wendreda**, at Town End, is
notable for its magnificent timber
roof, a double hammerbeam with 120
carved angels, a fine font and some
impressive gargoyles. John Betjeman
declared the church to be 'worth
cycling 40 miles into a headwind to
see'.

The **Nene-Ouse Navigation
Link** runs through the town,
affording many attractive riverside
walks and, just outside the town off
the B1099, **Dunhams Wood**
comprises four acres of woodland set
among the fens. The site contains an
enormous variety of trees, along with
sculptures and a miniature railway.

CHATTERIS

8 miles S of March off the A141

A friendly little market town, the
**Chatteris Museum and Council
Chamber** features a series of
interesting displays on Fenland life
and the development of the town.
Themes include education,
agriculture, transport and local trades,
along with temporary exhibitions and
local photographs, all housed in five
galleries.

The church of St Peter and St
Paul has some 14th century features
but is mostly more modern in
appearance, having been substantially
restored in 1909.

STONEA

3 miles SE of March off the B1098

Stonea Camp is the lowest 'hill'-
fort in Britain. Built in the Iron
Age, it proved unsuccessful against
the Romans. A listed ancient
monument whose banks and
ditches were restored after
excavations in 1991, the site is also
an increasingly important habitat
for wildlife.

WELNEY

4 miles SE of March off the A1101

The **Wildfowl & Wetlands Trust**
in Welney is a nature reserve that
attracts large numbers of swans and
ducks in winter. Special floodlit
'swan evenings' are held, and there
is also a wide range of wild plants
and butterflies to be enjoyed.

WISBECH

One of the largest of the Fenland
towns, a port in medieval times and
still enjoying shipping trade with
Europe, Wisbech is at the centre of
a thriving agricultural region. The
18th century in particular saw the
building of rows of handsome
houses, notably in North Brink and
South Brink, which face each other
across the river. The finest of all
the properties is undoubtedly
Peckover House, built in 1722
and bought at the end of the 18th
century by Jonathan Peckover, a
member of the Quaker banking
family. The family gave the building
to the National Trust in 1948.
Behind its elegant brick façade are
splendid panelled rooms, Georgian

fireplaces with richly carved overmantels, and ornate plaster decorations. At the back of the house is a beautiful walled garden with summerhouses, a Victorian fernery, pond and rose garden and an orangery with 300-year-old orange trees.

No 1 South Brink Place is the birthplace of Octavia Hill (1838-1912), co-founder of the National Trust and a tireless worker for the cause of the poor, particularly in the sphere of housing. The house is now the **Octavia Hill's Birthplace House** with displays and exhibits commemorating her work.

More Georgian splendour is evident in the area where the Norman castle once stood. The castle was replaced by a bishop's palace in 1478, and in the 17th century by a mansion built for Cromwell's Secretary of State, John Thurloe. Local builder Joseph Medworth built the present Regency villa in 1816; of the Thurloe mansion, only the gate piers remain.

The **Wisbech and Fenland Museum** is one of the oldest purpose-built museums in the country, and in charming Victorian surroundings visitors can view displays of porcelain, coins, rare geological specimens, Egyptian tomb treasures and several items of national importance, including the manuscript of Charles Dickens' *Great Expectations*, Napoleon's Sèvres breakfast set captured at Waterloo, and an ivory chess set that belonged to Louis XIV.

Museum Square, Wisbech

Other sights to see in Wisbech include **Elgoods Brewery**, a classic Georgian brewery on the banks of the River Nene. Visitors can see traditional brewing methods and sample the excellent brews, savour award-winning ales and enjoy a walk in the four-acre garden, which includes a maze and rockery. Another Wisbech attraction is the impressive 68-feet limestone memorial to Thomas Clarkson, one of the earliest leaders of the abolitionist movement. The monument was designed by Sir George Gilbert Scott in Gothic style.

Still a lively commercial port, Wisbech boasts a yacht harbour with facilities for small craft that include floating pontoons with berths for 75 yachts.

The Angles Theatre – the third-oldest working theatre in Britain – is a vibrant centre for the arts located in a Georgian building with a history stretching back over 200 years. Some of the best talent in the nation, from poets and musicians

Wisbech is the stage for East Anglia's premier church flower festival, with flowers in four churches, strawberry teas, crafts, bric-a-brac, plants and a parade of floats. The event takes place at the beginning of July. The most important of the churches is the church of St Peter and St Paul, with two naves under one roof and an independent tower with a peal of ten bells. Note the royal arms of James I and the 17th century wall monuments in the chancel.

267 ELGOOD'S
BREWERY &
GARDENS

North Bank, Wisbech

A 200 year old brewery
where visitors can observe
traditional brewing methods,
sample the finished product
and relax in thesuperb four
acre garden.

 see page 344

to dance, comedy and theatrical
troupes – come to perform in the
intimate 112-seat auditorium.

Wisbech's **Lilian Ream
Photographic Collection** is
named after a daughter of
Wisbech born in the late 19th
century who at the time of her
death in 1961 had amassed a
collection of over 100,000
photographs of Wisbech people,
places and events, making for a
unique and fascinating insight into
the history and culture of the
town. The collection is housed in
the Tourist Information Centre in
Bridge Street, and offers changing
exhibitions from this treasure trove
of pictorial memorabilia.

AROUND WISBECH

WEST WALTON AND WALTON HIGHWAY

3 miles NE of Wisbech off the A47/B198

Several attractions can be found
here, notably the Church of St
Mary the Virgin in West Walton
with its magnificent 13th century
detached tower that dominates the
landscape. Walton Highway is home
to the **Fenland and West Norfolk
Aviation Museum**, whose exhibits
include Rolls-Royce Merlin engines,
a Lightning jet, a Vampire and a
Jumbo jet cockpit simulator. The

museum is open on summer
weekends.

LEVERINGTON

1 mile NW of Wisbech off the A1101

The tower and spire of the church
of St Leonard date from the 13th
and 14th centuries. The most
exceptional feature of an
exceptionally interesting church is
the 15th century stained-glass Jesse
window in the north aisle. There
are many fine memorials in the
churchyard. Oliver Goldsmith
wrote *She Stoops to Conquer* while
staying in Leverington.

PARSON DROVE

6 miles W of Wisbech on the B1187

Parson Drove is a Fenland village
which Samuel Pepys visited in 1663.
He stayed at the village's **Swan Inn**,
and mentions it in his diaries, though
he was not complimentary. It was a
centre of the woad industry until
1914, when the last remaining woad
mill was demolished. Parson Drove
is most certainly not the '*heathen
place*' once described by Pepys!

The Parson Drove Visitors
Centre is set in the old Victorian
lock-up on the village green, a
building with an unusual 170-year
history. Photographs and documents
trace the story of this lovely Fens
village.

Advertising Section

236

Norfolk

The area that lies between the county capital of Norwich and the border with Suffolk is mainly flat farmland, with quiet villages, handsome old farmhouses and the charming towers and spires of churches (Norfolk has more than 600 medieval churches). The valleys of the Rivers Nar and Wensum offer some of the most enchanting scenery in the county, while the major centres of population include Diss, an old market town with a mix of Tudor, Georgian and Victorian houses, and Wymondham, with an Abbey church that can compare even with the majestic Norwich Cathedral. Norwich is a vibrant city that moves with the times while retaining many medieval buildings, a number of which are museums telling the fascinating history of the region. The area to the east of Norwich contains the unique Norfolk Broads, stretches of shallow, slow-moving rivers that are both Britain's favourite choice for boating holidays (120 navigable miles) and a sanctuary for many species of birds and wildlife. Wroxham is perhaps the most beautiful of the Broads, Hickling the largest, and Ranworth has one of Norfolk Wildlife Trust's most popular family destinations, where interpreted boardwalks promote an understanding of Broads ecology.

On the coast due east of Norwich is the old port and modern resort of Great Yarmouth, where the visitor will find miles of sandy beaches, a breezy promenade, two piers and all the fun of the fair, as well as a rich maritime heritage that lives on to this day. The beaches, the sea views and the bracing air await visitors all along the coast, which stretches from Great Yarmouth up to Cromer on the northern edge and west to Sheringham, Hunstanton and King's Lynn. The most important town on the northwest coast is the busy resort of Hunstanton, the only east coast resort that actually faces west. King's Lynn, on the Great Ouse three miles inland from The Wash, was one of England's most important ports in medieval times, sitting at the southern end of an underwater maze of sandbanks. Close to King's Lynn is the Royal Family's country estate of Sandringham, while further inland is the prosperous market town of Fakenham, around which is a remarkable variety of places on interest. To the north, the Shrine of Our Lady of Walsingham was in medieval times second only to Canterbury as a destination for pilgrims.

The main centres of population in the centre and south of the county are Dereham, Swaffham and Thetford. Thetford's position at the meeting of the Rivers Thet and Little Ouse made it a place of strategic importance for centuries, and excavations have revealed an Iron Age settlement that is thought to have been the Palace of Queen Boadicea (Boudicca). To the west of the town stretch the 90 miles of Thetford Forest, which include the Neolithic flint mines of Grimes Graves. The area of southwest Norfolk leading into Suffolk is known as Breckland, meaning an area of land once cultivated but reverting to heath after the soil has become exhausted. This quiet corner of the county is bounded by the Little Ouse and Waveney rivers, which separate Norfolk from Suffolk.

Boats on the Norfolk Broads

Food and Drink in Norfolk

The selection of establishments serving food and drink featured in this section includes restaurants, cafes, hotels, pubs, inns and tea & coffee shops. Each establishment has an entry number which is used to identify its location on the map below and its name and short address in the list below the map.

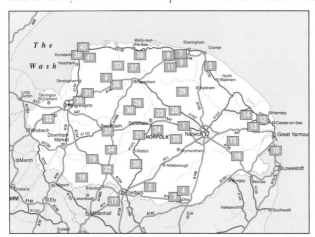

The entry number can also be used to find more information and contact details for the establishment in the ensuing pages. In addition full details of establishments serving food and drink featured in this section may be found on the Travel Publishing website –

www.travelpublishing.co.uk

This website has a large database of establishments serving food and drink covering the whole of Britain and Ireland.

FOOD AND DRINK

1   The Rembrandt, Easton
2   The Swan, East Harling
3   Fayre View Restaurant & Rooms, Diss
4   The Burston Crown, Burston
5   Elderton Lodge, Thorpe Market
6   The Dukes Head and Tham's Restaurant & Bar, West Rudham
7   The Red Hart Inn, Bodham
8   The Railway Tavern, Holt
9   The Hare & Hounds, Hempstead
10 The White Hart, Hopton-on-Sea
11 The Hunworth Bell, Hunworth
12 The Kings Head, Filby
13 The Ferry Inn, Stokesby
14 The Lion Inn, Thurne
15 The New Inn, Rockland St Mary
16 The King's Head, Loddon
17 The Elveden Inn, Elveden
18 The Lodge, Feltwell
19 The Crown Inn, Northwold
20 The Chequers Inn, Thompson

21 The Golden Dog, Shipdham
22 Lynford Country Hotel & Business Centre, Mundord
23 The Angel, Swanton Morley
24 The Mustard Pot, Whinburgh
25 The Bell, Barnham Broom
26 The Fox & Hounds, Lyng
27 The Norfolk Hero, Swaffham
28 The Mallard, Mileham
29 The Bell Inn, Cawston
30 The Bull Inn, Litcham
31 The Anvil, Congham
32 The Coach & Horses, Tilney St Lawrence
33 The Ostrich Inn, South Creake
34 The Swan, Hilborough
35 The Three Horseshoes, Roydon
36 The Crown , East Rudham
37 The Black Lion Hotel, Little Walsingham
38 The Carpenters Arms, Wighton
39 Georgie's Restaurant & Cellar Bar, Hunstanton
40 Neptune Inn & Restaurant, Old Hunstanton
41 The Gin Trap, Ringstead

1 THE REMBRANDT

Dereham Road, Easton, Norfolk NR9 5EH
☎ 01603 880010 Fax: 01603 880241

The Rembrandt is a popular, family-friendly fish & chips and pizza restaurant adorned with pictures of Norwich City FC. The menu also offers steaks, burgers and pies, along with a wide selection of lagers, beers, soft drinks, wines and spirits. Open from 4.30 Tuesday to Sunday, also lunchtime Wednesday, Friday and Saturday.

2 THE SWAN

Market Street, East Harling, nr Norwich,
Norfolk NR16 2AD
☎ 01953 717951
e-mail: clairepaul26@hotmail.com

Jamie in the kitchen and Claire behind the bar make a fine team at **The Swan**, a 15th century inn with beams, fireplaces and a garden. Home-cooked dishes cater for all tastes and there's a good choice of real ales. Tuesday is curry night, Wednesday quiz, live music twice monthly.

3 FAYRE VIEW RESTAURANT & ROOMS

Lower Denmark Street, Diss,
Norfolk IP22 4BE
☎ 01379 644684 Fax: 01379 644684
e-mail: thefayreview@aol.com

A short stroll from the centre of Diss brings visitors to **Fayre View**, a stunning setting for a meal or a stay. Owner Chris Gissing oversees every detail of the cooking, insisting on the finest and freshest of seasonal ingredients. A meal in the non-smoking restaurant brings delights  such as pigeon and pork terrine, fillet of beef poached in Barolo with thyme and garlic, and raspberry ripple crème brûlée, accompanied by a superb selection of wines. For guests staying overnight Fayre View has three very spacious en suite rooms.

4 THE BURSTON CROWN

Burston, nr Diss, Norfolk IP22 5TW
☎ 01379 741257 Fax: 01379 741257
e-mail: chris@burstoncrown.co.uk
🌐 www.burstoncrown.co.uk

Chris and Emily Targett retired from their professions as a doctor and nurse to run the **Burston Crown**, which he bought at the end of 2004. Tucked away a couple of miles north of Diss, this fine old country pub, which Chris runs with his wife Emily, excels in hospitality, food and drink. Stepping inside the bar, with its low oak beams, huge inglenooks and inviting sofas, is like taking a

step back in time. A chalkboard gives full details of gravity-fed real ales such as Adnam's Best Bitter, Elgood's Pageant Ale and Woodforde's Great Eastern.

Cooking is a passion with Chris, and he keeps the customers happy with a wide selection of dishes, from snacks to three-course meals. Everything is terrific, but the panini, tiger prawns, lasagne, lamb shanks and rib-eye steaks are particular favourites with the locals. The garden at the side of the pub is a great place for an alfresco drink, and there's plenty of room for the little ones to romp.

5 ELDERTON LODGE

Thorpe Market, Norfolk NR11 8TZ
☎ 01263 833547 Fax: 01263 834673
e-mail: enquiries@eldertonlodge.co.uk
⊕ www.eldertonlodge.co.uk

Once the shooting lodge of the adjacent Gunton Hall Estate, **Elderton Lodge** is now a thriving food-driven hotel with a warm, welcoming atmosphere. The transformation is largely due to the efforts of Rachel Lusher, who took over in 2001. Built in the latter half of the 18th century, the Grade II listed Lodge retains many original features, and the 11 individually decorated bedrooms, though traditional in style, are tastefully appointed to the highest modern standards. All rooms have en suite bath or shower rooms, central heating, television, telephone and tea/coffee trays.

The public rooms include a lounge bar, a charming conservatory and the elegant candlelit Langtry Restaurant. The emphasis here is on the very best seasonal produce with fish, lobsters, crabs and mussels from the nearby coast and game, including Gunton Park venison, from local estates. The fine food is complemented by an extensive cellar. Set in six acres of mature gardens, Elderton Lodge is a comfortable, secluded and very civilised base for discovering the many delights of rural North Norfolk.

6 THE DUKES HEAD AND THAM'S RESTAURANT & BAR

Lynn Road, West Rudham, nr King's Lynn, Norfolk PE31 8RW
☎ 01495 528628
⊕ www.thamsatdukeshead.co.uk

On the A148 between King's Lynn and Fakenham, **The Dukes Head** is a 17th century redbrick building with a light, airy interior and attractive open brickwork. Tham and his staff offer a warm welcome to drinkers and diners alike, but what sets this fine old inn apart is its food. Malaysian-born Tham and his chefs offer an exciting menu of Cantonese dishes with a Malaysian influence, freshly prepared from carefully sourced ingredients and free from Monosodium Glutamate. A lane beside the pub leads to November Cottage, which Tham has recently opened as a self-catering cottage for 4 guests.

7 THE RED HART INN

Bodham, Norfolk
☎ 01263 588270
e-mail: garethhamptongray@hotmail.com

Hearty home cooking is just one of the attractions of **The Red Hart Inn**, with beef & ale pie, lamb shanks and roast chicken among the popular choices. Pool and darts are played in the bar of this 17th century inn, which hosts a quiz every other Sunday. Beer garden and adjacent caravan site.

Explore Britain and Ireland with *Hidden Places* guides - a fascinating series of national and local travel guides.

www.travelpublishing.co.uk

0118-981-7777

info@travelpublishing.co.uk

8 THE RAILWAY TAVERN

Holt, Norfolk NR25 6BS
☎ 01263 712283
e-mail: awjonah@yahoo.co.uk

Holt is a regular finalist in the 'Anglia in Bloom' competition, and **The Railway Tavern** is one of many handsome buildings on the main street. Alan Jones, who took over the lease in the spring of 2005, has a friendly greeting for all his customers, and well-spaced tables allow plenty of room to enjoy a drink or a lunchtime snack or meal. A television screen shows Sky Sports events, and Alan has plans for quiz nights, theme nights and weekend entertainment.

9 THE HARE & HOUNDS

Holt Road, Hempstead, Norfolk NR25 6LD
☎ 01263 712329

A mile and a half from Holt on the Baconsthorpe road, **The Hare & Hounds** is a charming brick-and-flint building dating from about 1640. It has seen many changes down the years, but care has been taken to preserve its old-world appeal, the

beams and inglenook with wood-burning stove make a delightful setting for enjoying a drink (Woodforde Wherry cask ales are popular) and meal. In the two non-smoking dining areas daily changing menus offer a wide choice of meat, poultry, fish and vegetarian dishes, with lovely traditional desserts to finish. The pub has a large garden with plenty of room for children to play.

10 THE WHITE HART

Lowestoft Road, Hopton-on-Sea,
nr Great Yarmouth, Norfolk NR31 9AH
☎ 01502 730321
e-mail: paul@hoptonwhitehart.co.uk
🌐 www.hoptonwhitehart.co.uk

The White Hart is an 18th century coaching inn standing just seconds from the A12 between Lowestoft and Great Yarmouth. The mat is permanently out for visitors, and Paul, Jacqui and their family are the most conscientious of hosts, always striving to improve on what is a already a first-class offering. The substantial exterior of this free house is bright and cheerful, and the very spacious, well-designed interior comprises a lively bar, a family lounge, an intimate restaurant and a function room.

The pub is open all day for traditional ales, lagers, wines and spirits, and home-cooked food is served lunchtime and evening (all day in high season) and from 12 to 8 for the Sunday roasts. Light snacks cater for smaller appetites, while the main courses includes lots of pasta, all-day breakfast, curries, pies (shepherds, steak & ale, chicken & ham), barbecued ribs and giant Yorkshire pudding filled with sausage & mash or liver & bacon. The White Hart has a beer garden, and car parking at the front and rear.

241

11 THE HUNWORTH BELL

Hunworth, nr Holt, Norfolk NR24 2AA
☎ 01263 712300

Affable landlord Derek Feast has made many friends in the village and the surrounding area since taking over the reins at the **Hunworth Bell** in 1997. Overlooking the green in this picture-postcard village, the pub retains many original features from its 17th century origins, and a huge chalkboard menu in the beamed bar tempts with a very wide-ranging choice of dishes, from super fish and seafood specials to barbecued ribs, sausage & herb pie, chicken tikka and lamb cutlets with rosemary and a port sauce. There's a separate steak menu. The Hunworth Bell is open all day for drinks, including excellent real ales, and the food is served every lunchtime and evening.

12 THE KINGS HEAD

Main Road, Filby, Norfolk NR29 3HY
☎ 01493 730992

Open from noon onwards, **The Kings Head** is thriving under a mother-and-daughter team who took over in April 2005. Cosy, well furnished and full of character, the walls covered in prints of old Filby, the pub serves real ales and home-cooked food. Pool table; beer garden.

Looking for:
- *Places to Visit?*
- *Places to Stay?*
- *Places to Eat & Drink?*
- *Places to Shop?*

www.travelpublishing.co.uk

13 THE FERRY INN

Stokesby, Norfolk NR29 3EX
☎ 01493 751096 Fax: 01493 751245
e-mail: tbean74@aol.com

Off the A1064 west of Caister, **The Ferry Inn** is open all day, every day for drinks, meals and a happy, relaxed ambience. The interior is well designed, spacious and comfortable, with a long, solid wooden bar counter, low beams, an open fire and lots of copper and brass ornaments. Tenant Tracey Bean lives and breathes this delightful pub, and she keeps local residents and visitors happy with her excellent cooking. Rolls, jacket potatoes and light snacks take care of smaller lunchtime appetites, while the main courses (the choice changes daily) might include scampi, burgers, lasagne, beef stroganoff, chicken and smoky bacon pasta, and terrific suet puddings- steak & kidney or lamb & mint.

The pleasure lasts right through to desserts such as chocolate fudge cake or traditional apple pie. Adnams and guest ales head the list of drinks. This is the heart of the Broads, and as well as being easy to find from Caister or Great Yarmouth, it is very accessible to sailors: the River Bure runs alongside the beer garden, with moorings virtually on the doorstep. The Ferry Inn has a pool table, and hosts a monthly quiz. Guest accommodation might become available in the near future.

14 THE LION INN

Thurne, Norfolk NR29 3AP
☎ 01692 670796 Fax: 01692 670796

Tucked away off the B1152 between Billockby and Bastwick, **The Lion Inn** is the pride of Paul and Clare Denton. The welcome is equally warm for familiar faces and first-timers, and the pub is open from 11 o'clock onwards (from 12 on Sunday). The sturdy stone inn started life as a hunting lodge for Lord St Clair, and the bar, restaurant and family/function room have very comfortable, inviting feel.

Outside is a patio and beer garden, and

40 moorings are located just yards away. The choice for real ale drinkers is impressive, with Adnams, Flowers, Woodforde Wherry and Old Speckled Hen on tap, and the chalkboard menu provides a good choice of home-cooked dishes to please both traditional and more adventurous tastes. The Sunday carvery is always popular, and pizzas such as ham & mushroom or spicy Bolognese are also among the favourites. The special sweets board tempts with the likes of cool mint fling or strawberry indulgence. Out of season, the pub hosts a quiz every Sunday. An unusual amenity is a village shop located in the car park.

15 THE NEW INN

Rockland St Mary, nr Norwich, Norfolk NR14 7HP
☎ 01508 538403 Fax: 01508 538403
e-mail: stuartharrison@virgin.net

Stuart the chef and Ali behind the bar are making big changes at **The New Inn**, an 18th century coaching inn on the edge of the Broads, overlooking boats moored along the riverbank. The most important change is the bringing on stream of four spacious modern en suite bedrooms for Bed & Breakfast guests.

The inn, which is reached off the A146 a few miles southeast of Norwich, is open for drinks from 11 onwards (12 on Sunday), and food is served lunchtime and evening Tuesday to Saturday and all day Sunday. The regularly changing menu is always full of interest, ranging from starters/snacks such as cod & pancetta fishcakes or asparagus & gruyere flan to roast guinea fowl with rösti and a Grand Marnier sauce and chargrilled ribeye steak. The fine food is accompanied by an excellent wine selection. Booking is advisable at the weekend.

243

16 THE KING'S HEAD

**16 Bridge Street, Loddon,
Norfolk NR14 6EZ
☎ 01508 520330
e-mail: kingshead8th@yahoo.co.uk**

Local residents, holidaymakers and boating
people create a very relaxed, convivial
atmosphere at **The King's Head**, which
stands in a village on the River Chett, a
tributary of the Yare. Sue and Derick are
affable hosts, and in the bar, with beams, an
open fire, bench seating and military
memorabilia, the real ales include several local
brews. Sue is a very talented cook, and her
dishes range from light snacks and brunches
to splendid fish and seafood dishes to good
British
beef.
Great
wines
accompany
the fine
food.

17 THE ELVEDEN INN

**Brandon Road, Elveden, nr Thetford,
Norfolk IP24 3TP
☎ 01842 890378**

Open all day, every day, **The Elveden Inn**
stands on the 23,000-acre Iveagh Estate just
south of Thetford. Well-priced food includes
a popular Sunday roast lunch and regular hog
roasts in the marquee. The three guest
bedrooms all boast four-posters.

18 THE LODGE

**27/29 High Street, Feltwell,
Norfolk IP26 4AF
☎ 01842 828474**

In the village of Feltwell, on the B1112, **The
Lodge** is a free house with a delightful long-
serving owner who is also the chef. Mexican
food is her speciality, and draught San Miguel
is the perfect accompaniment.

19 THE CROWN INN

**30 High Street, Northwold,
Norfolk IP26 5LA
☎ 01366 727317**

The Crown Inn is a fine old whitewashed
stone building on the main street of
Northwold, just off the A134 northwest of
Thetford. The interior has a warm, inviting
old-world feel, and the blackboard menu
ranges from familiar pub classics to Caribbean
specials and super desserts. Four real ales.

20 THE CHEQUERS INN

**Griston Road, Thompson, nr Watton,
Norfolk IP24 1PX
☎ 01953 483360 Fax: 01953 488092**

The Chequers is a thatched 16th century
village inn whose customers enjoy a good
selection of real ales and a choice of home-
cooked dishes from bar and restaurant
menus. The public area has a traditional look,
and outside is a large beer garden. The
Chequers also offers accommodation in three
purpose-built bedrooms.

21 THE GOLDEN DOG

**High Street, Shipdham, nr Dereham,
Norfolk IP25 7PA
☎ 01362 820255**

Dating from the mid-16th century, **The
Golden Dog** stands on the A1075 a short
drive south of Dereham. Homely,
comfortable and friendly, this is a much-loved
local with an unpretentious appeal; that's the
way
owner
Peter
Claxton
likes it,
and
that's the
way his
regulars
like it.
The pub
is open
from
noon every day for drinks and
straightforward cooking. Pool and darts are
played in the bar, and the beer garden has
plenty of space for kids to play.

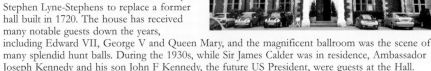

Mundford, nr Thetford,
Norfolk IP26 5HW
☎ 01842 878351 Fax: 01842 878252
e-mail: enquiries@lynfordhallhotel.co.uk
🌐 www.lynfordhallhotel.co.uk

Lynford Hall Country House Hotel & Business Centre is a distinguished Grade II listed mansion built in the Jacobean style. It was designed in the Jacobean style by William Burn and built between 1857 and 1862 by Stephen Lyne-Stephens to replace a former hall built in 1720. The house has received many notable guests down the years, including Edward VII, George V and Queen Mary, and the magnificent ballroom was the scene of many splendid hunt balls. During the 1930s, while Sir James Calder was in residence, Ambassador Joseph Kennedy and his son John F Kennedy, the future US President, were guests at the Hall.

The accommodation at the Hall comprises 21 luxurious en suite bedrooms, all individually

furnished and appointed in keeping with the Hall's heritage. The new owners Mansion House Weddings Limited plan to add many more rooms, and other new facilities in the pipeline include an organic centre and a sports centre. The Duvernay Restaurant (named after the great ballerina who married Stephen Lyne-Stephens) is an elegant room with ornate ceilings and fine views over the Hall's formal gardens and lake. The restaurant is renowned for dishes based on organic produce, including vegetables from the garden.

The Wellingtonia public bar offers a cosy, warm and friendly atmosphere in which to enjoy a drink by the roaring fire. When the weather is fine, the Terrace is a delightful spot for morning coffee or afternoon tea. Scenes from popular programmes such as *You Rang My Lord*, *Love on a Branch Line*, *Dads Army* and *Allo Allo* were filmed here, and the last is remembered by the recent opening of René's Café. Lynford Hall is one of the region's top conference, exhibition, banqueting and wedding venues, and the setting, in 27 acres of mature gardens within Thetford Forest Park, makes it an ideal place for a relaxing break or for touring the area. Leisure pursuits, including walking, cycling, horse riding, golfing and fishing, are all available nearby.

245

23 THE ANGEL

**66 Greengate, Swanton Morley,
Norfolk NR20 4LX
☎ 01362 637407 Fax: 01362 638316**

Three miles north of Dereham, close to Thetford Forest, **The Angel** is a fine old redbrick house with a history going back almost 400 years. Avril and Peter took over the reins in the autumn of 2003 and have embarked on a long-term plan to enhance the amenities of this splendid place. In the busy little bar with its roaring open fire real ale fans can enjoy the excellent Woodforde Wherry and two or three guest ales. Avril is in charge in the kitchen, using good fresh ingredients, locally sourced as far as possible, for her generously served dishes. Those in the know save room for scrumptious desserts such as jam or chocolate sponge, spotted dick and blackberry & apple crumble.

The Angel is said to incorporate the remains of a home that belonged to the ancestors of Abraham Lincoln. A framed notice tells that in 1615 Richard Lincoln made a will disinheriting his son Edward and prompting his son Samuel to emigrate to America in 1637. The rest, as they say, is history!

24 THE MUSTARD POT

**Dereham Road, Whinburgh,
Norfolk NR19 1AF
☎ 01362 692179**

Easy to spot with its cheerful mustard-coloured exterior, **The Mustard Pot** is a 17th century roadside inn with a cosy, relaxing ambience. Traditional ales and beers – including Wolf's Golden Jackal and Big Red – accompany home-cooked food: Mustard Pot chicken with honey, wholegrain mustard and special spicy potatoes is a great favourite.

25 THE BELL

**Barnham Broom, Norfolk NR9 4AA
☎ 01603 759619**

The Bell is a 15th century roadside inn with bubbly, welcoming tenants and a lively, sociable ambience. Real ales accompany good-value home cooked dishes, and entertainment includes pool, darts, karaoke on Thursday and live music on Saturday.

26 THE FOX & HOUNDS

**The Street, Lyng, nr Norwich,
Norfolk NR9 5AL
☎ 01603 872316 Fax: 01603 879030
e-mail: Webster.neil@talk21.com**

The Fox & Hounds has all the essentials of a traditional country inn: a charming village setting, friendly hosts, real ales, honest home cooking, pub games and a pleasant beer garden. the inn is open lunchtime and evenings Monday to Wednesday and all day Thursday to Sunday.

27 THE NORFOLK HERO

**Station Street, Swaffham,
Norfolk PE37 7HB
☎ 01760 723923
e-mail: thenorfolkhero@aol.com**

Colin and Jane Green, at the helm for 15 years, have a welcome for all visitors to **The Norfolk Hero** in Swaffham. Behind the attractive Victorian frontage a cosy, traditional interior is a pleasant setting for enjoying snacks and classic dishes such as shepherds pie, chilli or chicken curry.

The Street, Mileham, nr East Dereham,
Norfolk PE32 2RA
☎ 01328 700602 Fax: 01328 700061
e-mail: joscelin.colborne@mallard.co.uk

Joscelin Colborne has exchanged life as a commodity broker for owning and running self-catering holiday accommodation and a thriving wine business. **The Mallard** is a stunning development of farmhouse dwellings, where no expense has been spared into creating five superb self-catering units on a 3-acre site in the tucked-away village of Mileham. The tile-roofed redbrick buildings

are adorned with luxuriant greenery, and inside, top-quality modern equipment complements original features such as rough stone walls. Each unit contains a bedroom furnished in uncluttered, elegant style, a bathroom, a lounge and fully fitted kitchen.

The five units that make up The Mallard are each named after a member or relative of the duck family – Widgeon, Pintail, Mandarin, Grebe and Teal. The spacious grounds offer pleasant strolling, and residents can pass a happy hour in the on-site games room. Joscelin has made The Mallard unique by adding a wine centre to the two top units. Mallard's Fine Wines is an exclusive wine importing business, and guests have the unusual opportunity of browsing through the wine selection and choosing wines to quaff or to complement their meal literally on the doorstep.

In a triangle bounded by Fakenham, Swaffham and Dereham, The Mallard is well placed for exploring both the countryside, the villages and the towns of the region. Even the next villages have plenty of visitor attractions. Litcham, on the River Nar just along the B1145, has a fascinating Village Museum, and Gressenhall is home to one of the UK's rural life museums. And for anyone with an interest in churches, those at Beeston, Brisley, Tittleshall and East Dereham, all within a short drive, are well worth a visit. The Mallard is open all year round.

29 THE BELL INN

High Street, Cawston, Norfolk NR10 4AE
☎ 01603 871216
e-mail: drinabellinn@aol.com
🌐 www.bellinncawston.co.uk

The Bell Inn is a fine late 16th century
hostelry on the main street of Cawston,
whose attractions include one of the most
magnificent churches in the county. Behind
the freshly painted frontage the public rooms
are spacious and spotless, and outside there's
a roomy patio
and beer
garden.
Andreanna
Brookman's
cooking
attracts an
eager band of
regulars and
visitors, who

come here for steaks, pizzas, vegetarian
dishes and hearty blackboard specials that
could include lasagne, chicken & leek pie and
braised lamb shanks. Three en suite guest
rooms provide a comfortable base for
discovering the delights of the Norfolk
countryside.

31 THE ANVIL

St Andrews Lane, Congham,
nr King's Lynn, Norfolk PE32 1DU
☎ 01485 600615
e-mail: andreawsix@aol.com

Since arriving in the autumn of 2004, David
and Andrea Bunn have really made their mark
at **The Anvil**. The smartly modernised 18th
century house has a traditional look inside,
with horse
brasses
surrounding
the brick
hearth in
the bar-
lounge.
David
dispenses
good
conversation
and real

ales, while Andrea cooks pies, pasta, steaks
and fish and vegetarian specials to enjoy in
the pretty 24-cover restaurant. The Anvil is
open all day, every day.

30 THE BULL INN

Litcham, nr King's Lynn,
Norfolk PE32 2NS
☎ 01328 701340
e-mail: neilmilsom@aol.com

Manager Neil Milsom is overseeing a major
improvement programme at the **Bull Inn**,
which overlooks the green in the village of
Litcham on the B1145 equidistant from
Dereham
and
Fakenham.
Dating
from 1618,
the inn has
a smart
whitewashed
frontage
and

delightfully traditional interior with beams
and wooden floors. Classic pub dishes include
gammon, steaks and pies, and Greene King
IPA is the favourite ale. The main change for
the autumn of 2005 is the bringing on stream
of new bedrooms adding to the two already
available. Quiz Thursday.

32 THE COACH & HORSES

Tilney St Lawrence, nr King's Lynn,
Norfolk PE34 4RU
☎ 01945 880266

Located off the A47 six miles south of
King's Lynn, **The Coach & Horses** is a 17th
century country inn with some attractive
Dutch influences in its architecture. It's a
cosy, pleasant setting for enjoying the
hospitality provided by Rachel and Paul, and
Rachel's good honest home cooking is a real
bonus.

33 THE OSTRICH INN

1 Fakenham Road, South Creake,
nr Fakenham, Norfolk NR21 9PB
☎ 01328 823320 Fax: 01328 823192
e-mail: info@ostrichinn.co.uk
🌐 www.ostrichinn.co.uk

Simon and Emma welcome visitors to **The
Ostrich** Inn, complete with its original rustic
beams. It has been trading since the 1680s and
offers the same warm welcome today as it did
then! Real ales, fine wines and great food are
served in the bar and restaurants and there are
three comfortable en-suite guest rooms.

34 THE SWAN

Brandon Road, Hilborough, nr Swaffham,
Norfolk IP26 5BW
☎ 01760 756380

The Swan is a distinguished old coaching inn set back from the A1065 close to the village of Hilborough. Ray and Mary Nelson have owned the premises since 2002 and took over the running in the spring of 2005, ably assisted by their right-hand lady Kate. The oldest parts date back to the 17th century, and log fires create a homely, welcoming atmosphere in the bar, where the counter is fronted by some splendid ornate wood.

The Swan is open every session and all day Friday, Saturday and Sunday for drinks, which include three or four ales, with Greene King IPA

and Morland's Old Speckled Hen the regulars. The pub is also one of the best places in the area to enjoy a meal, and in the 50-cover non-smoking restaurant gnarled black beams contrast with immaculate white-painted walls. The printed menu and the specials board provide plenty of choice for all tastes and appetites, and because of the pub's popularity booking is necessary at the weekend. Picnic benches are set outside on the patio, and there's ample off-road parking space.

Food and drink are not the only reasons for visiting this fine old inn, as it also offers excellent Bed & Breakfast accommodation all year round. The nine en suite rooms, combining period charm with modern facilities, include a family room, and the two rooms on the ground floor are suitable for less mobile guests. The tariff includes a hearty breakfast, and the friendly owners and staff ensure a very pleasant, relaxing stay. All are welcome to join in the weekly quiz, which starts at 9 o'clock every Wednesday.

The village of Hilborough is situated between the old market towns of Swaffham and Thetford, and The Swan is a very civilised base for exploring the history of these towns and for exploring the lovely countryside of the region. One of the main attractions is Thetford Forest, the most extensive lowland forest in Britain, offering woodland walks and nature trails, cycling and a variety of other activities.

249

35 THE THREE HORSESHOES

Roydon, nr King's Lynn, Norfolk PE32 1AQ
☎ 01485 600362 Fax: 01485 600362

The Three Horseshoes is a handsome redbrick, tile-roofed 17th century building in a pleasant little village 2 miles east of the A148/A149 roundabout. Open all day, every day from noon onwards, the pub has an inviting, traditional bar with local history on display, and in fine weather the front patio and the rear garden are popular spots for enjoying a drink or a meal. Tony and Lin Metcalfe took over the reins in the spring of 2005, with Tony behind the bar and Lin and her daughter in the kitchen.

The food side of the business has really taken off since they arrived, and the old pool room is now an elegant 30-cover non-smoking restaurant. The choice runs from baguettes, jacket potatoes, ploughmans platters and hot and cold light bites to classic pub dishes such as battered cod, meat pies, steaks and lasagne (meat and vegetarian). Lunch is served between 12 and 2.30 every day, evening meals between 6 and 9 Monday to Saturday. It is probable that accommodation will be available some time in 2006, making The Three Horseshoes an ideal base for exploring the many places of scenic and historic interest in the region.

36 THE CROWN

The Green, East Rudham, nr King's Lynn, Norfolk PE31 8RD
☎ 01485 528292

The Crown is an attractive 17th century pub on the Green at East Rudham, a village on the A148 between King's Lynn and Fakenham. Wendy Land and David Hanna have built up an excellent reputation since taking over in 1990. Wendy is a serious cook whose home-cooked dishes are famous

throughout this area of Norfolk, and David does an equally fine job behind the bar, dispensing good cheer and good beer. The Crown has a loyal local following, and walkers and tourists are also always welcome. For overnight guests the pub has two letting bedrooms – a twin and a family room.

37 THE BLACK LION HOTEL

Friday Market Place, Little Walsingham, Norfolk NR22 6DB
☎ 01328 820235
e-mail: theresaathompson@aol.com
🌐 www.blacklionwalsingham.com

Just behind the main street in a village that attracts thousands of visitors every year, **The Black Lion Hotel** is a very pleasant spot for a drink, a meal or an overnight or longer stay. Run by sisters Christabel and Theresa, the premises date back as far as the 13th century

and there's plenty of period charm in the comfortably furnished bar-lounge overlooking the patio. In the restaurant, prime produce, mostly locally sourced, feature in dishes that range from carrot and ginger soup to cod & chips, mussels, steaks and venison pie. B&B accommodation comprises seven en suite bedrooms.

38 THE CARPENTERS ARMS

Wighton, nr Fakenham, Norfolk NR23 1PF
☎ 01328 820752

The Carpenters Arms has been providing good hospitality since 1861, and its appeal is wider than ever since business partners Matthew Higham and Stephen Franklin took over at the end of 2004. The new tenants have completely revamped the bar and restaurant, bringing contemporary touches to the decor; comfortable leather sofas greet visitors in the reception area, and eyecatching features include some attractive stained glass in the restaurant. Matthew is a talented and enthusiastic chef, and reports of his culinary

have quickly spread around the region, bringing a growing band of regulars to this pretty village.

Prime fresh ingredients are very much to the fore in dishes that include fish and seafood specials, curries and a super steak & ale pie. Woodforde Wherry is a favourite among a choice of real ales that increases to about 20 during the beer festival hosted by the pub in early June. Wighton is situated between Wells and the Walsinghams, and just outside the village the charming narrow-gauge Wells-Walsingham Light Railway makes its gentle way through the countryside.

39 GEORGIE'S RESTAURANT & CELLAR BAR

3 Lestrange Terrace, Hunstanton, Norfolk
☎ 01485 535565

Georgie's Restaurant & Cellar Bar is open lunchtime and evening, and all day in summer. The ground-floor restaurant and cellar below provide a good choice of snacks and popular dishes accompanied by a range of beers, lagers, wines and spirits. Wednesday and Saturday are karaoke nights; live music last Friday of the month.

Explore Britain and Ireland with *Hidden Places* guides - a fascinating series of national and local travel guides.

www.travelpublishing.co.uk

0118-981-7777

info@travelpublishing.co.uk

40 NEPTUNE INN & RESTAURANT

85 Old Hunstanton Road, Old Hunstanton, Norfolk PE36 6HZ
☎ 01485 532122
e-mail: reservations@theneptune.co.uk
🌐 www.theneptune.co.uk

Owners Paul and Hilary Berriff and head chef Jon Cleland make a great team at the **Neptune Inn & Restaurant**, a fine place for a meal and ideal base for exploring North Norfolk. Hilary has given the 1830s redbrick building a completely new look inspired by the New England coast of Maine, with mellow brown tones, white clapboard walls, replica boats and evocative black-and-white photographs; hand-made New England furniture graces the seven superbly equipped en suite bedrooms. Chef Jon's sophisticated menus make inspired use of the best local produce, and the American-style Sunday brunch is a popular feature. Fine wines and cask ales complement the terrific food.

6 High Street, Ringstead, nr Hunstanton,
Norfolk PE36 5JU
☎ 01485 525264 Fax: 01485 525321
e-mail: thegintrap@aol.com

Signposted off the A149 three miles east of
Hunstanton, Ringstead is a village of pretty
whitewashed houses in local carrstone. It's
also the home of **The Gin Trap**, a delightful
17th century coaching inn with a particularly
warm and inviting atmosphere. The beamed
bar, with its wood-burning stove, tables on
cast-iron frames and comfortable old chairs,
is an ideal spot for relaxing with a glass of
real ale from a choice that includes Adnams,
Greene King, Woodforde and some 'own-
label' brews. The wine list includes half a
dozen by the glass, to enjoy on their own or
to accompany a snack or a meal from the bar
menu.

Morning coffee, lunch and supper are served in the
bar, whose offerings run from filled baps and ciabatta
bread to ploughman's platters, wild boar sausages with red
onion gravy, meat and fish pies and delectable desserts.
The menu in the intimate candle-lit restaurant with its two
rosette award, reflects the abundance of produce from
the North Norfolk coast and countryside, including
oysters, mussels, crabs, samphire, fresh fish and game. To
accompany this fine choice of dishes both traditional and
contemporary (ending with a delectable list of desserts),
is an extensive, well-chosen wine list.

Ringstead is an ideal base for exploring North
Norfolk, and The Gin Trap has three beautifully
furnished guest bedrooms – two doubles with luxurious,
spacious bathrooms
with baths ands
separate shower
units, and a twin
with a shower room.

More bedrooms are being added, and two charming self-
catering cottages with access to a large garden are also
available. Margaret Greer has run the Gin Trap for 2 years,
while her husband Don is mainly responsible for the adjacent
Ringstead Gallery, housed in a lovely old whitewashed
stable building. The gallery and display areas are showcases
for the work of artists such as Lawrie Williamson, Jeremy
Barlow, Luis Frutos, Hugo Grenville and many more artists
evoking the beautiful local landscape. The gallery also features
limited editions and an exciting range of bronze sculptures by
Rosemary Cook and Sue Riley. The gallery, which is open
from 10 to 5 Monday to Saturday, hosts regular exhibitions
throughout the year.

Accommodation in Norfolk

The accommodation featured in this section includes hotels, inns, guest houses, bed & breakfasts and self catered establishments. Each establishment has an entry number which is used to identify its location on the map below and its name and short address in the list below the map. The entry number can also be used to find more information and contact details for the accommodation in the ensuing pages. In addition full details of all this accommodation may be found on the Travel Publishing website - www.travelpublishing.co.uk. This website has a comprehensive database of accommodation covering the whole of Britain and Ireland.

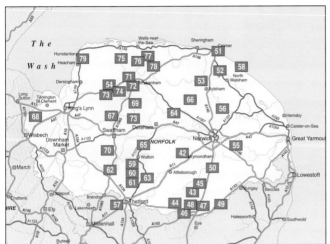

ACCOMMODATION

42	Kimberley Home Farm, Wymondham
43	Grove Farm, Gissing
44	Hazel Barn, Bressingham
45	Oakbrook, Great Moulton
46	Fayre View Restaurant & Rooms, Diss
47	Moor View, Dickleburgh
48	Walcot Green Farm Cottage, Walcot Green
49	Tom', 'Dick' and 'Harry', Withersdale
50	Foxhole Farm, Saxlingham Thorpe
51	The Knoll Guest House, Cromer
52	Elderton Lodge, Thorpe Market
53	Itteringham Mill, Itteringham
54	The Dukes Head and Tham's Restaurant & Bar, West Rudham
55	The New Inn, Rockland St Mary
56	Bridge House, Coltishall
57	The Elveden Inn, Elveden
58	The Durdans, Mundesley-on-Sea
59	College Farm, Thompson
60	The Chequers Inn, Thompson

61	The Thatched House, Thompson
62	Lynford Country Hotel & Business Centre, Mundord
63	Manor Farm, Great Hocking
64	Collin Green Cottages, Lyng
65	Pound Green Hotel, Shipdham
66	The Bell Inn, Cawston
67	Lodge Farm, Castle Acre
68	Black Barn House, Walpole St Peter
69	The Mallard, Mileham
70	The Swan, Hilborough
71	Manor Farm, Sculthorpe
72	Wensum House, Hempton
73	Lower Farm B&B, Harpley
74	The Crown, East Rudham
75	The Ostrich Inn, South Creake
76	The Black Lion Hotel, Little Walsingham
77	Berry Hall, Great Walsingham
78	Field House, Hindringham
79	The Gin Trap, Ringstead

42 KIMBERLEY HOME FARM

Barnham Broom Road, Wymondham,
Norfolk NR18 0RW
☎ 01953 603137 Fax: 01953 604836

Three rooms
provide quiet,
secluded and
very roomy
B&B
accommodation
at **Kimberley
Home Farm**.
Good
breakfasts, evening meals by arrangement.

43 GROVE FARM

Gissing, nr Diss, Norfolk IP22 5XA
☎ 01379 677232 Mobile: 07887 957142

Set among lawns and
woodland, **Grove Farm** is
a country farming estate
four miles north of Diss. A
luxurious self-catering
bungalow sleeping up to five in three bedrooms
offers seclusion, tranquillity and all the modern
comforts.

44 HAZEL BARN

Lodge Lane, Bressingham, nr Diss,
Norfolk IP22 2BE
☎ 01379 644396 Fax: 01379 644396
e-mail: hazelbarn@ukonline.co.uk

A purpose-built addition to a 16th century
barn provides a very quiet, civilised base for
Bed & Breakfast guests. Resident owners
Nigel and Pearl Dunscombe welcome visitors
to **Hazel Barn**, where the accommodation
comprises three bedrooms decorated and
furnished with uncluttered elegance and all
with modern
en suite
facilities,
television
and tea/
coffee tray.
All are on
the ground
floor, with
level access.

The barn is set in mature gardens with a
natural pond and a heated swimming pool. A
good choice for breakfast includes vegetarian
options. No smoking; no pets.

45 OAKBROOK

Frith Way, Great Moulton, nr Long Stratton,
Norfolk NR15 2HE
☎ 01379 677359
e-mail: simonandheather@btopenworld.com
🌐 www.norfolkbroads.com/oakbrook/

A short drive from the A140 at Long Stratton
brings visitors to **Oakbrook**, a new venture
for owners Simon and Heather Moss. They
arrived in April 2005 and set in progress a
room-by-room refurbishment of this
handsome redbrick building, which was a
village school and later a nursing home before
becoming a guest house. Accommodation
comprises nine bright, spacious bedrooms,

seven of them en suite. They range from singles to family
rooms; five are upstairs, four on the ground floor, and full
facilities are available for disabled guests. Rooms are let on a
Bed & Breakfast basis, but packed lunches and evening meals
can be provided with a little notice. Open throughout the year,
Oakbrook is a quiet, pleasant base for discovering the
rural delights and pretty villages of the region. And the
proximity of the A140 affords easy access to Norwich to the
north and Diss to the south.

46 FAYRE VIEW RESTAURANT & ROOMS

Lower Denmark Street, Diss,
Norfolk IP22 4BE
☎ 01379 644684 Fax: 01379 644684
e-mail: thefayreview@aol.com

A short stroll from the centre of Diss brings visitors to **Fayre View**, a stunning setting for a meal or a stay. Owner Chris Gissing oversees every detail of the cooking, insisting on the finest and freshest of seasonal ingredients. A meal in the non-smoking restaurant brings delights such  as pigeon and pork terrine, fillet of beef poached in Barolo with thyme and garlic, and raspberry ripple crème brûlée, accompanied by a superb selection of wines. For guests staying overnight Fayre View has three very spacious en suite rooms.

47 MOOR VIEW

Semere Green Lane, Dickleburgh,
Norfolk IP21 4NT
☎ 01379 741401
e-mail: vhooper@ukonline.co.uk
🌐 www.moor-view.com

Surrounded by unspoilt countryside on the A140 six miles north of Diss, Moor View is an excellent base for a relaxing break, for a walking holiday or for exploring the many local places of interest. Resident owners Viki and Michael Hooper offer a choice of accommodation, with well appointed  bedrooms for B&B guests in the renovated main house and a pretty two bedroom cottage fully equipped for self-catering. The owners produce excellent breakfasts, afternoon teas and evening meals, and packed lunches are always offered. No smoking inside. Pets are welcome, and purpose built kennels are available on site.

48 WALCOT GREEN FARM COTTAGE

Walcot Green, nr Diss, Norfolk IP22 5SU
☎ 01379 652806 Fax: 01379 652806
e-mail: walcotgreenfarm@fsmail.net
🌐 www.walcotgreenfarm.co.uk

On a working farm two miles from the centre of Diss, a tastefully converted cottage provides top-quality self-catering accommodation. The farm on which **Walcot Green Farm Cottage** stands is owned and run by Ken and Nannette Catchpole, who have been arable farmers throughout their working lives. The cottage has three bedrooms (one family room and two singles), a fully-equipped kitchen and a comfortable living area.

Guests have the use of other amenities including an indoor heated swimming pool, a spacious lawned garden and a patio area with a barbecue and garden furniture. Set in peaceful, idyllic countryside just two miles from John  Betjeman's favourite Norfolk town, this friendly, welcoming establishment is  an excellent base from which to explore local attractions such as Banham Zoo, the Steam Museum and Gardens at Bressingham and the 100th Bomb Group Museum at Dickleburgh. Walcot Green is a non-smoking establishment. Children welcome, but no pets.

49 'TOM', 'DICK' & 'HARRY'

Church Farm, Withersdale, nr Harleston,
Norfolk IP20 0JR
☎ 01379 588091 Fax: 01379 586009
e-mail: enquiries@bacatchurchfarm.co.uk
🌐 www.bacatchurchfarm.co.uk

'Tom', 'Dick' & 'Harry' are three delightful self-catering cottages in a tranquil, scenic setting halfway between Diss and Beccles. Converted from traditional farm buildings, each has a double bedroom ('Dick' has room for a cot and

single bed), bath or shower room, lounge/dining area and kitchen. Guests have the use of a landscaped garden area with garden furniture. The farm is surrounded by meadows grazed by cattle and sheep and farmed to encourage wildlife.

50 FOXHOLE FARM

Foxhole, Saxlingham Thorpe, nr Norwich,
Norfolk NR15 1UG
☎ 01508 499226 Fax: 01508 499226
e-mail: foxholefarm@hotmail.com

Pauline and John Spear welcome guests to their family home at **Foxhole Farm**, in a delightful rural setting. The house has two en-suite rooms for B&B – a twin and a double, both overlooking open countryside. Evening meal by prior arrangement. No smoking; no credit cards.

51 THE KNOLL GUEST HOUSE

23 Alfred Road, Cromer,
Norfolk NR27 9AN
☎ 01263 512753
e-mail: ian@knollguesthouse.co.uk
🌐 www.knollguesthouse.co.uk

The Knoll is a charming licensed guest house in the heart of Cromer, with walking, cycling and riding all available nearby. The five bedrooms are comfortable and well-appointed, and a hearty breakfast starts the day. Evening meals by arrangement. No smoking.

52 ELDERTON LODGE

Thorpe Market, Norfolk NR11 8TZ
☎ 01263 833547 Fax: 01263 834673
e-mail: enquiries@eldertonlodge.co.uk
🌐 www.eldertonlodge.co.uk

Once the shooting lodge of the adjacent Gunton Hall Estate, **Elderton Lodge** is now a thriving food-driven hotel with a warm, welcoming atmosphere. The transformation is largely due to the efforts of Rachel Lusher, who took over in 2001. Built in the latter half of the 18th century, the Grade II listed Lodge retains many original features, and the 11 individually decorated bedrooms, though traditional in style, are tastefully appointed to the highest modern standards. All rooms have en suite bath or shower rooms, central heating, television, telephone and tea/coffee trays.

The public rooms include a lounge bar, a charming conservatory and the elegant candlelit Langtry Restaurant. The emphasis here is on the very best seasonal produce with fish, lobsters, crabs and mussels from the nearby coast and game, including Gunton Park venison, from local estates. The fine food is complemented by an extensive cellar. Set in six acres of mature gardens, Elderton Lodge is a comfortable, secluded and very civilised base for discovering the many delights of rural North Norfolk.

53 ITTERINGHAM MILL

The Mill, The Common, Itteringham,
Norfolk NR11 7AR
☎ 01263 587688
e-mail: downspeter@talk21.com

Country-lovers, birdwatchers, walkers and
tourists all enjoy the hospitality in generous
supply at **Itteringham Mill**, which enjoys a
quiet, scenic setting in a tiny rural hamlet.

The 18th
century mill has
been stylishly
converted into
a distinguished
country
mansion where
owners Peter
and Lis Downs
have three very
spacious and comfortable bedrooms for Bed
& Breakfast guests. All rooms have river
views and ensuite facilities. A splendid multi-
choice breakfast is served in the lovely lounge
that also makes the most of the location.
Non-smoking. Cash and Cheques only
accepted.

54 THE DUKES HEAD AND THAM'S RESTAURANT & BAR

Lynn Road, West Rudham, nr King's Lynn,
Norfolk PE31 8RW
☎ 01495 528628
🌐 www.thamsatdukeshead.co.uk

On the A148 between King's Lynn and
Fakenham, **The Dukes Head** is a 17th
century redbrick
building with a
light, airy
interior and
attractive open
brickwork.
Tham and his
staff offer a
warm welcome

to drinkers and diners alike, but what sets this
fine old inn apart is its food. Malaysian-born
Tham and his chefs offer an exciting menu of
Cantonese dishes with a Malaysian influence,
freshly prepared from carefully sourced
ingredients and free from Monosodium
Glutamate. A lane beside the pub leads to
November Cottage, which Tham has recently
opened as a self-catering cottage for 4 guests.

55 THE NEW INN

Rockland St Mary, nr Norwich,
Norfolk NR14 7HP
☎ 01508 538403 Fax: 01508 538403
e-mail: stuartharrison@virgin.net

Stuart the chef and Ali behind the bar are
making big changes at **The New Inn**, an
18th century coaching inn on the edge of the
Broads, overlooking boats moored along the
riverbank. The most important change is the
bringing on stream of four spacious modern
en suite bedrooms for Bed & Breakfast
guests.

The inn, which is reached off the A146 a few
miles southeast of Norwich, is open for drinks from 11
onwards (12 on Sunday), and food is served lunchtime
and evening Tuesday to Saturday and all day Sunday.
The regularly changing menu is always full of interest,
ranging from starters/snacks such as cod & pancetta
fishcakes or asparagus & gruyere flan to roast guinea
fowl with rösti and a Grand Marnier sauce and
chargrilled ribeye steak. The fine food is accompanied
by an excellent wine selection. Booking is advisable at
the weekend.

56 BRIDGE HOUSE

High Street, Coltishall, Norfolk NR12 7AA
☎ 01603 737323 Fax: 01603 737323
🌐 www.bridge-house.com

Service, comfort and
hospitality are watchwords at
Bridge House, where
Sharon and Steve offer non-
smoking B&B in five en

suite rooms. One is in the 18th century family
home, the other in a barn conversion. The
garden leads to a private river frontage.

57 THE ELVEDEN INN

Brandon Road, Elveden, nr Thetford,
Norfolk IP24 3TP
☎ 01842 890378

Open all day, every day, **The Elveden Inn**
stands on the 23,000-acre Iveagh Estate just
south of Thetford. Well-priced food includes
a popular Sunday roast lunch and regular hog
roasts in the marquee. The three guest
bedrooms all boast four-posters.

59 COLLEGE FARM

Thompson, nr Thetford, Norfolk IP24 1QG
☎ 01953 483318 Fax: 01953 483318
e-mail: collegefarm@amserve.net

A 600-year-old farmhouse in rural Norfolk,
near Watton, makes an excellent base for
relaxing, enjoying the scenery, walking (the
Peddars Way is nearby) or touring the region.
Lavender
Garnier,
here for 30
years, has
three rooms
for B&B, all
very roomy
and
comfortable,
overlooking
the walled

gardens and the ponds. The immaculately
kept house, originally a college for priests,
retains many of its best period features; more
recently, one of the bedrooms was decorated
by Laura Ashley. Lavender offers a splendid
choice for breakfast. Prices start at £27.50

58 THE DURDANS

36 Trunch Road, Mundesley-on-Sea,
Norfolk NR11 8JX
☎ 01263 722225 Fax: 01263 722883
e-mail: info@thedurdans.co.uk
🌐 www.thedurdans.co.uk

Anyone in search of invigorating air, a superb
sandy beach and an unassuming resort, need
look no further than
The Durdans,
which enjoys a quiet,
secluded setting at
the end of a tree-
lined drive. Owners
Andrew and
Caroline Griffin

have devoted much time and energy in ensuring
that everything is of a high standard at their
Victorian residence, with tasteful decoration,
quality furniture and expensive bed linen. The
seven bedrooms (six en-suite, one with private
bathrokom) provide a very comfortable,
civilised base for Bed & Breakfast guests. Lawns
to the rear slope down to Mundesley Beck. A
fine breakfast starts the day.

60 THE CHEQUERS INN

Griston Road, Thompson, nr Watton,
Norfolk IP24 1PX
☎ 01953 483360 Fax: 01953 488092

The Chequers is a thatched 16th century
village inn whose customers enjoy a good
selection of real ales and a choice of home-
cooked dishes from bar and restaurant
menus. The public area has a traditional look,
and outside is a large beer garden. The
Chequers also offers accommodation in three
purpose-built bedrooms.

61 THE THATCHED HOUSE

Mill Road, Thompson, near Thetford,
Norfolk IP24 1PH
☎ 01953 483577
e-mail: thatchouse@amserve.com

One of the prettiest
properties in the
region. The three
guest bedrooms are
decorated and
furnished in period

style and Brenda's breakfasts make a great
start to the day.

62 LYNFORD HALL COUNTRY HOTEL & BUSINESS CENTRE

Mundford, nr Thetford, Norfolk IP26 5HW
☎ 01842 878351 Fax: 01842 878252
e-mail: enquiries@lynfordhallhotel.co.uk
🌐 www.lynfordhallhotel.co.uk

Lynford Hall Country House Hotel & Business Centre is a distinguished Grade II listed mansion built in the Jacobean style. It was designed in the Jacobean style by William Burn and built between 1857 and 1862 by Stephen Lyne-Stephens to replace a former hall built in 1720. The house has received many notable guests down the years, including Edward VII, George V and Queen Mary, and the magnificent ballroom was the scene of many splendid hunt balls. During the 1930s, while Sir James Calder was in residence, Ambassador Joseph Kennedy and his son John F Kennedy, the future US President, were guests at the Hall.

The accommodation at the Hall comprises 21 luxurious en suite bedrooms, all individually furnished and appointed in keeping with the Hall's heritage. The new owners Mansion House Weddings Limited plan to add many more rooms, and other new facilities in the pipeline include an organic centre and a sports centre. The Duvernay Restaurant (named after the great ballerina who married Stephen Lyne-Stephens) is an elegant room with ornate ceilings and fine views over the Hall's formal gardens and lake. The restaurant is renowned for dishes based on organic produce, including vegetables from the garden.

The Wellingtonia public bar offers a cosy, warm and friendly atmosphere in which to enjoy a drink by the roaring fire. When the weather is fine, the Terrace is a delightful spot for morning coffee or afternoon tea. Scenes from popular programmes such as *You Rang My Lord*, *Love on a Branch Line*, *Dads Army* and *Allo Allo* were filmed here, and the last is remembered by the recent opening of René's Café. Lynford Hall is one of the region's top conference, exhibition, banqueting and wedding venues, and the setting, in 27 acres of mature gardens within Thetford Forest Park, makes it an ideal place for a relaxing break or for touring the area. Leisure pursuits, including walking, cycling, horse riding, golfing and fishing, are all available nearby.

63 MANOR FARM

Vicarage Road, Great Hockham,
nr Thetford, Norfolk IP24 1PE
☎ 01953 498204 Fax: 01953 498204
e-mail: manorfarm@ukfnet
🌐 www.bed&breakfastsinnorfolk.co.uk

Escape to this 16th century farm B&B, just five minutes from the edge of Thetford Forest in the unique Brecks countryside. Try the award-winning breakfasts - traditional and healthy options. Home-made and home-grown and local produce. Gold award for Green Tourism

64 COLLIN GREEN COTTAGES

Collin Green, Lyng, nr Norwich,
Norfolk NR9 5LH
☎ 01603 880158 Fax: 01603 881228
e-mail: thomaslyng@supanet.com

Collin Green Cottages comprise a two-bedroom bungalow and a joined pair of farm cottages sleeping up to 6 guests in three bedrooms. Both properties have a lounge/sitting room and modern fitted kitchen, and are equipped with everything needed for a relaxing self-catering holiday.

66 THE BELL INN

High Street, Cawston, Norfolk NR10 4AE
☎ 01603 871216
e-mail: drinabellinn@aol.com
🌐 www.bellinncawston.co.uk

The Bell Inn is a fine late 16th century hostelry on the main street of Cawston, whose attractions include one of the most magnificent churches in the county. Behind the freshly painted frontage the public rooms are spacious and spotless, and outside there's a roomy patio and beer garden. Andreanna Brookman's cooking attracts an eager band of regulars and visitors, who come here for steaks, pizzas, vegetarian dishes and hearty blackboard specials that could include lasagne, chicken & leek pie and braised lamb shanks. Three en suite guest rooms provide a comfortable base for discovering the delights of the Norfolk countryside.

65 POUND GREEN HOTEL

Pound Green Lane, Shipdham,
Norfolk IP25 7LS
☎ 01362 820940 Fax: 01362 820940
e-mail: poundgreen@aol.com
🌐 www.poundgreenhotel.co.uk

Standing in its own grounds off the A1075 between Watton and Dereham, **Pound Green Hotel** (awarded 1AA rosette) is a very pleasant choice for a relaxing break and a fine base for touring the region. Most of the 11 comfortable bedrooms have en suite facilities, and can be booked on a B&B or Dinner B&B basis. In the Bay Tree Brasserie chef-patron David Ostle offers a  regularly changing menu that is always full of interest. The hotel has a function suite and a good-sized garden with a children's play area.

67 LODGE FARM

Castle Acre, nr King's Lynn,
Norfolk PE32 2BS
☎ 01760 755506 Fax: 01760 755103

Country-lovers Simon and Marigold Thompson have a warm welcome for one and all at **Lodge Farm**, where three spacious en suite bedrooms provide comfortable accommodation in the tranquil, scenic setting of a working farm. There's a good choice for breakfast, and packed lunches can be arranged.

68 BLACK BARN HOUSE

Chalk Road, Walpole St Peter,
Norfolk PE14 7PN
☎ 01945 781115
🌐 www.blackbarnhouse.co.uk

Located off the A47, A1101 or A17, **Black Barn House** is a modern B&B with roomy guest accommodation. The house has three rooms (1 en suite) with television and tea/coffee facilities, and a garden flat sleeping four. A swimming pool in the garden is a boon in summer.

69 THE MALLARD

The Street, Mileham, nr East Dereham,
Norfolk PE32 2RA
☎ 01328 700602 Fax: 01328 700061
e-mail: joscelin.colborne@mallard.co.uk

Joscelin Colborne has exchanged life as a commodity broker for owning and running self-catering holiday accommodation and a thriving wine business. **The Mallard** is a stunning development of farmhouse dwellings, where no expense has been spared into creating five superb self-catering units on a 3-acre site in the tucked-away village of Mileham. The tile-roofed redbrick buildings

are adorned with luxuriant greenery, and inside, top-quality modern equipment complements original features such as rough stone walls. Each unit contains a bedroom furnished in uncluttered, elegant style, a bathroom, a lounge and fully fitted kitchen.

The five units that make up The Mallard are each named after a member or relative of the duck family – Widgeon, Pintail, Mandarin, Grebe and Teal. The spacious grounds offer pleasant strolling, and residents can pass a happy hour in the on-site games room. Joscelin has made The Mallard unique by adding a wine centre to the two top units. Mallard's Fine Wines is an exclusive wine importing business, and guests have the unusual opportunity of browsing through the wine selection and choosing wines to quaff or to complement their meal literally on the doorstep.

In a triangle bounded by Fakenham, Swaffham and Dereham, The Mallard is well placed for exploring both the countryside, the villages and the towns of the region. Even the next villages have plenty of visitor attractions. Litcham, on the River Nar just along the B1145, has a fascinating Village Museum, and Gressenhall is home to one of the UK's rural life museums. And for anyone with an interest in churches, those at Beeston, Brisley, Tittleshall and East Dereham, all within a short drive, are well worth a visit. The Mallard is open all year round.

Brandon Road, Hilborough, nr Swaffham,
Norfolk IP26 5BW
☎ 01760 756380

The Swan is a distinguished old coaching inn set back from the A1065 close to the village of Hilborough. Ray and Mary Nelson have owned the premises since 2002 and took over the running in the spring of 2005, ably assisted by their right-hand lady Kate. The oldest parts date back to the 17th century, and log fires create a homely, welcoming atmosphere in the bar, where the counter is

fronted by some splendid ornate wood.

The Swan is open every session and all day Friday, Saturday and Sunday for drinks, which include three or four ales, with Greene King IPA and Morland's Old Speckled Hen the regulars. The pub is also one of the best places in the area to enjoy a meal, and in the 50-cover non-smoking restaurant gnarled black beams contrast with immaculate white-painted walls. The printed menu and the specials board provide plenty of choice for all tastes and appetites, and because of the pub's popularity booking is necessary at the weekend. Picnic benches are set outside on the patio, and there's ample off-road parking space.

Food and drink are not the only reasons for visiting this fine old inn, as it also offers excellent Bed & Breakfast accommodation all year round. The nine en suite rooms, combining period charm with modern facilities, include a family room, and the two rooms on the ground floor are suitable for less mobile guests. The tariff includes a hearty breakfast, and the friendly owners and staff ensure a very pleasant, relaxing stay. All are welcome to join in the weekly quiz, which starts at 9 o'clock every Wednesday.

The village of Hilborough is situated between the old market towns of Swaffham and Thetford, and The Swan is a very civilised base for exploring the history of these towns and for exploring the lovely countryside of the region. One of the main attractions is Thetford Forest, the most extensive lowland forest in Britain, offering woodland walks and nature trails, cycling and a variety of other activities.

71 MANOR FARM

Sculthorpe, nr Fakenham,
Norfolk NR21 9NJ
☎ 01328 862185 Fax: 01328 862033
e-mail: carol@manorfarmb&b.com
🌐 www.manorfarmb&b.com

Manor Farm has three beautifully appointed bedrooms, two en suite and one with private facilities, providing quiet, comfortable, Bed & Breakfast accommodation. The house and its stunning walled garden are on a 500-acre farm located off the A148 near Fakenham.

72 WENSUM HOUSE

4 Dereham Road, Hempton, Fakenham,
Norfolk NR21 7AD
☎ 01328 864490 Fax: 01328 853686

Wensum House, is a grade II listed building in a village near the River Wensum. Fishing, golf, racecourse nearby. Pets welcome. B&B and s/c annexe open all year.

74 THE CROWN

The Green, East Rudham, nr King's Lynn,
Norfolk PE31 8RD
☎ 01485 528292

The Crown is an attractive 17th century pub on the Green at East Rudham, a village on the A148 between King's Lynn and Fakenham. Wendy Land and David Hanna have built up an excellent reputation since taking over in 1990. Wendy is a serious cook whose home-cooked dishes are famous

throughout this area of Norfolk, and David does an equally fine job behind the bar, dispensing good cheer and good beer. The Crown has a loyal local following, and walkers and tourists are also always welcome. For overnight guests the pub has two letting bedrooms – a twin and a family room.

73 LOWER FARM B&B

Harpley, nr King's Lynn, Norfolk PE31 6TU
☎ 01485 520240 Fax: 01485 520240

Just off the A148 between King's Lynn and Fakenham, **Lower Farm** enjoys a quiet, scenic setting in lovely gardens amid wonderful trees. The bedrooms on this working farm are notably large and comfortable, and guests can look forward to a splendid farmhouse breakfast – for other meals a fine pub is conveniently close. This is good walking country, and golfing and other outdoor activities are available nearby. Houghton Hall is just a mile away with Sandringham 5 miles, and it's a 20-minute drive to the coast.

75 THE OSTRICH INN

1 Fakenham Road, South Creake,
nr Fakenham, Norfolk NR21 9PB
☎ 01328 823320 Fax: 01328 823192
e-mail: info@ostrichinn.co.uk
🌐 www.ostrichinn.co.uk

Simon and Emma welcome visitors to **The Ostrich** Inn, complete with its original rustic beams. It has been trading since the 1680s and offers the same warm welcome today as it did then! Real ales, fine wines and great food are served in the bar and restaurants and three comfortable en-suite guest rooms are available.

Looking for:

- *Places to Visit?*
- *Places to Stay?*
- *Places to Eat & Drink?*
- *Places to Shop?*

www.travelpublishing.co.uk

76 THE BLACK LION HOTEL

Friday Market Place, Little Walsingham,
Norfolk NR22 6DB
☎ 01328 820235
e-mail: theresaathompson@aol.com
🌐 www.blacklionwalsingham.com

Just behind the main street in a village that
attracts thousands of visitors every year, **The
Black Lion Hotel** is a very pleasant spot for
a drink, a meal
or an
overnight or
longer stay.
Run by sisters
Christabel and
Theresa, the
premises date
back as far as
the 13th

century, and there's plenty of period charm
in the comfortably furnished bar-lounge
overlooking the patio. In the restaurant,
prime produce, mostly locally sourced,
feature in dishes that range from carrot and
ginger soup to cod & chips, mussels, steaks
and venison pie. B&B accommodation
comprises seven en suite bedrooms.

78 FIELD HOUSE

Moorgate Road, Hindringham,
Norfolk NR21 0PT
☎ 01328 878726
e-mail: stay@fieldhousehindringham.co.uk
🌐 www.fieldhousehindringham.co.uk

Field House displays the love and care
lavished by proud owner Wendy Dolton. Bed
& Breakfast guests are offered two
immaculate guest rooms in the main house
and another, with facilities for disabled guests,
in the annexe. A brilliant breakfast starts the
day, and superb evening meals are available by
arrangement.

77 BERRY HALL

Great Walsingham, Norfolk NR22 6DZ
☎ 01328 820267

Having raised her family here over a period
of many years, Joan Sheaf now opens her
home to guests. Four large, traditionally
furnished rooms (two en suite, two with
private facilities) provide delightful Bed &
Breakfast accommodation at 16th century
Berry Hall, which stands in 4½ acres of
gardens and grounds. Joan provides a good
choice for breakfast, and evening meals are
available by arrangement. An alternative to
the B&B is a two-bedroom self-catering
cottage along the lane.

79 THE GIN TRAP

6 High Street, Ringstead, nr Hunstanton,
Norfolk PE36 5JU
☎ 01485 525264 Fax: 01485 525321
e-mail: thegintrap@aol.com

Signposted off the A149 three miles east of Hunstanton, Ringstead is a village of pretty whitewashed houses in local carrstone. It's also the home of **The Gin Trap**, a delightful 17th century coaching inn with a particularly warm and inviting atmosphere. The beamed bar, with its wood-burning stove, tables on cast-iron frames and comfortable old chairs, is an ideal spot for relaxing with a glass of real ale from a choice that includes Adnams, Greene King, Woodforde and some 'own-label' brews. The wine list includes half a dozen by the glass, to enjoy on their own or to accompany a snack or a meal from the bar menu.

Morning coffee, lunch and supper are served in the bar, whose offerings run from filled baps and ciabatta bread to ploughman's platters, wild boar sausages with red onion gravy, meat and fish pies and delectable desserts. The menu in the intimate candle-lit restaurant , with its two rosette award, reflects the abundance of produce from the North Norfolk coast and countryside, including oysters, mussels, crabs, samphire, fresh fish and game. To accompany this fine choice of dishes both traditional and contemporary (ending with a delectable list of desserts), is an extensive, well-chosen wine list.

Ringstead is an ideal base for exploring North Norfolk, and The Gin Trap has three beautifully furnished guest bedrooms – two doubles with luxurious, spacious bathrooms with baths ands separate shower units, and a twin with a shower

room. More bedrooms are being added, and two charming self-catering cottages with access to a large garden are also available. Margaret Greer has run the Gin Trap for 2 years, while her husband Don is mainly responsible for the adjacent **Ringstead Gallery**, housed in a lovely old whitewashed stable building. The gallery and display areas are showcases for the work of local artists such as Lawrie Williamson, Jeremy Barlow, Luis Frutos, Hugo Grenville and many more artists evoking the beautiful local landscape. The gallery also features limited editions and an exciting range of bronze sculptures by Rosemary Cook and Sue Riley. The gallery, which is open from 10 to 5 Monday to Saturday, hosts regular exhibitions throughout the year.

Places of Interest in Norfolk

The selection of places of interest featured in this section includes museums, galleries, castles, historic houses, gardens, churches, cathedrals, gardens, country parks and many other places worth visiting in Norfolk. Each place of interest has an entry number which is used to identify its

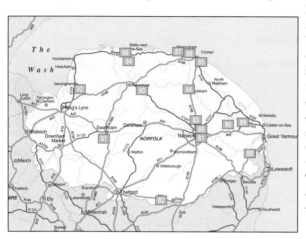

location on the map below and its name and short address in the list below the map. The entry number can also be used to find more information and contact details for the places of interest in the ensuing pages. In addition full details of places of interest in this section may be found on the Travel Publishing website – www.travelpublishing.co.uk This website has a large database of places of interest covering the whole of Britain and Ireland.

PLACES OF INTEREST

80 Dragon Hall, Norwich
81 The Plantation Garden, Norwich
82 Bressingham Gardens, Bressingham
83 City of Norwich Aviation Museum,
    Horsham St Faiths
84 Bure Valley Railway, Aylsham
85 Cromer Museum, Cromer
86 The Norfolk Shire Horse Centre, West Runton
87 Sheringham Museum, Sheringham
88 Fritton Lake Countryworld, Fritton
89 The Village Experience, Burgh St Margaret
90 Fairhaven Woodland & Water Garden, South Walsham
91 Swaffham Museum, Swaffham
92 Sandringham House, Sandringham
93 Pensthorpe Waterfowl Park & Nature Reserve,
    Pensthorpe
94 Walsingham Shirehall Museum & Abbey Grounds,
    Little Walsingham
95 Holkham Hall & Bygones Museum, Wells-next-the-Sea

80 DRAGON HALL

115-123 King Street, Norwich NR1 1QE
☎ 01603 663922

Dragon Hall is a magnificent medieval merchant's hall with an outstanding timber-framed structure. The 15th century Great Hall has a crown post roof with an intricately carved and painted dragon. Opening times: 2nd January to 31st March, Monday to Friday 10am-4pm; 1st April to 31st October, Monday to Saturday 10am-4pm; 1st November to 20th December, Monday to Friday 10am-4pm. Closed 21st December to 1st January and Bank Holidays. Admission prices and further information can be obtained from the telephone number above.

81 THE PLANTATION GARDEN

4 Earlham Road, Norwich, Norfolk
☎ 01603 621868
e-mail: chair@plantationgarden.co.uk
🌐 www.plantationgarden.co.uk

The Plantation Garden is a hidden treasure of Norwich, a green oasis just a few minutes walk from the city centre. It was created in the 19th century by Henry Trevor, a Norwich business man, who transformed an old chalk quarry into a most unusual and delightful garden. It fell into disrepair in the mid 20th century and was discovered overgrown in 1980. The Plantation Garden Preservation trust was formed to restore it. Within its 3 acres can be found a 'Gothic' fountain, Italianate terraces, 'medieval' terrace walls, woodland walkways and a rustic bridge as

well as mature trees, flower beds and lawns. It is a haven of peace and tranquility and a glimpse into a bygone age.

82 BRESSINGHAM GARDENS

Bressingham, Norfolk IP22 2AB
☎ 01379 688585 Fax: 01379 688490
www.blooms-online.com/about/
bressingham.php

A day to remember is guaranteed at **Bressingham**, where gardeners will be in paradise and children past and present can experience the thrill of the golden age of steam. Alan Bloom, one of the most respected plantsmen of his age, created the Dell Garden and its famous Island Beds between 1955 and 1962, and his garden is now world-renowned for its collection of nearly five thousand species and varieties of hardy perennials. The Garden Centre has a comprehensive collection of hardy perennials including the Blooms Heritage Collection, plus plants for the house and conservatory and all sorts of gardening gifts and accessories, as well as a café and bookshop.

83 CITY OF NORWICH AVIATION MUSEUM

Old Norwich Road, Horsham St Faiths, Norwich, Norfolk NR10 3JF
☎ 01603 893080

Follow the brown tourist signs from the A140 Norwich-Cromer road to find the **City of Norwich Aviation Museum**, a museum dedicated to keeping Norfolk's aviation heritage alive.

Dominating the museum's collection is a massive Avro Vulcan bomber, a veteran of the Falklands War of 1982.

Eight other military and civilian aircraft are on show, and although they are the main attraction for many visitors, the most fascinating feature is the display within the main exhibition building showing the development of aviation in Norfolk. From the pioneering days of aviation to present-day civilian and military operations,

every aspect is covered in a number of displays that are constantly being revised and expanded. The major roles played by Norfolk-based aircraft during the great air battles of World War II are remembered by exhibitions on the USAAF 8th Air Force and the role of the Royal Air Force in this conflict.

A special section is dedicated to the operations of RAF Bomber Command's 100 Group which flew on electronic counter measure, deception and night intruder missions from a number of Norfolk airfields.

84 BURE VALLEY RAILWAY

Aylsham Station, Norwich Road, Aylsham,
Norfolk NR11 6BW
☎ 01263 7338585 Fax: 01263 733814
e-mail: info@bvr.co.uk
🌐 www.bvrw.co.uk

Norfolk's longest narrow gauge heritage railway is a 15" gauge line operating between the old market town of Aylsham and Wroxham, a distance of nine miles. The line was built in 1989-1990 on the track bed of the former East Norfolk Railway, which opened in 1880. The Bure Valley Narrow Gauge Railway was opened in July 1990 with new station buildings and workshops at Aylsham and a new station adjacent to Hoveton and Wroxham station. The railway is operated primarily by four steam locomotives which carry passengers in 22 fully enclosed and luxuriously upholstered coaches, over a journey time of 45 minutes. At Aylsham the workshops are usually open to visitors; on site are a small museum and model railway, a well-stocked gift shop and the Whistlestop Restaurant. A shop selling confectionery and drinks is located at Wroxham station.

The Bure Valley Railway specialises in joint operations with other attractions. There is a regular boat train facility from Aylsham connecting with cruises on the Broads from Wroxham. In off-peak periods the Railway operates Steam Locomotive Driving Courses for beginners and the more experienced. The Bure Valley Railway operates regular services from April to October, Santa Specials towards Christmas and Day out with Thomas the Tank Engine events in May and September. The Railway is paralleled along its whole length by the scenic Bure Valley Walk and cycle path.

85 CROMER MUSEUM

East Cottages, Tucker Street, Cromer,
Norfolk NR27 9HB
☎ 01263 513543
e-mail: cromer.museum@norfolk.gov.uk
🌐 www.norfolk.gov.uk/leisure/museums/
cromer.htm

A row of restored fisherman's cottages houses **Cromer Museum**, where the look and feel of a fisherman's home life 100 years ago is enhanced by the gentle glow of real gas lights. The rooms inside tell the story of Cromer and the area from the bones of prehistoric animals to the

development of the town, the coming of the railway and the building of the grand Victorian hotels. There are thousands of pictures of old Cromer and visitors can find out about the geology and natural history of the local beaches. The Museum has a small, well-stocked shop.

86 THE NORFOLK SHIRE HORSE CENTRE

West Runton, Cromer, Norfolk NR27 9QH
☎ 01263 837339 Fax: 01263 837132
e-mail:
bakewekk@norfolkshirehorse.fsnet.co.uk
🌐 www.norfolk-shirehorse-centre.co.uk

Shires, Suffolk Punches and Clydesdales are among the stars of the show at the **Norfolk Shire Horse Centre**, and visitors can meet these wonderful, gentle giants at close quarters in the front yard stables. Two large museum sheds contain a video room and an indoor demonstration area, and also on show are carts, coaches, gypsy caravans and farm machinery of yesteryear. Next to the museum is a children's play area. A short walk through a meadow brings visitors to the area where the small animals are kept in their sheds and pens and aviaries. This really is a paradise for animal lovers.

87 SHERINGHAM MUSEUM

**Station Road, Sheringham,
Norfolk NR26 8RE
☎ 01263 821871**

Sheringham is the only place in the world to possess four of its original lifeboats. The **Sheringham Museum** Trust owns three and two are currently on display. A new museum is planned to house all three historic boats plus the existing social history museum. The latter has a wealth of interesting displays, from boat building, lifeboats, fishing and fishermen, to the war years, a local Roman kiln, beach finds and the Weybourne Elephant, dating back over one and a half million years. Other displays include one on golf - the first course was made in 1892 and had a cricket pitch in the middle! The museum is open Easter to October Tuesday to Saturday 10am-4pm and Sundays 2pm-4pm.

88 FRITTON LAKE COUNTRYWORLD

**Church Lane, Fritton, Great Yarmouth,
Norfolk NR31 9HA
☎ 01493 488288/488208
🌐 www.frittonlake.co.uk**

For an enjoyable day out in the country, **Fritton Lake Countryworld** has few rivals. The beautiful grounds offer a splendid contrast between natural woodland and formal Victorian gardens, and Fritton Lake has fishing and boating both available. A miniature railway runs by the lake, and among the many attractions are a family cycle trail, an orienteering course and giant outdoor board games. Also on site are a 9 hole par 3 golf course and an18-hole putting green, displays of falconry and basket-making, waterfowl, a children's farm and a heavy horse centre with working Suffolk Punches and Shires.

89 THE VILLAGE EXPERIENCE

**Burgh St Margaret, Fleggburgh,
Great Yarmouth, Norfolk NR29 3AF
☎ 01493 369770
🌐 www.thevillage-experience.com**

Set in over 30 acres of woodland, **The Village Experience** has something for all the family. Working steam and traditional fairground rides such as the Downhill Racer and Victorian Gallopers and unusual attractions like Fun with Science, Myths and Legends and Garden Golf ensure there's never a dull moment. Live shows include popular concerts and other entertainment takes in train rides, steam-hauled trailer rides, indoor soft play area, junior maze and adventure play area. Recent additions include

the Haunted Conservatory, the Swinging Chairs and the Wareham Bears. Food stops are plentiful, with a restaurant, BBQ, tearooms and traditional pub.

90 FAIRHAVEN WOODLAND & WATER GARDEN

South Walsham, Norwich,
Norfolk NR13 6EA

☎ 01603 270449

🌐 www.norfolkbroads.com/fairhaven

Nine miles north of Norwich on the B1140, this delightful and unique natural garden is environmentally managed for the benefit of all wildlife. A harmonious mix of wild and cultivated plants grows together, and the natural food chain takes care of any pests. It is a haven of peace and tranquillity, with three miles of paths under trees, over bridges and through sunny glades .

In winter and early spring there are snowdrops, followed by carpets of wild primroses, daffodils, skunk cabbage, butterbur, camellias and early rhododendrons in March and April. May sees the garden's spectacular Candelabra primulas, the largest naturalised collection in England, and the breathtaking blue of the wild bluebells. In June, July and August there are hostas, ligularia, astilbes, hydrangeas, foxgloves and wild flowers such as mullein and meadowsweet providing nectar for a variety of colourful butterflies. In autumn the glow of russet, red and gold leaves and bright berries provide the colour, while in winter the bare trees reveal views of the private Inner Broad that are hidden in other seasons.

The garden is accessible to wheelchairs except in wet weather; the tea room and toilet are also accessible, but visitors need to be able to board on foot the Edwardian-style river boat Beatrice for the Water Trail trip. The garden is open from 10am to 5pm all year and until 9 o'clock on Wednesday and Thursday evenings in May, June, July and August.

91 SWAFFHAM MUSEUM

Town Hall, 4 London Street, Swaffham,
Norfolk PE37 7DQ

☎ 01760 721230 Fax: 01760 720469

e-mail: swaffhammuseum@ic24.net

🌐 www.aboutswaffham.co.uk

Swaffham's Town Hall, a handsome redbrick building in the heart of the market place, is the setting for the excellent **Swaffham Museum**. The building itself has an interesting history: originally the home of 18th century brewer John Morse, it became the home of Swaffham Urban District Council in 1955; the Museum has been here since it opened in 1986. The Museum focuses on the social history of the town and the surrounding villages, and the collections cover many aspects of life including trade, industry and domestic life from prehistoric times to the present. This 'house of mystery and discovery' has many individual attractions. One of the highlights is the DM Symonds Collection of handmade figurines, donated by Mrs Ann Peal in memory of her father Derrick Maurice Symonds (1922-1993), author, teacher,

artist and craftsman. The collection consists of 66 hand-crafted figures or groups based on characters taken from the works of Tolkien, Dickens, Shakespeare and the Commedia dell'Arte. All the costumes were designed and made by Mr Symonds over a period of years.

Swaffham Museum offers excellent research and education facilities through a library of pictures, photographs, press cuttings and other documents, and staff are on hand to help with family trees or identifying objects found by visitors. The Museum and its souvenir shop are open Tuesday to Sunday from April to October.

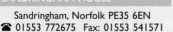
Sandringham, Norfolk PE35 6EN
☎ 01553 772675 Fax: 01553 541571
e-mail: enquiries@sandringhamestate.co.uk

Sandringham House is thecountry retreat of Her Majesty The Queen hidden in the heart of 60 acres of beautiful wooded gardens. All the main ground-floor rooms used by the Royal Family, full of their treasured ornaments, portraits and furniture, are open to the public. More family possessions, displayed in the Museum, include vehicles ranging from the first car owned by a British monarch, a 1900 Daimler, to a half-scale Aston Martin used by Princes William and Harry. A new display tells the tale of the Sandringham Company, who fought and died at Gallipoli in 1915, recently the subject of a television film *All the King's Men.*

HIDDEN PLACES GUIDES

Explore Britain and Ireland with *Hidden Places* guides - a fascinating series of national and local travel guides.

Packed with easy to read information on hundreds of places of interest as well as places to stay, eat and drink.

Available from both high street and internet booksellers

For more information on the full range of *Hidden Places* guides and other titles published by Travel Publishing visit our website on

www.travelpublishing.co.uk or ask for our leaflet by phoning **0118-981-7777** or emailing **info@travelpublishing.co.uk**

Pensthorpe, Fakenham, Norfolk NR21 0LN
☎ 01328 851465 Fax: 01328 855905

Southeast of Fakenham, off the A1067, the **Pensthorpe Waterfowl Park & Nature Reserve** is a 200-acre site with a world-renowned collection of waterfowl. As well as familiar native breeds, birds from all over the world are represented, including king eiders and harlequins from the Arctic; diminutive pygmy geese from tropical Africa; the Javan tree duck; and the sacred, glossy and scarlet ibises. The flock of endangered red-breasted geese, native to northern Siberia, is a special attraction, as is the unusual oldsquaw (long-tailed duck) that is the symbol of the Pensthorpe Waterfowl Trust.

Walk-through aviaries, bird hides and strategically sited feeding stations around the lakes allow close contact with the birds, and access to all areas is easy thanks to specially built colour-coded paths. Animal life as well as bird life abounds here, including otters, voles, red squirrels and the secretive, humble slow worm, and there is also a wide range of insect and plant life to be discovered. Among other attractions within the site are a children's adventure playground, exhibition centre, wildlife gift shop and licensed restaurant.

Pensthorpe Waterfowl Trust is a charitable trust whose aims are to protect waterfowl and wetland habitats; to encourage public appreciation of the importance of wetlands for wildlife; to work with young people and schools to develop a sense of enjoyment of the natural world and an appreciation of the need for wildlife conservation; and to provide facilities to promote the enjoyment of waterfowl and other wildlife on the Pensthorpe Reserve.

94 WALSINGHAM SHIREHALL MUSEUM & ABBEY GROUNDS

Common Place, Little Walsingham,
Norfolk NR22 6BP
☎ 01328 820510/820259
e-mail: walsingham.museum@farmline.com

The early 16th century building that now houses the **Walsingham Shirehall Museum** was used as a hostel for visitors to the Priory Church. In the 1770s it was converted into the shirehall for the quarter and the petty sessions. The courtroom has survived unaltered since it was last used and is now part of the 'hands-on' museum, which includes a comprehensive display on Walsingham as a place of pilgrimage since 1061, as well as
local artefacts and photographs. It is also the entrance to the Abbey grounds, which contain the remains of the Augustinian Priory.

95 HOLKHAM HALL & BYGONES MUSEUM

Wells-next-the-Sea, Norfolk NR23 1AB
☎ 01328 710227 Fax: 01328 711707
🌐 www.holkham.co.uk

In a lakeside deer park on the beautiful North Norfolk coast stands **Holkham Hall**, one of Britain's most majestic stately homes, seat of the Earls of Leicester. This classic 18th century mansion in Palladian style is a treasure house of artistic and architectural history, each
part with its
own character
and appeal,
from the
stunning
grandeur of the
Marble Hall and

the magnificence of the State Rooms to the old kitchen with its original pots and pans and the elegant formal gardens. In addition there is a Bygones Museum crammed with over 4,000 domestic and agricultural artefacts as well as nursery gardens, a pottery shop, restaurant and tearooms.

Suffolk

For much of its length the River Stour forms the county boundary between Suffolk and Essex, and here lies some of the most peaceful and attractive countryside in the county. The beauty is to a large extent unspoilt, and those travelling through the area will come upon a succession of picturesque, ancient wool towns and villages, historic churches, stately homes and nature reserves. Among the gems to be discovered are the wonderful preserved medieval town of Lavenham, the atmospheric old wool town of Long Melford, Sudbury, the largest of the wool towns and once a busy port on the Stour (and birthplace of the painter Thomas Gainsborough) and, perhaps above all, East Bergholt. This was the birthplace, in 1776, of the painter John Constable, and two of his most famous subjects – Flatford Mill and Willy Lott's Cottage – are visited by thousands of tourists and look very much the same as they did in the great artist's day. Much of inland Suffolk remains rich farmland, with ancient towns and along with some of the finest windmills and watermills in the country.

Founded long before the Norman Conquest, Bury St Edmunds is named after St Edmund, who was the last King of East Anglia and the patron saint of England before St George. Further west lies Newmarket, for centuries the centre of the Sport of kings. While Suffolk has few equals in terms of picturesque countryside and settlements, it is also very much a maritime county. With more than 50 miles of coastline. The whole stretch of the coast is a conservation area, with miles of waymarked walks and cycle trails and an abundance of nature reserves, wildlife and birdlife. This coast, which has for centuries been under attack from the sea, has long been a source of inspiration for writers, artists and musicians. Notable among these are the poet George Crabbe, who created the solitary fisherman Peter Grimes, and the composer Benjamin Britten, who wrote an

opera based on the life of Peter Grimes and who started the renowned Aldeburgh Festival. Among the contemporary artists who have made their mark is Maggie Hambling, whose tribute to Britten is a huge metal clam shell on the beach at Aldeburgh. Dunwich was once one of the most important coastal towns in England, but down the years the sea has taken almost all evidence of its former importance.

Between the major port of Ipswich, whose most famous son was Thomas Wolsey, Lord Chancellor under Henry VIII, and the fishing port of Lowestoft are some charming and popular resorts, including Aldeburgh and Southwold, which have done their best to avoid the brash commercialism that has spoiled so many English resorts. Felixstowe, which developed from a small fishing village, is now one of the biggest commercial ports in Europe. Suffolk has its fair share of architectural interest, with many fine town and country mansions and some superb churches. Among the latter are the masterpieces at Lavenham, Long Melford, Southwold, Blythburgh, Bury St Edmunds, Framlingham and Mildenhall.

History comes alive at many places in Suffolk, nowhere more graphically than at Sutton Hoo, sometimes referred to as 'page one of the history of England'.

Aldeburgh

273

Food and Drink in Suffolk

The selection of establishments serving food and drink featured in this section includes restaurants, cafes, hotels, pubs, inns and tea & coffee shops. Each establishment has an entry number which is used to identify its location on the map below and its name and short address in the list below the map. The entry number can also be used to find more information and contact details for the establishment in the ensuing pages. In addition full details of establishments serving food and drink featured in this section may be found on the Travel Publishing website – **www.travelpublishing.co.uk** This website has a large database of establishments serving food and drink covering the whole of Britain and Ireland.

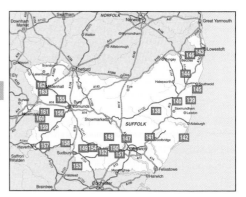

FOOD AND DRINK

96	The Maypole Inn, Wetherden
97	The White Horse, Badingham
98	The White Hart, Otley
99	The Queens Head, Brandeston
100	Forge Café, Restaurant & Gift Shop, Thornham Magna
101	The Railway Tavern, Mellis
102	The Ship Inn at Dunwich, Dunwich
103	The Griffin Inn, Yoxford
104	The Moon & Mushroom, Swilland
105	The Horse & Groom, Melton
106	The Sutton Plough Inn, Sutton
107	The Kings Head Inn, Orford
108	The Old Chequers, Friston
109	The Bull Hotel, Woodbridge
110	The Sorrel Horse Inn, Shottisham
111	The Commodore, Oulton Broad
112	The George Borrow Hotel, Oulton Broad
113	The Anchor, Walberswick
114	The Star Inn, Wenhaston
115	The Case is Altered, Bentley
116	The Racehorse, Westhall
117	The Swan Inn, Barnby
118	The Wild Man Inn, Sproughton
119	The Fleece, Boxford
120	The Fox & Hounds, Groton
121	The Linden Tree, Bury St Edmunds
122	Street Level, Bury St Edmunds
123	The Sorrel Horse Inn, Barham
124	The Lamarsh Lion, Lamarsh
125	The Greyhound Inn, Flempton
126	Scutchers, Long Melford
127	Red Lodge Inn, Red Lodge
128	The Five Bells, Cavendish
129	The Cock Bar & Restaurant, Clare
130	The Lion , Stoke by Clare
131	The Six Bells, Horringer
132	The White Horse, Kedington
133	The White Horse, Brandon
134	The Reindeer, Saxon Street
135	The Bull, Burrough Green
136	The Affleck Arms, Dalham
137	Worlington Hall Country House Hotel, Worlington

96 THE MAYPOLE INN

Stowmarket Road, Wetherden,
Suffolk IP14 3JP
☎ 01359 240300 Fax: 01359 240300
e-mail: wetherdenmaypole@aol.com

The Maypole Inn is a traditional 17th century Free House with a warm welcoming atmosphere. Well kept Real ales , fine wines and very good home-cooked food.

97 THE WHITE HORSE

Badingham, nr Woodbridge,
Suffolk IP13 8JR
☎ 01728 638280

Set back from the A1120 west of Yoxford, **The White Horse** has an inviting, traditional bar with old beams, flagstones, horse brasses and a wood-burning stove. Outside is a large secluded garden with plenty of picnic tables. Real ales accompany delicious home-cooked dishes listed on the blackboard.

98 THE WHITE HART

Helmington Road, Otley, nr Ipswich,
Suffolk IP6 9NS
☎ 01473 890312 Fax: 01473 890312

The White Hart is a cosy, friendly pub
dating from the 18th century. Ales include
Victoria Bitter from the Earl Soham Brewery,
and among the favourite dishes served in the
non-smoking restaurant are lasagne and the
Sunday roasts. Beer garden, car park. Closed
Sunday evening and Monday except Bank
Holidays.

Explore Britain and Ireland with
Hidden Places guides - a fascinating
series of national and local travel
guides.

www.travelpublishing.co.uk

0118-981-7777

info@travelpublishing.co.uk

99 THE QUEENS HEAD

The Street, Brandeston, nr Framlingham,
Suffolk IP13 7AD
☎ 01728 685307
e-mail: stensethhome@aol.com
⊕ www.brandestonqueenshead.co.uk

On the main street of Brandeston, **The
Queens Head** started life as a row of
redbrick cottages and has been a pub since
1811. Suzanne Stenseth, her Black Labradors
Stella and Artois and her cats provide the
warmest of welcomes at this unpretentious
country inn, which has won many accolades
for its food (Suffolk Food Pub of the Year
2003-2004). Local produce is put to excellent
use on menus that include pub classics and
Thai, Indonesian, Mediterranean and
vegetarian
dishes,
with
scrumptious
puds to
finish.
Adnams
ales, large
garden.

100 THE FORGE CAFÉ, RESTAURANT & GIFT SHOP

Thornham Magna, nr Eye, Suffolk IP23 8HH
☎ 01379 783035 Fax: 01379 783015
e-mail: rtunmer@aol.com
⊕ www.forgerestaurant.co.uk

Set in woodland just off the A143 at the
entrance to the Thornham Estate, **The Forge**
is a favourite place of refreshment for
walkers, naturalists and tourists. With 50
covers inside and another 25 outside, the
Forge serves
a day-long
selection of
snacks, main
meals, cream
teas and
home-made
desserts, all
freshly
prepared and
making use of locally sourced ingredients.
Opposite the café-restaurant stands the Gift
Shop selling a delightful variety of arts, crafts
and gifts.

101 THE RAILWAY TAVERN

The Common, Yaxley Road, Mellis, nr Eye,
Suffolk IP23 8DU
☎ 01379 783416
e-mail: info@mellistavern.co.uk
⊕ www.mellistavern.co.uk

**The Railway
Tavern** stands
on the largest
common in
Suffolk, a
conservation
area noted for
wild flowers.
Behind the
flower-adorned black and white exterior the
inn has the comfortable feel of a well-loved
local, and the there's no mistaking the warmth
of the welcome from licensees Ruth and
Denny Newman and their dogs Jess and
Mattie. Real ale enthusiasts have a choice of
half-a-dozen brews, and traditional pub dishes
are served Wednesday to Sunday lunchtimes
(book for the Sunday roasts) and Friday
nights. Folk music on the first Thursday of
the month, quiz on the second Thursday.

102 THE SHIP INN AT DUNWICH

Dunwich, nr Saxmundham,
Suffolk IP17 3DT
☎ 01728 648219 Fax: 01728 648675
e-mail: shipinn@tiscali.co.uk

One of the most delightful and distinctive inns on the east coast, **The Ship Inn at Dunwich** has a history dating back 500 years. Once the haunt of sea dogs and smugglers, it is now a firm favourite with both locals and the many visitors to this region of many attractions. A fine selection of real ales and wines is always available, and home-cooked dishes – including popular fish and seafood specials – are served every lunchtime and evening in the bar or dining room. Four comfortably furnished en suite bedrooms, with four more added for the

2005 season, provide an ideal base for walking, touring and exploring the coast.

103 THE GRIFFIN INN

High Street, Yoxford, Suffolk IP17 3EP
☎ 01728 668229 Fax: 01728 667040
e-mail: inquiries@thegriffin.co.uk
🌐 www.thegriffin.co.uk

The Griffin Inn started life in 1358, when it was the memorial court for the local Lord of the Manor. It became an inn two centuries later, and behind its black and white, slate-roofed exterior it retains a traditional look with high timbered walls and ceilings, a log fire and church pew seating in the bar. Thirsts are quenched by Adnams and guest brews, and locally sourced produce features prominently in the generously served dishes. Overnight accommodation comprises three beamed bedrooms that are popular with tourists and birdwatchers.

104 THE MOON & MUSHROOM

High Road, Swilland, Suffolk IP6 9LR
☎ 01473 785320 Fax: 01473 785320
e-mail: nikki@ecocleen.fsnet.co.uk

Real ales from independent East Anglian breweries bring connoisseurs of traditional beer to the **Moon & Mushroom**, a cosy 300-year-old inn on the main street of a village a short drive north of Ipswich. The inn also offers a warm welcome and hearty home-cooked food.

106 THE SUTTON PLOUGH INN

Main Street, Sutton, Suffolk IP12 3DU
☎ 01344 411785 Fax: 01344 411785
e-mail: suttonplough@aol.com

A warm welcome awaits at the **Sutton Plough Inn**, where a selection of well-kept real ales is on tap in the bar. Two dining areas make an elegant setting for enjoying light snacks to full meals (no food Tuesday). Tenants Anne and Stuart Gales also run a Post Office on the premises. Sutton lies between Woodbridge and the coast.

105 THE HORSE & GROOM

Yarmouth Road, Melton, nr Woodbridge,
Suffolk IP12 1QB
☎ 01394 383566

The Horse & Groom is a fine old coaching inn that once served passengers on the London-Yarmouth run. It's now a popular spot with locals and tourists, serving a wide range of real ales, tasty bar snacks and a full restaurant menu. It stands next to the Church of St Andrew

107 THE KINGS HEAD INN

Front Street, Orford, Suffolk IP12 2LW
☎ 01394 450271 Fax: 01394 459157
e-mail: ian_thornton@talk21.com
🌐 www.kingshead-orford-suffolk.co.uk

Period charm is in generous supply at **The Kings Head**, a 13th century inn, former smugglers inn. Adnams is the favourite brew, and the bar and restaurant menus feature a popular seafood platter and the produce of the neighbouring smokery. Three bedrooms for B&B.

Aldeburgh Road, Friston, Suffolk IP17 1NP
☎ 01728 688270

On a prominent corner site in the village of Friston, a short drive from Aldeburgh, **The Old Chequers** is a distinguished country inn long noted for outstanding hospitality. The inn has always had an enviable and well-justified reputation, but many of the regulars say that under the new team who took over in January 2005 the pub is better and more professionally run than ever. Alan and Lynn Bailey have very many years' experience in

the trade, and they have the invaluable assistance of their daughter and her partner Matt.

The appeal of the Old Chequers is evident even from the outside, with its very smart buttercup yellow frontage, grey-tiled roof, shuttered windows, hanging baskets, window boxes and picnic tables set out on the patio. Inside, Windsor-style stools are set at the brick-fronted bar counter, and the 55-cover restaurant has a non-smoking area. Lynn is number one in the kitchen, and her menus reflect the abundance of fine fresh produce that is to be found in the region. The land and the sea are both generous in their seasonal bounty, which is featured on the printed menu and on the daily specials. Pies of the day might include steak, lamb and pigeon, and among other typical delectable dishes could be asparagus, crab, lobster, Cumberland sausage served in a Yorkshire pudding, rabbit stew, lamb shanks braised in red wine, and scrumpy pork hock. Fine food deserves fine wines, and the list at the Old Chequers caters for all preferences. For beer-drinkers, Adnams, Broadside and guest ales are on tap. The pub is open lunchtime and evening, and all day, every day in the summer season. Food is served from 12 to 2 (till 3 on Sunday) and from 5.30 to 9.

Friston lies half a mile off the A1094, the road that links the main A12 and Aldeburgh. Aldeburgh, Thorpeness, Saxmundham and Snape Maltings are all a few minutes' drive away.

109 THE BULL HOTEL

2 Market Hill, Woodbridge,
Suffolk IP12 4LR
☎ 01394 382089 Fax: 01394 384902
e-mail: reception@bullhotel.co.uk
🌐 www.bullhotel.co.uk

On the picturesque square overlooking the Elizabethan Shire Hall, **The Bull Hotel** is a 16th century hostelry that was once a posting inn for the Union Stage between Ipswich and Norwich. The tradition of hospitality is carried on by hosts Paul and Heather Barker, who have enhanced The Bull's reputation as a cheerful 'local', a fine restaurant and a comfortable hotel. It's open all day, every day for drinks (Greene King IPA and Morelands Original are the favourite brews), and bar and restaurant menus are available for breakfast, lunch and dinner for residents and non-residents.

The 16 en suite guest bedrooms (two in outside chalets, two suitable for families) are all very well decorated and furnished, and equipped with television, direct-dial phone and tea/coffee tray. Rooms can be let on a B&B or Dinner, B&B basis. The Bull is a popular venue for private parties, wedding receptions and meetings. The coat of arms on the front of the building are those of King Victor Emmanuel II of Italy, who stayed here as the guest of the owner of the day, a noted breeder of horses.

110 THE SORREL HORSE INN

Hollesley Road, Shottisham, nr Woodbridge,
Suffolk IP12 3HD
☎ 01394 411617

The Sorrel Horse Inn is a delightful pub of Tudor origins, located in a tucked-away village between Woodbridge and the coast and close to the mouth of the River Deben. The pub is in the capable hands of Clive and Pauline, who have a wealth of experience in the licensed trade, and Pauline has quickly made her mark with her excellent home cooking. The printed menu and the specials board provide plenty of choice, and Pauline

uses local produce as much as possible. Two ales are served from the cask, and hand-pulled ales have become available with the construction of a new cellar.

The cellar is just one of the improvements Clive and Pauline are overseeing, and when the refurbishment of the stable block has been completed they will be offering Bed & Breakfast accommodation. At that point, the Sorrel Horse will be an ideal base for enjoying the scenic delights of coast and countryside that are all around. Wednesday is quiz night. The inn has very convivial bar and dining areas, a small front garden, a rear patio and an off-road car park.

111 THE COMMODORE

Commodore Road, Oulton Broad,
nr Lowestoft, Suffolk NR32 3NE
☎ 01502 565955

Good food, good ales and good staff make
The Commodore a popular choice with
both locals, tourists and holidaymakers. Warm
and cosy, with a traditional ambience, the pub
serves food and drink throughout the day.
The garden provides great views of the River
Waveney.

112 THE GEORGE BORROW HOTEL

Bridge Road, Oulton Broad, Lowestoft,
Suffolk NR32 3LL
☎ 01502 569245 Fax: 01502 568595

Named after a renowned Victorian writer and
traveller, the **George Borrow Hotel** provides
today's travellers and tourists with
comfortable accommodation in 12 rooms,
from singles to family suites. It's also open for
drinks and straightforward pub dishes. Live
music Friday, karaoke Sunday in the function
room.

114 THE STAR INN

Hall Road, Wenhaston, Suffolk IP19 9HF
☎ 01502 478240

Locals, walkers, cyclists, motorists and
tourists all enjoy the hospitality provided by
David and Denise at **The Star Inn**, a
delightful country pub located between
Halesworth and Blythburgh. Specialities on
Denise's menu include superb steaks from
beef reared by David at nearby Reydon.

115 THE CASE IS ALTERED

Capel Road, Bentley, nr Ipswich IP9 2DW
☎ 01473 310282 Fax: 01473 310311

In the village of Bentley, **The Case Is
Altered** is a welcoming redbrick pub with
flowers on the patio and a cosy, traditional
interior. Three real ales are always available,
and the chef takes his inspiration from
around the world for excellent dishes that
include fresh fish specials and the popular
Mongolian Lamb. The inn also serves as the
village Post Office.

113 THE ANCHOR

Walberswick, Suffolk IP18 6UA
☎ 01502 722112

Mark and Sophie Dorber welcome families,
artists, walkers, musicians, tourists and
everyone else to **The Anchor**, their pleasant
1920s pub in
the picturesque
village of
Walberswick.
The bar is light
and roomy, and
outside there's
a front terrace
and a lovely
rear garden

with a wood at the end and a path leading to
the beach. Sophie's cooking is a great
attraction here, and her menus are based on
the best ingredients including freshly caught
fish. The choice of beer and wine is also
excellent, and each dish on the menu is
matched with a wine or beer suggestion. The
Anchor is also a lovely holiday base with 11
guest rooms divided between the main
building and family chalets in the garden.

116 THE RACEHORSE

Westhall, nr Halesworth, Suffolk IP19 8RQ
☎ 01502 575706
e-mail:
racehorse@westhall1810.fsbusiness.co.uk

The Racehorse is looking very smart after a
top-to-toe refurbishment carried out by hosts
Jerry and Bella Aldred. The bar area features
beams, an open fire, darkwood furniture and
traditional trappings. Adnams Best is the
resident real ale, with seasonal beers from
Tindalls, a small local brewery. In the new
restaurant Jerry makes excellent use of fresh
local produce for his wide-ranging menus,
which run from snacks to a full à la carte
evening selection. Bella puts the seal on a
meal with her scrumptious desserts. The

Racehorse
is very
much the
hub of the
village and
fields pool
and darts
teams in
the local
leagues.

117 THE SWAN INN

Swan Lane, Barnby, Suffolk NR34 7QE
☎ 01502 476646 Fax: 01502 562513

Regular customers travel from all over the region to enjoy the superb fish dishes that are a speciality at **The Swan Inn**. Donny Cole chooses the fish daily from the local market, and the menu in the Fisherman's Cove Restaurant provides a truly impressive choice. Meat-eaters and vegetarians are not forgotten, and connoisseurs of real ale will also find an excellent selection. Tucked away in the village of Barnby, off the A146 east of Beccles, The

Swan has a two-bedroom self-catering apartment that provides an ideal base for walking and touring.

118 THE WILD MAN INN

Bramford Road, Sproughton,
nr Ipswich, Suffolk IP8 3DA
☎ 01473 742102 Fax: 01473 240447

The Wild Man Inn is located in the village of Sproughton, by junction 54 of the A14 and a mile west of Ipswich. Open lunchtime and evening, and all day Friday, Saturday and Sunday, the pub has recently been smartly refurbished by the new tenants Bob and Jean McGregor. Extensive A La Carte menu with vegetarian options and one of the few full carveries in Suffolk operates 7 days a week, together with a large choice of home made specials. Large parties catered for. Children are welcome, large car park.

119 THE FLEECE

8-10 Broad Street, Boxford, nr Sudbury,
Suffolk CO10 5DX
☎ 01787 210247

The Fleece is an 18th century coaching inn with an excellent tenant/chef in Jackie Heare. Her chalk menus offer plenty of variety, with typical dishes including lasagne, lamb & mint pudding, steak & kidney pie and sun-dried tomato and cheddar tart. Three real ales, pool table, beer garden, jazz on Friday. Closed Monday lunchtime except Bank Holidays.

120 THE FOX & HOUNDS

Groton, nr Boxford, Sudbury,
Suffolk CO10 4ED
☎ 01787 210474

The Fox & Hounds enjoys a scenic village location just north of Boxford. The oldest parts of the premises date back to the 14th century, and the interior is rich in old-world charm. The pub is open every lunch and evening for drinks (4 real ales), and the food runs from bar snacks to traditional dishes listed on the blackboard.

121 THE LINDEN TREE

7 Outnorthgate, Bury St Edmunds,
Suffolk IP33 1JQ
☎ 01284 754600 Fax: 01284 750619

Next to Bury railway station and once the station hotel, **The Linden Tree** is a smart, welcoming pub with a lovely leafy garden. Home cooked dishes provide something for everyone, and diners can eat in the bar or in the bright conservatory dining area.

122 STREET LEVEL

29 Abbeygate Street, Bury St Edmunds,
Suffolk IP33 1UN ☎ 01284 752941
e-mail: sales@streetlevelcafe.co.uk
🌐 www.streetlevelcafe.co.uk

With a bright modern interior behind a traditional frontage, **Street Level** appeals to all with a day-long choice of snacks and meals. Among the offerings are baguettes with interesting fillings, a wide breakfast selection, salads, fish, chicken dishes, grills and vegetarian options. No smoking.

123 THE SORREL HORSE INN

Old Norwich Road, Barham, nr Ipswich,
Suffolk IP6 0PG
☎ 01473 830327 Fax: 01473 833149
e-mail: enquiries@sorrelhorse.co.uk
🌐 www.sorrelhorse.co.uk

In a pleasant country setting, **The Sorrel Horse Inn** has been owned and run for many years by Bridget (Breda) Smith and her sons Matthew and Philip. The 17th century pink-washed, pantiled building first became an inn in about 1840, and the interior boasts original features such as wall and ceiling beams and open fireplaces. Hewn log-style

tables and rustic chairs assist the traditional look, and the dining areas feature interesting collections of miniatures and foreign banknotes.

Among the inn's many assets is a large lawned garden with plenty of picnic benches and parasols, a summer barbecue and a children's play area complete with slide and bouncy castle.

Expertly kept real ales – Adnams Bitter, Shepherd Neame Spitfire, Theakston's Bitter – keep cask connoisseurs happy, and fresh-air appetites are satisfied with an excellent selection of home-cooked dishes served in the two dining areas. Lasagne, chicken curry, steaks and savoury pies are at the top of the all-time favourites, and there's always a good choice of vegetarian dishes. Lighter options are available at lunchtime, and the inn is also open for breakfast.

With many attractions nearby (the magnificent Shrubland Hall and its Victorian gardens are almost on the doorstep), the cheerful, friendly Sorrel Horse is an excellent base for touring the region, and the nearby A14 provides easy access to all parts.

Eight bedrooms in a splendidly converted barn provide quiet, comfortable accommodation; most of the rooms have en suite facilities, and all are equipped with televisions, telephones and drinks trays.

Ground-floor rooms are old-fashioned in style, with original beams, while those above have a more modern look, with smart pine furniture. One room has facilities for disabled guests.

124 THE LAMARSH LION

Bures Road, Lamarsh, Suffolk CO8 5EP
☎ 01787 227918

A few miles south of Sudbury off the B1508 Colchester road, **The Lamarsh Lion** is a fine old country inn dating back to the 14th century. Overlooking open farmland, this friendly free house serves an excellent choice of real ales (including Old Growler, IPA and Painted Lady from the Nethergate Brewery) and fine wines, to enjoy on their own or to accompany a snack or a meal.

An open fire keeps things cosy in the bar, and at neatly laid tables in the dining area the dishes on the blackboard menu runs from garlic mushrooms, moules marinière and deep-fried brie with cranberry sauce to grilled plaice and skate, vegetable kiev, cottage pie and a great selection of roasts.

The Lamarsh Lion is a pleasant base for exploring the Stour Valley, with three well-appointed rooms for Bed & Breakfast guests. The inn has a patio and a beer garden with a children's play area.

125 THE GREYHOUND INN

The Green, Flempton, Suffolk IP28 6EL
☎ 01284 728400 Fax: 01284 728400
e-mail: boregamp@thegreyhound.freeserve.co.uk

Off the A1101 between Mildenhall and Bury St Edmunds, **The Greyhound Inn** is a substantial 18th century inn overlooking the green in the shadow of a very old church. The convivial bar area has an open fire and old oak tables, and one part of the dining area is designated non-smoking. Greene King IPA and Abbot Ale head the drinks list, and the good-value home-cooked dishes include Sunday roasts and kebabs (also available for takeaway). Sunday is quiz night, Tuesday pool, Wednesday cribbage, Thursday and Friday darts. For guests staying overnight, The Greyhound has three rooms with shared facilities.

126 SCUTCHERS

Westgate Street, Long Melford, nr Sudbury, Suffolk
☎ 01787 310200 Fax: 01787 375700
🌐 www.scutchers.com

Scutchers is a fine restaurant set in a 16th century hall house in historic Long Melford. Behind the mustard-coloured facade, the dining area has a lovely old-world look, an elegant setting for enjoying really excellent cooking. Nick and Di Barrett and their staff offer an interesting menu that might typically include crayfish and smoked haddock risotto, roast breast of duck with caramelised apples, and a classic steak au poivre. Superb desserts round things off in fine style, and the food is complemented by a superb wine list that includes lots of half-bottles. Scutchers, a non-smoking restaurant, is open lunchtime and evening Tuesday to Saturday.

127 RED LODGE INN

70 Turnpike Road, Red Lodge, nr Bury St
Edmunds, Suffolk IP28 8LB
☎ 018638 756531
e-mail: n.j.sandells@btinternet.com

The **Red Lodge Inn** is a new venture for Malcolm Sandells and Joanne Jones, who are well on the way to making it once again one of the most popular pubs in the area around Newmarket, Bury St Edmunds and Mildenhall. The site, on the Mildenhall road out of Newmarket, has been occupied by a hostelry since the 13th century, and the leafy setting is certainly promising, with the A11

and A14 both very close by, providing easy access in all directions.

The familiar red-painted exterior is made even more colourful in spring and summer by window boxes and hanging baskets, and the interior has abundant old-world charm; the huge brick hearth is a dominant feature in the intimate dining area, where the walls are hung with period photographs of the locality. The inn is open from 10.30 Monday to Saturday and from noon on Sunday, and both food and drinks are served throughout the day. Joanne's excellent cooking is proving to a great attraction, and her regularly changing menus provide something for everyone. Typical specials on the chalkboard run from soup of the day served with a crusty roll to fresh fish, liver & bacon, sweet & sour chicken, steaks, bourbon BBQ ribs and the splendid steamed puddings – steak & kidney, steak, ale & mushroom, chicken & mushroom, spinach with tomato and mozzarella.

As well as becoming a place to seek out as a destination restaurant, the Red Lodge Inn also retains its traditional role as the social hub of the village. Pool is the favourite pub game, and weekends see regular live music sessions. Malcolm, Joanne and their staff have a warm welcome for all the family (dogs included), and the beer garden has a children's play area.

128 THE FIVE BELLS

The Green, Cavendish, Suffolk CO10 8BA
☎ 01787 280547

The village of Cavendish is splendidly traditional, with its church, thatched cottages and almshouses, and many of its most attractive buildings are set around the village green. Among these is **The Five Bells**, a fine traditional pub where the hardworking manager Christine and her staff are now realising its true potential. Behind the substantial frontage adorned with window boxes and hanging baskets, the main public area has a brick-fronted bar counter, with old beams and plenty of comfortable seats.

This is an ideal spot for enjoying a glass of cask ale, while the newly refurbished non-smoking restaurant is an equally appealing setting for a snack or a meal. Food has become a major part of the pub's business, and lasagne and steak & kidney pie are among the classics on the menu. Other choices run from Newmarket sausages with egg, chips and beans to battered cod, half-pounder burger and salmon & spinach in a tarragon sauce, with baguettes for quicker snacks. Families are welcome at the Five Bells, which has a large beer garden and ample parking space. Pub hours are 11.30 to 2.30 and 5 to 11.30, with all-day opening Friday, Saturday and Sunday.

129 THE COCK BAR & RESTAURANT

Callis Street, Clare, nr Sudbury,
Suffolk CO10 8PX
☎ 01787 277391
e-mail: allyson@rogers-01.freeserve.co.uk

The Cock Bar & Restaurant is a handsome establishment open lunchtime and evening for a wide variety of well-conceived, freshly prepared dishes. Hardworking hosts Allyson and John Rogers have redecorated inside and out stage by stage, modernising the style whilst retaining all the traditional charm. Allyson's regularly changing menus run from bar snacks such as potato skins and ciabatta club sandwiches to a comprehensive restaurant menu including sticky BBQ ribs, fish pie with a root vegetable topping and stuffed peppers with couscous. Children's menu available. Weekly themed international evenings; beer garden.

130 THE LION

The Street, Stoke by Clare, nr Haverhill,
Suffolk CO10 8HP ☎ 01787 277571

With tenants Stuart and Irene Hales as ringmasters, **The Lion** has roared back into favour as a convivial hostelry with a warm welcome for locals and strangers. Hearty home cooking includes steak & ale pie and the Sunday roasts served with lots of fresh vegetables. Sundays see crib, dominoes and bingo nights, and The Lion has a large, secluded beer garden.

131 THE SIX BELLS

Horringer, Bury St Edmunds,
Suffolk IP29 5SJ
☎ 01284 735551
⊕ www.sixbellshorringer.co.uk

Carol Smith is the proprietor of **The Six Bells**, where a good selection of drinks and home-cooked food is served every day. Plush carpets cover the old wooden floors, and the little restaurant overlooks the beer garden. Three bedrooms are available for overnight guests.

132 THE WHITE HORSE

Sturmer Road, Kedington, Suffolk CB9 7NS
☎ 01440 763564

Dawn and Dave Tegg have a friendly greeting for visitors to **The White Horse**, which is located in a rural village near Haverhill. It's open for breakfast at 9 o'clock, and throughout the day for drinks and a good selection of favourite pub dishes. The White Horse also offers overnight accommodation in a twin room and a family room. Two bars, beer garden.

133 THE WHITE HORSE

White Horse Street, Brandon,
Suffolk IP27 0LB
☎ 01842 815767

New tenants Dave and Jeni have overseen a facelift outside and complete refurbishment inside **The White Horse**.

The bar is open all day, every day, and a choice of home-cooked pub food and bar snacks are prepared in the kitchen. Live entertainment   monthly.

135 THE BULL

Bradley Road, Burrough Green,
nr Newmarket, Suffolk CB8 9NH
☎ 01638 507480

Host Susanne and Esther previously ran a holiday camp in France

and have transferred the happy, relaxed atmosphere to **The Bull**, an 18 th coaching inn in a pretty village close to the A11. Real ale fans can take their pick from Greene King IPA, Abbot Ale, Old Speckled Hen and guests, and Susanne keeps the customers smiling with her heart home cooking – typical choices might be Newmarket sausages, chicken breast topped with mozzarella, moussaka and the very tempting fish specials. The Bull is closed Tuesday lunchtime; no food Monday and Tuesday evenings.

134 THE REINDEER

62 The Street, Saxon Street, nr Newmarket,
Suffolk CB8 9RS
☎ 01638 730989 Fax: 01638 730898
e-mail: thereindeer@msn.com
⊕ www.thereindeer.com

In a village a few miles south of Newmarket (off the B1061 or B1063), **The Reindeer** is a fine brick building with a covering of creeper, traditional public rooms and a lovely leafy garden. The pub, which dates back to the 18th century, is well known for the quality of its food, which range from bar snacks to a full à la carte menu, daily specials and Sunday roasts. There are seats for 80 inside and 25 outside. The Reindeer also has two superior

bedrooms, both en suite, for B&B guests. No smoking anywhere inside.

136 THE AFFLECK ARMS

1 Brookside, Dalham, nr Newmarket,
Suffolk CB8 8TG
☎ 01638 500306 Fax: 01638 500306
e-mail: denisepowell@waitrose.com

Local residents, tourists and racegoers at Newmarket make up the clientele at **The Affleck Arms**, where Denise Powell and her daughter Sam provide the warmest of welcomes. Picnic benches are set out in front of this charming old thatched pub, that features a vast brick hearth with a wood-burning stove. Real ales include some from small local breweries, and the interesting menus, including Sunday lunch, offer both traditional and contemporary dishes. A tastefully appointed en-suite room provides overnight accommodation. The pub is open

from 5pm Monday to Friday evenings, lunchtime and evening Saturday and all day Sunday.

137 WORLINGTON HALL COUNTRY HOUSE HOTEL

Worlington, Suffolk IP28 8RX
☎ 01638 712237 Fax: 01638 717631
e-mail: worlingtonhall@aol.com
🌐 www.worlingtonhall-hotel.co.uk

Business partners Joy O'Brien Miller and Sharon Parkinson welcome all visitors to **Worlington Hall Country House**, which is located on the B1102 west of Mildenhall. The Hall is a gentleman's residence dating from 1570 and set in five acres of tranquil grounds leading down to the River Lark.

The guest accommodation comprises eight individually designed bedrooms in the

main building and a private suite in the converted coach house in the courtyard. All rooms have toilet and either bath or shower en suite, and the comprehensive amenities include television, alarm clock radio, direct-dial telephone, hairdryer and tea and coffee making facilities. The original house, which acquired its beautiful Queen Anne facade in the early 18th century, retains many fine period features. Elizabethan carved-wood panelling adds greatly to the intimate character of the bar. Residents and non-residents are welcome to enjoy a snack in the bar at lunchtime, or to sit down to a full à la carte dinner in the lovely Willow Room or Oak Room. Sharon takes justified pride in her excellent, unfussy cooking, and her menus are available every session except Sunday evening.

The Willow Room can be booked for private dinner parties, working lunches or business meetings, and also provides a pleasant setting for breakfast. With its own private entrance from the garden and car park, the Garden Room is a perfect choice for larger gatherings: up to 150 guests can be accommodated in comfort, with ample room for dancing and separate bar facilities. Worlington Hall is well placed for a wide variety of local attractions, including Mildenhall, with its magnificent parish church and fascinating museum; Royal Worlington and Newmarket golf courses; horse riding and fishing; racing and associated attractions at Newmarket; and historic Bury St Edmunds.

Accommodation in Suffolk

The accommodation featured in this section includes hotels, inns, guest houses, bed & breakfasts and self catered establishments. Each establishment has an entry number which is used to identify its location on the map below and its name and short address in the list below the map. The entry number can also be used to find more information and contact details for the accommodation in the ensuing pages. In addition full details of all this accommodation may be found on the Travel Publishing website - www.travelpublishing.co.uk. This website has a comprehensive database of accommodation covering the whole of Britain and Ireland.

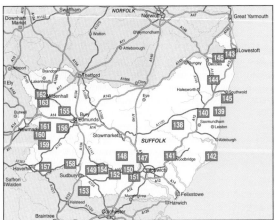

138 HIGH HOUSE FARM

Cransford Farm, Framlingham,
Suffolk IP13 9PD
☎ 01728 663461 Fax: 01728 663409
e-mail: info@highhousefarm.co.uk
⊕ www.highhousefarm.co.uk

Well away from the urban hustle and bustle, **High House Farm** is an elegant 15th century farmhouse offering traditional comfort in a choice of B&B and self-catering accommodation. A double with en suite shower and a family room with adjacent private bathroom are in the main house, which is set alongside 250 acres of rolling farmland. Resident owners Tim and Sarah Kindred, who run the family farm, also own the beautiful three-bedroom Woodlodge standing in gardens and woodland a short distance from the main house.

287

139 THE SHIP INN AT DUNWICH

Dunwich, nr Saxmundham,
Suffolk IP17 3DT
☎ 01728 648219 Fax: 01728 648675
e-mail: shipinn@tiscali.co.uk

One of the most delightful and distinctive inns on the east coast, **The Ship Inn at Dunwich** has a history dating back 500 years. Once the haunt of sea dogs and smugglers, it is now a firm favourite with both locals and the many visitors to this region of many attractions. A fine selection of real ales and wines is always available, and home-cooked dishes – including popular fish and seafood specials – are served every lunchtime and evening in the bar or dining room. Four comfortably furnished en suite bedrooms, with four more added for the

2005 season, provide an ideal base for walking, touring and exploring the coast.

140 THE GRIFFIN INN

High Street, Yoxford, Suffolk IP17 3EP
☎ 01728 668229 Fax: 01728 667040
e-mail: inquiries@thegriffin.co.uk
🌐 www.thegriffin.co.uk

The Griffin Inn started life in 1358, when it was the memorial court for the local Lord of the Manor. It became an inn two centuries later, and behind its black and white, slate-roofed exterior it retains a traditional look with high timbered walls and ceilings, a log fire and church pew seating in the bar. Thirsts are quenched by Adnams and guest brews, and locally sourced produce features prominently in the generously served dishes. Overnight accommodation comprises three beamed bedrooms that are popular with tourists and birdwatchers.

141 THE BULL HOTEL

2 Market Hill, Woodbridge,
Suffolk IP12 4LR
☎ 01394 382089 Fax: 01394 384902
e-mail: reception@bullhotel.co.uk
🌐 www.bullhotel.co.uk

On the picturesque square overlooking the Elizabethan Shire Hall, **The Bull Hotel** is a 16th century hostelry that was once a posting inn for the Union Stage between Ipswich and Norwich. The tradition of hospitality is carried on by hosts Paul and Heather Barker, who have enhanced The Bull's reputation as a cheerful 'local', a fine restaurant and a comfortable hotel. It's open all day, every day for drinks (Greene King IPA and Morelands Original are the favourite brews), and bar and restaurant menus are available for breakfast, lunch and dinner for residents and non-residents.

The 16 en suite guest bedrooms (two in outside chalets, two suitable for families) are all very well decorated and furnished, and equipped with television, direct-dial phone and tea/coffee tray. Rooms can be let on a B&B or Dinner, B&B basis. The Bull is a popular venue for private parties, wedding receptions and meetings. The coat of arms on the front of the building are those of King Victor Emmanuel II of Italy, who stayed here as the guest of the owner of the day, a noted breeder of horses.

142 VESTA COTTAGE

73 Broad Street, Orford, nr Woodbridge,
Suffolk IP12 2NQ
☎ 01394 450135 Fax: 01394 450097
e-mail: kaysorford@pobox.com
🌐 www.vestacottage.co.uk

In a quiet street near the centre of Orford,
Vesta Cottage provides comfortable self
catering accommodation for up to four guests
and a baby. The house is well equipped and
has a small garden.No smoking or pets.

143 THE GEORGE BORROW HOTEL

Bridge Road, Oulton Broad, Lowestoft,
Suffolk NR32 3LL
☎ 01502 569245 Fax: 01502 568595

Named after a renowned Victorian writer and
traveller, the **George Borrow Hotel** provides
today's travellers and tourists with
comfortable accommodation in 12 rooms,
from singles to family suites. It's also open for
drinks and straightforward pub dishes. Live
music Friday, karaoke Sunday in the function
room.

146 THE SWAN INN

Swan Lane, Barnby, Suffolk NR34 7QE
☎ 01502 476646 Fax: 01502 562513

Regular customers travel from all over the
region to enjoy the superb fish dishes that are
a speciality at **The Swan Inn**. Donny Cole
chooses the fish daily from the local market,
and the menu in the Fisherman's Cove
Restaurant
provides a
truly
impressive
choice.
Meat-
eaters and
vegetarians
are not
forgotten,
and
connoisseurs of real ale will also find an
excellent selection. Tucked away in the village
of Barnby, off the A146 east of Beccles, The
Swan has a two-bedroom self-catering
apartment that provides an ideal base for
walking and touring.

144 UGGESHALL MANOR FARM

Uggeshall, nr Southwold,
Suffolk NR34 8BD
☎ 01502 578367 Fax: 01502 578155

A handsome redbrick house at **Uggeshall
Manor Farm** has two well-equipped en suite
bedrooms for B&B guests. Alternatively, self-
catering accommodation is provided in two
stylishly converted barns, one with 4
bedrooms, the other with 3. The farm is
located by the A145 2 miles north of
Blythburgh and 3 miles from the sea.

145 THE ANCHOR

Walberswick, Suffolk IP18 6UA
☎ 01502 722112

Mark and Sophie Dorber welcome families,
artists, walkers, musicians, tourists and
everyone else to **The Anchor**, their pleasant
1920s pub in the picturesque village of
Walberswick. The bar is light and roomy, and
outside there's a front terrace and a lovely
rear garden with a wood at the end and a
path leading to the beach. Sophie's cooking is
a great attraction here, and her menus are
based on the best ingredients including
freshly caught fish. The choice of beer and
wine is also excellent, and each dish on the
menu is matched with a wine or beer
suggestion. The Anchor is also a lovely
holiday base with 11 guest rooms divided
between the main building and family chalets
in the garden.

289

147 THE SORREL HORSE INN

Old Norwich Road, Barham, nr Ipswich,
Suffolk IP6 0PG
☎ 01473 830327 Fax: 01473 833149
e-mail: enquiries@sorrelhorse.co.uk
⊕ www.sorrelhorse.co.uk

In a pleasant country setting, **The Sorrel Horse Inn** has been owned and run for many years by Bridget (Breda) Smith and her sons Matthew and Philip. The 17th century pink-washed, pantiled building first became an inn in about 1840, and the interior boasts original features such as wall and ceiling beams and open fireplaces. Hewn log-style

tables and rustic chairs assist the traditional look, and the dining areas feature interesting collections of miniatures and foreign banknotes.

Among the inn's many assets is a large lawned garden with plenty of picnic benches and parasols, a summer barbecue and a children's play area complete with slide and bouncy castle.

Expertly kept real ales – Adnams Bitter, Shepherd Neame Spitfire, Theakston's Bitter – keep cask connoisseurs happy, and fresh-air appetites are satisfied with an excellent selection of home-cooked dishes served in the two dining areas. Lasagne, chicken curry, steaks and savoury pies are at the top of the all-time favourites, and there's always a good choice of vegetarian dishes. Lighter options are available at lunchtime, and the inn is also open for breakfast.

With many attractions nearby (the magnificent Shrubland Hall and its Victorian gardens are almost on the doorstep), the cheerful, friendly Sorrel Horse is an excellent base for touring the region, and the nearby A14 provides easy access to all parts.

Eight bedrooms in a splendidly converted barn provide quiet, comfortable accommodation; most of the rooms have en suite facilities, and all are equipped with televisions, telephones and drinks trays.

Ground-floor rooms are old-fashioned in style, with original beams, while those above have a more modern look, with smart pine furniture. One room has facilities for disabled guests.

148 RIVERSIDE COTTAGE & STUDIO

Great Bricett, nr Ipswich, Suffolk IP7 7DQ
☎ 01473 658266
⊕ www.riversidecottagebandb.co.uk

Two Elizabethan thatched cottages make up
the accommodation at the **Riverside
Cottage & Studio**, which stands close to the
11th century church in the village of Great
Bricett. The main house has a double and a
twin bedroom,
both with en
suite facilities,
and the day
starts with a
good choice
for breakfast;
evening meals

are available by arrangement. Resident owners
Charles and Jane Horne also offer self-
catering accommodation in a self-contained
one-bedroom studio adjoining the thatched
house. The large garden provides gentle
strolls, pleasant views, a tree house and a
swimming pool. Riverside Cottage stands just
off the B1078 Needham Market to Bildeston
road.

150 COLLEGE FARM

Back Road, Hintlesham, nr Ipswich,
Suffolk IP8 3NT
☎ 01473 652253
⊕ www.smoothhound.co.uk/hotels/collegefarm
e-mail: bandb@collegefarm.plus.com

College Farm is a beamed Tudor building
once owned by Cardinal Wolsey and now
carefully modernised by Rosemary and Ian
Bryce to provide spacious Bed & Breakfast
accommodation. One room is an en suite
double, the other a double/twin/family room
with a private bathroom. Another room is on
the ground floor of the converted stables. An
Aga-cooked breakfast is served in the dining
room, and there are plenty of books and
games in the guest lounge. The working farm,
which also has a lovely quiet garden, is an
ideal base
for
exploring
the area.
Children
over 10
welcome.

149 JASMINE COTTAGE

The Heath, Lavenham Road, Great
Waldingfield, Suffolk CO10 0RN
☎ 01787 374665
⊕ : www.jasminecottage-b-and-b.co.uk

In the grounds of 18th century **Jasmine
Cottage**, Mike and Brenda Gander have two
rooms for B & B guests – both self-contained
units with en suite facilities. Breakfast is
between 7 and 10, and packed lunches can be
arranged. Guests have use of a pleasant
garden and a swimming pool.

Looking for:
- *Places to Visit?*
- *Places to Stay?*
- *Places to Eat & Drink?*
- *Places to Shop?*

www.travelpublishing.co.uk

151 THE GRANARY & STABLE COTTAGES

Chattisham Place, Chattisham, nr Ipswich,
Suffolk IP8 3QD
☎ 01473 652210 Fax: 01473 652210
e-mail: margaret.langton@talk21.com
⊕ www.farmstayanglia.co.uk/chattisham

Margaret and Hugo Langton welcome guests
to **The Granary & Stable Cottage**, which
provide top-quality self-catering
accommodation set round a courtyard.
Granary, Grade II listed, on stilts and with
exposed roof
timbers, sleeps up to
8 guests, Coachmans
Cottage 4 to 6 and
Stable Cottage 2 to
4; these two cottages
are wheelchair
accessible and have

adapted shower rooms. All are fully furnished
to a high standard, with fitted kitchens,
central heating and television with video and
DVD. Amenities include a laundry room,
tennis court, swimming pool and secure play
area for children.

291

152 EDGE HALL HOTEL

2 High Street, Hadleigh, Suffolk IP7 5AP
☎ 01473 822458 Fax: 01473 827751
e-mail: r.rolfe@edgehall-hotel.co.uk
🌐 www.edgehall-hotel.co.uk

At one end of Hadleigh's main street, **Edge Hall** is a family-run hotel offering sumptuous accommodation in very distinguished and civilised surroundings. The hotel is one of the oldest buildings still standing in the long High Street, dating from 1590 and remodelled to its present form in the early 1700s.

The bedrooms offer abundant character and comfort, and guests can relax in an elegant lounge. A splendid breakfast served in the stately dining room features home-grown and local produce, and the walled garden is a lovely spot for afternoon tea or a game of croquet in summer.

The main house is non-smoking, but an alternative to the main house, and the choice of guests with pets, is the budget accommodation – also of a very high standard – in Lodge House adjoining the flower garden.

153 THE LAMARSH LION

Bures Road, Lamarsh, Suffolk CO8 5EP
☎ 01787 227918

A few miles south of Sudbury off the B1508 Colchester road, **The Lamarsh Lion** is a fine old country inn dating back to the 14th century. Overlooking open farmland, this friendly free house serves an excellent choice of real ales (including Old Growler, IPA and Painted Lady from the Nethergate Brewery) and fine wines, to enjoy on their own or to accompany a snack or a meal.

An open fire keeps things cosy in the bar, and at neatly laid tables in the dining area the dishes on the blackboard menu runs from garlic mushrooms, moules marinière and deep-fried brie with cranberry sauce to grilled plaice and skate, vegetable kiev, cottage pie and a great selection of roasts.

The Lamarsh Lion is a pleasant base for exploring the Stour Valley, with three well-appointed rooms for Bed & Breakfast guests. The inn has a patio and a beer garden with a children's play area.

154 GROVE COTTAGES

Priory Green, Edwardstone,
Suffolk CO10 5PP
☎ 01787 211115
e-mail: mark@grovecottages.co.uk
⊕ www.grove-cottages.co.uk

In a lovely rural setting between Sudbury and
Hadleigh, **Grove Cottages**
provide the perfect choice for a quiet break.
Each of the six cottages has its own
personality: open fires, polished wood floors
and period furniture retain traditional charm,
while modern fittings provide everything
needed for a relaxed, hassle-free self-catering
holiday surrounded by unspoilt countryside
and an abundance of wildlife. Owner Mark
Scott, who is also the letting agent for four

other
properties,
has posted
full details of
the cottages
on a very
informative
website.

156 THE SIX BELLS

Horringer, Bury St Edmunds,
Suffolk IP29 5SJ
☎ 01284 735551
⊕ www.sixbellshorringer.co.uk

Carol Smith is the proprietor of **The Six
Bells**, where a good selection of drinks and
home-cooked food is served every day. Plush
carpets cover the old wooden floors, and the
little restaurant overlooks the beer garden.
Three bedrooms are available for overnight
guests.

157 THE WHITE HORSE

Sturmer Road, Kedington, Suffolk CB9 7NS
☎ 01440 763564

Dawn and Dave Tegg have a friendly greeting
for visitors to **The White Horse**, which is
located in a rural village near Haverhill. It's
open for breakfast at 9 o'clock, and
throughout the day for drinks and a good
selection of favourite pub dishes. The White
Horse also offers overnight accommodation
in a twin room and a family room. Two bars,
beer garden.

155 THE GREYHOUND INN

The Green, Flempton, Suffolk IP28 6EL
☎ 01284 728400 Fax: 01284 728400
e-mail:
boregamp@thegreyhound.freeserve.co.uk

Off the
A1101
between
Mildenhall
and Bury St
Edmunds,
**The
Greyhound
Inn** is a
substantial 18th century inn overlooking the
green in the shadow of a very old church.
The convivial bar area has an open fire and
old oak tables, and one part of the dining
area is designated non-smoking. Greene King
IPA and Abbot Ale head the drinks list, and
the good-value home-cooked dishes include
Sunday roasts and kebabs (also available for
takeaway). Sunday is quiz night, Tuesday pool,
Wednesday cribbage, Thursday and Friday
darts. For guests staying overnight, The
Greyhound has three rooms with shared
facilities.

293

158 EMBLETON HOUSE

Melford Road, Cavendish, Sudbury,
Suffolk CO10 8AA
☎ 01787 280447 Fax: 01787 282396
e-mail: silverned@aol.com
🌐 www.embletonhouse.co.uk

Edward Silver and his parents John and Rosemary look forward to welcoming you. Opened in August 2000 they have an excellent reputation for their friendly welcome, delicious local breakfasts, and comfortable relaxing rooms. **Embleton House** was built in 1932 for the village Doctor on this 1.6 acre plot which

he purchased from a local farmer. He had his dream house built with the provision of a Waiting Room and a Surgery on the ground floor, which are now used for two en-suite rooms.

The house is set well back from the road and with the help of many of the mature specimen trees and shrubs, some planted in the 1930s, it is secluded and peaceful. In addition to the beautiful gardens, there is a hard tennis court and a well heated outdoor swimming pool for guests to use by arrangement in the summer months. There are five large en-suite rooms in total, all carefully designed with comfort and relaxation in mind. Two large double/twins are on the ground floor, one with wheelchair access and both with their own entrances and parking spaces right outside, enabling guests to come and go with ease. Two doubles upstairs have beautiful Stour Valley views, and a wonderful Superior in the former games room has huge bay windows, a dressing area and luxury bathroom. Wake up in one of these to the sound of bird song and wander into the guests lounge with French doors to the garden or a roaring log fire to welcome you in winter.

Make your choice from Embleton's famous full Suffolk breakfast, with lots of really local produce slowly griddled for a fuller flavour - Farmers Market 100% pork sausages, Long Melford dry cure bacon, mushrooms, potatoes, English tomatoes and fresh free range eggs from Willow Farm Shop, one mile down the road. Along with bread from Clare Bakery and a wide selection of home-made jams and jellies from the garden.

Whether in Suffolk on business, touring by car, cycling or simply visiting friends and family, Embleton is the perfect base to relax and enjoy this special part of Suffolk. When you return, you will find a flask of fresh milk on your tea tray and some of Rosemary's home-made shortbread to tide you over until supper. When you want to eat there are two excellent places in Cavendish, both within a ten minute walk, and many more a short drive away. Whatever your plans Edward can supply you with extra information to make your visit more enjoyable; route maps, suggested restaurants and pubs, garden tours etc.

Embleton has four diamonds and a Silver Award from the English Tourism Council and has been recommended by Which? for four years. Edward and his parents really love what they do and this really shows through with their attention to detail and with all the extra little touches they will leave for you to discover.

159 THRIFT FARM

Cowlinge, nr Newmarket, Suffolk CB8 9JA
☎ 01440 783274 Fax: 01440 783274
e-mail: janoddy@yahoo.co.uk

Set in five acres of meadow and garden, **Thrift Farm** is the perfect place to relax in friendly, homely surroundings and an ideal base for walking or exploring this region of Suffolk. The family home offers superior Bed & Breakfast accommodation in two lovely guest bedrooms (one twin and one double). Owner Jan Oddy has lived here for 46 years; she is a welcoming and hospitable host, with a conscientious attention to service and quality. The farmhouse, a listed building believed to date from the 16th century, has been sensitively converted and refurbished to offer the highest standards of comfort. It is truly hidden away down a quiet country lane, so visitors are advised to ask directions in the village, or to ring for further information.

The double and twin are in the farmhouse, while the third room, a double/family room, is self-contained in the annexe. Tasteful decor and charming furnishings are the hallmark of this B&B, and the room are enhanced by artefacts brought from around the world by Jan's son Stuart. Breakfast is served by the Aga in the handsome country kitchen. Jan has three delightful dogs: a Labrador, a Labrador/Dalmatian cross and an enchanting Yorkshire terrier/Jack Russell cross called Kipling.

160 THE REINDEER

62 The Street, Saxon Street, nr Newmarket,
Suffolk CB8 9RS
☎ 01638 730989 Fax: 01638 730898
e-mail: thereindeer@msn.com
⊕ www.thereindeer.com

In a village a few miles south of Newmarket (off the B1061 or B1063), **The Reindeer** is a fine brick building with a covering of creeper, traditional public rooms and a lovely leafy garden. The pub, which dates back to the 18th century, is well known for the quality of its food, which range from bar snacks to a full à la carte menu, daily specials and Sunday roasts. There are seats for 80 inside and 25 outside. The Reindeer also has two superior bedrooms, both en suite, for B&B guests. No smoking anywhere inside.

161 THE AFFLECK ARMS

1 Brookside, Dalham, nr Newmarket,
Suffolk CB8 8TG
☎ 01638 500306 Fax: 01638 500306
e-mail: denisepowell@waitrose.com

Local residents, tourists and racegoers at Newmarket make up the clientele at **The Affleck Arms**, where Denise Powell, her daughter Sam and Jack the Jack Russell terrier provide the warmest of welcomes. Picnic benches are set out in front of this charming old thatched pub, and features a vast brick hearth with a wood-burning stove. Real ales include some from small local breweries, and the interesting menus offer both traditional and contemporary dishes. A tastefully appointed en-suite room provides overnight accommodation. The pub is open Monday to Friday evenings, lunchtime and evening Saturday and all day Sunday.

30 Wamil Way, Mildenhall, Suffolk IP28 7JU
☎ 01638 515417 Fax: 01638 713569
e-mail: mariabayley@holidaylets365.com
⊕ www.holidaylets365.com

Two very different properties in Mildenhall make up **Holiday Lets 365**, both owned and managed by Maria Bayley. **The Lodge**, in Wamil Way, is a very roomy, well-designed modern four-bedroom family home a very short walk from the centre, the shops and the restaurants. Beds are very luxurious and comfortable, and facilities include Sky Digital TV including American Sports Live, VCR, DVD, music centre and ceiling fans.

The kitchen has a capacious American fridge-freezer, a dishwasher and washer-dryer. One of the bedrooms is on the ground floor, wheelchair friendly, with bathroom en suite. The Lodge has good off-street parking and a large south-facing garden with a barbecue. **Mill Street Mews** is a small designer-decorated Mediterranean-style mews house tucked away in the heart of Mildenhall town centre. The vaulted and galleried bedroom has a 6-foot double bed, and equipment includes Sky Digital, DVD, VCR, ceiling fan and romantic lighting. Both properties have been refurbished to the highest standards, and guests will find everything provided, from towels to pots and pans and cutlery.

The state-of-the-art equipment in The Lodge and Mill Street Mews appeals to guests who insist on the best. Mildenhall USAAF base brings many American visitors to the town, and Holiday Lets is an ideal place to stay. The Museum in Mildenhall covers the whole history of the town and the surrounding area, from the natural history of the Fens and Breckland and the Roman presence to the RAF and American air bases that have been such a large part of life in the town. The other sight not to be missed is the magnificent Church of St Mary and St Andrew with its decorated east windows and some of the finest roof carvings in the country.

163 WORLINGTON HALL COUNTRY HOUSE HOTEL

Worlington, Suffolk IP28 8RX
☎ 01638 712237 Fax: 01638 717631
e-mail: worlingtonhall@aol.com
🌐 www.worlingtonhall-hotel.co.uk

Business partners Joy O'Brien Miller and Sharon Parkinson welcome all visitors to **Worlington Hall Country House**, which is located on the B1102 west of Mildenhall. The Hall is a gentleman's residence dating from 1570 and set in five acres of tranquil grounds leading down to the River Lark.

The guest accommodation comprises eight individually designed bedrooms in the

main building and a private suite in the converted coach house in the courtyard. All rooms have toilet and either bath or shower en suite, and the comprehensive amenities include television, alarm clock radio, direct-dial telephone, hairdryer and tea and coffee making facilities. The original house, which acquired its beautiful Queen Anne facade in the early 18th century, retains many fine period features. Elizabethan carved-wood panelling adds greatly to the intimate character of the bar. Residents and non-residents are welcome to enjoy a snack in the bar at lunchtime, or to sit down to a full à la carte dinner in the lovely Willow Room or Oak Room. Sharon takes justified pride in her excellent, unfussy cooking, and her menus are available every session except Sunday evening.

The Willow Room can be booked for private dinner parties, working lunches or business meetings, and also provides a pleasant setting for breakfast. With its own private entrance from the garden and car park, the Garden Room is a perfect choice for larger gatherings: up to 150 guests

can be accommodated in comfort, with ample room for dancing and separate bar facilities. Worlington Hall is well placed for a wide variety of local attractions, including Mildenhall, with its magnificent parish church and fascinating museum; Royal Worlington and Newmarket golf courses; horse riding and fishing; racing and associated attractions at Newmarket; and historic Bury St Edmunds.

297

Places of Interest in Suffolk

The selection of places of interest featured in this section includes museums, galleries, castles, historic houses, gardens, churches, cathedrals, gardens, country parks and many other places worth visiting in Norfolk. Each place of interest has an entry number which is used to identify its location on the map below and its name and short address in the list below the map. The entry number can also be used to find more information and contact details for the places of interest in the ensuing pages. In addition full details of places of interest in this section may be found on the Travel Publishing website – www.travelpublishing.co.uk This website has a large database of places of interest covering the whole of Britain and Ireland.

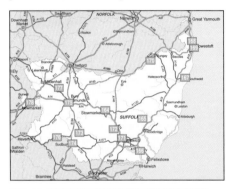

🏛 PLACES OF INTEREST

164	Museum of East Anglian Life, Stowmarket
165	Easton Farm Park, Easton
166	Sutton Hoo, Sutton Hoo
167	Southwold Pier, Southwold
168	Lowestoft Maritime Museum, Lowestoft
169	Somerleyton Hall & Gardens, Lowestoft
170	Norfolk & Suffolk Aviation Museum, Flixton
171	Ipswich Transport Museum, Ipswich
172	Baylham House Rare Breeds Farm, Baylham
173	The Guildhall Lavenham, Lavenham
174	Gainsborough's House, Sudbury
175	St Edmundsbury Cathedral, Bury St Edmunds
176	Clare Castle Country Park, Clare
177	West Stow Anglo-Saxon Village, West Stow
178	National Horseracing Museum, Newmarket

164 MUSEUM OF EAST ANGLIAN LIFE 🏛

Stowmarket, Suffolk IP14 1DL
☎ 01449 612229 Fax: 01449 672307
🌐 www.suffolkcc.gov.uk/central/meal

The Museum of East Anglian Life has collections of social, rural and industrial history including a number of historic buildings. Farm animals, adventure playground, picnic sites, café and gift shop.

165 EASTON FARM PARK 🏛

Easton, Woodbridge, Suffolk IP13 0EQ
☎ 01728 746475 Fax: 01728 747861
e-mail: easton@eastonfarmpark.co.uk
🌐 www.eastonfarmpark.co.uk

Comprising 35 acres of woodland walks, meadows and farmland, **Easton Farm Park** is one of Suffolk's greatest attractions. As well as the vast array of animals here, local tradional crafts are showcased. A great day out for the family.

166 SUTTON HOO 🏛

Tranmer House, Sutton Hoo, Woodbridge, Suffolk IP12 3DJ
☎ 01394 389700 Fax: 01394 389702

One of several large mounds was excavated in 1939 revealing the famous treasures, including a warrior's helmet, shield and gold ornaments in the remains of a burial chamber of a 90ft ship. A permanent display tells the story of Anglo-Saxon kings and the excavation, and includes a life size replica of the burial chamber.

167 SOUTHWOLD PIER 🏛

North Parade, Southwold, Suffolk IP18 6BN
☎ 01502 722105
🌐 www.southwoldpier.demon.co.uk

Voted Britain's Pier of the Year in 2002, **Southwold Pier** is the realisation of Chris and Helen Iredale's vision – a local project boasting dining, shops, unique hand made amusements and many other attractions at the pier pavilion and on the pier deck.

168 LOWESTOFT MARITIME MUSEUM

Sparrows Nest Park, Whapload Road,
Lowestoft, Suffolk NR32 1XG
☎ 01502 561963

Lowestoft Maritime Museum specialises in the history of the Lowestoft fishing fleet, from early sail to steam and through to the modern diesel-powered vessels. Methods of fishing are recorded, including trawling and

the no longer practised driftnet fishing for herring, and other displays depict the evolution of lifeboats and the town's association with the Royal Navy. A replica of the aft cabin of a steam drifter and a fine picture gallery are other attractions of this fascinating museum, where the attendants are ex-seamen and others interested in the port of Lowestoft. Open daily.

169 SOMERLEYTON HALL & GARDENS

Lowestoft, Suffolk NR32 5QQ
☎ 01502 730224 Fax: 01502 732143
⊕ www.somerleyton.co.uk

The stately home of Lord and Lady Somerleyton is a splendid early Victorian mansion virtually rebuilt from the Tudor and Jacobean house that stood on the site. The Oak Room, with 17th century panelling from

the original Jacobean hous, some outstanding wood carvings and an exquisite silver and gilt mirror made for the Doge's Palace in Venice, is one of several superb rooms in this grandest of houses. The splendour of the house is matched by the magnificent gardens. A miniature railway offers fine views of the Hall and surrounding parkland.

170 NORFOLK & SUFFOLK AVIATION MUSEUM

The Street, Flixton, Nr. Bungay,
Suffolk NR35 1NZ
☎ 01986 896644
⊕ www.aviationmuseum.net

Set in the picturesque Waveney Valley, the **Norfolk & Suffolk Aviation Museum** complex covers 7½ acres, with unique undercover exhibitions, military and civil, from the pioneer days through both World Wars, right up to the present day.

171 IPSWICH TRANSPORT MUSEUM

Old Trolleybus Depot, Cobham Road,
Ipswich, Suffolk IP3 9JD
☎ 01473 715666
⊕ www.ipswichtransportmuseum.co.uk

The collection at the **Ipswich Transport Museum** is thought to be the largest in the country. Some unusual exhibits include a road sweeper converted from a car, a horse drawn tower wagon and the oldest trolleybus in the world. Gift shop, tearoom and outdoor picnic area.

172 BAYLHAM HOUSE RARE BREEDS FARM

Mill Lane, Baylham, Suffolk IP6 8LG
☎ 01473 830264
⊕ www.baylham-house-farm.co.uk

Baylham House Rare Breeds Farm aims to help maintain the national stock of rare breed farm animals, providing the best possible care and proving people with an opportunity to meet these healthy and contented animals. Riverside walks, refreshments and gifts available.

173 THE GUILDHALL, LAVENHAM

Market Place, Lavenham, Suffolk CO10 9QZ
☎ 01787 247646
e-mail: almjtg@smtp.ntrust.org.uk

The Guildhall, built around 1530 by the prosperous Corpus Christi religious guild, is a fine example of close-studded timber framing, with exuberant carvings. In 1547 it became parish property and over the years had various uses including a workhouse. Now in the hands of the National Trust it houses a local history museum.

174 GAINSBOROUGH'S HOUSE

46 Gainsborough Street, Sudbury, Suffolk
CO10 2EU
☎ 01787 372958 Fax: 01787 376991
e-mail: mail@gainsborough.org
⊕ www.gainsborough.org

Gainsborough's House is the birthplace museum of Thomas Gainsborough (1727-1788), one of England's most celebrated artists. An exceptional collection of his paintings, drawings and prints is on display in this charming town house with a Georgian façade built by the artist's father. Around 25 oil paintings are on show, including a magnificent landscape of 1782 and a touching miniature of his wife, and among the Gainsborough memorabilia to be seen in the house are the artist's studio cabinet, his swordstick and his pocket watch. Two galleries and the garden showcase contemporary art.

175 ST EDMUNDSBURY CATHEDRAL

Angel Hill, Bury St Edmunds,
Suffolk IP33 1LS
☎ 01284 754933 Fax: 01284 768655
⊕ www.stedscathedral.co.uk

The site of Suffolk's Cathedral has been one of worship for almost 1,000 years. Today's church, started in 1503, is the successor to one built in the precinct of a Norman Abbey, of which little remains. Features include a monumental bishop's throne and a magnificent hammerbeam roof.

176 CLARE CASTLE COUNTRY PARK

Maltings Lane, Clare, Suffolk CO10 8NJ
☎ 01787 277491

Within **Clare Castle Country Park** are the remains of Clare Castle and Clare Railway Station. The former railway goods shed is now a visitor centre. There is ample open space for picnics and games, while children can enjoy an adventure playground. The riverside path and old railway line offer delightful walks.

177 WEST STOW ANGLO-SAXON VILLAGE

Icklingham Road, West Stow,
Bury St Edmunds, Suffolk IP28 6HG
☎ 01284 728718 Fax: 01284 728277
⊕ www.stedmundsbury.gov.uk/weststow.htm

Between 1965 and 1972 the low hill by the River Lark in Suffolk was excavated to reveal over 70 buildings from an early Anglo Saxon village. It was decided to carry out a practical experiment to test ideas about these buildings and part of the

village has been reconstructed on the site where the original was excavated, using tools and techniques that were available to the Anglo-Saxons. The displays show aspects of village life and the focal point is a series of life size reconstructions of costume, based upon grave finds in a nearby cemetery.

178 NATIONAL HORSERACING MUSEUM

99 High Street, Newmarket,
Suffolk CB8 8JL
☎ 01638 667333 Fax: 01638 665600
⊕ www.nationalstud.co.uk

At **The National Horseracing Museum** the story of racing throughout the ages is told through permanent collections, featuring the horses, people, events and scandals that make the sport so colourful. Highlights include the head of Persimmon, Royal Derby winner in 1896; the skeleton of Eclipse, ancestor of 90 per cent of modern thoroughbreds and items associated with Red Rum, Lester Piggott, Frankie Dettori and other heroes

of the Turf. In the Practical Gallery, visitors can learn everything there is to know about the horse and jockey, and a range of exciting temporary exhibitions, including paintings and other works of art with a racing theme.

Essex

Bordering the northern bank of the River Thames, Essex has long been a gateway to London. While the southern part contains much heavy industry, it also encompasses some delightful scenery and important marshland wildlife habitats. Epping Forest, a former royal hunting ground, provides walking and exploring on the edge of London, and there are nature reserves, superb gardens and other rural delights. History abounds in the part of the county that runs along the Thames. Henry VIII built the riverside block houses at East and West Tilbury that later became Coalhouse and Tilbury Forts. It was at West Tilbury that Queen Elizabeth I gave her famous speech to the troops assembled to meet the threat of the Spanish Armada. Throughout the centuries, the area has been subject to invasion: there are many Roman remains, and one of the most decisive battles in England's early history took place at Maldon in the 10th century when one of the English leaders was killed by invading Danes.

Southend-on-Sea has long been a great favourite with Londoners for a day by the sea, while Burnham-on-Crouch is a popular yachting centre. Chelmsford is the county town of Essex, but Colchester is older and has more to offer the visitor. First established in the 7th century, the country's oldest recorded town was the capital of Roman Britain until Boadicea, Queen of the Iceni, burned it to the ground. Other towns with long histories include Tiptree, home to the famous jam factory, Coggeshall, a well-known centre of lace production, and Saffron Walden, named after the saffron crocus plant that was raised here to produce dyestuffs. Thaxted, Great Dunmow and Stansted Mountfichet are among the loveliest towns and villages in the county, while Audley End is one of the most magnificent Jacobean mansions in the whole land.

Along the east coast, dubbed the 'Sunshine Holiday Coast', are the resorts of Clacton, Frinton and Waldon, all developed in the 19th century. Seafaring, fishing and shipbuilding were all once the mainstays of many of the settlements hereabouts, including Mistley, Manningtree and Harwich; there are Martello Towers – built to provide a coastal defence against Napoleon's armies – at Clacton and Walton, and Brightlingsea has the distinction of being the only limb of the Cinque Ports outside Kent and Sussex.

Northeast Essex has the true feel of East Anglia, particularly around the villages of the Stour Valley, part of which is known as Constable Country. The Stour Estuary and the Colne Estuary are renowned for seabirds and other wildlife, and many areas are protected nature reserves. Essex has many interesting churches, many built with wood and brick rather then stone. They range from the Saxon mission of St Peter-on-the-Wall at Bradwell and the oldest log-built church in Europe at Greensted to Thaxted's Church of St John, Waltham Abbey and the Cathedrals at Chelmsford and Braintree.

The heritage and scenery of Essex are very accessible not just to motorists but, with the mainly flat lie of the land, also to walkers and cyclists, and visitors will find an abundance of opportunities for relaxation and recreation.

Saffron Walden

Food and Drink in Essex

The selection of establishments serving food and drink featured in this section includes restaurants, cafes, hotels, pubs, inns and tea & coffee shops. Each establishment has an entry number which is used to identify its location on the map below and its name and short address in the list below the map. The entry number can also be used to find more information and contact details for the establishment in the ensuing pages. In addition full details of establishments serving food and drink featured in this section may be found on the Travel Publishing website – www.travelpublishing.co.uk This website has a large database of establishments serving food and drink covering the whole of Britain and Ireland.

FOOD AND DRINK

179 THE LION

Mersea Road, Langenhoe, nr Colchester,
Essex CO5 7LF
☎ 01206 735263
e-mail: d.kiddle@btconnect.com

The Lion was built as station offices in the 1880s for a railway that was never built and it became a pub in 1891. Debbie and Dougie Kiddle, together with talented chef Gary, have made the pub a destination for lovers of good food and those

who want to relax with a drink (Greene King IPA is the resident cask ale, augmented by two guests in summer). The choice of food is amazing with dishes from around the world, includingMaryland crab cakes, French cotriade and mahu-mahu with a red curry prawn sauce. Children are welcome and there is a delightful sun-trap courtyard patio.

180 THE WHITE HART INN

Nayland Road, West Bergholt,
nr Colchester, Essex CO6 3DD
☎ 01206 240331

The White Hart Inn is a fine old hostelry standing on its own in the village of West Bergholt, a short drive northwest of Colchester. The new leaseholders are Simon and Mandy Jones, who are continuing the long tradition of hospitality that brings visitors from Colchester and the surrounding towns and villages. The pub is open every session for drinks (real ales are Greene King IPA, Abbot Ale and a monthly changing guest) and food is served from 12 to 2 and 6 to 9 Monday to Saturday and from 12 to 3 on Sunday, with a special Sunday evening menu. The non-smoking restaurant has seats for 40, with another 40 seats in the bar, and the menu offers a

wide variety of home-cooked dishes to suit all tastes and appetites. Classic choices range from sole, scampi and plaice to sausage, egg & chips, chicken and lamb curries, lasagne and beef & stout pie, plus dishes not usually seen on pub menus, like moussaka or lamb steak with a blue cheese and cream sauce; Monday is steak night. The White Hart has a superb beer garden with a gas-fired barbecue, and an adjacent field is available for tents and caravans. Plans include creating three en suite bedrooms in the main building for B&B, and another in an outbuilding.

181 THE WIG & FIDGETT

Straight Road, Boxted, nr Colchester,
Essex CO4 5QX
☎ 01206 272227

The name, shared by no other pub in the land, is just one of the many appealing features of **The Wig & Fidgett**. It's a true hidden gem, reached by minor roads off the A134 or A12 5 miles north of Colchester. It's the first venture into the licensed trade for tenant Louise Robertson and her partner Malcolm, and they have lost no time in winning new friends since taking over the

reins in November 2004. The bar-lounge and seated dining area are delightfully and unpretentiously rustic, with lots of dark wood, beams and brasses. Open from 5 o'clock on Monday and all day Tuesday to Sunday, the pub offers an across-the-board menu served 12 to 3 and 5 to 8 Tuesday to Saturday and from 1 to 4 on Sunday. The Wig & Fidgett has a splendid beer garden to the rear and a smaller alfresco area to one side. All-comers are welcome for the Thursday quiz (starting at 8.30), and once a month, usually on a Friday, there's entertainment in the form of live music, karaoke or a disco.

182 THE CASTLE

**77 High Street, Earls Colne, nr Colchester,
Essex CO6 2QX ☎ 01787 222694
e-mail: queenjuliann2001@yahoo.co.uk**

Behind its smart yellow-painted frontage,
The Castle has a superb traditional interior
with beams, real fire, a mural of a medieval
drinking scene and memorabilia from a local
engineering works. The pub is open all day
for drinks, including three cask ales. Beer
garden, off-road parking, Sunday quiz.

183 THE BULL AT BLACKMORE END

**Blackmore End, nr Braintree,
Essex CM7 4DD ☎ 01371 851037
e-mail: blackmoreendbull@supanet.com**

With origins in the 14th century, **The Bull at
Blackmore End** has an abundance of
traditional charm. A choice of real ales is
served in the bar, and locally sourced
ingredients are the basis of the menus, which
range from baked potatoes and toasties to
steak and daily specials. There is a pool table,
large garden and parking.

184 THE ROSE & CROWN

**Crown Street, Dedham, nr Colchester,
Essex CO7 6AS
☎ 01206 322197**

A short walk from the centre of Dedham, on
the B1029 northeast of Colchester, **The
Rose & Crown** is easy to spot with its
steeply-raked tiled roof and tall redbrick
chimneys. Built in 1907 on the site of an
earlier hostelry, it has been run since the
beginning of 2005 by experienced leaseholder
Linda Lilley and her daughter Lisa. Linda's

cooking is winning many new friends, and the really good
news is that her food is available from noon to 9 o'clock
every day of the week. Home-cooked ham egg & chips
and a super steak & ale pie are already well-established
favourites, but the printed menu and daily specials offer a
very wide choice that could include stilton & walnut pâté,
an all-day breakfast, salmon hollandaise, sweet & sour
chicken and a rarely seen favourite of yesteryear – toad-
in-the-hole. The smartly traditional interior of the Rose &
Crown includes a bright conservatory dining area
overlooking the garden. Sunday is quiz night, and themed
food evenings take place monthly.

HIDDEN PLACES GUIDES

Explore Britain and Ireland with
Hidden Places guides - a fascinating
series of national and local travel
guides.

Packed with easy to read information
on hundreds of places of interest as
well as places to stay, eat and drink.

Available from both high street and
internet booksellers

For more information on the full range
of *Hidden Places* guides and other
titles published by Travel Publishing
visit our website on

www.travelpublishing.co.uk
or ask for our leaflet by phoning
0118-981-7777 or emailing
info@travelpublishing.co.uk

304

185 THE WOOLPACK INN

Church Street, Coggeshall, Essex CO6 1UB
☎ 01376 561235

The Woolpack Inn is a pub of great appeal, standing next to the church on the edge of the charming old cloth and lace town of Coggeshall. The town has many fine buildings, and The Woolpack is certainly among them, its splendid timbered frontage a landmark for more than 500 years; it is thought to be the oldest secular building in Coggeshall. The promise of the outside is more than fulfilled within, where copper and brass ornaments and a copper-hooded fire in a large brick hearth add to the old-world charm. Visitors can expect a really warm welcome from Maurice and Annie, who came as tenants in 2000. The Woolpack is open all day, every day for drinks (Greene King IPA and Adnams Bitter are the regular cask ales) and food is served lunchtime and evening except Sunday evening and all

Monday unless it's a Bank Holiday. Herbs from the pub's garden enhance many of the dishes, which range from light bar snacks to daily changing main courses such as cod and smoked bacon fishcakes served on spinach with a honey and mustard sauce, or Mediterranean lamb with tagliatelle. When the sun shines, the courtyard garden comes into its own.

186 THE BELL INN

The Street, Feering, nr Colchester, Essex CO5 9QQ
☎ 01376 570375 Fax: 01376 572862
e-mail: thebell@wilkinsonhouse.co.uk

Alan and Carole Nash and chef Keith Wilkinson make a great team at **The Bell Inn**, a fine 16th century inn overlooking the village green. Open lunchtime and evening and all day on Sunday, the inn serves London Pride and Greene king IPA, and Keith's excellent dishes are served every session except Sunday and Monday evenings.

187 THE HORSE & GROOM

Cornish Hall End, nr Finchingfield, Braintree, Essex CM7 4HF
☎ 01799 586306

The **Horse & Groom** is a 17th century country pub of wide appeal, serving as a convivial local and a good place to seek out by motorists, tourists and travellers using nearby Stansted Airport. It's very much a family affair, with Kelly and Geoff Bishop and Geoff's brother Daniel sharing the duties. Thirsts are quenched by

a choice of three real ales, and in the bar or spacious non-smoking restaurant food is served lunchtime and evening. The choice runs from snacks and classic pub dishes to an extensive list of daily specials and a Sunday carvery with 3 or 4 roasts. The pub is the spiritual home of the village cricket team and fields a darts team in the local league. Closed Monday except Bank Holidays.

Looking for:
- *Places to Visit?*
- *Places to Stay?*
- *Places to Eat & Drink?*
- *Places to Shop?*

www.travelpublishing.co.uk

305

6 Church Hill, Finchingfield,
Essex CM7 4NN
☎ 01371 810400 Fax: 01371 810400
e-mail: franktyler@excite.co.uk
🌐 www.red-lion-finchingfield.com

Frank and Zahra Tyler have brought their extensive hotel and catering experience to this quiet and picturesque corner of Essex and the impressive **Red Lion**. Here they have created a comfortable, cosy and convivial inn, as their enthusiasm for good food, good wine and good company is truly infectious. Here since 1996, and now 'assisted' by their three-

year-old son, Flynn, and one-year-old son Nathan, they and their friendly staff offer a warm welcome and great service to all their guests.

A hub of local community activity for this and the surrounding vilages, as well as attracting a number of foreign visitors (Stansted Airport is not all that far away), this quintessentially English inn – located in what has been called the country's prettiest village, boasting a number of antiques shops, craft shops and tearooms, and located near some excellent walking country – dates back to 1520 (though it was extensively 'modernised' in 1823).

The interior of the bar is a splendid mix of oak beams, brick and brass. The restaurant boasts real Georgian elegance. The pub has featured several times in *The Good Beer Guide* (1995-2003). The wide-ranging menu of over 50 different dishes features generously filled traditional Essex 'Huffers' and a full a la carte selection, all making the most of locally-supplied produce wherever possible. Traditional favourites such as sausage and mash, steaks and fresh fish dishes are augmented by special themed nights featuring French cuisine and other continental menus.

The three guest bedrooms are comfortably furnished with locally-produced and hand-painted pine furnishings, and make an excellent base from which to explore this part of Essex and the surrounding region. Open all day every day, this fine inn has been awarded 3 Diamonds

189 THE WHITE HOUSE

High Street, Halstead, Essex CO9 2AP
☎ 01787 476641
e-mail: Bradley@telco4u.net
⊕ www.whitehousehalstead.co.uk

The White House has graced the main street
of Halstead for more than 500 years, and its
history is full of interest. It probably started
life as a wool merchant's house, and it was
home to surgeons and an architect, a doctor's
surgery, a gift shop and a restaurant before
becoming today's home of the traditional
English tea and fine dining in elegant, civilised
surroundings. The facade is Georgian, the
windows Victorian, and the property has an original walled garden and an adjacent coach house. Ken
and Elaine Bradley came here in 1999 and transformed the place with a major refurbishment
programme, much of the work designed by Ken himself.

Elaine is a superb pastry chef, and her cakes and pastries are
always in demand. On the savoury side, the White House serves
sandwich platters, salads, light lunches, daily specials such as
chicken Milanese or seafood provençale, and traditional roasts for
Sunday lunch. Opening times are 10 to 5 Tuesday to Saturday, 12
to 3 on Sunday. The Coach House has its own access and can be
let on a self-catering basis: it has a bedroom, bathroom, sitting
room and superbly appointed kitchen.

190 THE LOCOMOTIVE

3 Butler Road, Halstead, Essex CO9 1LL
☎ 01787 472425
e-mail: locomotive@thelocomotive.co.uk
⊕ www.thelocomotive.co.uk

Prominently sited on one of Halstead's main
streets, **The Locomotive** is a fine old pub
with abundant character and wide appeal.
Mugs and tankards hang from beams in the
dining area, and the bar is filled with brasses,
period prints and photographs and a wealth
of little secrets to discover. Mic and Mo have
won many friends since taking over in 1993,
and the bar is open all day for drinks –

Boddingtons is the locals' favourite.

Food is served lunchtime and evening Thursday to
Saturday and from 12 to 4 on Sunday. The printed
menu and specials board provide plenty of choice for
meat-eaters, fish-eaters and vegetarians. Among the
most popular main courses are at least 20 sizzling
dishes – beef and steak, chicken, lamb, prawn – even
vegetarian. Food is also available Monday to Wednesday
only with advance booking. Dominoes, darts and pool
are the favourite games at this most sociable of pubs.

191 THE VICTORY INN & WICKHAM SHIP RESTAURANT

The Green, Wickham St Pauls, nr Halstead,
Essex CO9 2PT
☎ 01787 269364 Fax: 01787 269364
e-mail: info@thevictoryinn.net
🌐 www.thevictoryinn.net

The Victory Inn is an outstanding establishment with all the best features of a traditional country pub and a fine destination restaurant. It overlooks the green in the pretty village of Wickham St Pauls, off the B1058 or A131 a few miles south of Sudbury and a short drive north of Halstead. The

premises were in a state of neglect and might have closed, but two couples living in the village decided to save their pub and bought it in October 2004, appointing John Helps as landlord.

John brought many years' experience in the trade, and he has lost no time in turning round The Victory's fortunes and making it a very popular venue. The inn has a great deal of character: outside, timbers, small-paned windows and lots of flowers and greenery in the spring and summer; inside, stylish updating of the decor while retaining the traditional feel. The inn is open lunchtime and evening, and all day in the summer season. Greene King IPA and Adnams Bitter are the resident cask ales, augmented by two regularly rotating guests ales.

The Victory can seat up to 70 diners, 40 of them in the non-smoking **Wickham Ship Restaurant**. Food is served from 12 to 2.30 and 6.30 to 9.30 Monday to Saturday and from 12 to 4 on Sunday. The printed menu, the blackboard menu and the specials board provide a first-class choice of home-cooked dishes, and fresh fish and chargrilled dishes are great favourites. A typical selection from the boards might include filo crab parcels set on a bed of ruby chard dressed with balsamic vinegar; deep-fried sesame brie with a mixed berry coulis; tagliatelle carbonara; long-cooked lamb shank (kleftico); sweet & sour duck breast with mixed peppers; cod in a guest ale batter; rump steak with the Victory 'full monty'; and salmon and prawn risotto. Desserts include ice creams on their own menu. Everything tastes as good as it reads, and such is the popularity of the restaurant that booking is advisable at all times and essential at the weekend. The beer garden at the front overlooks the village green and pond – a perfect spot for enjoying a drink and making the most of the attractive setting.

192 THE RED LION

Clacton Road, Thorrington,
Essex CO7 8EX
☎ 01206 250664

In a pleasant rural setting between Colchester and Clacton, **The Red Lion** is a smart, spacious free house with a warm, convivial feel. The decor is a marriage of original 17th century and bright modern elements, and the menus, too, offer both tradition favourites and more contemporary choices. Three real ales.

193 THE NEW BELL INN

Outpart Eastward, Harwich,
Essex CO12 3EN
☎ 01255 503545 Fax: 01255 503545

Blue walls, red doors and white window surrounds make a patriotic sight at **The New Bell Inn**, an 18th century property between the river mouth and the sea. The cosy interior is a good spot for enjoying real ales (some for small local brewers) and freshly made snacks – dressed crab and huffers (large filled rolls) are among the favourites. Home-made soups a speciality.

195 THE RED LION

44 South Street, Manningtree,
Essex CO11 1BG
☎ 01206 395052

Dating from the 16th century, **The Red Lion** is a popular town pub offering fine home cooking (smoked salmon tart is a real winner), well-kept ales and excellent wines. The adjoining Victorian house has two rooms for B&B. Regular themed lunches and dinners, and varied entertainment.

196 MAZE

9 Market Place, Saffron Walden,
Essex CB10 1HR
☎ 01799 525429 (coffee shop)
01799 529255 (restaurant)

Many eating houses claim to cater for all tastes, but few succeed as well as the excellent **Maze** in Saffron Waldon. Chef-patron Lee Newsome runs an all-day coffee shop and sandwich bar, a pizza/pasta house and a splendid restaurant.

194 THE WHITE HART

Mill Street, St Osyth, Essex CO16 8EN
☎ 01255 820318
⊕ www.thewhitehartstosyth.co.uk

Simon Mallett and his mother Karen are the affable hosts at **The White Hart**, a fine old inn on the road from St Osyth to Point Clear. The old-world look is reinforced by old beams and wood-burning stoves in the bar, where a good choice of cask ales, beers, lagers, wines and spirits is available all day. In the non-smoking dining area they serve a variety of snacks and classic pub dishes, from baguettes, jacket potatoes and salads  to excellent steaks and Sunday roasts. The garden has a children's play area with swings and slides.

197 THE THREE HORSESHOES

Hellions Bumpstead, nr Saffron Walden,
Essex CB9 7AL
☎ 01440 730298

In a lovely little village straddling three counties – Essex, Cambridgeshire and Suffolk – **The Three Horseshoes** is a pleasant, welcoming pub dating from the 17th century. Behind the white-painted, slate-roofed  facade adorned in season by tubs and hanging baskets, the cosy, beautifully furnished interior provides the ideal ambience for relaxing with a drink and a chat, or for settling down to enjoy something from the menu of traditional dishes. The food, served Tuesday to Sunday lunchtime and Wednesday to Saturday evening, is accompanied by a very good wine list.

198 THE RED LION

8 Church Street, Steeple Bumpstead, Essex CB9 7DG
☎ 01440 731833

Major changes continue apace at **The Red Lion**, which stands opposite the lovely old Church of St Mary the Virgin in the picturesque Essex village of Steeple Bumpstead. Licensees Angela and Jim Webb previously ran a pub in London's Isle of Dogs; Angela is a keen horsewoman, Jim is a rugby and fishing enthusiast, and both are clearly dedicated to transforming this fine old brick building.

The year 2004 saw the total refurbishment of the interior, a huge task carried out by Jim that involved incorporating original beams into the smartly updated decor: in one part of the bars rustic tables on a flagstone floor are separated by low wooden screens, in another there are comfortable upholstered chairs. Exposed floorboards, a modern bar in light oak and a wood-burning stove in a fine brick fireplace are other features, while outside at the rear is an enclosed garden with children's amusements including a bouncy castle for the summer. Due to come on stream in the spring of 2006 is a 20-cover restaurant with a slate roof and sash windows – a look in keeping with the requirements of this conservation area. Until then, anywhere in the pub is available for enjoying traditional pub snacks, an à la carte menu and a traditional Sunday lunch with a choice of four roasts.

Greene King IPA is the resident cask ales, joined by regularly changing guest beers. The amenities of The Red Lion will be further enhanced in 2006 with the provision of guest accommodation. Two self-catering cottages adjoining the pub are due in the spring, and three rooms upstairs in the pub will be available in the autumn; facilities will be available for guests with restricted mobility.

When the accommodation opens, The Red Lion will be a popular and convenient base for both business and leisure visitors: Haverhill is a short drive to the north, and Saffron Walden is a few miles to the west, and the whole area is filled with places of scenic or historic interest.

199 THE CRICKETERS

22 Beaumont Hill, Great Dunmow,
Essex CM6 2AP
☎ 01371 873359

On the northern edge of Great Dunmow on the road to Thaxted, **The Cricketers** attracts a wide mix of customers, from a loyal local clientele to tourists, holidaymakers, business people and air travellers using nearby Stansted Airport. Sarah and Andi brought plenty of experience in the licensed trade when they took over the pub at the beginning of 2005, and the welcome they have for all their customers is warm and genuine.

The pub has several areas for eating and drinking, including public and lounge bars, the snug in the centre and the area by the old oven that has been preserved from the time when it was a bakery. Ridleys IPA, Old Bob, Prospect and Tolly Cobbold are among the cask ales on tap, to satisfy thirsts or

to accompany Andi's traditional home cooking. His menu caters for large and small appetites with a choice that runs from sandwiches and baguettes to jacket potatoes, salads lasagne (meat or vegetarian), fish & chips, steaks and mixed grill. Much of the decor has a cricketing theme, and the pub hosts an annual match in July between under-35 and over-35 local teams. Other activities at this very sociable pub include pool, darts, dominoes and regular quizzes.

The Cricketers is open from 12 to 11 (Sunday to 10.30) and food is served food 12 to 9 (Sunday lunch till 8).

200 THE VIPER

Mill Green Road, Mill Green, nr
Ingatestone, Essex CM4 0PT
☎ 01277 352010

Peacefully located down snaking country lanes north of Ingatestone, **The Viper** is a great place for all the family. Some of the ales are brewed specially for the pub, and food is served every lunchtime. The Viper has a superb garden and woods for children to romp in.

Explore Britain and Ireland with
Hidden Places guides - a fascinating
series of national and local travel
guides.

www.travelpublishing.co.uk

0118-981-7777

info@travelpublishing.co.uk

201 THE CRICKETERS

Mill Green, nr Ingatestone, Essex CM4 0JD
☎ 01277 352400
e-mail: thecricketers@tiscali.co.uk
🌐 www.thecricketersatfryerning.co.uk

Food is big business at **The Cricketers**, a fine little village pub dating from the early 19th century. The public rooms are tastefully decorated and furnished, with plenty of comfortable seats and some cricketing memorabilia. Daily specials add to the choice of excellent home-cooked dishes, which include fresh seafood and seasonal game. The pub sign shows players

in cricketing gear, but they're actually footballers – see if you can recognise them!

Swan Lane, Margaretting Tye,
Essex CM4 9JX
☎ 01277 840478 Fax: 01277 841178
e-mail: liz@thewhitehart.uk.com
🌐 www.thewhitehart.uk.com

Owner Liz Haines, chef Ting Sayer and friendly, hardworking staff have established the reputation of **The White Hart** as one of the very best pubs in the whole region. The rural setting lends itself to a number of excellent walks, which makes it a popular

choice of walkers, ramblers and cyclists as well as a favourite with local residents, travellers and tourists.

Swan Lane, which runs from Galleywood to Stock, is a Grade II listed street, and the White Hart is one of its most distinguished buildings. The frontage is adorned in spring and summer with flower boxes and hanging baskets, and in the public areas the heavily beamed vaulted ceiling and open fires add to the cosy, traditional ambience.

The White Hart is open every session and all day Saturday and Sunday, with food served lunchtime and evening. A choice of at least half a dozen real ales includes regulars Mighty Oak IPA, Adnams Best and Broadside, a choice that multiplies many times during the two annual beer festivals (50+ real ales in June, 20+ in October). These popular occasions include live entertainment and barbecues, and Liz also holds a charitable 'Village Day' in August, with live jazz on the green, barbecues, games and stalls. Chef Ting's excellent food can be enjoyed anywhere in the pub, and the choice really does cater for all tastes and appetites.

The food is a very popular and important side of the White Hart's business, and booking is recommended for all meals – and essential on Sunday. Outside, the pub has a large lawned garden, a safe children's play area and a pets corner with goats and other farm animals, an aviary and a large duck pond with a waterfall. Liz plans to extend the already impressive amenities of the White Hart by bringing on stream a number of rooms for Bed & Breakfast, which will make this a fine base for exploring the region.

203 THE WHITE SWAN

Main Road, Bicknacre, nr Chelmsford,
Essex CM3 4EX
☎ 01245 222826

On the B1418 southeast of Chelmsford, **The White Swan** is a traditional village pub. Greene King IPA, Brewers Gold and Oscar Wilde are the resident ales, and food ranges from bar snacks (served every session except Monday and Tuesday evenings) to an à la carte restaurant menu for Friday and Saturday, and Sunday lunch.

204 THE WHITE HART

The Street, Little Waltham, nr Chelmsford,
Essex CM3 3NY
☎ 01245 360487

Mo Gordon has a warm welcome for all the family at the **White Hart**, her delightful traditional pub on the main street of Little Waltham. Bar and restaurant menus cater for all tastes and appetites, and entertainment includes live music on Saturday and jam sessions on Thursday.

205 MILL BEACH

Goldhanger Road, Heybridge, nr Maldon,
essex CM9 4RA
☎ 01621 857157
e-mail: millbeachph@hotmail.com
🌐 www.millbeach.com

When Lee and Liz Pearson came here in 2002, **Mill Beach** was in a state of neglect. Now, thanks to their efforts, this mid-Victorian pub set back from the B1056 has been smartly refurbished, and visitors find a warm welcome, fine food and drink and weekend entertainment. Liz does the cooking, and her printed menu and specials board are available for summer lunches (including a Sunday carvery) and Saturday evening. The pub has a family room, a non-smoking restaurant, a games room with Sky Sports and a garden overlooking the Blackwater Estuary. Live entertainment summer Saturday night, pianist Sunday lunchtime.

206 THE BLUE BOAR HOTEL

Silver Street, Maldon, Essex CM9 4QE
☎ 01621 855888 Fax: 01621 856202
e-mail: blueboarhotel@hotmail.com
🌐 www.blueboarmaldon.co.uk

Owner John Wilsdon and manager David Shaw are justly very proud of their traditional English coaching inn, which has been a landmark in Maldon since the 14th century. Down the centuries **The Blue Boar** has provided hospitality for travellers, business people and tradesmen, and it now offers an equally warm welcome to tourists and holiday-makers. The hotel provides the expected up-to-date comfort and amenities while maintaining its old-world character, and antiques are a feature throughout (the hotel actually has an adjacent antiques shop).

The 28 guest bedrooms range from singles to doubles/twins and some splendid four-poster rooms, and behind the somewhat austere Georgian frontage the day rooms and reception rooms are contrastingly ornate, with ancient beams, striking paintings, chandeliers, pewter and brass, mirrors and oriental figures. The food options comprise lunchtime and evening bar snacks and a varied à la carte menu served in the restaurant. Well-chosen extras include a long gallery function room, a 40 space car park and connoisseurs of real ales will find at least three from the Blue Boar's own Farmers Microbrewery.

207 MALONES DINER

8 High Street, Maldon, Essex CN9 5PJ
☎ 01621 840007

Maldon is a fascinating town with a thousand years of history and a strong maritime tradition. The High Street and the alleys leading from it are filled with interesting shops, inns and places to eat, and among the lasts **Malones Diner** is one of the best. This very cheerful and relaxing place is run by Kelly and Stewart Swanborough, who offer their customers an impressive range of American-inspired dishes lunchtime and

evening seven days a week.

Favourites on the lunchtime menu include jacket potatoes and speciality sandwiches with tempting fillings such as smoked salmon and brie melt or steak served hot in ciabatta. The main menu runs the whole transatlantic gamut from buffalo wings, nachos and enchiladas to stuffed jalapeno peppers, chargrilled chicken, chilli, ribs, burgers, steaks and fishy delights such as tilapia, red snapper, salmon, scallops and swordfish. Malones has a full licence.

208 CHIGBOROUGH LODGE RESTAURANT

Chigborough Road, Heybridge, nr Maldon, Essex CM9 4RE
☎ 01621 853590
e-mail: chigboroughlodge@aol.com

In the tranquil North Essex countryside, amidst the beautiful lakes of the Chigboro' Fisheries, there is a hidden treasure waiting to be discovered. Search out the special delight of the friendly atmosphere and fine

dining at the **Chigborough Lodge Restaurant**. The restaurant is closed Sunday evening and all Monday and Tuesday. The a la carte menu is available from 6.30pm, while the lunch and lighter moments menus tempt the midday diner and breakfasts fill the fishermen.

209 THE HURDLEMAKERS ARMS

Post Office Road, Woodham Mortimer, nr Maldon, Essex CM9 6ST
☎ 01245 225169

In a pretty village off the A414 Maldon to Danbury road, **The Hurdlemakers Arms** is open every lunchtime and evening, and all day Saturday and Sunday in the summer months. Beams, rustic furniture and an open fire in a brick hearth create an inviting ambience in the bars, where Greene King IPA and Abbot Ale are the regular ales. Home-cooked food is served every session (book at the weekend) and in summer the barbecue in the lawned garden is a popular attraction.

Accommodation in Essex

T he accommodation featured in this section includes hotels, inns, guest houses, bed & breakfasts and self catered establishments. Each establishment has an entry number which is used to identify its location on the map below and its name and short address in the list below the map. The entry number can also be used to find more information and contact details for the accommodation in the ensuing pages. In addition full details of all this accommodation may be found on the Travel Publishing website - www.travelpublishing.co.uk. This website has a comprehensive database of accommodation covering the whole of Britain and Ireland.

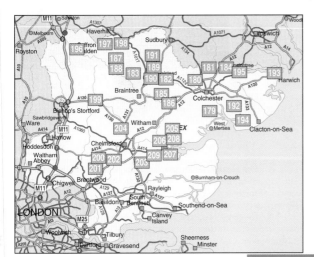

ACCOMMODATION

210   The White Hart Inn, West Bergholt
211   The White House, Halstead
212   The Red Lion, Finchingfield
213   The Red Lion, Manningtree
214   Archway Guest House, Saffron Walden
215   Hollingate Bed & Breakfast, Radwinter End
216   Garnish Hall, Margaret Roding
217   The Red Lion, Steeple Bumpstead
218   The White Hart, Margaretting Tye
219   The Blue Boar Hotel, Maldon

HIDDEN PLACES GUIDES

Explore Britain and Ireland with *Hidden Places* guides - a fascinating series of national and local travel guides.

Packed with easy to read information on hundreds of places of interest as well as places to stay, eat and drink.

Available from both high street and internet booksellers

For more information on the full range of *Hidden Places* guides and other titles published by Travel Publishing visit our website on

www.travelpublishing.co.uk
or ask for our leaflet by phoning
0118-981-7777 or emailing
info@travelpublishing.co.uk

210 THE WHITE HART INN

Nayland Road, West Bergholt, nr
Colchester, Essex CO6 3DD
☎ 01206 240331

The White Hart Inn is a fine old hostelry
standing on its own in the village of West
Bergholt, a short drive northwest of Colchester.
The new leaseholders are Simon and Mandy
Jones, who are continuing the long tradition of
hospitality that brings visitors from Colchester
and the surrounding towns and villages. The pub is open every session for drinks (real ales are
Greene King IPA, Abbot Ale and a monthly changing guest) and food is served from 12 to 2 and 6
to 9 Monday to Saturday and from 12 to 3 on Sunday, with a special Sunday evening menu. The
non-smoking restaurant has seats for 40, with another 40 seats in the bar, and the menu offers a

wide variety of home-cooked dishes to suit all tastes and
appetites. Classic choices range from sole, scampi and plaice to
sausage, egg & chips, chicken and lamb curries, lasagne and
beef & stout pie, plus dishes not usually seen on pub menus,
like moussaka or lamb steak with a blue cheese and cream
sauce; Monday is steak night. The White Hart has a superb
beer garden with a gas-fired barbecue, and an adjacent field is
available for tents and caravans. Plans include creating three en
suite bedrooms in the main building for B&B, and another in
an outbuilding.

211 THE WHITE HOUSE

High Street, Halstead, Essex CO9 2AP
☎ 01787 476641
e-mail: Bradley@telco4u.net
🌐 www.whitehousehalstead.co.uk

The White House has graced the main street
of Halstead for more than 500 years, and its
history is full of interest. It probably started
life as a wool merchant's house, and it was
home to surgeons and an architect, a doctor's
surgery, a gift shop and a restaurant before
becoming today's home of the traditional
English tea and fine dining in elegant, civilised
surroundings. The facade is Georgian, the
windows Victorian, and the property has an original walled garden and an adjacent coach house. Ken
and Elaine Bradley came here in 1999 and transformed the place with a major refurbishment

programme, much of the work designed by Ken himself.
Elaine is a superb pastry chef, and her cakes and pastries are
always in demand. On the savoury side, the White House serves
sandwich platters, salads, light lunches, daily specials such as
chicken Milanese or seafood provençale, and traditional roasts for
Sunday lunch. Opening times are 10 to 5 Tuesday to Saturday, 12
to 3 on Sunday. The Coach House has its own access and can be
let on a self-catering basis: it has a bedroom, bathroom, sitting
room and superbly appointed kitchen.

316

212 THE RED LION

6 Church Hill, Finchingfield,
Essex CM7 4NN
☎ 01371 810400 Fax: 01371 810400
e-mail: franktyler@excite.co.uk
⊕ www.red-lion-finchingfield.com

Frank and Zahra Tyler have brought their extensive hotel and catering experience to this quiet and picturesque corner of Essex and the impressive **Red Lion**. Here they have created a comfortable, cosy and convivial inn, as their enthusiasm for good food, good wine and good company is truly infectious. Here since 1996, and now 'assisted' by their three-

year-old son, Flynn, and one-year-old son Nathan, they and their friendly staff offer a warm welcome and great service to all their guests.

A hub of local community activity for this and the surrounding vilages, as well as attracting a number of foreign visitors (Stansted Airport is not all that far away), this quintessentially English inn – located in what has been called the country's prettiest village, boasting a number of antiques shops, craft shops and tearooms, and located near some excellent walking country – dates back to 1520 (though it was extensively 'modernised' in 1823).

The interior of the bar is a splendid mix of oak beams, brick and brass. The restaurant boasts real Georgian elegance. The pub has featured several times in *The Good Beer Guide* (1995-2003). The wide-ranging menu of over 50 different dishes features generously filled traditional Essex 'Huffers' and a full a la carte selection, all making the most of locally-supplied produce wherever possible. Traditional favourites such as sausage and mash, steaks and fresh fish dishes are augmented by special themed nights featuring French cuisine and other continental menus.

The three guest bedrooms are comfortably furnished with locally-produced and hand-painted pine furnishings, and make an excellent base from which to explore this part of Essex and the surrounding region. Open all day every day, this fine inn has been awarded 3 Diamonds

213 THE RED LION

44 South Street, Manningtree,
Essex CO11 1BG
☎ 01206 395052

Dating from the 16th century, **The Red Lion** is a popular town pub offering fine home cooking (smoked salmon tart is a real winner), well-kept ales and excellent wines. The adjoining Victorian house has two rooms for B&B. Regular themed lunches and dinners, and varied entertainment.

214 ARCHWAY GUEST HOUSE

Church Street, Saffron Walden,
Essex CB10 1JW
☎ 01799 501500 Fax: 01799 506003
e-mail: archwayguesthouse@ntlworld.com
🌐 www.smoothhound.co.uk/hotels/
archwayguest

With fine views of St Mary's church, **Archway Guest House** has 7 letting bedrooms, most with en-suite facilities. The ambience is friendly and relaxed, and the house is decorated in a highly original style, with striking paintings, rock and pop memorabilia and antique toys. Guests can take a nostalgia trip with the help of the 60s juke box.

Looking for:
- *Places to Visit?*
- *Places to Stay?*
- *Places to Eat & Drink?*
- *Places to Shop?*

www.travelpublishing.co.uk

215 HOLLINGATE BED & BREAKFAST

Radwinter End, nr Saffron Walden,
Essex CB10 2UD
☎ 01799 599184 Fax: 01799 599632
e-mail: enquiries@hollingate.co.uk
🌐 www.hollingate.co.uk

Two converted 19th century cottages provide Bed & Breakfast in excellent walking country. The bedrooms have been smartly refurbished, and a fine breakfast includes home-baked bread, and eggs from owners Graham and Sue Schneider's hens. Large garden. No smoking inside.

216 GARNISH HALL

Margaret Roding (on the A1060), Essex
☎ 01245 231209 Fax: 01245 231224
e-mail: peter@garnishhall.fsnet.co.uk
🌐 www.garnishhall.co.uk

Garnish Hall is a delightful rural retreat set in seven acres of lovely grounds that include a walled garden, a tennis court and a pond that's home to black swans. This marvellous 15th century manor house has three beautiful guest bedrooms decorated and furnished in traditional style and enjoying exquisite views.

All the rooms, including the two splendid sitting rooms, are non-smoking. Bed & Breakfast, with evening meals by arrangement.

318

217 THE RED LION

8 Church Street, Steeple Bumpstead, Essex CB9 7DG
☎ 01440 731833

Major changes continue apace at **The Red Lion**, which stands opposite the lovely old Church of St Mary the Virgin in the picturesque Essex village of Steeple Bumpstead. Licensees Angela and Jim Webb previously ran a pub in London's Isle of Dogs; Angela is a keen horsewoman, Jim is a rugby and fishing enthusiast, and both are clearly dedicated to transforming this fine old brick building.

The year 2004 saw the total refurbishment of the interior, a huge task carried out by Jim that involved incorporating original beams into the smartly updated decor: in one part of the bars rustic tables on a flagstone floor are separated by low wooden screens, in another there are comfortable upholstered chairs. Exposed floorboards, a modern bar in light oak and a wood-burning stove in a fine brick fireplace are other features, while outside at the rear is an enclosed garden with children's amusements including a bouncy castle for the summer. Due to come on stream in the spring of 2006 is a 20-cover restaurant with a slate roof and sash windows – a look in keeping with the requirements of this conservation area. Until then, anywhere in the pub is available for enjoying traditional pub snacks, an à la carte menu and a traditional Sunday lunch with a choice of four roasts.

Greene King IPA is the resident cask ales, joined by regularly changing guest beers. The amenities of The Red Lion will be further enhanced in 2006 with the provision of guest accommodation. Two self-catering cottages adjoining the pub are due in the spring, and three rooms upstairs in the pub will be available in the autumn; facilities will be available for guests with restricted mobility. When the accommodation opens, The Red Lion will be a popular and convenient base for both business and leisure visitors: Haverhill is a short drive to the north, and Saffron Walden is a few miles to the west, and the whole area is filled with places of scenic or historic interest.

218 THE WHITE HART

Swan Lane, Margaretting Tye,
Essex CM4 9JX
☎ 01277 840478 Fax: 01277 841178
e-mail: liz@thewhitehart.uk.com
🌐 www.thewhitehart.uk.com

Owner Liz Haines, chef Ting Sayer and friendly, hardworking staff have established the reputation of **The White Hart** as one of the very best pubs in the whole region. The rural setting lends itself to a number of excellent walks, which makes it a popular

choice of walkers, ramblers and cyclists as well as a favourite with local residents, travellers and tourists.

Swan Lane, which runs from Galleywood to Stock, is a Grade II listed street, and the White Hart is one of its most distinguished buildings. The frontage is adorned in spring and summer with flower boxes and hanging baskets, and in the public areas the heavily beamed vaulted ceiling and open fires add to the cosy, traditional ambience.

The White Hart is open every session and all day Saturday and Sunday, with food served lunchtime and evening. A choice of at least half a dozen real ales includes regulars Mighty Oak IPA, Adnams Best and Broadside, a choice that multiplies many times during the two annual beer festivals (50+ real ales in June, 20+ in October). These popular occasions include live entertainment and barbecues, and Liz also holds a charitable 'Village Day' in August, with live jazz on the green, barbecues, games and stalls. Chef Ting's excellent food can be enjoyed anywhere in the pub, and the choice really does cater for all tastes and appetites.

The food is a very popular and important side of the White Hart's business, and booking is recommended for all meals – and essential on Sunday. Outside, the pub has a large lawned garden, a safe children's play area and a pets corner with goats and other farm animals, an aviary and a large duck pond with a waterfall. Liz plans to extend the already impressive amenities of the White Hart by bringing on stream a number of rooms for Bed & Breakfast, which will make this a fine base for exploring the region.

219 THE BLUE BOAR HOTEL

Silver Street, Maldon, Essex CM9 4QE
☎ 01621 855888 Fax: 01621 856202
e-mail: blueboarhotel@hotmail.com
🌐 www.blueboarmaldon.co.uk

Owner John Wilsdon and manager David Shaw are justly very proud of their traditional English coaching inn, which has been a landmark in Maldon since the 14th century. Down the centuries **The Blue Boar** has provided hospitality for travellers, business people and tradesmen, and it now offers an equally warm welcome to tourists and holiday-makers. The hotel provides the expected up-to-date comfort and amenities while maintaining its old-world character, and antiques are a feature throughout (the hotel actually has an adjacent antiques shop).

The 28 guest bedrooms range from singles to doubles/twins and some splendid four-poster rooms, and behind the somewhat austere Georgian frontage the day rooms and reception rooms are contrastingly ornate, with ancient beams, striking paintings, chandeliers, pewter and brass, mirrors and oriental figures. The food options comprise lunchtime and evening bar snacks and a varied à la carte menu served in the restaurant. Well-chosen extras include a long gallery function room, a 40 space car park and connoisseurs of real ales will find at least three from the Blue Boar's own Farmers Microbrewery.

HIDDEN PLACES GUIDES

Explore Britain and Ireland with *Hidden Places* guides - a fascinating series of national and local travel guides.

Packed with easy to read information on hundreds of places of interest as well as places to stay, eat and drink.

Available from both high street and internet booksellers

For more information on the full range of *Hidden Places* guides and other titles published by Travel Publishing visit our website on

www.travelpublishing.co.uk
or ask for our leaflet by phoning **0118-981-7777** or
emailing **info@travelpublishing.co.uk**

Places of Interest in Essex

The selection of places of interest featured in this section includes museums, galleries, castles, historic houses, gardens, churches, cathedrals, gardens, country parks and many other places worth visiting in Norfolk. Each place of interest has an entry number which is used to identify its

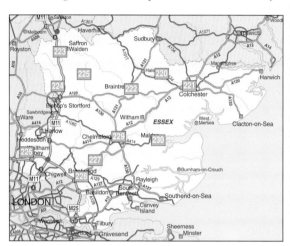

location on the map below and its name and short address in the list below the map. The entry number can also be used to find more information and contact details for the places of interest in the ensuing pages. In addition full details of places of interest in this section may be found on the Travel Publishing website – www.travelpublishing.co.uk This website has a large database of places of interest covering the whole of Britain and Ireland.

PLACES OF INTEREST

220 EAST ANGLIAN RAILWAY MUSEUM

**Chappel Station, nr Colchester,
Essex CO6 2DS
☎ 01206 242524**

The **East Anglian Railway Museum** is a fascinating and comprehensive collection of period railway architecture, engineering and memorabilia housed in beautifully restored station buildings. A grand day out for railway buffs young and old, this is the place to

try your hand at being a signalman and to admire the handsome engines and carriages. There is also a delightful miniature railway. Special steam days and events are held throughout the year.

221 COLCHESTER CASTLE

Castle Park, High Street, Colchester
☎ 01206 282939
🖥 www.colchestermuseums.co.uk

Colchester Castle is undeniably one of the most important historic buildings in the country, and today, a thousand years after it was built, it is still a living, vibrant place, a potent symbol of Britain's oldest recorded town. Colchester was the first capital of Britain and beneath the Castle's foundations are the remains of one of the most renowned Roman buildings, the Temple of Claudius, which was attacked in AD60 by rebels led by Queen Boudica (Boadicea). The town's citizens barricaded themselves in the temple but after two days were all killed. As many as 30,000 could have been killed during the sacking of Colchester.

Around 1076 King William I ordered a royal fortress to be built at Colchester, and the great stone base of the now ruined temple was an obvious foundation for the keep of the new castle. The great size of the temple dictated that of the keep, the largest ever built in Britain.

For most of its life the Castle was used as a prison; in 1645 Matthew Hopkins, the self-styled Witchfinder General, used the Castle to imprison and interrogate suspected witches. The Castle first opened its doors in the role of Museum in 1860 and today features many hands-on displays to help explain the town-people's experience of Colchester's varying fortunes. Visitors can slip into a toga, feel the weight of Roman armour, try on medieval hats and shoes and see treasures like the Roman bronze statue of Mercury and the Colchester Vase, one of the finest examples of Roman pottery found in Britain.

222 BRAINTREE DISTRICT MUSEUM

The Town Hall Centre, Market Place,
Braintree, Essex CM7 3YG
☎ 01376 328868 Fax: 01376 344345
e-mail: jean@bdcmuseum.demon.co.uk
🖥 www.enjoybraintreedistrict.co.uk

Housed in a beautifully converted Victorian school, **Braintree District Museum** has elegant exhibition areas and a faithfully re-created Victorian classroom, where role-play

lessons are provided for schools on a daily basis. The permanent galleries tell the fascinating story of the wool trade in North Essex of which Braintree was the medieval centre, and also of the development of engineering design. Country crafts such as straw plaiting are featured, along with the work of rural artists. A programme of changing exhibitions is a feature of the museum and a range of craft items are available for sale.

323

223 AUDLEY END STEAM RAILWAY

Brunketts, Wendens Ambo, Saffron Walden
CB11 4JL
☎ 01799 541354

Many people will have heard of Audley End Mansion just outside the charming town of Saffron Walden. Not so many people know of the nearby miniature railway. This is a 10¼ inch gauge line at Audley End that runs for about 1½ miles through Estate woodland crossing
the River
Cam twice.
Children
are
delighted
by the
large

number of teddies that inhabit the woods and adults enjoy a nostalgic trip back to the golden age of steam. Running every weekend from April to October and every afternoon during the school holidays, with Santa Specials running in December, this train journey is not one to be missed.

HIDDEN PLACES GUIDES

Explore Britain and Ireland with *Hidden Places* guides - a fascinating series of national and local travel guides.

Packed with easy to read information on hundreds of places of interest as well as places to stay, eat and drink.

Available from both high street and internet booksellers

For more information on the full range of *Hidden Places* guides and other titles published by Travel Publishing visit our website on

www.travelpublishing.co.uk
or ask for our leaflet by phoning
**0118-981-7777 or emailing
info@travelpublishing.co.uk**

224 MOUNTFITCHET CASTLE & NORMAN VILLAGE

Stansted, Essex CM24 8SP
☎ 01279 813237 Fax: 01279 816391
e-mail:
mountfitchetcastle1066@btinternet.com
⊕ www.gold.enta.net

This historic site gives visitors a glimpse into life as it was over 900 years ago in 1066. The careful reconstruction, as it would have appeared in the Domesday era, enables the study of an 11th century motte and bailey castle and the Norman village which was enclosed within its walls. You can learn about medieval life, early fortifications, weaponry, the construction of dwellings and much more.

Many of the animals and birds to be found in the grounds are rescued and represent those which would
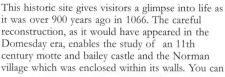
have been kept for food by the Normans, such as fallow deer, sheep, goats, chickens and geese. The Castle Shop carries a comprehensive range of gifts and souvenirs and is open
March to November 10am-5pm daily, as is the Castle.

Also here you will find the House on the Hill Toy Museum Adventure. An impressive collection of toys, games and books can be enjoyed by children of all ages and the museum has been greatly improved by the addition of sound effects, animation and hands-on opportunities. Permanent displays of film, theatre and rock'n'roll memorabilia have been added in recent years, as has an exhibition of seaside end-of-the-pier amusements.

225 THE THAXTED GARDEN FOR BUTTERFLIES

Aldboro' Lodge, Park Street, Thaxted,
Essex CM6 2ND
☎ 01371 830780

The Thaxted Garden for Butterflies is a Help the Aged Millenium award-winning project demonstrating how a retirement hobby garden of one acre could be developed to conserve our native British Butterflies and other local wildlife. The garden has proven to be successful by  attracting 23 species of butterflies, as well as rare moths, dragonflies, insects, grass snakes, newts, frogs, toads, muntjac deer, foxes and hedghogs. Since it opened to the public in 2000 many people have enjoyed its charm and tranquility, and learned about butterflies from seeing them, their habitat and the plants they and their caterpillars need.

Explore Britain and Ireland with *Hidden Places* guides - a fascinating series of national and local travel guides.

www.travelpublishing.co.uk

0118-981-7777

info@travelpublishing.co.uk

Looking for:
- *Places to Visit?*
- *Places to Stay?*
- *Places to Eat & Drink?*
- *Places to Shop?*

www.travelpublishing.co.uk

226 ROYAL GUNPOWDER MILLS

Powdermill Lane, Waltham Abbey,
Essex EN9 1BN
☎ 01992 767022 Fax: 01992 710341
🌐 www.royalgunpowdermills.com

The **Royal Gunpowder Mills** in Waltham Abbey is open to the general public after a 300 year history. Thanks to funding from the Heritage Lottery Fund and Ministry of Defence, this secret site which was home to gunpowder and explosive production and research for more than three centuries, has been developed to offer visitors a truly unique day out.

Gunpowder production began at Waltham Abbey in the mid 1660's on the site of a late medieval fulling mill. The gunpowder Mills remained in private hands until 1787, when they were purchased by the crown. From this date, the Royal Gunpowder Mills developed into the pre eminent powder works in Britain and one of the most important in Europe.

Set in175 acres of natural parkland and boasting 21 important historic buildings the regenerated site will offer visitors a unique mixture of fascinating history, exciting science and beautiful surroundings. Approximately 70 acres of the site, containing some of the oldest buildings and much of the canal network, will be open for visitors to explore freely. The remaining area of the site including the largest heronry in Essex has been designated as a Site of Special Scientific Interest and will be accessible to the public by way of special guided tours. Open April to September.

Ingatestone, Essex CM4 9NR
☎ 01277 353010 Fax: 01245 248979

Ingatestone Hall is a 16th century mansion and grounds, built by Sir William Petre, Secretary of State to four Tudor monarchs, and still occupied by his descendants. The house substantially retains its original form

and appearance (including two priests' hiding places) and contains furniture, pictures and family memorabilia accumulated over the centuries. A programme of special events is available on request and there is a gift shop and a tea room in the grounds. A picnic area is sited in Car Park Meadow. Open Saturday, Sunday and Bank Holiday afternoons from Easter to the end of September, plus Wednesdays, Thursdays and Fridays in the school summer holidays.

Kelvedon Hatch Lane, Brentwood,
Essex CM14 5TL
☎ 01277 364883   Fax: 01277 372562
e-mail: bunker@japar.demon.co.uk
🌐 www.japar.demon.co.uk

The **Kelvedon Hatch Secret Nuclear Bunker** was built in 1952 as a base from which the government and military commanders could have run operations, had there been a nuclear war. The labyrinth of rooms built into the hillside, 75 feet below ground and encased in 10foot thick concrete, is cleverly disguised from the outside by a rural bungalow.

Inside the bunker you will be able to see the areas where up to 600 personnel could have been housed, along with all the equipment they would have needed to co-ordinate the survival of civilians. There is a BBC radio studio, enormous power generators and water filtration system, a radar room and large dormitories and sickbay.

To add to your enjoyment of this attrcation, refreshments are available and there is a souvenir shop. Picnics can be taken amid the beautiful woodland setting. Opening times vary according to the time of year - phone for details.

229 CHELMSFORD MUSEUM & ESSEX REGIMENT MUSEUM

Oaklands Park, Moulsham Street,
Chelmsford, Essex CM2 9AQ
☎ 01245 615100 Fax: 01245 611250
e-mail: oaklands@chelmsfordbc.gov.uk
🌐 www.chelmsfordbc.gov.uk/leisure/
museums

Chelmsford Museum, founded in 1835, has since 1930 been located in a lovely Victorian mansion in a city-centre park. The history of Chelmsford and its people from prehistoric times right up to the present day is told through displays that include geology, natural history (with a live beehive!), costumes and coins. Fine and Decorative Arts are represented by works by Edward Bawden and other regionally based artists, the Tunstall Bequest of 18th century drinking glasses and flamboyant Victorian pieces from Castle Hedingham Pottery.

The Essex Regiment on the same site relates the story of the 44th and 56th Regiments from 1741 to the modern Royal Anglian Regiment. Among the many items on display are a tailcoat of 1785 with Pompadour purple collar and cuffs, a French eagle standard captured in battle in 1812, the Regimental silver and silver drums presented by the people of Essex, medals won by Essex men including four Victoria Cross winners, the Colours of the 44th Foot carried for 102 years, and an Essex Home Guard display. Regularly changing temporary exhibitions supplement the permanent displays at both Museums.

Also under the aegis of Chelmsford Borough Council is a developing Science and Industry project at Sandford Mill, Chelmer Village (Tel/Fax: 01245 475498) with visits by appointment or on open days and science weeks for local schools.

230 MALDON DISTRICT MUSEUM

47 Mill Road, Maldon, Essex CM9 5HX
☎ 01621 842688

Maldon Museum was originally founded in 1922 by a group of Borough Councillors and occupied an upstairs room above the Victorian Fire Station until this was demolished in 1938 to build a larger fire facility. The collection was then stored at the Coucil Offices until rescued thirty years later.

The museum then occupied various premises in Maldon High Street, always on an annual lease; there were several years when the artefacts were again in storage. In 1995 the Museum Association was offered by the District Council the use of the Edwardian building standing on the edge of Promenade Park, which had previously housed the Park keeper. This has allowed a greatly expanded display of the items held.

The core strength of the collection is in items relating to the social history of Maldon over the past three hundred years. These give pleasure to the many visitors to the town as well as being appreciated by the local residents. The museum is open each afternoon from the beginning of April to the end of October, except Mondays and Tuesdays, and on Bank Holidays. Special openeings can be arranged for schools and groups.

HIDDEN PLACES GUIDES

Explore Britain and Ireland with *Hidden Places* guides - a fascinating series of national and local travel guides.

Packed with easy to read information on hundreds of places of interest as well as places to stay, eat and drink.

Available from both high street and internet booksellers

For more information on the full range of *Hidden Places* guides and other titles published by Travel Publishing visit our website on

www.travelpublishing.co.uk
or ask for our leaflet by phoning **0118-981-7777** or emailing **info@travelpublishing.co.uk**

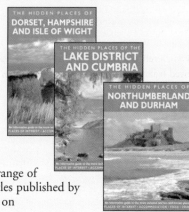

VISIT THE TRAVEL PUBLISHING WEBSITE

Looking for:

- *Places to Visit?*
- *Places to Stay?*
- *Places to Eat & Drink?*
- *Places to Shop?*

Then why not visit the Travel Publishing website...

- Informative pages on places to visit, stay, eat, drink and shop throughout the British Isles.

- Detailed information on Travel Publishing's wide range of national and regional travel guides.

www.travelpublishing.co.uk

Cambridgeshire

Cambridgeshire is a county with a rich rural heritage, with attractive villages strung along the banks of the Great Ouse and the flat land of the Fens, stretching north towards the Wash. Far removed from the hustle and bustle of modern life, the Fens are like a breath of fresh air; extending over much of Cambridgeshire from the Wash, these flat Fenland fields contain some of the riches soil in England. Before the Fens were drained, this was a land of mist, marshes and bogs, of small islands inhabited by independent folk who lived on the fish and waterfowl of this eerie, watery place. The massive project of draining this land has spanned the centuries, starting with the Romans, who were the first to construct embankments and drains to lessen the incidence of flooding. Throughout the Middle Ages, large areas of marsh and bog were reclaimed, with much of the work undertaken by the monasteries and later by Dutch settlers, whose influence lives on in some of the architecture and place names. After the English Civil War the New Bedford River was cut to provide more drainage. First windmills and then steam and finally electric pumping engines have been used to remove the water from the fields. The Fens offer almost unlimited opportunities for exploration on foot, by bicycle, by car or by boat. The jewel in the crown of the southern part of the Fens is Ely, with its magnificent Cathedral. A few miles to the south, Wicken Fen is the oldest nature reserve in the country – 600 acres of undrained fenland that is famous for its varied plant, insect and birdlife. On the western edge of the Fens is the second city of Cambridgeshire, Peterborough, with a history that can be traced back to the Bronze Age; its early days can be seen in the archaeological site at Flag Fen. Although a cathedral city, it is also a new town (designated in 1967), so modern development and expansion have vastly increased its amenities while retaining the quality of its historic heart.

The southeast of the county is dominated by the county town Cambridge and is rich in history, with a host of archaeological sites and monuments, as well as many important museums. Cambridge is one of the leading academic centres of the world and a place that needs plenty of time to explore – on foot, by bicycle or the more romantic option of a punt. The surrounding countryside is fairly flat and therefore ideal for walking and cycling. It contains a surprising variety of habitats, along with stately homes and windmills – a particular feature of East Anglia. The old county of Huntingdonshire lies at the heartland of the rural heritage of Cambridgeshire and the former county town, Huntingdon, is famous as the birthplace of Oliver Cromwell. Places associated with the great Parliamentarian abound, and many motorists follow the Cromwell Trail. There are also many ancient market towns and villages to discover, along with numerous nature reserves and prehistoric sites. The 26-mile Ouse Valley Way follows the course of the Great Ouse through pretty villages and a variety of natural attractions, and a gentle cruise can fill a lazy day to perfection.

Bridge of Sighs, Cambridge

329

Food and Drink in Cambridgeshire

The selection of establishments serving food and drink featured in this section includes restaurants, cafes, hotels, pubs, inns and tea & coffee shops. Each establishment has an entry number which is used to identify its location on the map below and its name and short address in the list below the map. The entry number can also be used to find more information and contact details for the establishment in the ensuing pages. In addition full details of establishments serving food and drink featured in this section may be found on the Travel Publishing website – www.travelpublishing.co.uk This website has a large database of establishments serving food and drink covering the whole of Britain and Ireland.

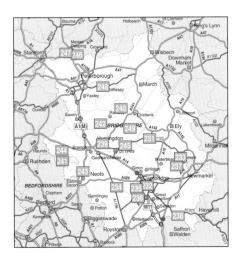

FOOD AND DRINK

231 THE THREE KINGS

6 Station Road, Haddenham, nr Ely, Cambridgeshire CB6 3XD
☎ 01353 749080

Starting life in the 17th century as a coaching inn, **The Three Kings** is located in the picturesque village of Haddenham, where the A1123 meets the A1421. Tenants Marie and Jamie Corless have made this one of the most popular pubs in the area, offering traditional hospitality, real ales and a fine across-

the-board selection of food, from generously filled sandwiches and baguettes to pub classics like haddock and chips or steak & Guinness pie and some excellent sauced meat and fish dishes. No smoking areas, benches in the courtyard, large car park.

233 THE PORTLAND ARMS

129 Chesterton Road, Cambridge CB4 3BA
☎ 01223 357268
e-mail: post@theportlandarms.co.uk
🌐 www.theportlandarms.co.uk

The Portland Arms is a substantial brick building with handsome public rooms and a sun-trap beer garden. Hosts Hayley and Steve provide excellent hospitality, an impressive list of cask ales and fine menus which include steak & Guinness pie and Sunday roasts.

233 THE FIVE BELLS

**High Street, Burwell,
Cambridgeshire CB5 0HD
☎ 01638 741404 Fax: 01638 741404**

On the main street of Burwell, **The Five Bells** has a popular public bar, a comfortable lounge and a non-smoking restaurant. Food ranges from snacks to full meals, and there's a choice of four real ales and good wines. Pub games; children's play area.

234 THE DUKE OF WELLINGTON

**Alms Hill, Bourn, Cambridgeshire CB3 7SH
☎ 01954 719364 Fax: 01954 719364
e-mail: alexandlynn@aol.com
www.duke-of-wellington.net**

The Duke of Wellington is a smartly renovated Georgian house run by Alex and Lynn Williams. Both are talented chefs, and in the spacious non-smoking dining area the menus offer an excellent choice. Fine wines and cask ales complement the food. Closed Sunday evening and all day Monday.

235 THE BARN TEA ROOMS

**Burwash Manor Farm, New Road, Barton,
Cambridgeshire CB3 7BD
☎ 01223 264821**

Morning coffee, lunch, afternoon tea – all can be enjoyed at **The Barn Tea Rooms**, part of a group of shops and amenities at Burwash Manor Farm a short drive from Cambridge. Owner Daniella Streek offers an excellent  choice of delicious home cooked lunches, salads, cakes and Traditional afternoon tea, using local produce in many of the dishes. There are seats for 40 inside, and a further 20 for outside eating in the summer. Small groups are welcome, and outside catering can be provided for any event. The Barn is open from 10 to 4.30 Monday to Friday, 10 to 5 Saturday and 11 to 5 Sunday.

236 THE WHITE HORSE INN

**118 High Street, Barton,
Cambridgeshire CB3 7BG
☎ 01223 262327
e-mail: tom.Williams@homecall.co.uk**

On the main street of Barton, a short drive from Cambridge and just half a mile from the M11, **The White Horse Inn** is a lovely old coaching inn of great charm and character. Tenants Tom, Thaisa and Mark pride themselves on providing a warm, friendly welcome to all who pass through the doors, and their passion  for real ales, fine wines and traditional, wholesome food brings visitors from near and far.

Two rotating guest ales (more in summer) and specialised bottled beers are favourites among the drinks available all day in the bars, and food is served all day Tuesday to Saturday and from 12

to 3.30 on Sunday, when a popular carvery operates. The bar and restaurant menus offer a wide-ranging choice, from sandwiches with generous hot or cold fillings and giant Yorkshire pudding with mince and gravy to super main dishes such as herb and lemon marinated trout served on buttered asparagus, classic steaks and wild mushroom casserole with herb dumplings. The White Horse also provides warm, comfortable accommodation in two en suite rooms available throughout the year. The pub is closed Monday lunchtime except Bank Holidays.

237 DYKES END INN

8 Fair Green, Reach,
Cambridgeshire CB5 0JD
☎ 01638 743816
e-mail: dykesend@aol.com

The **Dykes End** is an outstanding country inn overlooking the green and next to the church in the picturesque village of Reach. It takes its name from the nearby Devil's Dyke, built around 370, and the inn attracts visitors from the Dyke as well as from Cambridge and Newmarket, both about 8 miles away. But the inn is very much a destination in its own right, with a well-earned reputation for fine food, well-kept real ales and an excellent selection of wines.

Window boxes and hanging baskets adorn the white-painted facade in spring and summer, and the inn is fronted by a pleasant grassed area with grand old yew tress and picnic benches; at the back are a lovely secluded garden and a car park. The public rooms have an inviting, traditional look, with sturdy pine furniture, boards or parquet on the floor and candles on the dining tables. Three of four real ales – Adnams and guests – are always on tap, and the food choice really does offer something for everyone, from light lunchtime options to three-course meals served in the upstairs evening restaurant.

The menu makes mouthwatering reading, and results on the plate never disappoint. The chef and his team make judicious use of alcohol in several dishes such as spare ribs marinated in cola and bourbon, roast chicken with grappa and sweet potato mash, cod in ale batter, and roast breast of duck with a spiced port and orange sauce. Classic steaks come plain or sauced, and other choices might include potted ham, linguine with scallops and ricotta cake with honey and cardamom-roasted vegetables.

The Dykes End was saved a few years ago by the efforts of the villagers and subsequently bought by business partners Simon Owers and Frank Feehan, who run it with excellent staff and Banger the dog. A visit from the Prince of Wales commending the village for saving its pub is commemorated by a brass plate on display. The pub is closed Monday lunchtime, and food is not served Sunday or Monday evenings.

238 THE DOG & DUCK

63 High Street, Linton,
Cambridgeshire CB1 6HS
☎ 01223 891257
e-mail: doganduck@hotmail.com
⊕ www.dogandducklinton.co.uk

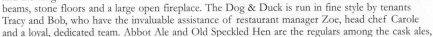

A riverside setting in the historic village of
Linton is one of the many assets of the
award winning **Dog & Duck**. This lovely old
thatched building, which dates back to the
16th century, has been a pub since the 1850s,
and the long bar features handsome oak
beams, stone floors and a large open fireplace. The Dog & Duck is run in fine style by tenants
Tracy and Bob, who have the invaluable assistance of restaurant manager Zoe, head chef Carole
and a loyal, dedicated team. Abbot Ale and Old Speckled Hen are the regulars among the cask ales,

and lunch and dinner menus offer a fine variety of home-
cooked dishes, with daily specials adding to the choice. Friday
is fish night, and Sunday lunch brings traditional roasts and a
few other choices. A bargain senior citizens lunch is served
Monday lunchtime, and the restaurant is open from 9.30
Monday to Saturday for coffee and tea mornings. Booking is
recommended to be sure of a table for Friday and Saturday
dinner and Sunday lunch. The non-smoking restaurant enjoys
a lovely view of the River Granta, and in summer the
riverside patio with its flowers and ducks is the place to be.

239 THE KING OF THE BELGIANS

27 Main Street, Hartford, nr Huntingdon,
Cambridgeshire PE29 1XU
☎ 01480 52030

Nobody seems to know how **The King of
the Belgians** got its name, but everyone
knows that hosts Jamie and Gwyneth extend
a right royal welcome to one and all. This fine
old inn is open lunchtime and evening
Monday to
Wednesday
and all day
Thursday
to Sunday.
Three
quality cask
ales are
always on
tap, and
food ranges

from hot and cold snacks to exciting
blackboard specials such as seafood
cannelloni, Thai cod & prawn fishcakes,
peppered duck and mozzarella & tomato
pudding. Live music first Saturday each
month.

240 THE GEORGE INN

1 Ramsey Road, Ramsey Forty Foot,
Cambridgeshire PE26 2XN
☎ 01487 812775

On a corner site by the river, **The George
Inn** is a delightful traditional inn with a beer
garden. Hosts Mandy and Bill offer a warm
welcome, three real ales all day in the bar and
good food served every session except
Sunday evening. Friday and Saturday are also
curry take-away evenings.

241 THE NEW SUN INN & RESTAURANT

20-22 High Street, Kimbolton, nr
Huntingdon, Cambridgeshire PE28 0HA
☎ 01480 860052 Fax: 01480 860052
e-mail: newsuninn@btinternet.com
⊕ www.newsuninn.co.uk

Steve and Elaine Rogers are the hosts at the
New Sun Inn & Restaurant in Kimbolton.
This delightful inn offers well-kept real ales,
wines and outstanding food, some with a
Mediterranean twist and some traditional.
Well-appointed, pleasant garden.

242 THE CROSS KEYS

High Street, Upwood,
Cambridgeshire PE26 2QE
☎ 01487 813384

The **Cross Keys** is a substantial white-painted inn on the main street of Upwood, reached by country roads off the A1(M) or A141. Jane behind the bar and Kevin at the stoves welcome old friends and new into the spotless, traditional lounge bar and restaurant, where they can enjoy cask ales (Adnams, Bass, John Smith)

and a fine selection of home-cooked snacks and main dishes to please carnivores, fish-eaters and vegetarians. Monthly theme nights feature the cuisine of different countries. The Cross Keys is open every session except Monday lunchtime (no food Monday evening).

243 THE ANCHOR INN

High Street, Little Paxton, nr St Neots,
Cambridgeshire PE19 6HA
☎ 1480 473199 Fax: 01480 408684

Close to the church in the village of Little Paxton, **The Anchor Inn** has been put firmly back on the map by tenants Tom and Sue Merritt. The inn is open all day for drinks (four rotating guest ales) and food is served from 12 to 7.30 and until 5.30 on Sunday. Sue is an accomplished cook, and her traditional British dishes include several based on old regional recipes. The premises date back to the early 18th century, and the interior has been

carefully modernised to retain its period appeal. Outside, the inn has a large off-road car park, a beer garden and a pétanque piste.

244 THE RACEHORSE COUNTRY INN

43 High Street, Catworth, nr Huntingdon,
Cambridgeshire PE28 0PF
☎ 01832 710123 Fax: 01832 710123

On the main street of Catworth, half a mile south of the junction 16 of the A14, **The Racehorse Country Inn** serves both the local community and visitors to the area in fine style. David and Julie Gibson brought ten years experience in the trade when they took over in November 2004, and with their right-hand lady Carly they have raised the profile of this excellent inn. Behind the smart white-painted front, the interior is very smart and

inviting, with ancient beams, a wood-panelled bar front, a feature stone fireplace and a variety of comfortably upholstered seats.

Theakstons Bitter is the regular brew among the four on tap, and the quality of the home cooking means that it's always best to book a table in the restaurant (bar snacks are also available). The Racehorse is also a splendid place for an overnight or longer stay, and the five en suite guest bedrooms are in a converted barn next to the inn. Three of the rooms are on the ground floor, and one is adapted for disabled guests. Rooms can be let on a B&B or room only basis.

245 THE QUEEN'S HEAD

High Street, Needingworth, nr St Ives,
Cambridgeshire
☎ 01480 463946

Linda and Fraser Macrae keep the welcome
mat on the door of the **Queen's Head**,
which lies off the A1123 on the main street
of Needingworth. The inn dates from the
18th century, and recent refurbishment inside
and out has updated the decor without losing
the inviting, traditional feel of a much-loved
local. This is a very good place for real ale
enthusiasts, with Greene King IPA, Abbot
Ale, Mann's Bitter and Old Speckled Hen

among
the choices.
Fraser heads the kitchen team producing excellent food
for every session, from lunchtime light bites to a good
spread of main dishes: these range from old favourites like
lasagne, burgers, fish & chips and steaks to composite salads
and daily specials such as pan-fried chicken breast topped
with bacon and melted cheese. The Queen's Head is also
very much at the heart of social life, with pool and darts
played at one end of the bar, a quiz on Monday evenings
and live music once a month.

246 THE GOAT

Frognall, Deeping St James,
nr Peterborough, Lincolnshire PE6 8SA
☎ 01778 347629

The Goat is a smart, white-painted, slate-
roofed pub set back from the B1166 in the
tiny hamlet of Frognall. Graham, Debbie and
their staff
welcome all
visitors, and
the bar has a
warm,
inviting feel,
with
handsome
brickwork,

darkwood furniture and a real fire. A
minimum of four real ales are always
available, which rises to around 20 during the
late-July beer festival. Whisky connoisseurs
can choose from almost 50 malts. Food is an
important factor in the success of The Goat,
and the printed menu and specials board
provide a fine choice of hot and cold home-
cooked dishes. The pub has an attractive beer
garden and plenty of off-road parking.

247 DEEPING COFFEE HOUSE

8 The Precinct, Market Deeping,
nr Peterborough PE6 8DL
☎ 01778 380410

Deeping Coffee House
provides welcome
refreshment throughout the
day. The varied menu
includes speciality breads and
bagels, soups, jacket potatoes
and homemade cakes.

248 THE BOAT INN

2 Ramsey Road, Whittlesey, nr
Peterborough PE7 1DR
☎ 01733 202488
e-mail: quinnboatinn@aol.com

Phil and Maria welcome visitors to **The Boat
Inn**, which is open for drinks all day six days
a week and from 4 o'clock on Tuesday. In the
cheerful bar they serve an impressive
selection of real ales. Five guest bedrooms
can be let on a B&B or room only basis.

249 THE BLACK BULL

89 High Street, Somersham, nr Huntingdon,
Cambridgeshire PE28 3EE
☎ 01487 843681

On the B1050 in the main street of Somersham, **The Black Bull** started life in the late-18th century. Gary Hartley, in the business for 20 years, has been the leaseholder here since 1999 and is ably assisted by Restaurant Manager Vicki; they and their staff have made this a pub with a wide and varied appeal – a cheerful local, a great place to take a break on a journey, and a place to seek out to relax over a leisurely meal. The interior of the inn has been smartly modernised, and the well-spaced tables allow plenty of room for enjoying a drink and a snack or a meal.

The Black Bull is open every day for drinks (real ales are Greene King IPA, Courage Best and a guest) and food is available lunchtime and evening and all day on Sunday. The two separate dining areas (non-smoking) can be combined into one for big get-togethers, and customers can also eat in the bar. The lunchtime menu is headed by light bites or starters such as soup, chicken liver pâté and devilled whitebait, baguettes and jacket potatoes, while main courses are mainly familiar classics like ham or sausage with egg and chips, omelettes, lasagne, cod & chips and steak & ale pie. The evening menu brings a wider selection of main courses including lots of ways with prime chicken supremes, spaghetti carbonara, chargrilled steaks and whole baked sea bass.

Gary buys fish fresh from the market on Friday mornings, so the fish specials on the Friday and Saturday specials board are always in demand. Sky Sports coverage is provided on a big screen,

and a quiz starts at 8 o'clock on the last Monday of every month. The Black Bull is a popular venue for functions and parties, and the management and staff are happy to discuss arrangements for special occasions large and small. Somersham, easily reached from either Huntingdon or St Ives, is famous not just for The Black Bull but also as the home of the Raptor Foundation, a refuge for owls and other birds of prey.

Accommodation in Cambridgeshire

The accommodation featured in this section includes hotels, inns, guest houses, bed & breakfasts and self catered establishments. Each establishment has an entry number which is used to identify its location on the map below and its name and short address in the list below the map. The entry number can also be used to find more information and contact details for the accommodation in the ensuing pages. In addition full details of all this accommodation may be found on the Travel Publishing website - www.travelpublishing.co.uk. This website has a comprehensive database of accommodation covering the whole of Britain and Ireland.

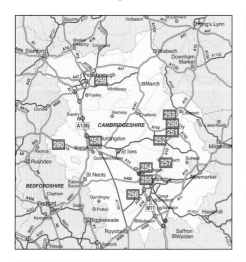

ACCOMMODATION

250	Post House, Ely
251	Chapel Cottage, Ely
252	Sharps Farm, Wilburton
253	Bury House, Little Downham
254	Rose Corner, Impington
255	Amber Lodge, Cambridge
256	The White Horse Inn, Barton
257	Goose Hall Farm, Waterbeach
258	Manor House, Great Stukeley
259	The Boat Inn, Whittlesey
260	The Racehorse Country Inn, Catworth

250 POST HOUSE

12a Egremont Street, Ely,
Cambridgeshire CB6 1AE
T 01353 667184
e-mail: nora@covell.fsbusiness.co.uk

Owner Nora Covell welcomes all to the **Post House**, where she has four spacious, spotless B&B rooms with central heating, television and tea/coffee tray. This modern house with precious off-road parking is an easy walk from the Cathedral. No smoking, no credit cards.

251 CHAPEL COTTAGE

11 Chapel Street, Ely,
Cambridgeshire CB6 1AD
☎ 01353 668768

Daphne Mortimer offers quiet, civilised Bed & Breakfast accommodation in two comfortable, charming guest rooms in a distinguished cottage with a history dating back 1,000 years. **Chapel Cottage** is very close to the Cathedral and river with a delightful conservatory and secluded courtyard garden. No smoking inside.

252 SHARPS FARM

Twentypence Road, Wilburton, nr Ely,
Cambridgeshire CB6 3PU
☎ 01353 740360 Fax: 01353 740360
e-mail: sharpsfarm@yahoo.com
🌐 www.sharpsfarm.co.uk

In a charming rural location, **Sharps Farm** promises a quiet, relaxing break in three well-appointed bedrooms. B&B or room only basis, evening meals by arrangement. Horses, dogs, cats and chickens live on the farm, and guests can stroll in the delightful garden. No smoking inside.

253 BURY HOUSE

11 Main Street, Little Downham, nr Ely,
Cambridgeshire CB6 2ST
☎ 01353 698766 Fax: 01353 698089

Bury House offers spacious Bed & Breakfast accommodation in comfortable, homely surroundings. The two rooms have central heating, TV and hot drinks tray. The day starts with a delicious farmhouse breakfast.

254 ROSE CORNER

42 Woodcock Close, Impington,
nr Cambridge, Cambridgeshire CB4 9LD
☎ 01223 563136 Fax: 01223 233886
e-mail: wsalmon.rosecorner@virgin.net
⊕ www.rose-corner.co.uk

In a peaceful village setting, **Rose Corner** provides a pleasant home from home in five modern bedrooms, three en suite. An outstanding breakfast starts the day, and guests have the use of a quiet lounge and garden.

255 AMBER LODGE

664 Newmarket Road, Cambridge CB5 8RS
☎ 01223 293481
e-mail: amberlodgecambridge@yahoo.co.uk
⊕ www.amberlodgecambridge.co.uk

Amber Lodge is a quiet, comfortable Bed & Breakfast guest house on the eastern outskirts of Cambridge. Open all year round, the Lodge has seven guest rooms, four of them with en suite facilities, all with television and tea/coffee facilities. The double room on the ground floor has patio doors overlooking the garden. A quality breakfast is included in the tariff. Children are welcome, and the Lodge has off-road parking for six cars.

256 THE WHITE HORSE INN

118 High Street, Barton,
Cambridgeshire CB3 7BG
☎ 01223 262327
e-mail: tom.Williams@homecall.co.uk

On the main street of Barton, a short drive from Cambridge and just half a mile from the M11, **The White Horse Inn** is a lovely old coaching inn of great charm and character. Tenants Tom, Thaisa and Mark pride themselves on providing a warm, friendly welcome to all who pass through the doors, and their passion

for real ales, fine wines and traditional, wholesome food brings visitors from near and far.

Two rotating guest ales (more in summer) and specialised bottled beers are favourites among the drinks available all day in the bars, and food is served all day Tuesday to Saturday and from 12

to 3.30 on Sunday, when a popular carvery operates. The bar and restaurant menus offer a wide-ranging choice, from sandwiches with generous hot or cold fillings and giant Yorkshire pudding with mince and gravy to super main dishes such as herb and lemon marinated trout served on buttered asparagus, classic steaks and wild mushroom casserole with herb dumplings. The White Horse also provides warm, comfortable accommodation in two en suite rooms available throughout the year. The pub is closed Monday lunchtime except Bank Holidays.

257 GOOSE HALL FARM

Ely Road, Waterbeach,
Cambridgeshire CB5 9PG
☎ 01223 860235 Fax: 01223 860235
e-mail: goosehall@lockn.freeserve.co.uk
⊕ www.goosehallfarm.co.uk

Guests at **Goose Hall Farm** have a choice
of Bed & Breakfast and self-catering
accommodation in scenic surroundings. The
en suite double and twin B&B rooms are in
the modern farmhouse, and two self-catering
cottages for up to 5 overlook the paddock.

259 THE BOAT INN

2 Ramsey Road, Whittlesey, nr
Peterborough PE7 1DR
☎ 01733 202488
e-mail: quinnboatinn@aol.com

Phil and Maria welcome visitors to **The Boat
Inn**, which is open for drinks all day six days
a week and from 4 o'clock on Tuesday. In the
cheerful bar they serve an impressive
selection of real ales. Five guest bedrooms
can be let on a B&B or room only basis.

258 MANOR HOUSE

Owl End, Great Stukeley, nr Huntingdon,
Cambridgeshire PE28 4AQ
☎ 01480 458967

Jan Tilden welcomes B&B guests to her 17th
century home, **Manor House**.
Accommodation comprises
three rooms with shared
facilities, TV and tea/coffee
tray. Evening meals by
arrangement. No smoking,
no credit cards.

Explore Britain and Ireland with
Hidden Places guides - a fascinating
series of national and local travel
guides.

www.travelpublishing.co.uk

0118-981-7777

info@travelpublishing.co.uk

260 THE RACEHORSE COUNTRY INN

43 High Street, Catworth, nr Huntingdon,
Cambridgeshire PE28 0PF
☎ 01832 710123 Fax: 01832 710123

On the main street of Catworth, half a mile
south of the junction 16 of the A14, **The
Racehorse Country Inn** serves both the
local community and visitors to the area in
fine style. David and Julie Gibson brought ten
years experience in the trade when they took
over in November 2004, and with their right-
hand lady Carly they have raised the profile
of this excellent inn. Behind the smart white-
painted front, the interior is very smart and
inviting, with ancient beams, a wood-panelled

bar front, a feature stone fireplace and a variety of
comfortably upholstered seats.
Theakstons Bitter is the regular brew among the four on
tap, and the quality of the home cooking means that it's
always best to book a table in the restaurant (bar snacks are
also available). The Racehorse is also a splendid place for an
overnight or longer stay, and the five en suite guest bedrooms
are in a converted barn next to the inn. Three of the rooms
are on the ground floor, and one is adapted for disabled
guests. Rooms can be let on a B&B or room only basis.

Places of Interest in Cambridgeshire

The selection of places of interest featured in this section includes museums, galleries, castles, historic houses, gardens, churches, cathedrals, gardens, country parks and many other places worth visiting in Norfolk. Each place of interest has an entry number which is used to identify its location on the map below and its name and short address in the list below the map. The entry number can also be used to find more information and contact details for the places of interest in the ensuing pages. In addition full details of places of interest in this section may be found on the Travel Publishing website – www.travelpublishing.co.uk This website has a large database of places of interest covering the whole of Britain and Ireland.

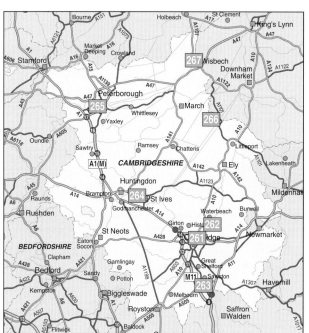

Looking for:

- *Places to Visit?*
- *Places to Stay?*
- *Places to Eat & Drink?*
- *Places to Shop?*

www.travelpublishing.co.uk

261 CAMBRIDGE & COUNTY FOLK MUSEUM

2-3 Castle Street, Cambridge,
Cambridgeshire CB3 0AQ
☎ 01223 355159

Housed in a late 15th century timber-framed building that was formerly the White Horse Inn, the **Cambridge & County Folk Museum** takes a nostalgic, warm-hearted look at the everyday lives of people from Cambridge and the surrounding area from 1700 onwards. Topics include Crafts &

Trades, Town & Gown, Witchbottles, Skating and Eels, and throughout the year themed talks and exhibitions take place. The Museum Shop stocks an interesting range of games and puzzles, books and many other items that make ideal Christmas stocking fillers, all with a nostalgic feel.

262 FARMLAND MUSEUM & DENNY ABBEY

Ely Road, Waterbeach,
Cambridgeshire CB5 9PQ
☎ 01223 860489
e-mail: f.m.denny@tesco.net
⊕ www.dennyfarmlandmuseum.org.uk

The stone-built farmhouse at the heart of this site is actually the remains of a 12th century Benedictine Abbey. The superb Norman interior has been beautifully preserved and restored, and visitors can see the nuns' refectory and the rooms converted for their founder, the Countess of Pembrokeshire. Displays tell the story of how Denny has evolved down the centuries. On the same site, and run by English Heritage as a joint attraction, is the Farmland Museum. Old farm buildings have been splendidly renovated and converted to tell visitors about the rural history of Cambridgeshire from early days to modern times.

263 IMPERIAL WAR MUSEUM DUXFORD

Duxford, Cambridgeshire CB2 4QR
☎ 01223 835000 Fax: 01223 837267

A branch of the **Imperial War Museum**, Duxford is Europe's premier aviation museum. Built on a former RAF and USAF fighter base that saw service during the Second World War, its preserved hangars, a control tower and operations room retain a period atmosphere. Visitors to Duxford can see the biplanes and Spitfires, Concorde and Gulf War jets that are among the 180 historic aircraft on

show. A major exhibition on the Battle of Britain charts events of 1940, and another building houses the American Air Museum with aircraft both on the ground and suspended from the roof as though in flight. Tanks and artillery are on show and regular air shows feature resident aircraft, current military aircraft and civilian display teams.

341

CAMBRIDGESHIRE - PLACES OF INTEREST

Houghton, Huntingdon,
Cambridgeshire PE28 2AZ
☎ 01480 301494 Fax: 01480 46964
🌐 www.nationaltrust.org.uk/
Houghtonmill

The National Trust-owned **Houghton Mill**
deserves its reputation as a popular tourist
attraction. There has been a mill on this site for
some 1,000 years. The present mill dates from the
18th century. This impressive five-story brick and
clapboard structure stands on a tributary of the

River Ouse midway between Huntingdon and St Ives.

The mill is one of the last and the most complete to survive in the area. As such it is the most
important of the very few remaining mills. It has recently had its wheel restored, as part of a 1.2
million pound restoration project and is fully operational. This has provided improved facilities for
visitors. Open days during the summer months
offer visitors the chance to see the mill in action,
and to appreciate the different forms of sustainable
energy - a water turbine which generates electricity
for the site and for other National Trust properties,
and the waterwheel at work to produce
stoneground flour. Milling takes place on Sundays
and Bank Holiday Mondays, and the site also
contains an art gallery, miniature millstones to turn
by hand, and a tea room. In addition, the area to the
north of the mill is an unusual survival of
undeveloped Ouse riverbank, which the Trust
intends to protect for its ecological interest and
landscape value as an appropriate setting for this
fine mill.

Britain's Bronze Age Centre, The Droveway,
Northey Road, Peterborough PE6 7QJ
☎ 01733 313414 Fax: 01733 349957
e-mail: office@flagfen.freeserve.co.uk
🌐 www.flagfen.com

Flag Fen is one of Europe's most important
Bronze Age sites; this archaeological jewel is
situated on the outskirts of the Cathedral City of
Peterborough. This Bronze Age religious site pre
dates the Cathedral by nearly 2000 years. The
Museum of the Bronze Age contains artefacts

found on the site over the last 20 years of excavating.

The park is entered through a uniquely designed 21st Century roundhouse; this visitor centre is
your portal to the past, with information boards, and pictures. Once out on the park you will be
stepping back into the past, and have the chance to see how your ancestors used to live, as you
explore the Bronze Age and Iron Age
roundhouses in their landscape setting.

The Preservation Hall contains
undercover archaeology, along with a 60
metre mural painting depicting life in the
Bronze Age in the Fens. During the
summer months, archaeologist's can often
be seen at work, uncovering
Peterborough's past.

Workshops and Lectures are among
our full programme of events, which
include Sword and Bronze Casting, Flint
Knapping and Theatre in the Park

Hundred Foot Bank, Welney, Wisbech,
Cambridgeshire PE14 9TN
☎ 01353 860711
e-mail: welney@wwt.org.uk
⊕ www.org.uk

The Wildfowl & Wetland Trust Welney is a
wetland paradise of international importance with
something to offer whatever the season. In winter,
enjoy the magic of hundreds of Whooper and
Bewick's Swans accompanied by flocks of
thousands of ducks. During the day, carpets of
Wigeon graze this precious wetland, while flocks of Pintail, Teal, Gadwall and Shoveler dabble in
the pools and lagoons.

Late afternoon is a special time as flocks of swans flight-in to claim their night roosting sites.
Summer brings an atmosphere of peace
and tranquillity broken only by the
piping calls of waders, drumming Snipe
and the chatter of warblers. Lush
meadows are bordered by a dazzling
display of Purple Loosestrife, Great
Willowherb and Marsh Woundwort.
Visitors can stroll along the boardwalks
through rustling reedbeds, and spend a
while pond-dipping for water beasts.
The Visitor Centre houses displays,
educational facilities and a well-stocked
gift shop. WWT Welney also runs a
packed programme of special events
throughout the year.

HIDDEN PLACES GUIDES

Explore Britain and Ireland with
Hidden Places guides - a fascinating series of national and local
travel guides.

Packed with easy to read information on hundreds of places of
interest as well as places to stay,
eat and drink.

Available from both high street
and internet booksellers

For more information on the full range of
Hidden Places guides and other titles published by
Travel Publishing visit our website on

www.travelpublishing.co.uk
or ask for our leaflet by phoning **0118-981-7777** or
emailing **info@travelpublishing.co.uk**

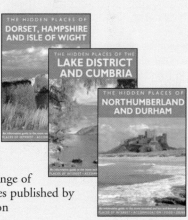

267 ELGOOD'S BREWERY & GARDENS

North Brink, Wisbech,
Cambridgeshire PE12 1LN
☎ 01945 583160 Fax: 01945 587711

Elgood's Brewery is a 200-year-old classic Georgian brewery situated on the bank of the River Nene. This friendly and relaxing place is set amid true rural splendour.

The brewery was established in 1795, and was one of the first in this style to be built outside London. It is a lively and welcoming establishment, the perfect setting in which to savour a pint of one of their famous award-winning ales, enjoy a range of delicious snacks and home-made cakes in the cafe, or stroll around the gardens.

Visitors can also enjoy observing traditional brewing methods, which use original open copper vessels - and can then sample a selection of real ales.

Famous locally and further afield for its welcoming hospitality and classic ales, Elgood's is not just for real ale enthusiasts - though there's plenty here to delight them as well. Behind the brewery is a four-acre garden with 150-year-old specimen trees, herbaceous borders, a lake, rockery, water features, exotics house, rose and herb gardens, and boasting many original Georgian and Victorian features. Beyond the walled gardens, there are lawns leading to the Millennium Maze, planted in the winter of 1992/93 - photographs of its progress are in the Visitors' Centre. The resident team of gardeners are happy to answer any questions. There is no 'formal route' to follow; visitors are

welcome to roam at will, enjoying this marvellous garden, as have the Elgoods for many years.

This family-owned business is still run by the Elgoods: Nigel, his wife Anne and their three daughters. Belinda Sutton and Jennifer Everall are responsible for the Brewery and Claire Simpson, who is qualified in garden design, has re-landscaped and planted the garden. Other amenities and attractions to delight the visitor include the café and licensed bar, gift and plant shop. The staff are helpful and friendly; in the garden shop they are happy to offer advice.

Gardens open: April to September - Tuesday, Wednesday and Thursday 11.30am to 4.30pm; brewery tours Tuesday, Wednesday and Thursday 2 pm. Please phone for more details.

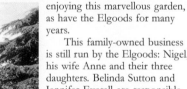

Tourist Information Centres

CAMBRIDGESHIRE

CAMBRIDGE

Wheeler Street
Cambridge
Cambridgeshire
CB2 3QB
Public enquiries: 0906 586 2526
Fax: 01223 457549
e-mail: tourism@cambridge.gov.uk

ELY

Oliver Cromwell's House
29 St Mary's Street
Ely
Cambridgeshire
CB7 4HF
Public enquiries: 01353 662062
Fax: 01353 668518
e-mail: tic@eastcambs.gov.uk

HUNTINGDON

The Library
Princes Street
Huntingdon
Cambridgeshire
PE29 3PH
Public enquiries: 01480 388588
Fax: 01480 388591
e-mail: Hunts.TIC@huntsdc.gov.uk

PETERBOROUGH

3-5 Minster Precincts
Peterborough
Cambridgeshire
PE1 1XS
Public enquiries: 01733 452336
Fax: 01733 452353
e-mail: tic@peterborough.gov.uk

ST NEOTS

The Old Court
8 New Street
St Neots
Cambridgeshire
PE19 1AE
Public enquiries: 01480 388788
Fax: 01480 388791
e-mail: stneots.tic@huntsdc.gov.uk

WISBECH

2-3 Bridge Street
Wisbech
Cambridgeshire
PE13 1EW
Public enquiries: 01945 583263
Fax: 01945 427199
e-mail: tourism@fenland.gov.uk

WITHERNSEA

131 Queen Street
Withernsea
HU19 2DJ
Public enquiries: 01964 615683
Fax: 01964 615683
e-mail: withernsea.tic@eastriding.gov.uk

ESSEX

BRAINTREE

Town Hall Centre
Market Place
Braintree
Essex
CM7 3YG
Public enquiries: 01376 550066
Fax: 01376 344345
e-mail: tic@braintree.gov.uk

BRENTWOOD

Pepperell House
44 High Street
Brentwood
Essex
CM14 4AJ
Public enquiries: 01277 200300
Fax: 01277 202375
e-mail: tic@brentwood.gov.uk

CHELMSFORD

County Hall
Market Road
Chelmsford
Essex
CM1 1GG
Public enquiries: 0870 225 4801
Fax: 01245 430 705
e-mail: chelmtic@essexcc.gov.uk
website: www.welcometoessex.co.uk

CLACTON-ON-SEA

Town Hall
Station Road
Clacton-on-Sea
Essex
CO15 1SE
Public enquiries: 01255 423400
Fax: 01255 253842
01255 253200
e-mail: emorgan@tendringdc.gov.uk

COLCHESTER

Tymperleys Clock Museum
Trinity Street
Colchester
Essex
CO1 1JN
Public enquiries: 01206 282920
Fax: 01206 282924
e-mail: vic@colchester.gov.uk

FLATFORD

Flatford Lane
Flatford
East Bergholt
Suffolk
CO7 6UL
Public enquiries: 01206 299460
Fax: 01206 299973
e-mail: flatfordvic@babergh.gov.uk

HARWICH

Iconfield Park
Parkeston
Harwich
Essex
CO12 4EN
Public enquiries: 01255 506139
Fax: 01255 240570
e-mail: harwichtic@btconnect.com

MALDON

Coach Lane
Maldon
Essex
CM9 4UH
Public enquiries: 01621 856503
Fax: 01621 875873
e-mail: tic@maldon.gov.uk

SAFFRON WALDEN

1 Market Place
Market Square
Saffron Walden
Essex
CB10 1HR
Public enquiries: 01799 510444
Fax: 01799 510445
e-mail: tourism@uttlesford.gov.uk

WALTHAM ABBEY

Unit B
2-4 Highbridge Street
Waltham Abbey
Essex
EN9 1DG
Public enquiries: 01992 652295
Fax: 01992 652295
e-mail: tic@walthamabbey.org.uk

SOUTHEND-ON-SEA

Pier Entrance
Western Esplanade
Southend-on-Sea
Essex
SS1 1EE
Public enquiries: 01702 215620
Fax: 01702 611889
e-mail: vic@southend.gov.uk

NORFOLK

AYLSHAM

Bure Valley Railway Station
Tourist Information Centre
Norwich Road
Aylsham
Norfolk
NR11 6BW
Public enquiries: 01263 733903
Fax: 01263 733922
e-mail: aylsham.tic@broadland.gov.uk

DISS

Meres Mouth
Mere Street
Diss
Norfolk
IP22 3AG
Public enquiries: 01379 650523
Fax: 01379 650838
e-mail: dtic@s-norfolk.gov.uk

GREAT YARMOUTH

25 Marine Parade
Great Yarmouth
Norfolk
NR30 2EN
Public enquiries: 01493 846345
e-mail: tourism@great-yarmouth.gov.uk

HOVETON

Station Road
Hoveton
Norfolk
NR12 8UR
Public enquiries: 01603 782281
Fax: 01603 782281
e-mail: hovetoninfo@broads-authority.gov.uk

KING'S LYNN

The Custom House
Purfleet Quay
King's Lynn
Norfolk
PE30 1HP
Public enquiries: 01553 763044
Fax: 01553 819441
e-mail: kings-lynn.tic@west-norfolk.gov.uk

MUNDESLEY

2 Station Road
Mundesley
Norfolk
NR11 8JH.
Public enquiries: 01263 721070
Fax: 01263 722796

HUNSTANTON

Town Hall
The Green
Hunstanton
Norfolk
PE36 6BQ
Public enquiries: 01485 532610
Fax: 01485 533972
e-mail: hunstanton.tic@west-norfolk.gov.uk

NORWICH

The Forum
Millennium Plain
Norwich
Norfolk
NR2 1TF
Public enquiries: 01603 727927
Fax: 01603 765389
e-mail: tourism@norwich.gov.uk

SHERINGHAM

Station Approach
Sheringham
Norfolk
NR26 8RA
Public enquiries: 0871 200 3071
e-mail: sheringhamtic@north-norfolk.gov.uk

HOLT

3 Pound House
Market Place
Holt
Norfolk
NR25 6BW
Public enquiries: 0871 200 3071
Fax: 01263 713100
e-mail: holttic@north-norfolk.gov.uk

347

CROMER

Prince of Wales Road
Cromer
Norfolk
NR27 9HS
Public enquiries: 0871 200 3071
Fax: 01263 513613
e-mail: cromertic@north-norfolk.gov.uk

WELLS-NEXT-THE-SEA

Staithe Street
Wells-next-the-Sea
Norfolk
NR23 1AN
Public enquiries: 0871 200 3071
Fax: 01328 711405
e-mail: wellstic@north-norfolk.gov.uk

BURNHAM DEEPDALE

Deepdale Farm
Burnham Deepdale
Norfolk
PE31 8DD
Public enquiries: 01485 210256
Fax: 01485 210158
e-mail: info@deepdalefarm.co.uk

SWAFFHAM

The Shambles
Market Place
Swaffham
Norfolk
PE37 7AB
Public enquiries: 01760 722255
Fax: 01760 723410
e-mail: swaffham@eetb.info

DOWNHAM MARKET

The Priory Centre
78 Priory Road
Downham Market
Norfolk
PE38 9JS
Public enquiries: 01366 383287
Fax: 01366 385 042
e-mail: downham-market.tic@west-
        norfolk.gov.uk

THETFORD

4 White Hart Street
Thetford
Norfolk
IP24 2HA
Public enquiries: 01842 820689
Fax: 01842 820986
e-mail: info@thetfordtourism.co.uk

WYMONDHAM

Market Cross
Market Place
WYMONDHAM
Norfolk
NR18 0AX
Public enquiries: 01953 604721
Fax: 01953 604721
e-mail: wymondhamtic@btconnect.com

SUFFOLK

ALDEBURGH

152 High Street
Aldeburgh
Suffolk
IP15 5AQ
Public enquiries: 01728 453637
Fax: 01728 453637
e-mail: atic@suffolkcoastal.gov.uk

BECCLES

The Quay
Fen Lane
Beccles
Suffolk
NR34 9BH
Public enquiries: 01502 713196
Fax: 01502 713196
e-mail: becclesinfo@broads-authority.gov.uk

BURY ST EDMUNDS

6 Angel Hill
Bury St Edmunds
Suffolk
IP33 1UZ
Public enquiries: 01284 764667
Fax: 01284 757084
e-mail: tic@stedsbc.gov.uk

FELIXSTOWE

91 Undercliff Road West
Felixstowe
Suffolk
IP11 2AF
Public enquiries: 01394 276770
Fax: 01394 276984
e-mail: ftic@suffolkcoastal.gov.uk

IPSWICH

St Stephens Church
St Stephens Lane
Ipswich
Suffolk
IP1 1DP
Public enquiries: 01473 258070
Fax: 01473 432017
e-mail: tourist@ipswich.gov.uk

LAVENHAM

Lady Street
Lavenham
Suffolk
CO10 9RA
Public enquiries: 01787 248207
Fax: 01787 249459
e-mail: lavenhamtic@babergh.gov.uk

LOWESTOFT

East Point Pavilion
Royal Plain
Lowestoft
Suffolk
NR33 0AP
Public enquiries: 01502 533600
Fax: 01502 539023
e-mail: touristinfo@waveney.gov.uk

NEWMARKET

Palace House
Palace Street
Newmarket
Suffolk
CB8 8EP
Public enquiries: 01638 667200
Fax: 01638 667415
e-mail: tic.newmarket@forest-heath.gov.uk

SOUTHWOLD

69 High Street
Southwold
Suffolk
IP18 6DS
Public enquiries: 01502 724729
Fax: 01502 722978
e-mail: southwold.tic@waveney.gov.uk

STOWMARKET

Wilkes Way
Stowmarket
Suffolk
IP14 1DE
Public enquiries: 01449 676800
Fax: 01449 614691
e-mail: tic@midsuffolk.gov.uk

SUDBURY

Town Hall
Market Hill
Sudbury
Suffolk
CO10 1TL
Public enquiries: 01787 881320
Fax: 01787 242129
e-mail: sudburytic@babergh.gov.uk

WOODBRIDGE

Station Buildings
Woodbridge
Suffolk
IP12 4AJ
Public enquiries: 01394 382240
Fax: 01394 386337
e-mail: wtic@suffolkcoastal.gov.uk

Towns, Villages and Places of Interest

Y

TRAVEL PUBLISHING ORDER FORM

To order any of our publications just fill in the payment details below and complete the order form. For orders of less than 4 copies please add £1 per book for postage and packing. Orders over 4 copies are P & P free.

Please Complete Either:

I enclose a cheque for £ [   ] made payable to *Travel Publishing Ltd*

Or:

Card No: [   ]   Expiry Date: [   ]

Signature: [   ]

Name: [   ]

Address: [   ]

Tel no: [   ]

Please either send, telephone, fax or e-mail your order to:
Travel Publishing Ltd, 7a Apollo House, Calleva Park, Aldermaston, Berkshire RG7 8TN
Tel: **0118 981 7777**   Fax: **0118 982 0077** e-mail: info@travelpublishing.co.uk

	Price	Quantity
HIDDEN PLACES REGIONAL TITLES		
Cornwall	£8.99	....
Devon	£8.99	....
Dorset, Hants & Isle of Wight	£8.99	....
East Anglia	£8.99	....
Lake District & Cumbria	£8.99	....
Northumberland & Durham	£8.99	....
Peak District	£8.99	....
Sussex	£8.99	....
Yorkshire	£8.99	....
HIDDEN PLACES NATIONAL TITLES		
England	£11.99	....
Ireland	£11.99	....
Scotland	£11.99	....
Wales	£11.99	....
HIDDEN INNS TITLES		
East Anglia	£7.99	....
Heart of England	£7.99	....
North of England	£7.99	....
South	£7.99	....
South East	£7.99	....
Wales	£7.99	....
West Country	£7.99	....
Yorkshire	£7.99	....

	Price	Quantity
COUNTRY PUBS AND INNS		
Cornwall	£8.99	....
Devon	£8.99	....
Sussex	£8.99	....
Wales	£8.99	....
COUNTRY LIVING RURAL GUIDES		
East Anglia	£10.99	....
Heart of England	£10.99	....
Ireland	£11.99	....
North East	£10.99	....
North West	£10.99	....
Scotland	£11.99	....
South of England	£10.99	....
South East of England	£10.99	....
Wales	£11.99	....
West Country	£10.99	....
OTHER TITLES		
Off the Motorway	£11.99	....

Total Quantity: [   ]

Post & Packing: [   ]

Total Value: [   ]

HIDDEN PLACES GUIDES

Explore Britain and Ireland with *Hidden Places* guides - a fascinating series of national and local travel guides.

Packed with easy to read information on hundreds of places of interest as well as places to stay, eat and drink.

Available from both high street and internet booksellers

For more information on the full range of *Hidden Places* guides and other titles published by Travel Publishing visit our website on

www.travelpublishing.co.uk
or ask for our leaflet by phoning **0118-981-7777** or emailing **info@travelpublishing.co.uk**

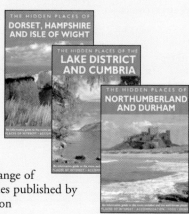

VISIT THE TRAVEL PUBLISHING WEBSITE

Looking for:

- *Places to Visit?*
- *Places to Stay?*
- *Places to Eat & Drink?*
- *Places to Shop?*

Then why not visit the Travel Publishing website...

- Informative pages on places to visit, stay, eat, drink and shop throughout the British Isles.

- Detailed information on Travel Publishing's wide range of national and regional travel guides.

www.travelpublishing.co.uk

364

READER REACTION FORM

The *Travel Publishing* research team would like to receive reader's comments on any visitor attractions or places reviewed in the book and also recommendations for suitable entries to be included in the next edition. This will help ensure that the *Hidden Places series of Guides* continues to provide its readers with useful information on the more interesting, unusual or unique features of each attraction or place ensuring that their visit to the local area is an enjoyable and stimulating experience. To provide your comments or recommendations would you please complete the forms below and overleaf as indicated and send to:

**The Research Department, Travel Publishing Ltd,
7a Apollo House, Calleva Park, Aldermaston, Reading, RG7 8TN.**

Your Name:

Your Address:

Your Telephone Number:

Please tick as appropriate:

Comments ☐   Recommendation ☐

Name of Establishment:

Address:

Telephone Number:

Name of Contact:

READER REACTION FORM

COMMENT OR REASON FOR RECOMMENDATION:

....

....

....

....

....

....

....

....

....

....

....

....

....

....

....

....

....

....

Index of Advertisers

NORFOLK

ACCOMMODATION

FOOD AND DRINK

PLACES OF INTEREST

SUFFOLK

ACCOMMODATION

FOOD AND DRINK

PLACES OF INTEREST

ESSEX

ACCOMMODATION

FOOD AND DRINK

369

CAMBRIDGESHIRE